MW00615791

The Story of God Bible Commentary
Series Endorsements

"Getting a story is about more than merely enjoying it. It means hearing it, understanding it, and above all, being impacted by it. This commentary series hopes that its readers not only hear and understand the story, but are impacted by it to live in as Christian a way as possible. The editors and contributors set that table very well and open up the biblical story in ways that move us to act with sensitivity and understanding. That makes hearing the story as these authors tell it well worth the time. Well done."

Darrell L. Bock
Executive Director of Cultural Engagement, Howard G. Hendricks
Center for Christian Leadership and Cultural Engagement,
Senior Research Professor of New Testament Studies
Dallas Theological Seminary

"The Story of God Bible Commentary series invites readers to probe how the message of the text relates to our situations today. Engagingly readable, it not only explores the biblical text but offers a range of applications and interesting illustrations."

Craig S. Keener
Professor of New Testament
Asbury Theological Seminary

"I love the Story of God Bible Commentary series. It makes the text sing, and helps us hear the story afresh."

John Ortberg
Senior pastor of Menlo Park Presbyterian Church,
and author of *Who Is This Man?*

"In this promising new series of commentaries, believing biblical scholars bring not only their expertise but their own commitment to Jesus and insights into today's culture to the Scriptures. The result is a commentary series that is anchored in the text but lives and breathes in the world of today's church with its variegated pattern of socioeconomic, ethnic, and national diversity. Pastors, Bible study leaders, and Christians of all types who are looking for a substantive and practical guide through the Scriptures will find these volumes helpful."

Frank Thielman
Professor of Divinity
Beeson Divinity School

"The Story of God Bible Commentary series is unique in its approach to exploring the Bible. Its easy-to-use format and practical guidance brings God's grand story to modern-day life so anyone can understand how it applies today."

Andy Stanley
Senior Pastor
North Point Ministries

"I'm a storyteller. Through writing and speaking I talk and teach about understanding the Story of God throughout Scripture and about letting God reveal more of His story as I live it out. Thus I am thrilled to have a commentary series based on the Story of God—a commentary that helps me to Listen to the Story, that Explains the Story, and then encourages me to probe how to Live the Story. A perfect tool for helping every follower of Jesus to walk in the story that God is writing for them."

Judy Douglass
Author, Speaker, Encourager
Office of the President, Cru
Director of Women's Resources, Cru

"The Bible is the story of God and his dealings with humanity from creation to new creation. The Bible is made up more of stories than of any other literary genre. Even the psalms, proverbs, prophecies, letters, and the Apocalypse make complete sense only when set in the context of the grand narrative of the entire Bible. This commentary series breaks new ground by taking all these observations seriously. It asks commentators to listen to the text, to explain the text, and to live the text. Some of the material in these sections overlaps with introduction, detailed textual analysis and application, respectively, but only some. The most riveting and valuable part of the commentaries are the stories that can appear in any of these sections, from any part of the globe and any part of church history, illustrating the text in any of these areas. Ideal for preaching and teaching."

Craig L. Blomberg
Distinguished Professor of New Testament
Denver Seminary

SERMON ON
THE MOUNT

The Story of God Bible Commentary

SERMON ON THE MOUNT

Scot McKnight

Tremper Longman III & Scot McKnight
General Editors

ZONDERVAN

Sermon on the Mount
Copyright © 2013 by Scot McKnight

This title is also available as a Zondervan ebook. Visit www.zondervan.com/ebooks.

Requests for information should be addressed to:

Zondervan, *Grand Rapids, Michigan 49530*

Library of Congress Cataloging-in-Publication Data

McKnight, Scot.
    The Sermon on the mount / Scot McKnight.
        p. cm. — (Story of God Bible commentary; 21)
    Includes bibliographical references.
    ISBN 978-0-310-32713-4
    1. Sermon on the mount — Commentaries. I. Title.
    BT380.3.M43 2013
    226.9'07 — dc23   2013000731

Cover design: Ron Huizinga
Cover imagery: iStockphoto®

Printed in the United States of America

13 14 15 16 17 18 19 20 /DCI/ 20 19 18 17 16 15 14 13 12 11 10 9 8 7 6 5 4 3 2

For David and Linda Parkyn

Old Testament series

New Testament series

Contents

Acknowledgments

This commentary was written at the end of seventeen wonderful years as a faculty member at North Park University, where I was honored to be the Karl Olsson Professor in Religious Studies. In my last few years at North Park we were led by one of Olsson's successors, President David Parkyn. David and Linda became friends to Kris and me, in part no doubt because we were the same age with similar experiences in life, not the least of which are grandchildren and aging parents. Alongside those experiences was David's leadership at North Park. David and I can't neglect mentioning Linda and her infectious joy each time we met, which exemplifies Christian leadership at a university— theologically alert, economically wise, and an exceptional communicator. But most of all I simply enjoyed David and Linda for how they followed Christ with grace and kindness. Not only are they fellow anabaptists with a love for liturgy, but they knew that the way to lead was cruciform. David was the first person at North Park I told when Northern Seminary knocked on my door and David opened his home to me not long after his surgery to discuss my final decision to leave. I miss David and Linda immensely.

Others were involved in this book by offering suggestions. Thanks especially belongs to my close colleague at North Park, Joel Willitts, and to fellow editors Lynn Cohick, Mike Bird, and Katya Covrett. At Zondervan, Verlyn Verbrugge's attention to details along with theology continues to amaze me. Seventeen years at North Park meant seventeen years of conversations with Greg Clark, a fellow anabaptist of whom I seemed to bounce all my big ideas, some of which were blown into the memories of things I'm glad to have forgotten. Also I thank Jeff Greenman, now at Regent College, for detailed comments on the introduction, and also to Jeff Cook for the same.

Never dare I sign off on a preface without expressing my love for Kris. As we have aged, we have learned that her more introverted personality and my need for quiet to write have become a match made in providence. As this book comes into the light of day, we are beginning to celebrate our fortieth year of splendid marriage.

The Story of God Bible Commentary Series

The Word of God may not change, but culture does. Think of what we have seen in the last twenty years: we now communicate predominantly through the internet and email; we read our news on iPads and computers; we can talk on the phone to our friends while we are driving, while we are playing golf, while we are taking long walks; and we can get in touch with others from the middle of nowhere. We carry in our hands small devices that connect us to the world and to a myriad of sources of information. Churches have changed; the "Nones" are rising in numbers and volume, and atheists are bold to assert their views in public forums. The days of home Bible studies are waning, there is a marked rise in activist missional groups in churches, and pastors are more and more preaching topical sermons, some of which are not directly connected to the Bible. Divorce rates are not going down, marriages are more stressed, rearing children is more demanding, and civil unions and same-sex marriages are knocking at the door of the church.

Progress can be found in many directions. While church attendance numbers are waning in Europe and North America, churches are growing in the South and the East. More and more women are finding a voice in churches; the plea of the former generation of leaders that Christians be concerned not just with evangelism but with justice is being answered today in new and vigorous ways. Resources for studying the Bible are more available today than ever before, and preachers and pastors are meeting the challenge of speaking a sure Word of God into shifting cultures.

Readers of the Bible change, too. These cultural shifts, our own personal developments, the progress in intellectual questions, as well as growth in biblical studies and theology and discoveries of new texts and new paradigms for understanding the contexts of the Bible—each of these elements works on an interpreter so that the person who reads the Bible today asks different questions from different angles.

Culture shifts, but the Word of God remains. That is why we as editors of The Story of God Bible Commentary series, a commentary based on the New International Version 2011 (NIV 2011), are excited to participate in this new series of commentaries on the Bible. This series is designed to address this generation with the same Word of God. We are asking the authors to explain what the Bible says to the sorts of readers who pick up commentaries so they can understand not only what Scripture says but what it means for today. The Bible does not change, but relating it to our culture changes constantly and in differing ways in different contexts.

When we, the New Testament editors, sat down in prayer and discussion to choose authors for this series, we realized we had found fertile ground. Our list of potential authors staggered in length and quality. We wanted the authors to be exceptional scholars, faithful Christians, committed evangelicals, and theologically diverse, and we wanted this series to represent the changing face of both American and world evangelicalism: ethnic and gender diversity. I believe this series has a wider diversity of authors than any commentary series in evangelical history.

The title of this series, emphasizing as it does the "Story" of the Bible, reveals the intent of the series. We want to explain each passage of the Bible in light of the Bible's grand Story. The Bible's grand Story, of course, connects this series to the classic expression *regula fidei*, the "rule of faith," which was the Bible's story coming to fulfillment in Jesus as the Messiah, Lord, and Savior of all. In brief, we see the narrative built around the following biblical themes: creation and fall, covenant and redemption, law and prophets, and especially God charge to humans as his image-bearers to rule under God. The theme of God as King and God's kingdom guides us to see the importance of Israel's kings as they come to fulfillment in Jesus, Lord and King over all, and the direction of history toward the new heavens and new earth, where God will be all in all. With these guiding themes, each passage is examined from three angles.

Listen to the Story. We believe that if the Bible is God speaking, then the most important posture of the Christian before the Bible is to listen. So our first section cites the text of Scripture and lists a selection of important biblical and sometimes noncanonical parallels; then each author introduces that passage. The introductions to the passages sometimes open up discussion to the theme of the passage while other times they tie this passage to its context in the specific book. But since the focus of this series is the Story of God in the Bible, the introduction leads the reader into reading this text in light of the Bible's Story.

Explain the Story. The authors follow up listening to the text by explaining each passage in light of the Bible's grand Story. This is not an academic series, so the footnotes are limited to the kinds of texts typical Bible readers and preachers readily will have on hand. Authors are given the freedom to explain the text as they read it, though you should not be surprised to find occasional listings of other options for reading the text. Authors explore

biblical backgrounds, historical context, cultural codes, and theological interpretations. Authors engage in word studies and interpret unique phrases and
clauses as they attempt to build a sound and living reading of the text in light
of the Story of God in the Bible.

Authors will not shy away from problems in the texts. Whether one is
examining the meaning of "perfect" in Matthew 5:48, the problems with
Christology in the hymn of Philippians 2:6–11, the challenge of understanding Paul in light of the swirling debates about the old, new, and post-new
perspectives, the endless debates about eschatology, or the vagaries of atonement theories, the authors will dive in, discuss evidence, and do their best to
sort out a reasonable and living reading of those issues for the church today.

Live the Story. Reading the Bible is not just about discovering what it
meant back then; the intent of The Story of God Bible Commentary series
is to probe how this text might be lived out today as that story continues to
march on in the life of the church. At times our authors will tell stories about
what this looks like; at other times they may offer some suggestions for living
it out; but always you will discover the struggle involved as we seek to live out
the Bible's grand Story in our world.

We are not offering suggestions for "application" so much as digging
deeper; we are concerned in this section with seeking out how this text, in
light of the Story of God in the Bible, compels us to live in our world so that
our own story lines up with the Bible's Story.

SCOT MCKNIGHT, general editor New Testament
LYNN COHICK, JOEL WILLITTS, and MICHAEL BIRD, editors

Abbreviations

AB	Anchor Bible
ABD	*Anchor Bible Dictionary*
ABRL	Anchor Bible Reference Library
ACCS: *Matthew*	Ancient Christian Commentary on Scripture: *Matthew*
ASV	American Standard Version
b.	*Babylonian Talmud*
BDAG	Bauer, Danker, Arndt, and Gingrich, *A Greek-English Lexicon of the New Testament and Other Early Christian Literature* (3rd ed.)
BECNT	Baker Exegetical Commentary on the New Testament
BJS	Brown Judaic Studies
CEB	Common English Bible
DJG	*Dictionary of Jesus and the Gospels*
EDEJ	*The Eerdmans Dictionary of Early Judaism*
EJ	*The Encyclopedia of Judaism*
ICC	International Critical Commentary
IVPWBC	*The IVP Women's Bible Commentary*
JBL	*Journal of Biblical Literature*
JSNTMS	Journal for the Study of the New Testament Monograph Series
KNT	N.T. Wright's Kingdom New Testament
KJV	King James Version
m.	*Mishnah*
NAC	New American Commentary
NICNT	New International Commentary on the New Testament
NIV	New International Version
NPNF	*Nicene and Post-Nicene Fathers*
NRSV	New Revised Standard Version
NTS	*New Testament Studies*
SNTSMS	Society for New Testament Studies Monograph Series
TLNT	*Theological Lexicon of the New Testament*
TNIV	Today's New International Version
WBC	Word Biblical Commentary

The Sermon on the Mount is not a statement to be treated
in a cavalier fashion—by saying that this or that isn't right
or that here we find an inconsistency.
Its validity depends on its being obeyed.
This is not a statement that we can freely choose to take or leave.
It is a compelling, lordly statement.

DIETRICH BONHOEFFER

What Jesus teaches in the sayings collected in the Sermon on the
    Mount
is not a complete regulation of the life of the disciples,
and it is not intended to be;
rather, what is taught here is symptoms, signs, examples,
of what it means when the kingdom of God breaks into
the world which is still under sin, death, and the devil.
You yourselves should be signs of the coming kingdom of God,
signs that something has already happened.

JOACHIM JEREMIAS

A man comes forth in Israel to make today's prophetic vision
tomorrow's agenda;
one for whom the teachings of Mount Sinai do not suffice
because he wishes to penetrate beyond to the original divine intent;
one who, despite war and tyranny, dares to pursue
the biblical love of neighbor to its ultimate consequence
in order to brand all our souls with an ideal of human possibility
that no longer allows us to be content with the threadbare,
run-of-the-mill persons we are
but need not be.   PINCHAS LAPIDE

[Jesus'] life is but a commentary on the sermon,
and the sermon is the exemplification of his life.

STANLEY HAUERWAS

The Sermon on the Mount has a strange way of making us
better people or better liars.   DEAN SMITH

Introduction

The Sermon on the Mount is the moral portrait of Jesus' own people. Because this portrait doesn't square with the church, this Sermon turns from instruction to indictment. To those ends—both instruction and indictment—this commentary has been written with the simple goal that God will use this book to lead us to become in real life the portrait Jesus sketched in the Sermon.

The contrast between Jesus' vision and our life bothers many of us. Throughout church history many have softened, reduced, recontextualized, and in some cases abandoned what Jesus taught—ironically, in order to be more Christian! Pinchas Lapide, an Orthodox Jew who wrote a short commentary on the Sermon on the Mount, described this history in these terms:

> In fact, the history of the impact of the Sermon on the Mount can largely be described in terms of an attempt to domesticate everything in it that is shocking, demanding, and uncompromising, and render it harmless.[1]

Harsh words, to be sure. But the history is there, and all you have to do is spend a day or a week reading how the Sermon has been (re)interpreted. Note Lapide's quote of Karl Barth's famous words: "It would be sheer folly to interpret the imperatives of the Sermon on the Mount as if we should bestir ourselves to actualize these pictures."[2]

So, what do these (re)interpretations look like?[3] First, some have said the Sermon is really Moses or the law ramped up to the highest level and that

---

1. P. Lapide, *The Sermon on the Mount: Utopia or Program for Action?* (trans. A. Swidler; Maryknoll, NY: Orbis, 1986).

2. Ibid., 4.

3. For an exceptional study of how the Sermon has been interpreted by major theologians, see J. P. Greenman et al., *The Sermon on the Mount through the Centuries: From the Early Church to John Paul II* (Grand Rapids: Brazos, 2007). A more complete sketch can be found in C. Bauman, *The Sermon on the Mount: The Modern Quest for Its Meaning* (Macon, GA: Mercer University Press, 1990); H. D. Betz, *The Sermon on the Mount* (Hermeneia; ed. A. Collins; Minneapolis: Fortress, 1995), 5–44. For a brief sketch of three major interpreters of the Sermon (William Stringfellow, David Lipscomb, and sixteenth-century Anabaptists), see R. Hughes, "Dare We Live in the World Imagined in the Sermon on the Mount?" in *Preaching the Sermon on the Mount: The World It Imagines* (ed. D. Fleer and D. Bland; St. Louis: Chalice, 2007). Also see G. Strecker, *The Sermon on the Mount: An Exegetical Commentary* (trans. O. C. Dean; Nashville: Abingdon, 1988), 15–23; W. Carter, *What Are They Saying about Matthew's Sermon on the Mount?* (Mahway, NJ: Paulist, 1994); C. Quarles, *Sermon on the Mount: Restoring Christ's Message to the Modern Church* (NAC Studies in Bible and

Jesus' intent is not to summon his followers to do these things but to show just how wretchedly sinful they are and how much they are in need of Christ's righteousness. The Sermon, then, is nothing but a mirror designed to reveal our sinfulness. Second, others assign the sayings of Jesus in the Sermon to the private level, sometimes as little more than disposition or intention or striving and other times to how Christians live personally and privately as a Christian but not how they live publicly. The Sermon, then, is a code for private morality. Third, others think these sayings belong only to the most committed of disciples, whether monk, nun, priest, pastor, or radical. If they are designed only for the hypercommitted, the ordinary person can pass them by. The Sermon is for the elite Christian. Fourth, the tendency today is to see the Sermon as *preceded by something*, and that something is the gospel and that gospel is personal salvation and grace. That means that the Sermon is a sketch of the Christian life but only for those who have been so transformed by grace that they see the demands not as law but as grace-shaped ethics that can only be done by the person who lives by the Spirit. The Sermon, then, is Christian ethics, but it can only be understood once someone understands a theology of grace.

This tendency today is respectable Christian theology and only the one who turns back an apple pie from Mom would disagree. But the danger is obvious: *those who take this approach more often than not end up denying the potency of the Sermon and sometimes simply turn elsewhere — to Galatians and Romans and Ephesians — for their Christian ethical instruction.* What many such readings of the Sermon really want is Paul, and since they can't find Paul in the Sermon, they reinterpret the Sermon and give us Paul instead.[4] It is far wiser to ask how Paul relates to the Sermon than to make Jesus sound like Paul, and many today are showing that Paul's ethics and Jesus' ethics — their theologies — are not as far apart as some have made them out to be.[5] Even more important, when we seek to "improve" the words of Jesus in the Sermon

Theology; Nashville: Broadman & Homan, 2011), 4–11; R. Schnackenburg, *All Things Are Possible to Believers: Reflections on the Lord's Prayer and the Sermon on the Mount* (trans. J. S. Currie; Louisville: Westminster John Knox, 1995), 10–21.

4. Two classic German examples: J. Jeremias, *The Sermon on the Mount* (Facet; trans. N. Perrin; Philadelphia: Fortress, 1963); E. Thurneysen, *The Sermon on the Mount* (trans. W. C. Robinson; Richmond, VA: John Knox, 1964). Two recent examples, one better than the other: G. H. Stassen, *Living the Sermon on the Mount: A Practical Hope for Grace and Deliverance* (Enduring Questions in Christian Life; San Francisco: Jossey-Bass, 2006). Stassen maintains a balance of finding a theological, or soteriological, context while affirming the demand of the Sermon. But Carl Vaught (*The Sermon on the Mount: A Theological Investigation* [Waco, TX: Baylor University Press, 2001]) seemingly can't find Jesus saying what he thinks Jesus ought to have said, so he works hard to show that Jesus can be made to be say what he wants him to say. Vaught might instead have written a commentary on Romans.

5. I have attempted to show this in *The King Jesus Gospel*. Of the many studies, see D. Wenham, *Paul: Follower of Jesus or Founder of Christianity?* (Grand Rapids: Eerdmans, 1995); J. R. Daniel Kirk,

on the Mount by setting them in a larger theological context, we too often ruin the words of Jesus. There is something vital—and this is a central theme in this commentary—in letting the demand of Jesus, expressed over and over in the Sermon as imperatives or commands, stand in its rhetorical ruggedness. Only as demand do we hear this Sermon as he meant it to be heard: as the claim of Jesus upon our whole being.

What these proposals for the Sermon do is force us to ask a set of questions:

- How did Jesus "do" ethics?
- What framework did Jesus use when it came to discipleship?
- Were his moral teachings truly requirements for salvation? For entrance into the kingdom? Necessary for salvation?

The Sermon and Moral Theory

The Sermon on the Mount remains the greatest moral document of all time.[6] To justify this claim I want to probe Jesus' moral vision by comparing Jesus' Sermon to other moral theorists.[7] From Moses to Plato and Aristotle to Augustine and Aquinas to Luther and Calvin, and then into the modern world of thinkers like Kant and Mill all the way to contemporary moral theorists like Richard and Reinhold Niebuhr, John Howard Yoder and Stanley Hauerwas, and also Oliver O'Donovan and Alasdair MacIntyre, some of the finest thinkers have applied their energies to ethics. How does Jesus fit into that history?[8]

Jesus Have I Loved, but Paul? A Narrative Approach to the Problem of Pauline Christianity (Grand Rapids: Baker Academic, 2011).

6. J. Pelikan, *Divine Rhetoric: The Sermon on the Mount as Message and as Model in Augustine, Chrysostom, and Luther* (Crestwood, NY: St Vladimir's Seminary Press, 2000).

7. For an older study, H. K. McArthur, *Understanding the Sermon on the Mount* (New York: Harper & Brothers, 1960), 105–48. Here are McArthur's twelve approaches: absolutist, modification [of the absolutist approach], hyperbole, general principles, attitudes-not-acts, double standard, two realms, analogy of Scripture, interim ethics, modern [now classic] dispensationalist, repentance, and unconditional divine will.

8. The literature here is overwhelming: S. Hauerwas, *The Peaceable Kingdom: A Primer in Christian Ethics* (Notre Dame, IN: University of Notre Dame Press, 1983); R. J. Mouw, *The God Who Commands* (Notre Dame, IN: University of Notre Dame Press, 1990); J. P. Wogaman, *Christian Ethics: A Historical Introduction* (Louisville: Westminster John Knox, 1993); O. O'Donovan, *Resurrection and Moral Order: An Outline for Evangelical Ethics* (Grand Rapids: Eerdmans, 1994); D. Willard, *Renovation of the Heart: Putting on the Character of Christ* (Colorado Springs: NavPress, 2002); S. Wells, *Improvisation: The Drama of Christian Ethics* (Grand Rapids: Brazos, 2004); S. Hauerwas and S. Wells eds., *The Blackwell Companion to Christian Ethics* (Oxford: Blackwell, 2006); W. C. Reuschling, *Reviving Evangelical Ethics: The Promises and Pitfalls of Classic Models of Morality* (Grand Rapids: Brazos, 2008); N. T. Wright, *After You Believe: Why Christian Character Matters* (New York: HarperOne, 2010); S. Wilkens, *Beyond Bumper Sticker Ethics: An Introduction to Theories of Right and Wrong* (Downers Grove, IL: InterVarsity Press, 2011).

In the history of discussion about ethics there have been some major proposals, and I want to sketch three of the most important, show how each can
be used to explain Jesus, offer critical pushback against each, and then offer
what I think is a more helpful approach to understanding the ethics of Jesus.

Virtue Ethics

The person with whom virtue ethics begins is ultimately Aristotle, whose
theory has been influential both in wider culture and in the church. It was
especially influential in Aquinas and the monastic tradition of the Catholic
Church, including devotional and spiritual greats like Benedict and Bonaventure. Others come to mind: Alasdair MacIntyre and N. T. Wright and Stanley
Hauerwas are each, in one way or another, deeply influenced by Aristotle's
virtue ethics. So we need to drill down a bit deeper to see just what Aristotle
had to say in order to grasp the core of virtue ethics.

Three ideas will give us handles on Aristotle's ethics. First, the goal of life
was human *flourishing* (Greek word *eudaimonia*). Second, a moral, reasonable
person could only become a virtuous person in the context of *friendship*. Put in
broader categories, virtue ethics are defined by and take shape within a community.[9] Third, Aristotle's approach was to practice the habits that made virtue the
core of one's *character*. The word "virtue," then, is tied to the word "character,"
and character forms as the result of good habits. The good person (character)
does what is good (virtues), and doing good (virtues, habits) over time produces
good character. The question, then, is not so much "What should I do?" but
"Who should I be?" or "What does it look like to be a virtuous person?"

Again, Christian ethicists have their own version of virtue ethics, and I would
call to our attention at this point the emphasis in Dallas Willard's spiritual formation studies: his acronym is "VIM."[10] That is, a person with vision and intention needs to practice the habitual means of the spiritual disciplines to become
a person with character sufficient for a flourishing (or blessed) life. In important
ways Willard's theory of spiritual formation is a radically revised version of virtue
ethics reshaped by the Christian theology of revelation and grace.[11]

---

9. This is a major point of A. MacIntyre, *After Virtue* (Notre Dame, IN: University of Notre
Dame Press, 1984). Also S. Hauerwas, *A Community of Character: Toward a Constructive Christian
Social Ethic* (Notre Dame, IN: University of Notre Dame Press, 1981).

10. Willard, *Renovation of the Heart*, 85.

11. Nikki Coffey Tousley and Brad J. Kallenberg, "Virtue Ethics," in *Dictionary of Scripture and
Ethics* (ed. J. B. Green; Grand Rapids: Baker Academic, 2011), 814–19. Their definition summarizes Aristotle's approach but shows how adaptable virtue ethics can be: "Virtues are (1) habituated
dispositions involving both an affective desire for the good and the skill to both discern and act
accordingly; (2) learned through practice within a tradition (i.e., a historical community with a rich
account of the 'good'); and (3) directed toward this tradition's particular conception of the good
(making virtues 'teleological')" (p. 814).

The question I will ask below and in this commentary is this: Was Jesus a virtue ethicist? Or, is virtue ethics the best or a sufficient way of thinking of how Jesus "did" ethics? I will argue that virtue ethics push us to the rim of the inner circle but do not completely come to terms with Jesus in his Jewish world. The fundamental problem with virtue ethics is that Jesus does not overtly talk like this; he does not teach the importance of habits as the way to form character.

The Categorical Imperative

The famous German philosopher Immanuel Kant, whose work reshaped all philosophical thought in the Western world, sought to establish ethics on the basis of reason alone, and his normative theory, often called deontological ethics (*deon* means "ought, duty, or obligation"), landed on the "categorical imperative." Kant framed the categorical imperative in a number of ways:[12]

> Act only in accordance with that maxim through which you can at the same time will that it become a universal law. [The focus here is on the *universality* of true ethics.]
>
> ... so act that you use humanity, whether in your person or in the person of any other, always at the same time as an end, never merely as a means. [Here the emphasis is treating humans *as humans deserving of profound respect*.]
>
> ... the idea of the will of every rational being as a will giving universal law. [And here we are to see that *each person, as an individual*, can be an expression of the universal ethic.]

These three statements — universality, humanity, individuality — are each variations and developments of the categorical imperative: what is true for one must be true for all, and if we treat others as an end and therefore value humanity inherently, we will act in such a way to live rationally and ethically. Two more ideas: At work here (1) are both *intention* and *practice*, with intention having even more weight than practice. Also at work, because Kant thinks of ethics in terms of universality, is (2) that what "I" ought to do becomes a *right* for everyone else as well as my *duty* to other people.

Was Jesus Kantian? It could be argued that Kant's categorical imperative is a variant on the Golden Rule (Matt 7:12) or the Jesus Creed (Mark 12:18–32), but this is inaccurate. In fact, Kant's categorical imperative is far more useful in telling us what not to do — do not lie — than what to do —

---

12. Reuschling, *Reviving Evangelical Ethics*, 31–41.

make promises and live by them. The ethicist Hauerwas levels Kant: "Kant's statement of the categorical imperative is an attempt to free us of the need to rely on forgiveness and, more critically, a savior. Kant's hope was to makes us what our pride desires, that is, that we be autonomous."[13]

Utilitarian Ethics

Two English thinkers, Jeremy Bentham (1748–1832) and John Stuart Mill (1806–1873), offered what is usually called *utilitarian* ethics. Classic utilitarianism can be said to have three leading points: it is consequentialist, universalist, and (in some cases) hedonist. It is consequentialist in that what makes an action right is the consequences of that action. It is universalist in that a utilitarian judges the consequences for *everyone* affected by the action. It is hedonist in that the classic utilitarian (and here we are thinking of Bentham, not Mill) identifies "good" with "pleasure" and "bad" with "pain." So an action is right if, and only if, it produces (thus, consequentialist) the greatest good (hedonism), and for the greatest number (universalist). We are asking if Jesus fits into such a scheme of ethical thinking.

Christian thinking can in some ways adapt or even colonize consequentialism and reframe ethics into that which brings the greatest pleasure of all, namely, glorifying God. I would not restrict John Piper's famous *Desiring God* project, which permeates all of his work, to an ethic of consequentialism, but there is a strain of this approach to ethics in his emphasis on God's glory.[14] In addition, one has to begin to think of Christian eschatology, including the final judgment as well as the new heavens and the new earth, as the final consequence toward which all ethics need to be shaped.[15] A kind of consequentialism plays an important element in the ethical theory of Jesus, but it needs to be said that the utilitarian model secularizes, flattens, and rationalizes eschatology. Furthermore, consequentialist ethics entail a major issue that postmodernity has brought to the fore: *Who* decides which ethic is most consequential? What groups do we include when we say the "greatest number"? It must be said once again: far too often we discover an ethic shaped and controlled by the privileged and powerful.

---

13. S. Hauerwas, *Matthew* (Brazos Theological Commentary on the Bible; Grand Rapids: Brazos, 2006), 88.

14. John Piper, *Desiring God: Meditations of a Christian Hedonist* (rev. ed.; Colorado Springs: Multnomah, 2011).

15. One good example is G. H. Stassen and D. P. Gushee, *Kingdom Ethics: Following Jesus in Contemporary Context* (Downers Grove, IL: InterVarsity Press, 2003).

Jesus and the Ethical Theories

I am convinced Jesus doesn't fit neatly into any of these theories, and the Sermon on the Mount requires a better "theory."[16] However, each of these theories—virtue, deontological, and utilitarian ethics—does say something true about how Jesus "did" ethics. But using these categories runs the serious risk of colonizing Jesus into the history of philosophical thinking. It might be wiser for us to begin by wondering what Jesus sounded like—morally, that is—in a first-century Galilean Jewish world.

This warning about imposing philosophical categories to Jesus leads to a warning against theologians doing the same. There is something about the Sermon on the Mount that makes Christians nervous, and in particular it makes Protestants nervous, especially those whose theology's first foot is a special understanding of grace. Now I don't want to say grace is not an important foot in the dance, but for some grace has to be said first or nothing works right. This realization leads many theologians to say something like this: "Nothing in the Sermon can be understood until you know that you are saved by grace and that, as a result of God's regenerative work in your inner person, you can listen to Jesus and follow Jesus." Or they may pose law (Sermon without grace) against gospel (grace leading to Sermon). No one said this more poignantly than John Wesley: "If they [the words of the Sermon] are considered as commandments, they are parts of the law; if as promises, of the gospel." And Kenneth Cain Kinghorn, who edited Wesley's sermons on the Sermon, put it this way: "Wesley taught that the moral law is the gospel presented in the form of a requirement, and the gospel is the law presented in the form of a promise."[17]

However this posture of introducing the Sermon is expressed, the Sermon still makes many Christians nervous. Why? Because Jesus doesn't "do" ethics the way many want him to do them. You can squeeze some texts all you want, but Jesus doesn't say, "First grace, then obedience." He dives right in. There may be—indeed *is*—a reason Jesus simply dove in. Stanley Hauerwas

---

16. This is not to say they don't each contribute to reading the Sermon. Charles Talbert's *Reading the Sermon on the Mount: Character Formation and Decision Making in Matthew 5–7* (Grand Rapids: Baker Academic, 2004) is framed through virtue ethics rather than through norms for decision-making. The same is true of N. T. Wright's *After You Believe*. My criticism is that Jesus isn't *speaking in this manner when he teaches his norms, morals, or ethics*. Virtue ethicists focus on character (or virtue), not on norms or commands; Jesus focuses on the latter. That is what is in need of theoretical explanation. I will contend it is found in Christology: his demands confront us with who he is, the Lord, the Messiah/King.

17. K. C. Kinghorn, *John Wesley on the Sermon on the Mount* (Nashville: Abingdon, 2002), 19. On Wesley, see Mark Noll, in J. P. Greenman et al., *The Sermon on the Mount through the Centuries*, 153–80.

recognizes that Jesus' new wine doesn't fit into the ethical-theory wineskins: "Virtue may be its own reward, but for Christians the virtues, the kind of virtues suggested by the Beatitudes, are names for the shared life made possible through Christ."[18] Or later, "Yet Christians are not called to be virtuous. We are called to be disciples."[19]

To sketch Jesus' "theory" I want to suggest first that Jesus "did" ethics from four angles: Ethics from Above, Ethics from Beyond, Ethics from Below, and then setting each of these into the context of Jesus' messianic ethics designed for the messianic community in the power of the Spirit.[20]

Ethics from Above: Torah

Jesus emerges out of a history, and that history is Israel's history. One of the central elements of that history is that God speaks to humans in the Torah — the law of Moses. The paradigmatic story is found in Exodus 19–24, with the Ten Commandments found in Exodus 20, all rehearsed in a new form in Deuteronomy. What strikes a reader is that this is top-down communication from God: God descends to the top of Mount Sinai and *reveals* divine law for Israel through Moses. That God spoke, of course, was nothing new, nor did God speak only once to Israel. The singular expression of the prophet, still known in the King James Version, is "Thus saith the LORD." Everything about Jesus' ethics emerges from this history of God having spoken directly to Israel.

Perhaps the most astounding feature of Jesus' ethics is that while Jesus clearly speaks for God and Jesus clearly fits the profile of a prophet, Jesus never says, "Thus saith the Lord." He speaks directly *as the voice of God*. His words are no less than an Ethics from Above. The Sermon on the Mount ends with words to this effect: "When Jesus had finished saying these things, the crowds were amazed at his teaching, because he taught as one who had authority, and not as their teachers of the law" (7:28–29).

No one in the last two hundred years seems to have grasped this self-authoritative dimension of the ethics of Jesus, namely, the encountering force of God-with-us in Jesus as King and Lord and Savior, like Dietrich Bonhoeffer did in his *Discipleship*.[21] This classical book blows apart the common

---

18. Hauerwas, *Matthew*, 65.

19. Ibid., 75.

20. I have a slightly more academic outline of this approach in the forthcoming revised *Dictionary of Jesus and the Gospels* (Downers Grove, IL: InterVarsity Press, 2014), s.v. "Ethics of Jesus."

21. D. Bonhoeffer, *Discipleship* (Dietrich Bonhoeffer Works 4; trans. B. Green; Minneapolis: Fortress, 1996). On Bonhoeffer's Sermon on the Mount, see S. Hauerwas, "Dietrich Bonhoeffer and John Howard Yoder," in *The Sermon on the Mount through the Centuries* (ed. J. P. Greenman; Grand Rapids: Brazos, 2007), 207–22.

distinction between justification and sanctification, and that move enabled Bonhoeffer to get closer to the heart of the Sermon than most. (If someone entered my house and stole every book I own, Bonhoeffer's *Discipleship* would be the first one I'd purchase the next morning—if I waited that long.)

Classic virtue, Kantian, and utilitarian ethics never make the claim to be divinely revealed words, but this is at the heart of the ethic of Jesus (and the Bible). When Christians express Christian ethics through such philosophical theories, they have to modify and reformulate both the content and the theory to make the theory fit.

Variations on this Ethics from Above are found in the Christian tradition. Perhaps the strongest form is divine command theory. This theory of ethics emphasizes divine revelation as the first word in all ethical discussions, with the added emphasis that what makes a moral demand right is that God issues that demand.[22] The ancient philosophical debate in Plato was whether an act was good because God commanded it or whether God commanded it because it was (already) good. But divine command theory today has found a way out of that thicket to make the claim that because God is good God's demands are good and right and loving.[23]

The newest kid on the block when it comes to ethical theory is narrative ethics, and by this we mean theories of ethics that contend we are part of a story, that such a story formed our ethics and is designed to shape us yet further. Stanley Hauerwas's capturing of ethics into an ecclesial narrative is perhaps the best-known example of a narrative-shaped ethic, but our point here is that *this story is a revelation, that is, the story in which we dwell comes to us from God*, and we appropriate this story as divine revelation through Scripture, the tradition, the Spirit, and the church.[24] Christian narrative ethics, then, require an Ethics from Above.

I would contend as well that N.T. Wright's virtue ethics work so well because of his commitment to Story and a biblical eschatology, one that takes seriously the created order as continuous in some ways with the new heavens and the new earth. Thus, Wright substantively reshapes virtue ethics in part by an Ethics from Above that is shaped by a kind of narrative ethics.[25] I have myself framed Jesus' gospel and the apostolic gospel as making sense only in the context of the Story of the Bible, the Story of Israel, and that the fulfillment of

---

22. W. C. Reuschling, "Divine Command Theories of Ethics," in *Dictionary of Scripture and Ethics* (ed. J. B. Green; Grand Rapids: Baker Academic, 2011), 242–46.

23. See Mouw, *The God Who Commands*.

24. See Hauerwas, *Peaceable Kingdom*; idem, *Community of Character*.

25. Wright, *After You Believe*. In other words, Wright's virtue ethics is a modified virtue ethics. Wright's serious work of appropriating creation can be explored further in O'Donovan, *Resurrection and Moral Order*.

that Story is the Story of Jesus.[26] That is, the gospel itself is a way of narrating God's Story in this world as moving from Adam through Abraham and Israel and David to Jesus and then beyond Jesus into the church of the prophets and apostles. If Jesus is the Messiah of that Story, and that is the gospel itself, then all ethics for Jesus involve at least, as one element, an Ethic from Above in the form of that narrative.

But narrowing how Jesus "did" ethics to a divine command posture or, better yet in his day and in his terms, to a Torah posture won't adequately capture how Jesus' ethics operated. Yes, to be sure, God speaks to us through Jesus, no more ethically than what we find in the Sermon on the Mount, but simply a vertical movement of words from God to us isn't sufficient for the fullness of Jesus' ethic.

Ethics from Beyond: Prophets

The genius of Israel's prophets was that they revealed God's will to his people, and at the heart of the prophets' ethic was bringing God's future to bear on the present. This is what I mean by an Ethics from Beyond, and it takes us one step beyond an Ethics from Above and one step closer to how Jesus "did" ethics. There is little corresponding ethic in modern ethical theory to this Ethics from Beyond except perhaps in a social contract that sustains a society into its future, or a progressive ethic that hopes beyond hope in some form of a world getting better and better, or a green ethic that urges humans to live now in light of the earth's future (or catastrophe). But social-contract, progressive, and ecological theories run out of steam just where Jesus began: his ethical posture toward the present was robustly shaped by a certain knowledge of God's future. Jesus' ethics flowed directly from God's kingdom; they are kingdom ethics.

The sheer force of Jesus' kingdom language, found more than a hundred times in the Synoptic Gospels and then advanced to some degree by John's conceptualization of kingdom in his expression "eternal life" and then crystallized in several Pauline observations (like Phil 2:6–11 or 1 Cor 15:20–28) and then gloriously sketched in Revelation 20–22, puts the listener of Jesus' ethic up against an eschatological ethic, a set of norms grounded in his belief of what is to come. What is to come for the person is consequentialist in that the future determines how one lives in the here and now. His ethic was an ethic for now in light of the kingdom to come. In the words of Stanley Hauerwas, "The sermon is the reality of the new age made possible in time."[27] Or, as

---

26. S. McKnight, *The King Jesus Gospel: The Original Good News Revisited* (Grand Rapids: Zondervan, 2011).

27. Hauerwas, *Matthew*, 60.

Joe Kapolyo framed it, "These disciples have the responsibility of living their lives in terms of the values that prevail in the kingdom of heaven."[28] We often call this "inaugurated" eschatology, and that means Jesus' kingdom ethic is an inaugurated-kingdom ethic.

The most notable element of Jesus' Ethics from Beyond was that the future had already begun to take effect in the present. This is the point of Matthew 4:17, words that butt up against the Sermon on the Mount and propel the words of Jesus throughout: "From that time on Jesus began to preach, 'Repent, for the kingdom of heaven has come near.'"

Over and over again in the Sermon and in Jesus' teaching, the future impinges on the present in such a way that a new day is already arriving in Jesus. Thus, "these are not ordinary ethics, nor are they merely an extension of intensification of Jewish ethics ... They are the ethics of the kingdom."[29]

The utilitarian, consequentialist ethic of Mill is a dry bone when compared to Israel's prophets and Jesus, for their consequentialism is not just a better world or even personal happiness, but ultimately the glory of God when God establishes his kingdom in this world. And a virtue ethic with no eschatology, which is what Aristotle offered to the world, can't be compared to the virtue ethic that one finds in Jesus. Here I think of how NT ethics are unfolded in Tom Wright's *After You Believe*, in Oliver O'Donovan's magisterial *Resurrection and Moral Order*, and in Glenn Stassen and David Gushee's *Kingdom Ethics*. An ethic unshaped by eschatology is neither Jesus' nor Christian.

But once again, there's a dimension of Jesus' ethics that is neither covered by an Ethics from Above or an Ethics from Beyond, but which is inherent to Israel's Story and, in fact, have become the predominant form of ethical reflection in the history of humankind.

Ethics from Below: Wisdom

This third dimension of Jesus' ethic emerges from a dimension of the Bible and Jewish history that is too often ignored in contemporary ethical theory, and it is an irony that a discipline known as the "love of wisdom" (*philosophia*) so rarely today lets itself become absorbed in wisdom motifs. An example of a moral philosopher who does, however, is Martin Buber, whose work *I and Thou* remains monumental.[30] Those familiar with Israel's wisdom

---

28. J. Kapolyo, "Matthew," in *Africa Bible Commentary* (ed. T. Adeyemo; Grand Rapids: Zondervan, 2006), 1117.

29. D. A. Hagner, "Ethics and the Sermon on the Mount," *Studia Theologica—Nordic Journal of Theology* 51/1 (1997): 48.

30. M. Buber, *I and Thou* (New York: Charles Scribner's Sons, 1958).

tradition, and Buber was, will know that there is a striking absence, or at least a major de-emphasis, of a Torah-shaped ethic and a revelatory-based set of commands.

Wisdom was not an Ethic from Above or, since it lacked an eschatological shaping, an Ethic from Beyond. The wisdom writers, and here I'm thinking of Proverbs, Ecclesiastes, Job, and the noncanonical Ben Sirach, don't say, "God says do this"; neither do they say, "Here comes God, better shape up!" No, the wisdom tradition anchors itself in *human observation*. Wisdom, then, is how to live in God's world in God's way, but this kind of wisdom can only be acquired by those who are humbly receptive to the wisdom of society's sages. As well, a wisdom culture trusts human observation and through intuition discerns God's intentions for this world.

Jesus, too, frequently teaches his followers how to live in light of inductive observation. In the Sermon this is clear, for instance, in going the second mile in Matthew 5:38–42, or in 6:19–34, where Jesus teaches a single-minded righteousness. Each day has enough gripes, so why engage today in tomorrow's griping?

Yet this earthy, horizontal, and inductive — dare one say empirical? — framing of ethics too often leads to the elimination of an Ethic from Above and an Ethic from Beyond.[31] One sees this in Aristotle, of course, but also in Kant, who wanted to frame all ethics on the basis of reason alone; one sees it in Bentham and Mill; one sees it in the egoistic ethical theory of Ayn Rand, our modern world's obsession with cultural relativism in which belief in a revelation or a kingdom has been surrendered; one sees it even more in evolutionary ethics that seek to frame ethics on the basis of what is natural to human evolution; one sees it in B. F. Skinner's behaviorism, which, in fact, all but surrendered anything like ethics. A good example of that struggle is Bernard Gert's attempt to establish moral theory on reason alone.[32] As my friend Greg Clark observed to me, perhaps we first learn about the futility — but ultimate cynical posture — of framing ethics entirely from below in the Bible itself, in Ecclesiastes, which reminds us that so much of human striving is nothing but vanity.

But others are extending through discernment Jesus' Ethics from Below in light of how the Bible speaks about a variety of pressing topics, and I think here of both William Webb, in his *Slaves, Women, and Homosexuals*, where he thoroughly maps his "redemptive-movement hermeneutic," and of Samuel Wells, in his *Improvisation*, where he contends that the proper posture of

---

31. Wilkens, *Beyond Bumper Sticker Ethics*.
32. B. Gert, *Common Morality: Deciding What to Do* (New York: Oxford University Press, 2004).

the Christian is to improvise rather than simply to perform the script.[33] The reason I assign Webb and Wells to an Ethics from Below is because they singularly focus on learning to discern, in wisdom, how to live out the Bible in our world in a way that breaches the script in order to advance a Christian ethic into new territory. Any use of the Sermon on the Mount that does not extend it into our world by plowing new ground converts into a mere Ethics from Above and fails to embrace that Jesus himself "did" Ethics from Below. How we can we "follow" Jesus and not learn to do ethics as he did?

Jesus' Ethical Theory: Messianic, Ecclesial, Pneumatic

I want to propose, then, that Jesus' ethic is a combination of an Ethics from Above, Beyond, and Below — the Law, the Prophets, and the Wisdom Literature. But there's more because those three elements for his ethics are tied to his messianic vocation, his conviction that an ethic can only be lived out in community (the kingdom manifestation in the church) and through the power of the Spirit now at work. The above, beyond, and below are each reshaped because it is Jesus' ethic, because this ethic is for his followers, and because the Spirit has been unleashed.

Jesus' ethic is distinct because Jesus saw himself as Israel's Messiah, and because at its core Jesus offered nothing other than a Messianic Ethic.[34] Nothing makes sense about the Sermon until we understand it as messianic vision, and once we understand it as messianic we can understand it all — especially its radical elements.[35] Thus, Tom Wright gets it exactly right when he says: "The Sermon ... isn't just about how to behave. It's about discovering the living God in the loving, and dying, Jesus, and learning to reflect that love ourselves into the world that needs it so badly."[36] Or, as the German New Testament scholar and Lutheran bishop Eduard Lohse, put it: "Jesus' word is not separable from the one who speaks it."[37]

At the core of Jesus' ethics, then, is a belief about himself, that he indeed was the one who brought the Old Testament Law and the Prophets (as well as Wisdom Literature) to their completion or defining point in who he was,

---

33. W. J. Webb, *Slaves, Women and Homosexuals: Exploring the Hermeneutics of Cultural Analysis* (Downers Grove, IL: InterVarsity Press, 2001); Wells, *Improvisation*. Also, W. J. Webb, *Corporal Punishment in the Bible: A Redemptive-Movement Hermeneutic for Troubling Texts* (Downers Grove, IL: InterVarsity Press, 2011), 57 – 73.

34. There are a number of books exploring Jesus' self-consciousness (who did he think he was?); N. T. Wright, *Simply Jesus: A New Vision of Who He Was, What He Did, and Why He Matters* (New York: HarperOne, 2011); McKnight, *King Jesus Gospel*, 100 – 111.

35. Talbert, *Reading the Sermon on the Mount*, 10 – 20.

36. N. T. Wright, *Matthew for Everyone* (2 vols.; Louisville: Westminster John Knox, 2002), 1:53.

37. E. Lohse, *Theological Ethics of the New Testament* (trans. E. Boring; Minneapolis: Fortress, 1991).

what he did, and what he taught. There is a Torah dimension; there is a Wisdom dimension; and there is a Prophet dimension. But King Jesus pushes each of these to a new level where Jesus himself is the Torah, the Wisdom, and the Prophet who was to come. Only in association or relationship with Jesus does the Sermon make sense. Jesus does not offer abstract principles or simply his version of the Torah for a new society. Instead, he offers himself to his disciples, or, put differently, he summons them to himself and in participation with Jesus and his vision the disciples are transformed into the fullness of a kingdom moral vision.

But Jesus' Messianic Ethic is not for isolated individuals. Transcending what Aristotle meant in his discussions of friendship and recapturing Israel's own sense of family identity, this ethic of Jesus was to be lived out in the context of a kingdom community, the ecclesia. As the Messiah formed a community of followers, so the ethic of Jesus is a messianic and kingdom-community ethic. The Sermon on the Mount is supremely and irreducibly ecclesial. Few have emphasized this theme as central to Christian ethics like John Howard Yoder.[38] Or, as Hauerwas said it, "The sermon, therefore, is not a list of requirements, but rather a description of the life of a people gathered by and around Jesus."[39] Church, then, forms the context for the ethic of Jesus.[40]

But there's more in the pages of the New Testament as ethical reflection lumbers toward the second century: Jesus' ethical vision was only practicable through the power of the Pentecostal gift of the Holy Spirit who took human abilities to the next level and human inabilities and turned them into new abilities. This Spirit-driven ethic was to be sustained in the ecclesia by sacraments, by Word, by the gifts of the Spirit, and by memory of our common Story. Much more could be said, but this sketches how Jesus did ethics.

Preliminaries to Reading the Sermon on the Mount in Matthew

There are two versions of the Sermon, one in Matthew 5–7 (the text this commentary will expound) and one in Luke 6:20–49. Since our focus will be on Matthew's version of the Sermon, we need to sketch a brief introduction to Matthew and its Sermon, though when this series is completed

---

38. Yoder's only study of the Sermon on the Mount, presented in 1966 in Uruguay, found the "political axioms" of the Sermon to be an ethic of repentance, discipleship, testimony, fulfillment, perfect love, excess, and reconciliation. See "The Political Axioms of the Sermon on the Mount," in J. H. Yoder, *The Original Revolution: Essays on Christian Pacifism* (Scottdale, PA: Herald, 2003), 34–51.

39. Hauerwas, *Matthew*, 61.

40. See a helpful emphasis in Reuschling, *Reviving Evangelical Ethics*.

there will be a more complete introduction to Matthew in the volume on Matthew.[41]

The Question of Authorship

After more than three decades of teaching Matthew and the Sermon, I have come to this conclusion: it is impossible to prove who wrote Matthew's gospel. By that I mean it is as impossible to prove that he (Matthew, the tax collector of Matt 9:9–13) didn't do as that he did. It has been customary to lay on the table one's claim: undeniably, Matthew is the traditional author. Then lay next to that claim the many and various criticisms of that claim, then respond to each criticism—often done with admirable detail—and then conclude that since none of the criticisms are sufficiently demonstrated, Matthew is the author. The logical problem here needs more attention by those who use this approach: disproving criticisms is not the same as proving the claim that the tax collector wrote the gospel. The reason I say that is because the critics of the traditional claim perform a similar procedure: they lay on the table the claim, then argue against the claim by offering their criticisms, and then conclude that *Matthew did not write the gospel.* Knocking down arguments does not a case make.

The arguments *for* Matthew, the tax collector, writing this gospel eventually wind down to the simple fact that Matthew has been connected to this gospel from the earliest surviving evidence. The earliest manuscripts of this gospel have *Kata Maththaion,* "according to Matthew." Many today have for a variety of reasons chosen to be suspicious of any early church claim like this, but I cannot share that suspicion. In fact, I am inclined to trust early church attributions.[42]

The authorship question can be rooted in the *question of sources.* For more than two hundred years, but particularly for the last century, how the Synoptic Evangelists got their material has been a constant discussion. Some think the canonical order is the chronological order (Matthew, then Mark, then Luke), while others argued that Augustine got it more or less right when he said Matthew was first, Luke was second, and Mark combines and reduces

---

41. See S. McKnight, "Gospel of Matthew," *DJG,* 526–41. For a recent study, R. T. France, *The Gospel of Matthew* (Grand Rapids: Eerdmans, 2007), 1–22. On the structure, see Talbert, *Reading the Sermon on the Mount,* 21–26. On rhetoric, H. Betz, *Sermon on the Mount,* 44–70. For the purpose and setting, see Carter, *What Are They Saying,* 56–77. On empire criticism, see W. Carter, "Power and Identities: The Contexts of Matthew's Sermon on the Mount," in *Preaching the Sermon on the Mount* (eds. D. Fleer and D. Bland; St. Louis: Chalice, 2007), 8–21. For evaluation, S. McKnight and J. B. Modica, eds, *Jesus Is Lord, Caesar Is Not: Evaluating Empire in New Testament Studies* (Downers Grove, IL: InterVarsity Press, 2013).

42. C. S. Keener, *A Commentary on the Gospel of Matthew* (Grand Rapids: Eerdmans, 1999), 38.

Matthew and Luke into a shorter gospel. This theory, today called the Gries-bach Hypothesis, is a minority viewpoint. The standard hypothesis, which I prefer to call the Oxford Hypothesis because it was framed at Oxford University about one century ago through the detailed work of B. H. Streeter and others, is that Mark and a hypothetical source called "Q" (from the German word *Quelle*, "source") were at the bottom of the Synoptics. Both Matthew and Luke each used both Mark and Q independently of one another, and they each probably had access both to other written sources as well as to oral traditions. I will assume this theory, which is the majority viewpoint today, in what follows. Though this will not be the focus of this commentary, at times we will observe how "Matthew" has edited his sources to reflect the theology we can detect in the first gospel.[43]

By way of additional note, if Matthew used Mark, we have now "dated" Matthew after Mark, and since most date Mark in the late 60s to early 70s, Matthew was probably written sometime in the 70s or even 80s, but a slightly earlier date for Mark (say the early 60s) makes it entirely possible for Matthew to have been written before AD 70. Any proposal for dating Matthew must remain tentative.[44]

If our source-critical conclusion is accepted, we have another piece of evidence for considering the authorship question. If Matthew used Mark, and if Matthew is the tax collector, then Matthew copied Mark's story of Matthew's own conversion story.

Mark 2:14	Matthew 9:9
As he walked along, he saw Levi son of Alphaeus sitting at the tax collector's booth. "Follow me," Jesus told him, and Levi got up and followed him.	As Jesus went on from there, he saw a man named Matthew sitting at the tax collector's booth. "Follow me," he told him, and Matthew got up and followed him.

There is nothing here that can really prove or disprove Matthew's author-ship, but it strikes more than a few readers today odd that an author, in this case Matthew, would copy someone else's version of his own conversion even if he changed the name from "Levi" to "Matthew." It is possible that Matthew had two names, Levi and Matthew, but that doesn't relieve the oddity of copy-ing someone else's record of your own conversion.

The evidence is not compelling in any direction. Craig Keener has

---

43. For my own take, see S. McKnight, "Source Criticism," in *Interpreting the New Testament: Essays on Methods and Issues* (ed. D. A. Black and D. S. Dockery; Nashville: Broadman & Holman, 2001), 74–105.

44. See Keener, *Matthew*, 42–44.

summed this up well: "Matthew's claim to authorship on any level [is] the weakest among the four canonical Gospels."[45] Yes, and with Keener I would contend that this argument comes down to whether or not we trust the earliest evidence and that a reasonable view is that Matthew is either the original deposit of this gospel or the author of the whole gospel. I will call the author "Matthew" because I think that is the most likely conclusion we can draw.

The *question of structure* for the Sermon is incapable of any kind of firm resolution.[46] There are a few proposals for the structure of the Sermon, the most intriguing being the one that suggests from the Lord's Prayer on we have expositions of each line in the Lord's Prayer.[47] The evidence in Matthew 6 and 7, though, must be stretched to fit those lines. The safest way to read and preach this Sermon is to recognize clearly discernible topics about discipleship that move one to another. The opening lines about disciples gathering around Jesus (5:1) with the ending having crowds (7:28) suggests to many that Matthew has composed a sermon based on sayings given by Jesus about ethics from a variety of his ministry locations.

---

45. Ibid., 39.
46. A dense summary of proposals can be seen in ibid., 163.
47. R. A. Guelich, *The Sermon on the Mount: A Foundation for Understanding* (Waco, TX: Word, 1982), 363–81.

Resources for Those Teaching or Preaching the Sermon

C ommentaries abound, and the number of works on the Sermon staggers. So I will list studies only on the Sermon that have risen to the top in my own study. In the process of writing this commentary I began always with Luther and Calvin, dipped into the Ancient Christian Commentary on Scripture, and then read through representative commentaries on offer today: Dale Allison, P. Lapide, Ulrich Luz, Don Hagner, David Garland, J. Nolland, R. T. France, David Turner, and Craig Keener. When I was all done, I read Stott's and Bonhoeffer's expositions. In writing this commentary I realized time and time again how many items I have read over the years on Matthew and this Sermon, many written by friends and colleagues, but in this context I have chosen to restrict dramatically those with whom I will interact. Here is a list of six significant items for those who want to build a library.

Bonhoeffer, D. *Discipleship*. Dietrich Bonhoeffer Works 4. Minneapolis: Fortress, 1996.

Allison, D. C. J. *The Sermon on the Mount: Inspiring the Moral Imagination*. New York: Herder, 1999.

Talbert, C. H. *Reading the Sermon on the Mount: Character Formation and Decision Making in Matthew 5–7*. Grand Rapids: Baker Academic, 2004.

Guelich, R. A. *The Sermon on the Mount: A Foundation for Understanding*. Waco, TX: Word, 1982.

Lapide, P. *The Sermon on the Mount: Utopia or Program for Action?* Maryknoll, NY: Orbis, 1986.

Greenman, J. P., T. Larsen, and S. R. Spencer, eds. *The Sermon on the Mount through the Centuries: From the Early Church to John Paul II*. Grand Rapids: Brazos, 2007.

CHAPTER 1

Matthew 5:1 – 2 and 7:28 – 29

 ## LISTEN[1] to the Story

⁵:¹Now when Jesus saw the crowds, he went up on a mountainside and sat down. His disciples came to him....

⁷:²⁴ "Therefore everyone who hears these words of mine and puts them into practice is like a wise man who built his house on the rock. ²⁵The rain came down, the streams rose, and the winds blew and beat against that house; yet it did not fall, because it had its foundation on the rock. ²⁶But everyone who hears these words of mine and does not put them into practice is like a foolish man who built his house on sand. ²⁷The rain came down, the streams rose, and the winds blew and beat against that house, and it fell with a great crash."

²⁸When Jesus had finished saying these things, the crowds were amazed at his teaching, ²⁹ because he taught as one who had authority, and not as their teachers of the law. ⁸:¹When Jesus came down from the mountainside, large crowds followed him.

Listening to the text in the Story: Matthew 4:23 – 25 and 9:35; 17:1 – 8; John 6:3; Exodus 19:3; 24:12 – 13; 34:1 – 2, 4; Deuteronomy 9:9; 10:3.

It is against every known method of reading, but we must begin reading the Sermon on the Mount by listening carefully to the ending of the Sermon (7:24 – 27 and 7:28 – 8:1) and tie that ending to the beginning at 5:1 – 2. As we begin at the end, we also must listen to how Matthew sets the *context* for the Sermon at 4:23 – 25 and 9:35.[2]

First the context. When the gospel of Matthew was written, no chapter divisions were used. To indicate transitions authors in the ancient world

---

1. It is good to learn to read this Sermon well for public hearing. See D. Dewey, "Great in the Empire of Heaven: A Faithful Performance of Matthew's Sermon on the Mount," in *Preaching the Sermon on the Mount: The World It Imagines* (eds. D. Fleer and D. Bland; St. Louis: Chalice, 2007).
2. Carter, *What Are They Saying*, 35 – 55.

used a quarry of devices, one of which was summary statements. Matthew's summary statement in 4:23–25 is nearly repeated verbatim in 9:35 and 10:1.

> [4:23]Jesus went throughout Galilee, *teaching in their synagogues, proclaiming the good news of the kingdom, and healing every disease and sickness among the people.* [24]News about him spread all over Syria, and people brought to him all who were ill with various diseases, those suffering severe pain, the demon-possessed, those having seizures, and the paralyzed; and he healed them. [25]Large crowds from Galilee, the Decapolis, Jerusalem, Judea and the region across the Jordan followed him.

> [9:35]Jesus went through all the towns and villages, *teaching in their synagogues, proclaiming the good news of the kingdom and healing every disease and sickness.*

> [10:1]Jesus called his twelve disciples to him and gave them authority to drive out impure spirits and *to heal every disease and sickness.*

The italicized connections are obvious, but they are even more obvious in Greek. The only three places where these Greek words are used together in Matthew are in these three sets of verses, which leads me to this observation: Matthew 4:23–25 outlines what Matthew will tell us about Jesus' ministry (teaching, preaching, healing) in Matthew 5–9, Matthew 9:35 tells us that Matthew has completed his sketch of Jesus' ministry of teaching, preaching, and healing, and then Matthew 10:1 shows that Jesus empowered his twelve apostles to extend that sketched ministry of Jesus to others.

Put together, here's what we get: Matthew 4:23–9:35 is a *sketch of the mission and ministry of Jesus*: he teaches and preaches in Matthew 5–7 and he heals in Matthew 8–9. The Sermon on the Mount, then, is a comprehensive sketch of the teaching and preaching message of Jesus. In the context of Matthew's narrative, the Sermon is a *presentation of Jesus' moral vision, his ethic.* You could say Matthew is saying to his audience who listens to Matthew 4:23–9:35: "Here's Jesus, here's his message [5–7], here are his actions [8–9]. You can now decide."

Second, the ending of the Sermon on the Mount provides a fundamental clue on how to read the Sermon. We will provide commentary on 7:24–27 at the end of this commentary, but for now we must observe that *Jesus ends the Sermon by calling people to do what he has taught.* Some soften his words: "He said, 'Do this,' but he didn't mean we have to obey his words." Others see a different motive: "Jesus' aim is to drive us to our knees, not make us obey his words." These common approaches fail the words of Jesus because in the Sermon Jesus calls his followers to do what he teaches. Those who don't do what he says, in fact, are condemned as foolish. The entire Sermon on the Mount, which Augustine said was the "perfect standard of the Christian life,"[3] then drives home one haunting question:

Will you follow me?

The Sermon presents Jesus' moral vision and summons us to follow him, and the Sermon is designed to prompt one to make a decision about Jesus. Thus, we are led to think immediately of an Ethic from Above.[4] John Stott finishes off his splendid and influential commentary on the Sermon with these words: "So Jesus confronts us with himself, sets before us the radical choice between obedience and disobedience, and calls us to an unconditional commitment of mind, will and life to his teaching."[5] Theologically speaking, the Sermon is grounded in a Christology, a view of who Jesus is, and that Christology begins at 5:1.

EXPLAIN the Story

As God (through Moses) did not give the Torah in Egypt but waited until the Israelites were deep in the wilderness, so Jesus waited. In Matthew's narrative we observe that Jesus waited for crowds to gather around what he was doing before he set out his own moral vision. Jesus had already been baptized and been tempted, and he had returned to Galilee and called four disciples to follow him (Matt 3:1 – 4:22). Furthermore, Matthew makes it clear that Jesus was on a public tour of Galilee, teaching in synagogues, preaching about God's kingdom, and healing all sorts of people (4:23 – 25), and with crowds gathering he set forth his moral vision.

Surrounding the Sermon are notations of crowds (4:25; 5:1; 7:28; 8:1). "When Jesus saw the crowds" in 5:1, presumably the crowds of 4:25, he began to teach. The "crowds" would have included males and females as well as adults and children.[6] There is a bit of a complication here for which there is no compelling solution: Jesus sees the crowds, sits down, and his disciples (not the crowds) gather around him, but when the Sermon is over we are told "the crowds were amazed" (7:28). The simple solution is that the crowds gathered around the disciples as Jesus taught his disciples, but it is just as possible to

---

3. Augustine, *Our Lord's Sermon on the Mount* (*NPNF*; ed. P. Schaff; Grand Rapids: Eerdmans, 1979), 3 (1.1).

4. See introduction, pp. 8 – 10.

5. J. R. W. Stott, *The Message of the Sermon on the Mount* (The Bible Speaks Today; Downers Grove, IL: InterVarsity Press, 1985), 205. On Stott, see Greenman et al., *The Sermon on the Mount through the Centuries*, 266 – 79.

6. R. M. Dowsett, "Matthew," in *IVPWBC*, 525.

think Matthew has collected teachings of Jesus from various settings, some restricted and some more open to the crowds.[7]

How Jesus begins the Sermon opens up vistas: "He went up on a mountainside [more accurately, 'into the mountain'] and sat down" (5:1). Saying Jesus went onto a "mountain" could be no more than a casual, (almost) meaningless geographical observation, and that Luke says Jesus taught from a flat place (Luke 6:17) supports such a casual view for some.[8] Or, as so many of the early fathers thought, it could be a geographical symbol of higher reality.[9] But anyone who reads the Bible as the Story of God suspects there is more at stake. Bible readers connect *mountain* with Moses. We agree: Matthew presents Jesus as a new Moses figure. As Moses ascended the mountain, as Moses sat on the mountain, as Moses descended the mountain, and as Moses taught the Torah, so Jesus does the same. Some Moses themes were set before Jesus ascended the mountain: both Jesus and Moses had a dream connected to their births, the slaughter of children is connected to their births, both narrowly escaped the clutches of a despot, both had to flee and then only later could return to the land — and, like Moses, Jesus was in the wilderness, fasted forty days, was tested by God, and passed through the Jordan (though Moses died before the Jordan).[10]

There is, then, plenty of evidence to see Matthew's description as more than accidental allusions to Moses.[11] The expression "he went up on a mountainside" is used many times in the Old Testament, especially for Moses' ascent onto the mountain (see, e.g., Exod 19:3; 24:12–13; 34:1–2, 4; Deut 9:9; 10:3). Moses also descended the mountain, as does Jesus in Matthew 8:1, and Matthew's words here are almost verbatim from Exodus 34:29. In addition, in the Sermon itself Jesus and Moses are explicitly connected if not contrasted at 5:17–48. Jesus' teachings are set in the context of the Torah of Moses as their completion.

Not to be forgotten is that the posture of a lawgiver is sitting. As those

---

7. On other occasions there is a contrast of crowds and disciples in Matthew (cf. 13:10–11, 34, 36; 17:14, 19). The term "disciple" is best seen as a "mirror" of all followers of Jesus. While most of the instances of this term refer to the Twelve, there are others that clearly don't (e.g., 27:57; 28:19). On this, Guelich, *Sermon on the Mount*, 53.

8. For "hills," France, *Matthew*, 156–57. KNT: "hillside."

9. M. Simonetti, *Matthew 1–13* (Ancient Christian Commentary on Scripture; ed. T. Oden; Downers Grove, IL: InterVarsity Press, 2001), 77–78. Jerome: "The Lord goes up to the mountains to draw the crowds toward deeper matters with himself, but the crowds are not capable of ascending" (from Jerome, *St. Jerome: Commentary on Matthew* [The Fathers of the Church; trans. T. P. Scheck; Washington, DC: Catholic University of America Press, 2008], 74–75).

10. David E. Garland, *Reading Matthew: A Literary and Theological Commentary on the First Gospel* (New York: Crossroad, 1993), 51–52. Garland cautions against seeing too much Moses.

11. D. C. Allison Jr., *The New Moses: A Matthean Typology* (Minneapolis: Fortress, 1993), 172–80; Keener, *Matthew*, 164. For an opposing view, see Guelich, *Sermon on the Mount*, 52.

with legal authority sat in the seat of Moses (Matt 23:2; cf. Luke 4:16, 20), so Jesus "sat down" to teach (Matt 5:1). Jesus is compared to both Moses and Elijah in 17:1 – 8. The early church saw Jesus taking Moses to an entirely new level, and no text is perhaps more pointed than Eusebius, *Demonstration of the Gospel* 3.2:[12]

> Moses was the first leader of the Jewish race. He found them attached to the deceitful polytheism of Egypt, and was the first to turn them from it, by enacting the severest punishment for idolatry. He was the first also to publish the theology of the one God, bidding them worship only the Creator and Maker of all things. He was the first to draw up for the same hearers a scheme of religious life, and is acknowledged to have been the first and only lawgiver of their religious polity. **But Jesus Christ too**, like Moses, only on a grander stage, was the first to originate the teaching according to holiness for the other nations, and first accomplished the rout of the idolatry that embraced the whole world. He was the first to introduce to all men the knowledge and religion of the one Almighty God. And He is proved to be the first Author and Lawgiver of a new life and of a system adapted to the holy.
>
> And with regard to the other teaching on the genesis of the world, and the immortality of the soul, and other doctrines of philosophy which Moses was the first to teach the Jewish race, **Jesus Christ** has been the first to publish them to the other nations by His disciples in a far diviner form. So that Moses may properly be called the first and only lawgiver of religion to the Jews, **and Jesus Christ** the same to all nations, according to the prophecy which says of Him: "Set, O Lord, a lawgiver over them: that the Gentiles may know themselves to be but men." [Ps. ix. 20.]
>
> Moses again by wonderful works and miracles authenticated the religion that he proclaimed: **Christ likewise**, using His recorded miracles to inspire faith in those who saw them, established the new discipline of the Gospel teaching. Moses again transferred the Jewish race from the bitterness of Egyptian slavery to freedom: **while Jesus Christ** summoned the whole human race to freedom from their impious Egyptian idolatry under evil daemons. Moses, too, promised a holy land and a holy life therein under a blessing to those who kept his laws: **while Jesus Christ** says likewise: "Blessed are the meek, for they shall inherit the earth," promising a far better land in truth, and a holy and godly, not the land of Judaea, which in no way excels the rest (of the earth), but the heavenly country which suits souls that love God, to those who follow out the

---

12. For more texts, Allison, *New Moses*, 103 – 6.

life proclaimed by Him. And that He might make it plainer still, He proclaimed the kingdom of heaven to those blessed by Him. **And you will find other works done by our Saviour with greater power than those of Moses, and yet resembling the works which Moses did**. As, for example, Moses fasted forty days continuously, as Scripture witnesses, saying: "And (Moses) was there with the Lord forty days and forty nights [Exod. xxxiv. 28.]; he did neither eat bread nor drink water." **And Christ likewise**: For it is written: "And he was led by the Spirit into the wilderness, being forty days tempted of the devil; and in those days he did eat nothing." [Luke iv. 1 – 2.][13]

And so on goes Eusebius as he connects Jesus to Moses in one detail after another and offers to his readers a stunning display of fulfillment in Christ. The noxious fumes of supersessionism[14] in Eusebius fill the air and in fact have driven many Christians from seeing the importance of a Mosaic Christology. In Matthew 5:1 Jesus is presented as the new Moses, not by replacing Moses but by fulfilling Moses.

The implication is significant: Jesus is teaching the new law as the new Moses for the new people of God. As such, it partakes in an Ethic from Above, but since this ethic is so tied to Jesus, it is also a messianic ethic. Once again we are back to what we said in the introduction: this theme of Jesus' completing Israel's Story is at the heart of the Story of the gospel. The gospel is the completion of Israel's Story in the Story of Jesus, and from the get-go in the Sermon on the Mount we are ushered into the gospel reality that Israel's Torah/moral vision has now come to its completion in Jesus' moral vision. This is why the context of the Sermon (i.e., 4:23 – 25 and 9:35) is so important. It guides us to see in the Sermon not simply a moral vision but Jesus himself, the Jesus who is the new Moses with a new moral vision for God's new people.

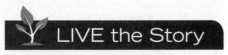

LIVE the Story

A New Kind of Evangelism

I used to teach at North Park University, a Christian college that does not require a student to be a Christian for admission. But two courses in biblical and theological studies are required for graduation, one of which is a survey of

---

13. www.ccel.org/ccel/pearse/morefathers/files/eusebius_de_05_book3.htm (accessed 7/27/2010). The boldfaced type emphasizes comparisons with Moses.

14. The belief that the church has absolutely replaced Israel as the people of God in such a manner that God's covenant with Israel is no longer viable.

the Bible. It is not uncommon for a student of another faith to enroll in our Bible survey class. One such student was Hindu. She actually did her best to convince me and others not to require her to take the class on religious grounds, but what's required at a Christian college entails something about the Christian faith. She was none too happy in the first few weeks of class; then I began to detect some more interest, and by November she was participating in class discussions. She came to me near the end of the semester and said, "Professor McKnight, I want to take your class called 'Jesus of Nazareth' because I think Jesus is really interesting and I want to learn more about him." She did take that class and made significant strides in understanding the Christian faith.

This Hindu student of mine *was attracted to Jesus because of the Story of Jesus she read in the Gospels.* She did not make appointments with me to discuss the gospel or how to get saved. She did not hear a plan of salvation in class. Instead, through reading the Bible she was exposed to Jesus. What attracted her was Jesus.

The Sermon on the Mount, when read from the special contextual clues Matthew provides at 4:23 – 25 and 9:35, which in Matthew's narrative is a sketch of Jesus' teaching, preaching, and healing ministries, is just that: *it is a compelling presentation of Jesus and his moral vision.* Pushed to the next level, what this means is that *reading or teaching or preaching the Sermon on the Mount is evangelism.*

A New Kind of Teacher

What do we learn about Jesus? We learn from our passage that he is the Teacher, the new Moses. Matthew emphasizes this theme perhaps more than any of the Gospels: 8:19; 9:11; 10:24 – 25; 12:38; 17:24; 19:16; 22:16, 24, 36; 23:8; 26:18. Furthermore, the Sermon begins and ends on the theme of Jesus as Teacher (5:2; 7:29), and its contextual markers are about teaching (4:23; 9:35). But Jesus isn't just an ordinary teacher in the Sermon: he is presented as the new Moses, the new law-giving teacher. Matthew 5:21 – 48 will make this abundantly clear.

Furthermore, as Moses taught the Torah, so Jesus, the new Moses, teaches his disciples the new Torah. It is no stretch to see here something profoundly messianic: the longed-for messianic era entailed a hope that a new Torah and a new obedience would accompany the Messiah,[15] and we see this in Jeremiah's famous new covenant passage (Jer 31:31 – 34). By presenting Jesus as that new Moses, Matthew is laying down a messianic claim for Jesus. This new kind of teacher is the messianic, new Moses.

---

15. W. D. Davies, *The Setting of the Sermon on the Mount* (BJS; Atlanta: Scholars Press, 1989).

John Stott is right to discuss the multidimensional authority of the Jesus who teaches the Sermon on the Mount. Stott expounds the authority of Jesus as Teacher, as the Messiah, as the Lord, as the Savior, as the Judge, as the Son of God, and as God incarnate. The most genuine readings of the Sermon lead the reader to ask: "Who is this teacher and who is this preacher? Who does he think he is?"[16] Or, as Richard Bauckham puts it, "The only Jesus we can plausibly find in the sources is a Jesus who, though usually reticent about it, speaks and acts for God in a way that far surpassed the authority of a prophet in the Jewish tradition."[17]

A New Posture

What does this mean for us? If Jesus is the new Moses/law-giving teacher for the new people of God, then there is one proper response: we are to assume the posture of a student.

The *posture* of a student, and nothing is more apropos at this point in studying the Sermon, is to sit and listen. Three gospel texts illustrate how students gathered around a teacher, the teacher stood to read the Torah, and then sat down to teach. Luke 10:39 tells us that Mary, unlike the too-busy Martha, "sat at the Lord's feet listening to what he said," and when Paul describes his education, he tells us that he sat at the feet of Gamaliel (Acts 22:3).[18] And Mark 3:31–35 describes "students" or disciples of Jesus in a circle around Jesus. We can do this in simple ways: we need to read the Bible in the posture of a student, namely, in a spirit of humble reverent reception of what God says. We can commit ourselves for a season to "sit at the feet" of Jesus again by reading the Gospels in a disciplined manner—from beginning to end a time or two.

The president of North Park University, David Parkyn, in the baccalaureate address of 2012, told us that during a recent recovery from surgery, he read through each of the Gospels in one sitting. He mentioned it was a life-transforming experience listening to and watching Jesus in the pages of the Gospels. Soaking ourselves with the words and actions of Jesus by reading the Gospels is the posture of a student of Jesus.

A recent event impressed me about this posture. Kris and I are part of Church of the Redeemer North Shore, an evangelical Anglican Church. In the church's tradition there are scheduled readings from the Bible for each Sunday: one from the Old Testament, one from the Psalms, and then a New Testament lesson followed by "the Gospel," which is a reading from the Gos-

---

16. Stott, *Message*, 212–22.

17. R. Bauckham, *Jesus: A Very Short Introduction* (Oxford/New York: Oxford University Press, 2011), 93–94.

18. The NIV: "I studied under Gamaliel" translates what could be more literally translated as "educated at the feet of Gamaliel." See also Luke 8:35, 41; 17:16; Acts 10:25.

pel text for the day. Amanda, a deacon, reads the Gospel each week. In reading Mark 10:46 – 52 Amanda came to the dramatic words of Jesus when blind Bartimaeus ran to Jesus. Jesus asked him a question that all of humanity wants to be asked by God. Amanda struggled emotionally to read the words of this liberating question. She then read: 'What do you want me to do for you?' Jesus asked." That is the question at the heart of many as we look to Jesus and hear the Gospel read. It is the question all the needy want to hear from Jesus, and it comes from the one person who can make the blind man see.

As the reader of the Gospel lesson, Amanda holds the text aloft so that we are all in the posture of students below the words of Jesus. The reading doesn't begin until she says, "The Holy Gospel of our Lord Jesus Christ." To which we say, "Glory be to you, O Lord." When she finishes she says, "The Gospel of the Lord." Our response, and on the day she read about the blind man a particularly hearty response was given, "Praise to you, Lord Jesus Christ."

We encountered Jesus Christ in the simple reading of the Gospel lesson. We did so because we sat as students at the feet of the Word of the Lord.

A New Obedience

In addition to this posture, the proper response to the Sermon is to *follow, or obey,* its teachings. While we will need to examine just how we can best follow Jesus' first-century teachings in a twenty-first-century world in the pages that follow, it is wise for us now to get our focus clear: we are called to do what Jesus teaches. This is the plain teaching of Matthew 7:13 – 27; 12:49 – 50; and 28:16 – 20. This new obedience leads to an entirely new life. Stanley Hauerwas captures this in words that sum up the whole of Jesus' vision and propel us into the rest of the Sermon:

> When he called his society together Jesus gave its members a new way of life to live. He gave them a new way to deal with offenders — by forgiving them. He gave them a new way to deal with violence — by suffering. He gave them a new way to deal with money — by sharing it. He gave them a new way to deal with problems of leadership — by drawing on the gift of every member, even the most humble. He gave them a new way to deal with a corrupt society — by building a new order, not smashing the old. He gave them a new pattern of relationship between man and woman, between parent and child, between master and slave, in which was made concrete a radical new vision of what it means to be a human person. He gave them a new attitude toward the state and toward the "enemy nation."[19]

---

19. Hauerwas, *Matthew*, 67 – 68.

The Sermon on the Mount crystallizes what Jesus gave to his disciples as the new way of life, the kingdom way of life in a world surrounded by the power brokers of empire. From the mountain, the posture of Moses, Jesus utters forth God's will for kingdom people, and as Jesus descended he gave those who heard the option of following. That same option stands before every reader of the Sermon.

LISTEN to the Story

¹His disciples came to him, ²and he began to teach them.¹
He said:

³ "Blessed are the poor in spirit,
  for theirs is the kingdom of heaven.
⁴Blessed are those who mourn,
  for they will be comforted.
⁵Blessed are the meek,
  for they will inherit the earth.
⁶Blessed are those who hunger and thirst for righteousness,
  for they will be filled.
⁷Blessed are the merciful,
  for they will be shown mercy.
⁸Blessed are the pure in heart,
  for they will see God.
⁹Blessed are the peacemakers,
  for they will be called children of God.
¹⁰Blessed are those who are persecuted because of righteousness,
  for theirs is the kingdom of heaven.

¹¹"Blessed are you when people insult you, persecute you and falsely say all kinds of evil against you because of me. ¹²Rejoice and be glad, because great is your reward in heaven, for in the same way they persecuted the prophets who were before you."

Listening to the text in the Story: Leviticus 26–27; Deuteronomy 28; Psalm 1; Isaiah 61.

---

1. Translations are interesting here. A literal translation would be "And opening his mouth Jesus began to teach them." The NIV, like the NRSV, simplifies by having only "he began to teach them," dropping the apparently redundant "opening his mouth." Older translations (KJV, ASV) and standard translations in other languages (French, German, Spanish) have "opening his mouth." Tom

Beginning Jesus' greatest Sermon with a list of the good guys implies (and the parallel at Luke 6:20–26 makes it explicit) a corresponding list of bad guys. Matthew will provide for us in Matthew 23's "woe" sayings an alternative list of bad guys. Not only that, Jesus finds all the "wrong" people on God's side and all the "right" people against God. Dallas Willard calls this a list of "God-based inversion" and the "hopelessly blessables" and finds at work a "gospel for the silly world."[2] Such a list is the way both to get your audience's attention and to force introspection. Or as Tom Wright cleverly put it, Jesus here takes us through the sound barrier, where things begin to work backwards.[3] Rosemary Dowsett observed that these blessings do not call attention to your typical manly characteristics but instead to those that in some cultures would be called "womanly."[4] Those who first heard this list of the truly blessed by God immediately began to wonder about themselves by asking, "Am I in or out?" The Beatitudes are a radical manifesto of a kingdom way of life because Jesus reveals who is in and who is not.

Two mutations of Israel's story occur in the Beatitudes. First, Jesus joins the prophetic voices, like Isaiah, who contend that not all of Israel is on God's side and that the remnant, or the faithful, are the true Israel. Jesus redefines who the remnant are. Second, Jesus stands here at least as more than a prophet. Jesus is the Lord, and Jesus pronounces who is on God's side. The natural response to Jesus' list of the blessed is to ask, "Who does this man think he is?!"

Listings like this at the time of Jesus had two basic orientations: one list rolled out the names of the saints, usually describing their behaviors, while another list focused on the characteristics of those who were observant of Torah and approved by God. For the first, I mention the list of noble ancestors in the Old Testament apocryphal book, Sirach 44; later in the New Testament we find a similar listing of saints in Hebrews 11. The other way of categorizing people, by characteristics of piety, can be found in later rabbinic texts, like *Mishnah ʾAbot* 5:12:

Wright's new translation (KNT) offers a helpful translation: "He took a deep breath, and began his teaching." Another translation of the Beatitudes worthy of consideration is that of T. D. Howell, *The Matthean Beatitudes in Their Jewish Origins: A Literary and Speech Act Analysis* (Studies in Biblical Literature; New York: Lang, 2011), 181–82. Here are his principal findings: "spiritually destitute," "those who experience sorrow," "humbled while on earth," "longing for and needing what is right," "showing mercy," "hearts of devotion," "who make peace," and "treated badly because of associating with the right."

2. D. Willard, *Divine Conspiracy: Rediscovering Our Hidden Life in God* (San Francisco: HarperSanFrancisco, 1998), 121–23.

3. Wright, *Matthew for Everyone*, 1:35.

4. Dowsett, "Matthew," 525.

A. There are four types of disciples:
B. (1) quick to grasp, quick to forget—he loses what he gains
C. (2) slow to grasp, slow to forget—what he loses he gains;
D. (3) quick to grasp, slow to forget—a sage;
E. (4) slow to grasp, quick to forget—a bad lot indeed.[5]

Jesus' list diverges from both of these lists and blesses the most unlikely of people. Instead of congratulating the Torah observant or the rigorously faithful or the heroic, he blesses the marginalized who stick with God through injustice.

Beginning with this list shapes the entire Sermon because it jolts us all into listening more attentively. We ask, "If these are the people who are in, what does that mean for me? If this is how the in-group lives, how should I live?" Jesus does not stand foursquare with the tradition of listing the saints, nor does he stand alongside the rabbis who saw humans through Torah observance. Instead, Jesus approached morals through the lens of *people who were (actually) living out the kingdom vision.* The Beatitudes, then, are a radical revisioning of the people of God. As Warren Carter frames it:

> In the beatitudes, Jesus has the disciples imagine a different world, a different identity for themselves, a different set of practices, a different relationship to the status quo. Why imagine? Not because it is impossible. Not because it is escapist. Not because it is fantasy. But because it begins to counter patterns imbibed from the culture of the imperial world.[6]

⚡ EXPLAIN the Story

What the disciples hear in the list is a revolutionary new basis for approval. Jesus tells the world that this motley crew around him is the true people of God, those who will populate the kingdom and enjoy the bounty of that kingdom. Maybe it is because I am privileged in our world, but those chosen by Jesus for inclusion make me nod my head in approval of his list. But my nodding is short-lived because as we proceed through this Sermon we will all eventually shift from nodding to wondering, if not disapproving. As Lucy

---

5. For the Mishnah, see Jacob Neusner, *The Mishnah: A New Translation* (New Haven, CT: Yale University Press, 1988). A list is found in the Dead Sea Scrolls at 4Q525 2.2.1 – 6 (the blessing here is for faithfulness to the Torah as the community interpreted it).

6. Carter, *What Are They Saying,* 21. Along this line of thinking Charles Campbell likens the Sermon to "folly" and Jesus to a "jester," pushing forward the radicality of Jesus' alternative society; see C. Campbell, "The Folly of the Sermon on the Mount," in *Preaching the Sermon on the Mount: The World It Imagines* (ed. D. Fleer and D. Bland; St. Louis: Chalice, 2007), 59 – 68.

Lind Hogan once asked us to consider as we read this Sermon, "When did the nodding stop?"[7]

The Meaning of "Blessed"

The word "blessed" is a blessed problem. Translations have done their best to find the perfect English word to translate the underlying Greek word (*makarios*) or sometimes the hypothetical Hebrew or Aramaic word Jesus actually used (perhaps *'ašrê*, as in Ps 1:1; 32:1, or *bārûk*, as in Gen 14:19 or Deut 28:3). Furthermore, the entire history of the philosophy of the "good life" and the late modern theory of "happiness" is at work when one says, "Blessed are...." Thus, this swarm of connections leads us to consider Aristotle's great Greek term *eudaimonia*, which means something like happiness or human flourishing, but it also prompts us to consider modern studies of what makes people happy.[8]

All of this gets bundled into the decision of which English word best translates the Greek word *makarios* ("blessed" in the NIV) now in the Beatitudes. An adventurous journey across the terrains of possible English words would be fun if this term were found in a subordinate clause in an otherwise insignificant verse in the Bible. But on this one word the entire passage stands and from this one word the whole list hangs. Get this word right, the rest falls into place; get it wrong, and the whole thing falls apart. We need to drill down to get it right.

The secret is to see this term in light of the Bible's story about who is blessed and who is not. Once we get that story's perspective, we are given parameters and content for understanding this term in this context, and once that happens we can examine the history of the quest for the good life and happiness. There are at least five major themes at work in this word "blessed."

First, the one who is "blessed" is blessed *by the God of Israel*. The entire biblical Story is in some sense shaped by God's watching over his elect people Israel, evaluating their covenant observance and either approving or disapproving of them in tangible ways. This theme has two primary points of origin: Leviticus 26–27 and Deuteronomy 28 as well as the Wisdom tradition, where it refers to a tangible, flourishing life rooted in common sense, hard work, and listening to one's elders (Pss 1; 32:1–2; Prov 3:13; 8:32; 20:7; 28:20). The theme of God's blessing on the obedient shapes the historical

---

7. L. L. Hogan, "You Be the Judge? Matthew 7:1–6," in *Preaching the Sermon on the Mount: The World It Imagines* (ed. D. Fleer and D. Bland; St. Louis: Chalice, 2007), 152.

8. On the history of happiness, D. McMahon, *Happiness: A History* (New York: Atlantic Monthly Press, 2006); I have an essay on happiness studies: "Happiness: Given, Lost, Regained," *Books & Culture* (Nov/Dec, 2008): 44–46, online at: www.booksandculture.com/articles/2008/novdec/14.44.html.

books like Judges, 1 and 2 Samuel, 1 and 2 Kings, 1 and 2 Chronicles, Ezra, and Nehemiah; it clearly reverberates throughout the prophets and in many ways gave rise to the sectarian movements at the time of Jesus, like the Pharisees and Essenes, who were seeking God's blessing.

Second, there is a clear *eschatological* focus in the word "blessed."[9] If a focus of the Old Testament was on present-life blessings for Torah observance, there is another dimension that deconstructs injustice and sets the tone for Israel's hope: the future blessing of God in the kingdom when all things will be put right; no text in the Old Testament fits more here than Isaiah 61.[10] This second dimension shapes the Beatitudes because Jesus' focus is on future blessing. The tense used in the promises for the blessing is often future, as in "they will be . . ." in verses 4–9. Notably, the present tense of the first and eighth blessing (5:3, 8), where we find the identical promise ("theirs *is* the kingdom"), surrounds the future tenses, perhaps indicating the certainty of those future promises.[11] As Dale Allison correctly points out, "We have here [in the Beatitudes] not commonsense wisdom born of experience but eschatological promise which foresees the unprecedented: the evils of the present will be undone and the righteous will be confirmed with reward."[12] This blessing, while its focus is future, begins now (Matt 11:6; 13:16).

A third theme at work is *conditionality*: those blessed are marked by specific attributes or characteristics and those who are implicitly not blessed (the Bible's word is "cursed"; see Luke 6:20–26; cf. Deut 28) are marked by the absence of those characteristics and by the presence of the opposite characteristics. But a word of caution is in order: clearly these blessings of Jesus are not directed at ethical attributes, as if this is Jesus' version of Paul's fruit of the Spirit (Gal 5:22–23), nor is this a virtue list by which to measure our moral progress. Instead, these blessings are heaped on *people groups* who are otherwise rejected in society, which means the blessings console those whom many would consider hopeless.

Thus, the conditionality here is not to be seen as a covert command for something we are to do, as if those who want blessing need to work at poverty of spirit or meekness. We are not to go out and become poor or start mourning or

---

9. Tom Wright's "You're going to . . ." and "You will . . ." in his KNT gets at this eschatological dimension well.

10. Stassen, *Living the Sermon*, 41–62. Stassen makes the following alignments with Isaiah 61: Matt 5:3 (Isa 61:1); 5:4 (61:2); 5:5 (61:1, 7); 5:6 (61:3, 8, 11); 5:8 (61:1); 5:10 (61:1); 5:11–12 (61:10–11).

11. D. C. Allison Jr., *The Sermon on the Mount: Inspiring the Moral Imagination* (Companions to the New Testament; New York: Crossroad/Herder & Herder, 1999), 42.

12. Ibid.

get ourselves persecuted.[13] Instead, Jesus here blesses people groups. The Beatitudes reveal that Jesus' ministry, as can be seen so clearly in Jesus' so-called inaugural sermon (Luke 4:16–30), focuses on the down-and-out and oppressed. Jesus is casting a vision so that his audience will come to know that things are not what they think they are. Instead, God's eyes are on all and God knows those who are living properly, regardless of their circumstances and conditions. The Beatitudes force the listener to *expand and contract who is in the kingdom of God.*

At the funeral of his father, Hauerwas preached a sermon on Revelation 7:9–17 and the Beatitudes of Matthew. He observed:

> Too often those characteristics [of the Beatitudes] … are turned into ideals we must strive to attain. As ideals, they can become formulas for power rather than descriptions of the kind of people characteristic of the new age brought by Christ.… Thus Jesus does not tell us that we should try to be poor in spirit, or meek, or peacemakers. He simply says that many who are called into the kingdom will find themselves so constituted.[14]

The "conditionality" of the Beatitudes is a reversal of typical conditions because it has the omniscience of God in knowing who is in and who is out.

Fourth, this list concerns the person's *relational disposition.* It is easy to think of the "blessed" as those who are in proper relation to God alone. But what stands out in the Beatitudes is one's relation to God as well as to self and others. When Matthew adds "in spirit" to "poor," we find what we also find in the third blessing ("meek"): an inner disposition that relates to God and others because of a proper estimation of oneself. Furthermore, some blessings are for those who relate to others in a loving disposition: "mourn" and "merciful" and "peacemakers." Others are concerned more directly with one's relation to God: "hunger and thirst for righteousness" and "pure in heart" and probably those who are persecuted. But the blessed people are noted by godly, loving relations with God, self, and others.

A final theme: *reversal* or *contrast.* Here we beg the reader's patience in appealing to the way Luke records the Beatitudes. Luke lists not only those who are blessed but also those who are cursed (Luke 6:20–26). Anytime someone blesses a group as Jesus does here, one is non-blessing others. Luke's curse list is implicit in Matthew, but this contention gains support from the oddity of those who are blessed: it is unconventional to bless those who are persecuted or those who meek. It gains even more strength from the radical presence of Jesus' unconventional ways of relating to "all the wrong people" (e.g., Matt 9:9–13)

---

13. Willard, *Divine Conspiracy,* 97–106, 114–25.
14. S. Hauerwas, *Hannah's Child: A Theologian's Memoir* (Grand Rapids: Eerdmans, 2010), 38–39.

and for the sorts of people he included among the apostles (4:18 – 22; 10:1 – 4). What Jesus blesses is countercultural and revolutionary and so turns culture inside out and society upside down. This can be seen simply by comparing Matthew 5:3 – 12 with a conventional list in Sirach 14:20 – 27 and 25:7 – 11:

> [14:20]Happy is the person who meditates on wisdom
> and reasons intelligently,
> [21]who reflects in his heart on her ways
> and ponders her secrets,
> [22]pursuing her like a hunter,
> and lying in wait on her paths;
> [23]who peers through her windows
> and listens at her doors;
> [24]who camps near her house
> and fastens his tent peg to her walls;
> [25]who pitches his tent near her,
> and so occupies an excellent lodging place;
> [26]who places his children under her shelter,
> and lodges under her boughs;
> [27]who is sheltered by her from the heat,
> and dwells in the midst of her glory.
>
> [25:7]I can think of nine whom I would call blessed,
> and a tenth my tongue proclaims:
> a man who can rejoice in his children;
> a man who lives to see the downfall of his foes.
> [8]Happy the man who lives with a sensible wife,
> and the one who does not plow with ox and ass together.
> Happy is the one who does not sin with the tongue,
> and the one who has not served an inferior.
> [9]Happy is the one who finds a friend,
> and the one who speaks to attentive listeners.
> [10]How great is the one who finds wisdom!
> But none is superior to the one who fears the Lord.
> [11]Fear of the Lord surpasses everything;
> to whom can we compare the one who has it?

Clearly, Jesus goes against the grain. Instead of blessing the one who pursues wisdom and reason and develops a reputation as a sage, and instead of blessing the one who has a good family, who observes the whole Torah, or the one who has all the right friends and develops a reputation as righteous or as a leader, Jesus blesses those whom no one else blessed. The genius of the

Beatitudes emerges from this contrastive stance: they are a countercultural revelation of the people of the kingdom.

If we add all this together, we get something like this: a "blessed" person is someone who, because of a heart for God, is promised and enjoys God's favor regardless of that person's status or countercultural condition.

This leads us back again to the translation issue: since no one English word will do the job in a completely adequate way, I prefer the word "blessed" because of its richer, covenantal, and theological contexts and because the only other real alternative, "happy" (CEB), often results in a focus on psychological happiness and gets associated easily with shallow discussions of happiness in contemporary culture and language.[15] A fulsome translation would be "God's favor is upon...."

One final observation about the word "blessed." *Jesus is the one who says who is and who is not blessed.* Our customary belief in Jesus somehow leads us at times to miss such a basic point, but one cannot fail to see that Jesus here steps into the pages of Israel's history as someone who speaks uniquely for God, and he does so with a truth claim so vital that one sees him as more than God's prophet.

The Blessed Ones

There are two "versions" of the Beatitudes of Jesus, and most scholars think the two versions derive from the hypothetical early Christian source called Q. Listing the two versions of the Beatitudes reveals both similarities and dissimilarities. Here are the two lists, and we italicize the beatitudes found only in Matthew:

Matthew 5:3–12	Luke 6: 20–23
1. Poor in spirit	1. Poor
2. Mourn	3. Weep now
3. *Meek*	
4. Hunger/thirst for righteousness	2. Hunger now
5. *Merciful*	
6. *Pure in heart*	
7. *Peacemakers*	
8. *Persecuted for righteousness*	
9. Insulted, persecuted, false statements	4. Hated, excluded, rejected

---

15. Guelich, *Sermon on the Mount*, famously translated the word "Congratulations!" and used that to define the blessing of salvation (pp. 109–11). "Joyful" is the proposal of Stassen, *Living the Sermon*, 39. Stott weighs in against translating the term with "happy," in Stott, *Message*, 33. Also D. A. Hagner, *Matthew 1–13* (WBC; Dallas: Word, 1993), 91; Keener (*Matthew*, 166) translates

Most notably, Luke has not only beatitudes but "woe" statements that match the beatitudes in reverse: rich, well fed, laugh, and speaking well of you. One cannot know for sure, but it is reasonable to think Matthew "collected" other beatitudes of Jesus and brought them together here. It also seems likely that Matthew has "airbrushed" some of the beatitudes, as can be seen in adding "in spirit" in #1 and "for righteousness" in #4, but in so doing he has clarified the original intent rather than leaving a beatitude or two open to misunderstanding.

It is risky to venture something new when it comes to organizing the Beatitudes, but I will try.[16] They have no apparent logical or consecutive order, though a few scholars have done their best to convince others that there is an order; one of the more pastorally common suggestions is that they begin on our need of redemption.[17] Dietrich Bonhoeffer saw instead a list of renunciations:[18] the call of Jesus leads to a life of renunciation (v. 3), and this leads to renunciation of happiness and peace (v. 4), rights (v. 5), our own righteousness (v. 6), our own dignity (v. 7), our own good and evil (v. 8), and violence and strife (v. 9); and they finish with a renunciation summary (v. 10).

Another suggestion has come from Mark Allan Powell, who believes the first four beatitudes promise reversal for those who are unfortunate (vv. 3–6) while the second four promise eschatological rewards to the virtuous (vv. 7–10), with verses 11–12 functioning as a concluding comment. He believes the second four blessings are addressing those who show mercy to the unfortunate ones in the first four.[19] A final suggestion is that the first four pertain to God and the second four to our relationship with others.[20] If I were to venture a suggestion here, it would be this: group the beatitudes into threes.[21] Thus, three on the *humility* of the poor ("poor in spirit," "mourn," "meek"), three on those who pursue *justice* ("hunger and thirst …," "merciful," "pure

---

"ultimately be well"; France, *Matthew*, 160–61. Also, D. L. Turner, *Matthew* (BECNT; Grand Rapids: Baker Academic, 2008), 146–47.

16. The Beatitudes are read through four basic lenses: eschatological promises, entrance requirements, Wisdom tradition, and an epitome of Jesus' ethics; for a sketch, see T. D. Howell, *Matthean Beatitudes*, 3–6. Our view sees the Beatitudes more ecclesially; that is, they focus on who constitutes the kingdom of God.

17. A good example is to see in them a "spiritual progression of relentless logic," as can be seen in Stott, *Message*, 46.

18. Bonhoeffer, *Discipleship*, 101–9.

19. M. A. Powell, *God with Us: A Pastoral Theology of Matthew's Gospel* (Minneapolis: Fortress, 1995), 119–40.

20. Garland, *Reading Matthew*, 54.

21. A humorous comment by J. Pelikan on Augustine's lining of seven beatitudes with seven requests in the Lord's Prayer, then multiplying them (to 49) and adding one (divine nature, after all) to get 50, for Pentecost ends with this: "Could it have been otherwise?" See Pelikan, *Divine Rhetoric*, 63.

in heart"), and three on those who create *peace* ("peacemakers," "persecuted
...," "insult you ..."). Thus, the three central moral themes of the Beatitudes
are humility (of the poor), justice, and peace.

More important than order we need to see this list in the context of Jesus'
major ethical idea. In another project of mine, a book called *The Jesus Creed*,
I argued that Jesus understood the entire Torah through two basic commandments, to love God and to love others (Matt 22:34–40). When Jesus did this,
he "amended" a standard Jewish moral creed called the *Shema*, "Hear," which
derives from Deuteronomy 6:4–9. The love-others commandment comes
from Leviticus 19:18, which says "Love your neighbor as yourself." Adding
the two together permits his followers to understand God's basic demands as
love of God and love of others. I call this combination the Jesus Creed.

But there's an element of ethics in the Jesus Creed that is sometimes overlooked. Love of neighbor in Leviticus 19:18 is rooted in proper love of self:
"love your neighbor *as yourself.*" The Golden Rule, the other great reduction of the Torah by Jesus (Matt 7:12), also rings the bell of self-love: "So in
everything, do to others *what you would have them do to you*, for this sums
up the Law and the Prophets." There is then, as many have seen, including
New Testament ethicist Rudolf Schnackenburg,[22] a threefold dimension to the
essence of Jesus' moral vision: love of God, love of self, love of others. If Jesus
explicitly reduces the Torah to loving God and loving others as oneself, then
every ethical statement of Jesus somehow needs to be connected to the double
commandment of love. I want to use the threefold grid (love of God, self,
and others) to examine the Beatitudes, partly as a test case and partly because
I'm convinced this is one of the best ways to see into the essence of why Jesus
blesses these people.

Space permits only a brief commentary on each beatitude, which will
begin with a description of how to define each people group, a sketch of the
evidence shaping our understanding, and then a sketch of the promise for
each people group. Because the first beatitude has drawn so much discussion,
I will treat it in more depth.

Three Blessings for the Humility of the Poor

#1. Blessed are the poor in spirit (5:3). The "poor in spirit" (for which Luke has
only "poor," Luke 6:20) describes an economically, physically impoverished,
or oppressed person who not only recognizes her or his need but also trusts in
God for full redemption.[23] This sort of person thus comprehends that he or

---

22. Schnackenburg, *All Things Are Possible*, 33–34.
23. Guelich, *Sermon on the Mount*, 67–72, though I disagree with him on the *Anawim* question
(see below). For other definitions, see U. Luz, *Matthew 1–7: A Commentary* (Hermeneia; trans.

she must be faithful in the midst of oppression and also form solidarity with other oppressed people. In other words, the poor in spirit love God enough to trust God, love the self aright, and love others enough to form alliances of hope, compassion, and justice. The antithesis of the "poor in spirit" is the rich oppressor; one hears this antagonism in James 1:9 – 11; 2:1 – 13; and 4:13 – 5:6. We need to remind ourselves that each beatitude is a reversal of cultural values: the self-dependent or wealthy oppressor is at odds with the economy of the kingdom.

Christian Bible readers have often gone to one extreme or the other with Matthew 5:3, seeing in this beatitude either little more than the oppressed poor or nothing besides spiritual dependence on God.[24] This dispute arises because of Luke's version: "Blessed are you who are poor." Luke can be read as reducing this beatitude to simple economics. The question then becomes whether Matthew has "spiritualized" the poverty to spiritual neediness/poverty alone,[25] or whether a straight line can be drawn from economic poverty to spiritual trust in God. The second view finds strong support elsewhere in Matthew (see 11:5; 19:21; 26:9, 11). So, rather than being forced to choose between economic or spiritual poverty, it is wisest to see here a both/and: both spiritually dependent and economically needy.[26] Moreover, the socioeconomic rootedness of the word "poor" (*ptōchos*) does not permit exclusively the spiritual poverty interpretation, and the "in spirit" demands that this be more than simple economic oppression.

This both/and interpretation makes sense in the Jewish context. Jesus has in mind the *Anawim*, a group of economically disadvantaged Jews (Ps 149:4; Isa 49:13; 61:1 – 2; 66:2).[27] Historians of Jewish history now mostly agree that the *Anawim* had three features: they were economically poor and yet trusted in God, they found their way to the temple as a meeting place, and they longed for the Messiah, who would finally bring justice. The archetype persons of the *Anawim* are Simeon in Luke 2:25 – 35 and Anna in 2:36 – 38, and I would add Jesus' mother, Mary, whose *Anawim* hope we encounter in

---

J. E. Crouch; Minneapolis: Fortress, 2007), 191 – 93; Allison, *Sermon on the Mount*, 45; Hagner, *Matthew 1 – 13*, 91; Keener, *Matthew*, 168 – 69; France, *Matthew*, 165.

24. E.g., Martin Luther, *The Sermon on the Mount (Sermons) and The Magnificat* (Luther's Works; ed. J. Pelikan; St. Louis: Concordia, 1956), 12. On Luther, see Pelikan, *Divine Rhetoric*, 81 – 94. Emerging from this line of thinking some have seen "poor in spirit" as the fundamental virtue and then have even found development from the first beatitude to the ninth. See those cited by Allison, *Sermon on the Mount*, 45. Also Talbert, *Reading the Sermon on the Mount*, 50.

25. As does Stott, *Message*, 32, 39; Quarles, *Sermon on the Mount*, 44.

26. Kapolyo, "Matthew," 1118.

27. Careful study of the exile texts of Isaiah 40 – 66 could suggest that those blessed by Jesus are the economically challenged returning exiles of Isaiah now applied, in an end-of-exile manner, to his followers. On the *Anawim*, J. D. Pleins, "Poor, Poverty," *ABD*, 5:411 – 13.

the Magnificat at Luke 1:46–55.[28] Roughly at the time of Jesus the Qumran community saw themselves as the "poor" who were trusting in God. A good example can be found in this fragment:

> ... [the] humble He has not spurned, and He has not overlooked the needy in trouble, He has kept his eyes on the weak, and paid attention to the cry of orphans for help. He has listened to their cry, and because of His abundant mercies, has shown favor to the meek. He has opened their eyes to see His ways and their ears to hear. (4Q434 f1i:2)

Our conclusion is that "poor in spirit" is a perfect blend of the economically destitute who nonetheless trust in God and put their hope for justice and the kingdom of God in God.

To "the poor in spirit" is promised "the kingdom of heaven." This expression pulls together the entire hope of Israel's Story for the messianic age. It involves a King (Messiah), a land, a holy, loving people (Israel), and a redemptive power that will create holiness, love, and peace. The "kingdom" describes the fullness of God's blessing. Those who are poor now, who nonetheless trust in God and wait for God's Messiah with faithfulness, are and will be the ones who populate God's kingdom. That kingdom has already begun to make its presence felt from the days of John and Jesus (11:11–12; 12:28), but it still awaits a future glorious consummation (7:21; 8:11; 19:23–24; 26:29). Notably, Jesus will later say the rich struggle to enter the kingdom (19:23–24).[29]

#2. Blessed are those who mourn (5:4). Those who "mourn" both grieve in their experiences of tragedy, injustice, and death, and reach out to others in grief and compassion when they experience injustice, sin, evil, tragedy, and death. In other words, they suffer and they love those who suffer. It is reasonable to think "those who mourn" are *Anawim*. But this kind of mourning is also directed at God in a kind of "How long, O Lord?" plaint that waits on God to act in justice. Once again Jesus is countercultural. Jesus has in mind those who respond to exile properly. Exile for the mourner didn't mean adaptation, accommodation, activism, and apostasy but instead grief, faithfulness, suffering, and hope.

---

28. R. E. Brown, *The Birth of the Messiah* (ABRL; rev. ed.; New York: Doubleday, 1993), 350–55.

29. On kingdom, see G. E. Ladd, *The Presence of the Future: The Eschatology of Biblical Realism* (Grand Rapids: Eerdmans, 1974). A shorter sketch can be found in G. E. Ladd and D. A. Hagner, *A Theology of the New Testament* (Grand Rapids: Eerdmans, 1993), 42–132. The literature is enormous: J. D. G. Dunn, *Jesus Remembered* (Christianity in the Making 1; Grand Rapids: Eerdmans, 2003), 383–487; N. T. Wright, *Jesus and the Victory of God* (Christians Origins and the Question of God 2; Minneapolis: Fortress, 1996); G. R. Beasley-Murray, *Jesus and the Kingdom of God* (Grand Rapids: Eerdmans, 1986). Also D. C. Allison Jr., "Kingdom of God," *EDEJ*, 860–61.

The meaning of this beatitude depends on what these blessed people are mourning about. Are they mourning for their loved ones? Israel's condition in exile or oppression? Injustices they have experienced? The lack of love, peace, holiness, and justice in the land? Or, as so many have claimed, are they mourning over their own sins? The answer to this set of questions is found by exploring the historical context.[30] We must begin with Isaiah 61:1–4 (in the context of the hope in chs. 40–66):

> The Spirit of the Sovereign LORD is on me,
>   because the LORD has anointed me
>   to proclaim good news to the poor.
> He has sent me to bind up the brokenhearted,
>   to proclaim freedom for the captives
>   and release from darkness for the prisoners,
> to proclaim the year of the LORD's favor
>   and the day of vengeance of our God,
> *to comfort all who mourn,*
>   and provide for those who grieve in Zion—
> to bestow on them a crown of beauty
>   instead of ashes,
> *the oil of joy*
>   *instead of mourning,*
> and a garment of praise
>   instead of a spirit of despair.
> They will be called the oaks of righteousness,
>   a planting of the LORD
>   for the display of his splendor.
> They will rebuild the ancient ruins
>   and restore the places long devastated;
> they will renew the ruined cities
>   that have been devastated for generations. (Isa 61:1–4, emphasis
>   added; cf. Ps 126:2–6).

This text clearly suggests that the mourners are those who are grieved over both Israel's and their own exile, who are teamed with one another in grief, and who long for Israel's return, for the temple to be restored, and for God's favor to return on Israel. It is a longing for grace and justice and for kingdom, and at the same time a commitment to faithfulness and hope.

Jesus promises the mourners that God will comfort them by satisfying the longing of their hearts. Knowing God's faithfulness and final justice, and

---

30. Turner, *Matthew*, 150–51.

anchoring one's hope in what God will certainly do empower the "mourner" to carry on faithfully. One thinks of Paul in Romans 5:3 or 8:37–39 and of John in Revelation 21:4.

#3. Blessed are the meek (5:5). The "meek" are those who suffer and who have been humbled, and yet they do not seek revenge but God's glory and the welfare of others. In other words, they lovingly trust God and hope in God's timing and God's justice. An overemphasis in the first beatitude ("poor in spirit") on humility leads to a near synonym with the third beatitude, which is a solid clue to keep the economic dimension of the first. Perhaps it is easiest to define "meek" by saying Jesus was meek: "for I am *gentle* [same word as our beatitude] and humble[31] in heart" (11:29). Moreover, in entering Jerusalem on a donkey, Jesus fulfilled an Old Testament expectation of the meek king (21:5).

In addition, we must take into consideration what the meek are promised: they will inherit the Land (more below). Because meekness connects here to land inheritance, and because the Beatitudes are so inherently countercultural, we suggest that meekness is framed over against wrath, anger, violence, acquisitiveness, rapaciousness, theft, violent takeovers, and brutal reclamations of property. The meek are unlike the Zealots, who used violence to seize the land. The meek choose to absorb unjust conditions in a form of nonviolent, nonretaliatory resistance that creates a calm, countercultural community of love, justice, and peace.[32]

The promise stands out: "for they will inherit the earth [Land]." Clearly the promise evokes both the land promise in Genesis 12 and the promises to the oppressed and waiting in Psalm 37:11 ("the meek will inherit the land and enjoy peace and prosperity"); 37:22 ("those the LORD blesses will inherit the land"); and 37:34 ("he will exalt you to inherit the land"). The Qumran community prized Psalm 37.[33] While it has been customary for Christians to see in the NIV's word "earth" a synonym for "world" now or in the new heavens and earth,[34] there is little likelihood that Jesus would have "world" in mind.[35] We must wrap our minds around the Bible's Story for the first-century Jew: those to whom Jesus spoke didn't care two figs for owning Italy or Gaul. They simply wanted shalom in the Land of Israel. The fundamental promise to

---

31. The Greek term behind "humble" here is *tapeinos*; behind "poor" in 5:3 it is *ptōchos*. Both words evoke the humble poor, the *Anawim*.

32. See Keener, *Matthew*, 168, for a full display of references. Also Powell, *God with Us*, 125–26.

33. See 4QpPs 37 [= 4Q171], and the pesher/comment on Ps 37:11 reads: "This refers to the company of the poor who endure the time of error but are delivered from all the snares of Belial. Afterwards they will enjoy all the […] of the earth [Heb., *hāʾāreṣ*, 'land'] and grow fat on every human [luxury]" (lines 8–11a).

34. Quarles, *Sermon on the Mount*, 56–58.

35. Hagner, *Matthew 1–13*, 92; Talbert, *Reading the Sermon on the Mount*, 52. On land, B. H. Amaru, "Land, Concept of," *EDEJ*, 866–68.

Abraham, and a promise that shapes everything about exile and return and hope and promise (e.g., Deut 28) is dwelling in peace and holiness in the land God promised them. Or read Luke 1:67–79 to see that Zechariah's idea of salvation is the elimination of enemies so Israel could dwell in the Land and worship in the temple in peace and holiness. This is the right context, so that this beatitude should be translated, "for they will inherit the Land."

If we put these first three beatitudes together, we find Jesus blessing the oppressed and the poor for their powerful trust in God, their willingness to wait on God for justice and the kingdom, and for their devotion that runs so deep they mourn over the condition of Israel and implicate themselves in the causes of that condition. These are the sorts of people, not the typical ones, that are (and will be) in the kingdom.

Three Blessings on Those Who Pursue Righteousness and Justice

#4. Blessed are those who hunger and thirst for righteousness (5:6). Those who "hunger and thirst for righteousness" are those who love God and God's will (revealed in Torah as love and justice) with their heart, soul, mind, and strength. Because they love God and others, they are willing to check their passions and will in order to do God's will, to further God's justice, and to express their longing that God act to establish his will and kingdom.[36] Their appetites, instead of being sated by the pleasures of food, sensualities, passions, and lusts, are satisfied only in communion with God, knowing and doing God's will and seeking the welfare of others. One thinks of Mary's Magnificat (Luke 1:46–55), but one also thinks of Abraham, who abandoned his home to strike out for God's land; of Moses, who learned the hard way to be devoted to God; of Samson, whose erratic life embedded yearning for God's will; and of the apostles Peter, Paul, and John, each of whom left a life to follow God's way and will.

Once again, like the first beatitude, comparison with Luke's version of this beatitude turns up significance: Luke has "who hunger now" (Luke 6:21), and Matthew edits this to "for righteousness." Has Matthew spiritualized an originally socioeconomic issue? No.[37] Again, we are to think of the poor and hungry who are chasing not just food but even more God's will being done on earth (as it is in heaven)—and their blessing is that they will be given that and more.[38]

Everything hinges on the meaning of the word "righteousness." We can only sketch some basics; I will begin with the two basic options for the

---

36. Powell, *God with Us*, 127.
37. Hagner, *Matthew 1–13*, 93, sees the two accounts as nearly the same.
38. So Guelich, *Sermon on the Mount*, 83–84, 87–88.

meaning of "righteousness." The *behavior* view emphasizes the Jewish Torah context and sees in this word "conformity to God's will as expressed in Torah and its interpretation," or simply "covenant faithfulness."[39] The *gift* view emphasizes God's grace and salvation and understands "righteousness" as one's "right standing before God [on the basis of Christ's meritorious life, death, and resurrection]." The English word "righteousness" complicates things because it is used to translate a word that can mean either "just" (righteous behavior) or "justification" (declared righteous).

The Jewish context[40] prior to Paul overwhelmingly suggests the term meant "covenant faithfulness" or "Torah observant." But Paul took all of this to a new level because he was involved in a completely different context, the Gentile mission. Paul shifted the focus of the term toward gift, toward "*declared* righteous [justified]." But with Jesus things are still pre-Pauline, and we would do well to remind ourselves of that. Instances in Matthew that almost certainly cannot mean "declared righteous" are 5:10, 20, 45; 6:1; 10:41; 13:17, 43, 49; 21:32; 23:28, 29, 35; 25:37, 46; 27:19. What clinches the case is that 5:10, which is to be read in conjunction with 5:6, cannot mean anything other than behavior that conforms to God's will. A profound example of the "covenant faithfulness" sense of this term is Joseph, Jesus' "father," in 1:19, who, because he was *Torah observant/righteous*, chose to divorce Mary because he wanted to remain observant.

The moment one defines righteousness as conformity to Torah or to God's Word in Scripture, three things happen. First, the scope of Scripture, especially as we find the prophetic texts, focuses our minds on big issues like justice, mercy, peace, faithfulness, worship, holiness, and love. Second, we are pushed into seeing how Jesus himself understood Torah observance, and here we think immediately of two texts, the Jesus Creed of 22:34–40 and the Golden Rule of 7:12, so that for Jesus a "righteous" person was someone who loved God and loved others as himself. Third, we are pressed into considering the antitheses of 5:17–48, where surpassing righteousness refers to kingdom behaviors.

To those who pursue righteousness Jesus promises "they will be filled," and the word "filled" means "sated," "slaked," "bloated," or "filled to overflowing." The metaphor expresses absolute and utter satisfaction: they will find a kingdom society where love, peace, justice, and holiness shape the entirety of creation.

#5. Blessed are the merciful (5:7). The "merciful" are those who, because they do to others as they would want done to themselves and because they

---

39. E.g., Luz, *Matthew 1–7*, 195–96; France, *Matthew*, 167–68; Turner, *Matthew*, 151. See the discussion in Talbert, *Reading the Sermon on the Mount*, 63–65.

40. B. Przybylski, *Righteousness in Matthew and His World of Thought* (SNTSMS 41; Cambridge: Cambridge University Press, 1980).

have experienced God's merciful love, empathize and show compassion to others. Inherent in works of mercy is the self-denying virtue of entering into the injustices and tragedies experienced by others. Once again, Jesus is countercultural to some trends in his world: merciful people are like the good Samaritan, whose love interrupts his trip; like Jesus, who is constantly interrupted by those in need (9:13; 12:7; 15:21–28); or like Jesus in the (not canonical) incident with the woman caught in sin (John 7:53–8:11); and like James, the brother of Jesus, who sees the abusive treatment of the poor in the synagogue and speaks out on their behalf (Jas 2:1–13). Jesus was radical enough to suggest that mercy needed to be shown to enemies (Matt 5:43–48).

The fifth beatitude complements the fourth beatitude, and perhaps even helps clarify the fourth, when we consider *to whom* the merciful show compassion. The answer can be heard the moment we begin the question: *those in need, those suffering injustice, those who are poor, those who are oppressed, and those who have failed.* In addition, the word "merciful" does not describe the ubiquitous and shallow virtue of "niceness" or "tolerance" in Western culture, but concrete actions of love, compassion, and sympathetic grace to those who are oppressed or to those who have sinned (cf. Gal 6:1). The writer of Hebrews depicts Jesus' priestly relation to us in terms of mercy (Heb 2:17). James said the same thing in other words:

> Speak and act as those who are going to be judged by the law that gives freedom, because judgment without mercy will be shown to anyone who has not been merciful. Mercy triumphs over judgment. (Jas 2:12–13)

To the merciful is promised divine mercy at the judgment, that is, entrance into the kingdom. While this blessing creates disturbance for us at times about works righteousness, its design is to remind us that mercy is fundamental to a proper love of God and others (23:23; cf. 25:31–46).

#6. Blessed are the pure in heart (5:8). If our suggestion of grouping the beatitudes into threes holds, this blessing is connected to the previous two around the theme of pursuing God's will. The "pure" in heart know the temptation of externalism and the social honor that comes with being pure in hands, or in observance, or in reputation (15:1–20; 23:25–28).[41] But the pure in heart see God as a person to be loved, so their first priority is God, and this love leads to loving others well. The best commentary on "pure in heart" is 6:1–18, where religious actions are done not for the praise of others but in order to engage with God, and 6:21, where the disciple is not shaped

---

41. France, *Matthew*, 168; Turner, *Matthew*, 152. See also Stott, *Message*, 49. Also, J. Klawans, *Impurity and Sin in Ancient Judaism* (Oxford/New York: Oxford University Press, 2000).

by wealth or possessions. James reveals an almost uncanny connection to the Beatitudes without giving so much as a hint in James 3:17–18.

This blessing, as with the others, comes with a history. One thinks immediately of Psalm 24's profound questions: "Who may ascend the mountain of the LORD? Who may stand in his holy place?" And the answer? "The one who has clean hands and a pure heart" (24:3–4). It is hard not to think that Paul's spirit-flesh battle emerges out of such Jewish thinking (Gal 5:13–26). Purity of heart avoids double-mindedness (Jas 4:8).

Christian history shows an interest in the "beatific vision" when we read, "for they will see God" (5:8).[42] Thus, Bonaventure's *Journey of the Mind to God*, the finale to Dante's *Divine Comedy*, and Bunyan's pilgrim, who discovers the land beyond the Jordan in *Pilgrim's Progress*, are major examples. The Bible both affirms a beatific vision (see Job 19:26; Ps 11:7; 1 John 3:2; Rev 22:4) and yet seems to deny its genuine possibility (e.g., Exod 33:20; 1 Tim 6:16). There is an immensity and an unapproachability to God that prevents humans from ever gazing directly into the being of God, but we can see and admire a glory surrounding God as we engage in intoxicating, ecstatic worship (e.g., Exod 3:2; Isa 6:1–5; Dan 7:9–10).[43]

Three Blessings on Those Who Create Peace

#7. Blessed are the peacemakers (5:9). The "peacemaker" is someone who is reconciled to God, knows God is for peace, and seeks reconciliation instead of strife and war.[44] Jewish expectations for the messianic kingdom were for peace; hence, a peacemaker is a kingdom person (Isa 9:5–6; Zech 9:9–10). That is, the Beatitudes look at people now through the lens of an Ethic from Beyond. Kingdom realities are now occurring through the peacemakers.[45]

Once again, Jesus is countercultural for some. There was a surging development in the first century in the rise of vigilante-like zealotry into a full-blown movement of Zealots, who were a part of Jewish resistance movements.[46] This beatitude turns its focus on those who, instead of seeking justice through violence, which remained a Christian temptation (see Jas 1:19–20; 4:1–3),

---

42. Allison, *Sermon on the Mount*, 51–54; also see his *Studies in Matthew* (Grand Rapids: Baker Academic, 2005), 43–63, where he sketches seven elements in the history of interpretation: an embodied deity, a christological interpretation, a mystical encounter, a metaphor for insight, God in perfected creation, God in perfected self and neighbor, and a present and future experience.

43. "Anonymous" in the *Incomplete Work on Matthew*, Homily 9, understands this vision of God in two ways: the one who sees Jesus sees God and does good works, while in the kingdom God will be seen directly (see ACCS: *Matthew*, 87).

44. Kapolyo, "Matthew," 1119.

45. Augustine: "Thereby they themselves [peacemakers] become the kingdom of God" (see ACCS: *Matthew*, 88–89).

46. James S. McLaren, "Resistance Movements," *EDEJ*, 1135–40.

turn from retaliation to reconciliation. The zealotry threat was resisted by the rabbis: "Hillel says, 'Be disciples of Aaron, "loving peace and pursuing peace, loving people and drawing them near to the Torah" (*m. 'Abot* 1.12).[47] Bonhoeffer sketched what would in reality become his own virtue and fate: "But their peace will never be greater than when they encounter evil people in peace and are willing to suffer from them."[48]

Peacemaking is neither being "nice" (as defined today), nor is it "tolerance" (again as defined today); rather, it is an active entrance into the middle of warring parties for the purpose of creating reconciliation and peace.[49] But neither is it soft-pedaling around real but not identical differences — that is, between those who have experienced apartheid and those who inflicted apartheid, between those who split a church and those who choose to remain, between a husband and wife who are struggling to get along, between two colleagues at the office, or between parents and children who can't seem to find enough common ground to trust one another. The peacemaker, as the person whom Jesus blesses, seeks to reconcile — not by pretending there are no differences or by suppressing differences, but by creating love of the other that transcends differences or that permits the people to join hands in spite of differences. Jesus will speak of reconciliation on other occasions, and these perhaps are the best commentary on "peacemakers" (5:21 – 26, 43 – 48; 6:14 – 15; 18:21 – 35). His framing of moral relations in terms of love (22:34 – 40) and servanthood (20:20 – 28) provide foundations for peacemaking.

Issues arise precisely because some Christians have taken these words so seriously. Two views deserve to be mentioned. First, does this beatitude teach pacifism or at least nonviolent resistance? This view has been attached to the Anabaptist tradition[50] and is sometimes accused of being utopian or unrealistic, but this is precisely the point: pacifism was the way of the earliest Christians — and participation in war was clearly frowned on by nearly all early Christians — because it was the way of Jesus, and the way of Jesus is the kingdom, realistic or not. The question for the pacifist is not, "Does it work in the world?" but "What does it mean to follow Jesus in this concrete situation?"

---

47. On the anti-Zealot perspective, see Hagner, *Matthew 1 – 13*, 94.

48. Bonhoeffer, *Discipleship*, 108. E. Bethge observed that Bonhoeffer was led into pacifist thinking through Jean Lasserre; see his *Dietrich Bonhoeffer: A Biography. Theologian, Christian, Man for His Times* (Minneapolis: Fortress, 2000), 153 – 54. Bonhoeffer's decision to cooperate with the resistance to Hitler seemingly strains themes in *Discipleship*.

49. Turner, *Matthew*, 152 – 53.

50. J. Denny Weaver, *Becoming Anabaptist* (2nd ed.; Scottdale, PA: Herald, 2005); W. R. Estep, *The Anabaptist Story* (3rd ed.; Grand Rapids: Eerdmans, 1996).

Second, there is another reading of these words of Jesus, that his words are about interpersonal relations and not international bodies; in other words, Christians shouldn't use violence in their personal life but they can participate in international/military violence (just war). This is the view of Augustine, Luther, and Calvin. To this one can respond pointedly that what applies to each of us as a follower of Jesus *must also* apply to anything in which we participate if we are consistently following Jesus. Privatizing one's kingdom ethics is not the way of Jesus.

So what do we think? Regardless of our posture toward the state, the military, or other countries, the *goal* of the follower of Jesus is peace. But we are to admit that the *means* is not as clear. That is, while we should all desire peace, *how we get there* may differ. Some Christians think the best way to get there is through military strength sufficient enough to intimidate other countries into dropping their military plans, while others (I join them) think the way of Jesus requires us to drop our military intimidation and negotiate in love for justice and peace.[51]

Jesus promises peacemakers that they will be "called children [sons] of God" (5:9) at the final judgment. The word "son/sons" was used in the Jewish world to connect a person with an attribute[52] or a person. Thus, a "son of God" here denotes someone who is on God's side, implying that God is a God of peace (Rom 16:20).

Peacemaking and justice/righteousness, which follows in verse 10, belong together in the Jewish world of Jesus. What makes this connection secure are these kinds of texts:

Love and faithfulness meet together;
  righteousness and peace kiss each other. (Ps 85:10)

Of the greatness of his government and *peace*
  there will be no end.
He will reign on David's throne
  and over his kingdom,
establishing and upholding it
  with justice and righteousness
  from that time on and forever.

---

51. The best book I've read from the pacifist side is R. J. Sider, *Christ and Violence* (Scottdale, PA: Herald, 1979); the classic is J. H. Yoder, *The Politics of Jesus* (2nd ed.; Grand Rapids: Eerdmans, 1994). But one should not neglect A. Trocmé, *Jesus and the Nonviolent Revolution* (trans. M. H. Shank and M. E. Miller; Scottdale, PA: Herald, 1973). Options are discussed in R. G. Clouse et al., *War: Four Christian Views* (Downers Grove, IL: InterVarsity Press, 1991), and in A. F. Holmes, *War and Christian Ethics* (2nd ed; Grand Rapids: Baker Academic, 2005).

52. See Matt 8:12; 9:15; 13:38; 23:31.

The zeal of the LORD Almighty
  will accomplish this. (Isa 9:7)

The fruit of that righteousness will be *peace*;
  its effect will be quietness and confidence forever. (Isa 32:17,
    emphasis added in the above)

#8 and #9. Blessed are those who are persecuted ... (5:10 – 12). Matthew doubles up on the theme of persecution. First, he has a blessing for those who are persecuted because they seek God's justice/righteousness (5:10). Second, Matthew then expands the eighth blessing by adding another blessing for the persecuted, this time spelling out the specifics in the direction of both verbal harassment and injustice, and no doubt again this suffering has to do with following and associating with Jesus: "because of me" (5:11; cf. 10:39; 16:25; 19:29; 24:9).[53] If verse 10 promises the "kingdom," verse 12a has "great is your reward."[54] The notion here is that one's eternal/kingdom state correlates with one's response to God in the present life. This isn't works righteousness but instead the moral call to responsibility in light of eternal correlation. Jesus later teaches that the disciple's reward far outstrips the correlation (cf. 20:1 – 16).

Blended together, the "persecuted" are those who seek God's will in spite of what others want, who love God so much they are faithful to God when oppressed, and who follow Jesus so unreservedly they suffer for him. Inherent in persecution, then, are both a love of God and a denial of self. The premier example, of course, is Jesus, and next to him is John the Baptist, but one also thinks of Jesus' words in 23:33 – 39 or those in Hebrews 11. If Jesus was reviled and then raised, so the disciple knows he or she will suffer the same fates (Matt 10:24 – 25).

LIVE the Story

Texts heavy with tradition and lit up with meaning for Christians of all times, like the Beatitudes, present their own challenges for the teacher. I suggest that we focus on the big ideas. Perhaps Bonhoeffer sets us on the proper

---

53. Matt 5:11 – 12 is not the same form as vv. 3 – 10. Not only is it "Blessed are you *when* ..." but the person changes from third person ("they") to second person ("you").

54. On reward in Matthew, see 5:46; 6:1, 2, 5, 16; 10:41 – 42; 20:1 – 16; 25:31 – 46. Recent scholarship has shown that Judaism shifted from conceptualizing sin as a burden to sin as indebtedness, which led in the centuries around Jesus to seeing good works in terms of credit. One should be wary, in other words, of inferring a works-based righteousness in Judaism on the basis of this shift from burden to debt. See G. A. Anderson, *Sin: A History* (New Haven, CT: Yale University Press, 2009).

course: "Here at the end of the Beatitudes the question arises as to where in this world such a faith-community actually finds a place ... at the cross. The faith-community of the blessed is the community of the Crucified. With him they lost everything, and with him they found everything."[55]

Happiness Deconstructed

The most important word in this text is "blessed," and it needs to be discussed over against modernity's pursuit of happiness. When the Continental Congress drafted the Declaration of Independence in June and July of 1776, the framers put into words what had been percolating in Europe for most of the century: "We hold these truths to be self-evident, that all men are created equal, that they are endowed by their Creator with certain unalienable Rights, that among these are Life, Liberty and *the pursuit of Happiness*." Most in the Western world believe that the pursuit of happiness is a right. But something has changed: more and more we think *being happy* is our right.

This leads to the question of what happiness means. Here one might toss in a hundred or so quotes, but eventually we will agree that "happiness" is about inner contentedness and material flourishing. That is, many today think it is a right not only to have life but to have a good life.[56] Here are several suggestions now about what happiness means.

1. Primarily happiness is understood as a subjective "feeling good about oneself and one's life and one's situation."
2. Happiness has become both a right and achievable now.
3. The pursuit of happiness never ends; it is instead a "hedonic treadmill." Once the center is pleasure or feeling good, that center becomes a source of unending demand for more and more.
4. Happiness research shows that it is largely the comparative that satisfies the subjective: that is, one becomes happy by comparing herself or himself with others who have less, and as long as one has more, one is happy. But those studies also show that diminishment in happiness enters once one has more than the necessities of life.
5. We also have learned that happiness is rooted in genetics: certain temperaments and dispositions are more capable of achieving this subjective sense of feeling good than are others: those who are sociable, active, stable, and conscientious tend to be more "happy." Not only is happiness genetic, but it is connected to our life span:

---

55. Bonhoeffer, *Discipleship*, 109.
56. I rely here on the piece I wrote for *Books & Culture* (November/December 2008): "Happiness: Given, Lost, Regained."

we reach the nadir of happiness at age 44 and after that it's a gentle stroll of increasing happiness all the way home.

6. Happiness can be generated falsely by the imagination. Our capacity to dream and to put things in the context of what we think our reality eventually will be creates greater chances of happiness, whether that imagined future ever occurs or not.

Here is my point. The term *happiness* today, because it rests on these kinds of observations, is not the best word for translating the Greek word *makarios* in the Beatitudes. The happiness of the Beatitudes is not about *feeling* good but about *being* good, and being good is defined by Jesus and shaped by one's relationship with God through him. Being blessed by Jesus may have nothing to do with one's observable condition in life and everything to do with whether one loves God, loves self, and loves others as the self. That, along with the behaviors that emerge out of that kind of love, makes one blessed.

A Revolution in Evaluation

Jesus here blesses three kinds of people:

- those who are the humble poor
- those who pursue righteousness and justice
- those who create peace

I wonder if we might examine once again the sort of people that measure up to our standards. How do we measure piety? How do we measure spirituality? How do we measure true Christianity? Jesus measures it by the standard of whether a person loves God, loves self, and loves others. He sees this in people who are the humble poor, who work for righteousness and justice, and who create reconciliation.

His standard and our standard are often at odds. In my experience in churches, I see these sorts of standards to measure followers:

- those who read their Bible and pray daily
- those who attend church regularly
- those who tithe
- those who know a lot about the Bible
- those who preach well
- those who exercise the spiritual gifts
- those who exercise the spiritual disciplines
- those who evangelize
- those who have great stories of conversion
- those who write books

- those who separate themselves from the world
- those who have succeeded in business
- those who run for public office
- those who serve in the military

Most of us would say apart from one or two of our quibbles, Christians do these things. But here's the problem: By what standard do we measure spirituality? By what we can see or by the inner qualities Jesus seems to be teaching? That is, do we see spirituality in those whose love for God and others has so worked into their inner fabric that they are humble in spite of their poverty and the suffering of injustice, that they are doing all they can to bring about justice in this world, and that they are seeking to reconcile those who are at odds? Are our standards those of Jesus?

The Beatitudes of Jesus are nothing short of a revolution of evaluation. We see in those whom Jesus blesses those who truly are the Jesus people of this world, and what he calls to our attention about them are not the sort of elements that often go into our evaluation methods.

Looking and Loving

In the Beatitudes the good life, the life that leads to blessing and to flourishing, is the life lived by looking constantly to God for both approval and sustenance, and a life lived before God as the judge and vindicator of God's true people. The Beatitudes provide a divine perspective on the true people of God, and Jesus is the Lord Messiah who declares who these people are.

Those who are on the scout for analogies of those blessed by Jesus will need to look into the cracks of culture and the corners of the church. As in Jesus' day, so in ours: Jesus was able to find those who had surrendered themselves to God because he wasn't in the flow of the powerful in his culture. Those who oppressed others surely thought they were justified and perhaps even had wisdom and Torah on their side, but Jesus saw things from a different angle. And it is that angle we need to have if we are to find the blessed in our culture. They are people whose fabric is the interweaving of love of God, love of others, and love of self. Time and time again we saw in the Beatitudes that Jesus' own hermeneutic of the Jesus Creed was at work under and behind the individuals whom Jesus blessed. Sometimes it is the simple person who loves her neighbor well, and other times it is the mother or father who has framed their life in a sacrificial way.

You know someone like this. As a child there was an old woman in our church whom we called Miss Meyers. She had to be ninety years old, though a preteen's judgment on age is hardly infallible. What I remember of Miss Meyers is that she was loving and was constantly serving others; she taught us—her Sunday School kids—to love plants and to pray and love God and love others. She taught us the Bible as if it were alive, which it was for her. I remember to this day that she could grow a cactus in her home. As one who had only read about a cactus in schoolbook descriptions about desert places, I marveled at her abilities. What I recall is her gentle nature when it came to plants. So she cut off a bit, gave it to me, and told me how to care for it, which I didn't do well because I wanted to care for it more than it needed. (That is, I wanted to water it because the sandy grit she planted it in was too dry—it wasn't.) In the annals of Freeport, Illinois' list of great Christians Miss Meyers may not be mentioned, but she was one whom Jesus blessed and she blessed us.

The Beatitudes teach us to look to Jesus not only as the one who thunders "Blessed!" before those who needed to hear it, but also as the one who embodied each beatitude in singular form. If the Story of the Bible teaches us anything, it teaches us to see the Story of Israel coming to completion and fulfillment in Jesus. The one who is blessed by God is Jesus, and those whom he blesses are those who take on his ways, his manners, and his love and extend it to others. Jesus was poor and humble; Jesus burned up his days pursuing righteousness and justice; and Jesus created God's peace everywhere he went. But paradoxically his kind of love is so sacrificial it cost him his life, so that learning to read the Beatitudes in their Jewish context must give way to reading them in the context of the Crucified.

The Christian and Law

It is hard not to point a finger at Martin Luther for creating a counterforce between law and gospel. In fact, contrasting the two—one to condemn and one to bring grace—is at the heart of the Lutheran dialectic, or how the Lutheran is taught to read the Bible. Nothing can be achieved by obedience to the law; all that can be achieved is achieved in Christ. The Reformed, those who follow from Calvin, involved themselves in a more nuanced way in the issue of how the law and the gospel are related. A good example of this approach is found in a statement by John Stott: "the law sends us to Christ to be justified, and Christ sends us back to the law to be sanctified."[57] There is considerable debate over this issue among evangelicals today.[58]

This problem is created by tidy systematic formulas, and I appreciate the nuances and discussions and light that systematicians sometime shed, but in this case something has gone terribly wrong. The immediate problem is that the debate often assumes that law demands performance while the gospel

---

57. Stott, *Message*, 36.
58. W. G. Strickland, ed., *Five Views on Law and Gospel* (Grand Rapids: Zondervan, 1996).

expects only faith. Beside the importance of what the New Perspective on Paul brings to this discussion, not the least of which is a radical reshaping of how Judaism worked as a religion and that "works of the law" are not just Torah but the special laws that separated the Jew from the Gentile, the contrast Paul makes between works of the law and faith does not result in the latter not having law or performance. After all, in one of his quintessential statements in Ephesians 2:8 – 10, Paul overtly argues Christians are created by God "to do good works" (which is performance by any other name).

As one sympathetic to the Anabaptists I believe in salvation by faith and not by works, and to their credit the Anabaptists have always taught the demand of discipleship in a way more emphatically central than most. Radical distinctions, often made by major theologians in the Protestant traditions, between justification and sanctification are unwise because they are not grounded in the Bible. The Torah is God's revelation to God's people and to be read as God's gracious demand. God graciously reveals what God wants, but God unfolds that demand over time so that it is completely revealed only in Christ; God graciously provides the power for us to do what Jesus teaches as we live in the Spirit in the light of the coming kingdom; and God graciously demands how God wants us to live in the Sermon and in the ethical exhortations of the New Testament.

In other words, in Jesus' demand to live righteously, which runs through the Sermon, we see an Ethic from Above, from Below, and from Beyond — but it is an ethic his followers are to perform. The best way to preach the Sermon is to preach what it is: a demand on the disciple.

CHAPTER 3

Matthew 5:13 – 16

 LISTEN to the Story

> ¹³"You are the salt of the earth. But if the salt loses its saltiness, how can it be made salty again? It is no longer good for anything, except to be thrown out and trampled underfoot.¹
>
> ¹⁴ "You are the light of the world. A town built on a hill cannot be hidden. ¹⁵Neither do people light a lamp and put it under a bowl.² Instead they put it on its stand, and it gives light to everyone in the house. ¹⁶In the same way, let your light shine before others, that they may see your good deeds³ and glorify your Father in heaven."
>
> *Listening to the text in the Story:* Genesis 1:26 – 27; Exodus 19:4 – 6; Psalm 8; Isaiah 51:4; 60:3; 61:6; Matthew 19:28; Romans 5:12 – 21 (esp. v. 17); 2 Timothy 2:8 – 13; 1 Peter 2:1 – 12; Revelation 1:5 – 6; 5:9 – 10; 20:4 – 6.

It is easier to think of salt and light as clever metaphors and then assume their meanings are clear to spin off into practical living exercises, than it is to think of the metaphors in the context of the Bible's big Story. This text encourages us to *reimagine our role in the world as God's agents of redemption.* Again, it is simpler to reimagine that role in this world as "moral influence" than through the biblical notion that is at work in the metaphors of salt and light. Because the moral-influence theory is instinctive for us, I have provided a long list of texts immediately below the citation of 5:13 – 16. I would urge you to read them all.

A brief sketch of those passages in the Bible assigns a particular role to Adam and Eve (Gen 1:26 – 27; Ps 8:1 – 6), then to Abraham (Gen 12), then through him to Israel (Exod 19:4 – 6), and eventually to Jesus and through him to his disciples as the church (Matt 19:28; 1 Pet 2:1 – 12). But this role

---

1. KNT: "You might as well throw it out and walk all over it."
2. KNT: "bucket."
3. KNT: "what wonderful things you do."

is given to the church only after Jesus Christ has actually performed that role perfectly (Rom 5:12–21; 2 Tim 2:8–13). What role is this? The role of being both *priests and kings* on behalf of God in this world. A simple probing of the final kingdom reveals that God's people will be mediating and ruling in the world in the kingdom (Rev 1:5–6; 5:9–10; 20:4–6). This conclusion to history leads us to a powerful and practical orientation in life: we are to mediate and rule now in light of the task we will be assigned in the kingdom.[4] Again, we are looking at an Ethic from Beyond mediated to us through the ruling King Jesus.

Keep this front and center: *our mediating and ruling roles are only done in Christ, who is the Mediator and Lord.* In Christ we are assigned a role, and salt and light are dimensions of that role. Only once we are on the right road (mediating, ruling) can we grip the wheel and guide our vehicle through the metaphors of salt and light.[5]

EXPLAIN the Story

What is implicit in 5:13–16, and buried inside the "you are ...," is that Jesus assumes his disciples will be salt and light because they are the followers of 4:18–22, the blessed of 5:3–12, and the obedient ones of 5:17–48 and beyond. They are not salt or light automatically but only to the degree that they "are" followers of Jesus.[6] Furthermore, perhaps we should give emphasis to the "you" in "you are"[7] because Jesus singles out his own followers and in so doing chooses against the standard Jewish options: *they* are the salt and light, not the temple, Jerusalem, the Torah, or the Pharisees. Paul knows that Israel thought it was the light to the world (Rom 2:17), but Jesus assigns this task exclusively to his followers as they indwell him who is the light of the world (John 8:12; 9:5; 13:35).

Both salt and light are images for impact on something else: salt impacts, for instance, meats, while light impacts darkness. While the specific sort of impact may not be clear, one would have to think both salt and light pertain

---

4. I disagree, then, with the classic view of John Stott that this refers to our evangelism and social action, even if I agree with him on the relation of these two and their fundamental importance in Christian witness; see his *Message*, 57–68. For a diamond-cutting discussion of this theme in Stott's career, see J. Greenman, "John R.W. Stott," in *The Sermon on the Mount through the Centuries* (ed. J. P. Greenman et al.; Grand Rapids: Brazos, 2007), 266–79. Greenman's conclusion resonates with my own experience of the same time period.

5. For discussion, see Wright, *After You Believe*, 73–100.

6. W. D. Davies and D. C. Allison Jr., *A Critical and Exegetical Commentary on the Gospel according to Saint Matthew* (ICC; 3 vols.; Edinburgh: T&T Clark, 1988), 1:471.

7. Note that in the Greek of vv. 13 and 14, "you" is emphatic.

to gospel teaching as well as to behavioral witness as impacting those who hear and see. Thus one can render these statements more actively as "You salt the earth" and "You enlighten the world."

Salt of the Earth (Land)

When we examined the third beatitude ("Blessed are the meek, for they will inherit the land"), we suggested that the common translation "earth" or "world" was probably not in mind. The same applies here: it is unlikely that "earth" means "world" but instead translates Jesus' use of the word "Land" ('ereṣ). Jesus is referring to the land of Israel. We will shortly also suggest that "world" in the second metaphor ("light of the world") anticipates a Gentile mission. In other words, one metaphor (salt) speaks of the role of Jesus' people to Israel and the other (light) to the Gentile world. The Israel-focused mission (the salt metaphor) is seen in Matthew at 10:5 – 6, 23, and 15:24. We might need to remember that there were two missions among the earliest followers of Jesus: one to Jews and one to Gentiles (see Acts 15:27 – 29; Gal 2:1 – 10).

Jesus' concern in the salt metaphor is the potential of diminishing one's impact, and so he crafts the metaphor of salt as one expressing negative possibilities. Thus, salt, if not treated properly or put to good use, will become insipid — "lose its saltiness" — and become good for nothing, or what John Stott calls "road dust."[8] The text is a poetic warning about judgment if one does not sustain one's saltiness — that is, if one is not faithful.[9]

Scholars as well as preachers, students as well as readers, have vexed themselves in discerning in what manner the followers of Jesus are salty. Salt, which was obtained from the shores of the Dead Sea, was added to sacrifices and thus was covenant salt (Lev 2:13); salt purified things (Exod 30:35). Salt flavored things (Job 6:6), and seasoning is found in the parallel at both Mark 9:50 and Luke 14:34, and it was a preservative. Salt was a necessity of life. Furthermore, possibly carrying on a theme in the Beatitudes, salt was connected with peace and friendship (Mark 9:50; Col 4:6). The image begs its listeners to use its evocative powers for the various ways Jesus' followers can influence their communities.

We are wise to avoid narrowing "saltiness" to only one sense; instead, we should use it as a general metaphor urging us to think carefully both about *how* we influence as well as *the possibility of diminishing our influence*. But we would also be wise to connect the sorts of influence we are to have to the themes of Jesus and, in particular, to the themes emerging from the Beatitudes (humble poor, pursuit of righteousness and justice, and creating peace and

---

8. Stott, *Message*, 60.
9. Kinghorn, *Wesley on the Sermon*, 111 – 13.

reconciliation). These would be the earliest "applications" made by followers of Jesus when they heard Jesus say they were the salt in Israel.[10] Bonhoeffer said it well: "When Jesus calls his disciples 'the salt,' instead of himself, this transfers his efficacy on earth to them. He brings them into his work." But he adds the warning of Jesus: "The call of Jesus Christ means being salt of the earth or being destroyed."[11]

Light of the World

This second metaphor comes with a short paragraph that explores three different images that illustrate light impacting darkness: a city on a hill (whose lights are visible in the dark), a small terra-cotta oil lamp (which gives light in a dark room), and then light as a metaphor for good works. Lights are designed to shine; they are not to be hidden.

In the Bible and the ancient world light is connected to knowledge, truth, revelation, and love. It was not uncommon in the Jewish world to use the word "light" for people who passed on the light of God to others. A good example is Daniel 12:3: "Those who are wise will shine like the brightness of the heavens, and those who lead many to righteousness, like the stars for ever and ever." But the image of "light" impacting darkness was connected to Israel telling of their God to the "nations" (Gentiles, world) in Isaiah. Here are two primary texts:

> Listen to me, my people;
>   hear me, my nation:
> Instruction will go out from me;
>   my justice will become a light to the nations (Isa 51:4).

> Nations will come to your light,
>   and kings to the brightness of your dawn (60:3).

Here is where reading the Sermon on the Mount in light of the Bible's Story reshapes both what we look for and what we see in the text. These texts suggest that "light of the world" is not a generic metaphor for moral influence in our local context, but actually anticipates the Gentile mission. With the general context of Israel's light-bearing witness from Isaiah in our mind, we come to Matthew's text to think again what he means by "you are the light of the world." But before we even get to this verse, we bump into 4:14–16, where we find "Galilee," "Gentiles," as well as "light" and "darkness" by appealing once again to the same prophet, Isaiah. We have good

---

10. Luz, *Matthew 1–7*, 208; Keener, *Matthew*, 172–73.
11. Bonhoeffer, *Discipleship*, 111–12.

reasons, then, to think that with "light of the world," Matthew taps into this great theme from Isaiah. Here are the words from Isaiah 9:1 – 2 Matthew cites at 4:14 – 16:

> Nevertheless, there will be no more gloom for those who were in distress. In the past he humbled the land of Zebulun and the land of Naphtali, but in the future he will honor Galilee of the nations [Gentiles], by the Way of the Sea, beyond the Jordan —
>
> The people walking in darkness
>   have seen a great light;
> on those living in the land of deep darkness
>   a light has dawned.

We suggest, then, that with "light of the world" in Matthew 5:14 Jesus is pointing to the Gentile mission when the gospel is taken beyond the land of Israel to the whole world.

Again, Jesus' concern is with the inevitable impact of light in darkness. As a town full of lights cannot be hidden (and it is possible he means Jerusalem,[12] but in Galilee one could see, for example, lights in Tiberias from Capernaum) and as people don't light a candle and then put it under a bowl so that its light is snuffed out or at least diminished beyond value, so the disciples are to see the inevitability of their impact on the Gentile world.

The metaphor gives way to direct communication in 5:16: light means good works, or as the CEB has it: "the good things you do." Jesus exhorts his disciples to be people of good works in a manner that attention and glory go to God the Father. Peter will later utter something similar about the impact of good works:

> Dear friends, I urge you, as foreigners and exiles, to abstain from sinful desires, which wage war against your soul. Live such good lives among the pagans that, though they accuse you of doing wrong, they may see your good deeds and glorify God on the day he visits us. (1 Pet 2:11 – 12)

Works witness, but this gives rise to a subtle but soluble problem. Here Jesus summons his disciples to do things publicly in order to impact others, while in 6:1 – 18 Jesus pushes against doing things publicly to be seen. The difference is at the level of intent: in the latter, the intent is to be noticed and congratulated by others as someone who is righteous or pious, while here the act is to be done publicly but in order to mediate God's redeeming presence

---

12. Isa 2:2 – 3; Ezek 5:5. That Jerusalem is in mind is a common observation: see, e.g., Garland, *Reading Matthew*, 59.

in Christ and thus to glorify God. The paradox is deeper: in the brutal reality of Bonhoeffer's own witness, he asked, "Is the cross not something which became outrageously visible in complete darkness?"[13]

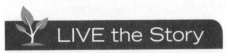

LIVE the Story

Once we connect this passage to the Story of God and once we see the role of God's people in that Story, this passage finds greater clarity. The text affirms our role as God's priests and rulers. Jesus seeks to clarify that role by using the metaphors of salt and light.

Discipleship Means Mission

We can dispute the precise connotations of both salt and light, and we can dispute whether one refers to the disciples' mission to Israel and also to the Gentiles. But one thing cannot be disputed: the follower of Jesus is summoned into a mission on behalf of and for God in this world. Salt and light both evoke the impact a follower of Jesus is to have on others.

Impact results from being missional, and it might be good for us to remind ourselves of a trend in contemporary theology, namely, to see the church and therefore individual Christians as *missional*. The fundamental insight here derives from the studies of theology on the part of missionaries and missiologists who spoke long ago of the *missio Dei*, or the mission of God. What we have to ask is not so much what *our* mission is but what *God's* mission is. I prefer to express this in this way: God's mission is to redeem a broken creation (as a result of sin and disobedience) through the life, death, resurrection, and exaltation of Jesus, through the gift of the Spirit to God's people, in order to bring creation into its perfect order. Of course, we speak here of God's final kingdom, but the challenge of God's people is to live into that kingdom now.

Once we grasp the bigness of this mission of God, we are led to see the church not so much as having one dimension of its duties wrapped up under the heading of "Mission," which more or less means evangelism. The church's mission is God's mission given to the church. A possible indicator of how we understand "mission" can be examined by looking at the church budget to see if the item called "Mission" is only about outreach. Instead, the church *is missional*. The church, in its very being and in everything it does, is missional: it is caught up in God's mission. This theology has been cleverly captured in this expression: because God has a mission, there is a church.

I was invited to speak at New Covenant Fellowship in Champaign, Illi-

---

13. Bonhoeffer, *Discipleship*, 114.

nois, one weekend. What Kris and I encountered there is perhaps the most missional church I have ever experienced. A friend of ours who is part of this fellowship said to me that they were missional before they knew what that meant! The only way I can describe this church is to say the boundaries between church and community are porous. The church is an offering to the community and the community seeps into the church. There are no real "members"; those who attend are part of the fellowship, those who participate can participate as the Lord leads, and any and all are welcome to their services and their serving.

A contrast might help. For many of us our church, whether it tries to or not, creates a serious boundary between those who are "in" and those who are "out." New Covenant has no such boundary. What New Covenant does is to minister to the local community—and we experienced some homeless folks, a middle-aged woman who showed signs of schizophrenia, some Jewish neighbors who thought the topic of my teaching was of interest to them— and whatever the local community needs is what shapes what New Covenant does. The church has become an open table—everyone is welcome to come hear about Jesus, to worship God, and to participate as each one desires. New Covenant wants to do in Champaign what God wants done in Champaign. They don't care who does it; they don't care what it takes; they want to participate in God's mission.

The Story and the salt and light metaphors reveal that the church's fundamental task is to mediate God's presence as priests and to rule on behalf of God as kings and queens under God, serving God in God's mission. Our task is to represent God—to mediate God's goodness, God's grace, God's holiness, and God's justice to this world as those who represent God. Salt and light, then, are about not just what we do but who we are.

Mission Includes Both Jews and Gentiles

Many Christians today, and I mean across the entire spectrum, want a Jesus who is as Jewish as one can make him. I once heard a veteran Jesus scholar say we are all trying to "out-Jewish-Jesus one another." This orientation arose after the discovery of the Dead Sea Scrolls, in reaction to the German history of religions school's emphasis on Greek and Roman religious influences on the New Testament authors, and through the brilliant work of New Testament scholars who illuminated the messages of both Jesus and Paul. One can say there is a fascination with all things Jewish. I have sketched a way of reading the salt and light metaphors in that context, but it is not enough to anchor Jesus into a credible Jewish world. His Jewishness has a missional intent.

Jesus' summons to his disciples was to embody the kingdom vision so thoroughly that both Jews and Gentiles would see the behavior of his followers. In fact, they were to impact both Jews and Gentiles and were to draw both of them into praise of his Father.

This mission to Jews and to Gentiles requires both a behavioral and a verbal mission. The behavioral refers to "good works," and in that world it would have meant almsgiving, visiting the sick, showing hospitality to foreigners, helping a newly married poor couple outfit a new home, sharing expenses and provisions for a wedding or funeral, and grieving with the suffering.[14] In our day it can take on even more forms, like caring for the suffering in Haiti, establishing hospitals for those with AIDS, providing compassion and guidance for the undocumented, funding food, provisions, and education for orphans, as well as helping in a local food pantry. Each and any other kind of behavioral compassion is a way of being both "salt" and "light." Nothing goes straighter to the heart of those in need like love.

Works witness, but those with such works are to witness to Jesus Christ as well. Some today are fond of the word *missional* because it may let them get off the hook of evangelism. The word is far more robust than that, and that is why so many (including this writer) are in favor of it. But behavior is not enough. The only way Jesus' Jewish context or the later Gentile context can be people who "glorify *your* Father in heaven" is to know the connection of the behaviors to the God who summons them. In other words, the behavior of the missional follower of Jesus leads the missioner to witness to Jesus Christ and to the Father. John Dickson's new book about promoting the gospel[15] provides an exceptional balance in this discussion. He is right in emphasizing that not all are called to be constant verbal evangelists, but we are all called to *promote* the gospel with our deeds, with our money, with our church, and with our words.

And our text calls us to promote the gospel *to all, both Jews and Gentiles*. Since missional work with Gentiles is the most common, I will ignore this aspect and focus on missional work with Jews. I spent more time than I care to admit doggedly reading and cataloguing Jewish conversion stories, the most recent and popular of which is Lauren Winner's must-read *Girl Meets God*,[16] and I'd like here to deposit conclusions from that study.[17] It begins with the

---

14. If one can read German, there is an exceptional sketch of Jewish information in H. Strack and P. Billerbeck, *Kommentar zum Neuen Testament* (Munich: C.H. Beck'sche Verlagsbuchhandlung/ Oskar Beck, 1928), 4.1.559–610.

15. J. Dickson, *The Best Kept Secret of Christian Mission: Promoting the Gospel with More than Our Lips* (Grand Rapids: Zondervan, 2010).

16. Lauren Winner, *Girl Meets God on the Path to a Spiritual Life* (Chapel Hill, NC: Algonquin, 2002).

17. You can find this study in ch. 2 of my *Finding Faith, Losing Faith* (with Hauna Ondrey; Waco, TX: Baylor University Press, 2008), 65–122.

observation that in our world, post-Holocaust and post-centuries of Christian anti-Semitism, conversion from Judaism to Jesus Christ (or the church) involves a challenge to the very identity of a Jew in a way perhaps unparalleled in any other kind of conversion. This is a standard Jewish perception: to be Jewish is not to be Christian; to be Christian is to betray one's Jewishness. That is the context for contemporary Jewish conversion, and it makes the move for the Jew anguishing.

While some Jews convert to Jesus Christ—and become messianic Jews—because of the power of a charismatic figure, because of some psychological healing, because of a tragedy, because of a mystical experience, or simply because of a general dissatisfaction in life, the most important factor involved in a Jewish conversion is something that Gentiles almost never consider. The fundamental issue is that Jews must be convinced that Jesus is the Messiah. So, nearly every Jew who converts to Christ becomes a student of Jewish Scriptures, particularly the Prophets, to see if what those Scriptures say about the Messiah matches what we know about Jesus. Once this examination is complete, and once one concludes that Jesus fits the bill, the process of conversion is already over. That admission makes the person a follower of Jesus.

Alongside this fundamental issue is one that follows: once a Jew becomes convinced that Jesus is the Messiah, that same Jew develops the belief that forgiveness of sins comes to them through Jesus' death and resurrection. Notice the order: the typical Jewish converts I have studied rarely are in a quest to find forgiveness of sins, and I believe this is because Jews have a robust belief in atonement, and they enact it and participate in it every year at Yom Kippur, the Day of Atonement. So, the *problem* for a Jew is not the need for forgiveness but whether or not Jesus is the Messiah. If Jesus is the Messiah, then forgiveness comes through him. So, my own wisdom for missional work among Jews is to live a life of love and justice and to learn the Prophets well enough to provoke questions among Jewish friends about whether Jesus is the Messiah. The rest will follow.

I make only one more point: it is unnecessary to require Jews to surrender their Jewishness in order to convert to Jesus as the Messiah. The earliest followers of Jesus were Jews, and they did not cease being Jews when they converted but became *messianic Jews*, or Yeshua-following Jews. There's so much more to say here, but this should suffice.[18]

---

18. I recommend Dan Cohn-Sherbok, *Messianic Judaism* (New York: Cassell, 2000), and M. S. Kinzer, *Post-Missionary Judaism* (Grand Rapids: Brazos, 2005); D. Rudolph and J. Willitts, eds., *Introduction to Messianic Judaism: Its Ecclesial Context and Biblical Foundations* (Grand Rapids: Zondervan, 2013).

Danger of Diminishment

This passage comes with a powerful warning, and that warning concerns diminished witness. Jesus uses a metaphor here: when salt loses its saltiness, it is tossed aside for road grit. With light Jesus speaks less about judgment and more about the incomprehensibility of something being lit and then covered so that the light's value is undone. But the image of being "thrown out" uses a word that is connected to judgment in Matthew's gospel:

"thrown into the fire" (3:10; 6:30; 7:19; cf. 18:8)
"thrown into prison" (5:25; 18:30)
"thrown into hell" (5:29; cf. 5:30; 18:9)
"threw the bad away" (13:48)
"throw them into the blazing furnace" (13:50)

Jesus' language is shaped to warn the followers of Jesus of the consequences of diminishing their impact: saltless salt is thrown away and covered lights are useless.

With this as our basis, we can consider the implications for us: to live this Story today we must take to heart what Jesus says. If we damage the impact we already have, that impact may never be regained (as is the case with some leaders who have fallen, with parents who have sacrificed their integrity in a family or neighborhood through morally reckless behaviors, etc). What's worse, Jesus evidently warns of judgment. I am less concerned here with the Calvinist-Arminian debate on whether or not a person can "lose his/her salvation" than I am with the rhetorical power of the image Jesus uses. Consequences follow in the Story of the Bible for those who are unfaithful to God's covenant blessings, and we can begin with the implicit warning of God walking between the cut up animals in Genesis 15, the blessings and curses of Deuteronomy 28, the sad collapse of leaders like Saul and Solomon, the diminished leadership of David, and the exile of both the northern and the southern kingdoms into Assyria and Babylon, respectively.

Instead of dwelling on the debatable, the text ultimately guides us to think about the need to be faithful—and again the Story of the Bible gives us powerful examples of covenant faithfulness, like Joseph, Moses, Joshua, Ruth, David, Isaiah, and Esther, and like Mary, Jesus, Paul, Peter, and Junia. No one is perfect, but all are called to remain faithful to Jesus.

CHAPTER 4

Matthew 5:17–20

 ## LISTEN to the Story

> [17]"Do not think that I have come to abolish the Law or the Prophets; I have not come to abolish them but to fulfill them. [18]For truly I tell you, until heaven and earth disappear, not the smallest letter, not the least stroke of a pen, will by any means disappear from the Law until everything is accomplished. [19]Therefore anyone who sets aside one of the least of these commands and teaches others accordingly will be called least in the kingdom of heaven, but whoever practices and teaches these commands will be called great in the kingdom of heaven. [20]For I tell you that unless your righteousness surpasses that of the Pharisees and the teachers of the law, you will certainly not enter the kingdom of heaven."

Listening to the text in the Story: Exodus 19–24; Deuteronomy 5–8; Jeremiah 31:31–34; Hebrews

There are two ways of reading the Bible so that we can live before God properly. One way reads the Bible from front to end as the gospel Story, and the other way reads the Bible from Genesis to Malachi with no preconceived Christian beliefs, no gospel orientation, and in a historical manner.[1] The moral life that follows from each reading will vary. The question for the second one is simple: What did this passage mean in its day? The question for the first one is different and looks like this: What does this passage say in light of the Story of the Bible and how do I live faithfully? If Jesus is the goal of that Story from Genesis 1 to Revelation 22, then reading the "Old Testament" without reference to Jesus will be a misreading. But this means learning to read the Bible the way Jews, Jesus, and the apostles did.[2]

---

1. A good introduction to this issue is Edward Klink III and Darian R. Lockett, *Understanding Biblical Theology* (Grand Rapids: Zondervan, 2012).

2. For Jewish texts, see Garland, *Reading Matthew*, 61. The least-exploited source for evaluating how the early Christians understood Scripture is Jewish evidence. For a place to begin, *EDEJ*, 1041–42 (Pentateuch) and 1316–17 (Torah); another sketch in "Scripture in Classical Judaism," in

Our passage is the most significant passage in the entire Bible on how to read the Bible, with a nod to Luke 24:13–49; Galatians 3:19–25; Romans 9–11; and the book of Hebrews, because Jesus tells us here how to read the Bible. The entire Old Testament or, in Jesus' Jewish shorthand summary, the Law and the Prophets, *aim at and are completed in/fulfilled in Jesus as Messiah*. Yet these words, "completed" and "fulfilled," do not mean "abolished." Rabbi Pinchas Lapide makes this potent observation: "In all rabbinic literature I know of no more unequivocal, fiery acknowledgement of Israel's holy scripture than this opening to the Instruction on the Mount."[3] This Jewish scholar thinks these words "acknowledge" — he means "affirm" — the Bible of Israel. This passage is also the thematic statement for what follows in Matthew 5:21–48; that is, we will be treated to five cases of how to read the Bible: about murder, adultery, oaths, retaliation, and love for enemies. Bible reading is at the heart of Jesus' mission, and this passage reveals what makes that heart beat.

So we need to be listening more carefully in our churches to this question: How do church folks read the Bible?[4] Some people read the Bible *formationally*; they read with the heart open to receive from God at a spiritual, intuitive, devotional, and relational level. Others read the Bible *informationally*; they read it to know what it said — and many such people have acquired the original languages so they can examine tenses, cases, and sentence structure. Others read the Bible *canonically*; they read it with their ears open to the rest of the Bible. Others read the Bible *historically*; they only want to know what Jesus' intent was in his world or what Matthew's intent was in his context. Others read the Bible *socio-pragmatically*; they read it to foster and further their own political, theological, ideological, or social agenda. Others read the Bible *according to what their guru says*; they read it — usually in a group, or a church, a sect, or a school of thought — according to how their favorite teacher or prophet or charismatic leader teaches the Bible. Thus, a "Catholic," a "Calvinist," an "Arminian," a "Barthian," a "Hauerwasian," an "N.T. Wrightian," or a "John Piperian" reading of the Bible, so they say, would look like this — you can fill in the blank.

Is there a right way? Or are there only *ways* of reading the Bible? Are some ways better than others, or do we simply read the Bible for ourselves? We can learn to transcend our own readings of the Bible by focusing on how Jesus read the Bible. What does he say?

EJ, 3:1302–9. One book of colossal importance here is C. H. Dodd, *According to the Scriptures: The Sub-Structure of New Testament Theology* (Welwyn, Hertfordshire: James Nisbet, 1961).

3. Lapide, *Sermon on the Mount*, 14.

4. S. McKnight, *The Blue Parakeet: Rethinking How You Read the Bible* (Grand Rapids: Zondervan, 2008), 22–79.

⚡ EXPLAIN the Story

There are four elements to our passage, and they need to be put in outline form perhaps to see how this passage is put together:

First, the *claim of fulfillment* (5:17).
Second, an *elucidation of the claim* (5:18).
Third, the *consequences of the elucidated claim* (5:19).
Fourth, an *elucidation of the consequences* (5:20).

Here's a more concrete, straightforward outline:

First, Jesus fulfills the Torah and Prophets (5:17).
Second, everything in the Torah is true (5:18).
Third, everything therefore must be observed (5:19).
Fourth, your obedience therefore must surpass the experts (5:20).

Whenever I read or teach this passage, I paraphrase a statement attributed to Mark Twain but which never shows up in his many writings: "It ain't those parts of the Bible that I can't understand that bother me; it is the parts I do understand." Whoever said that may well have been thinking about Matthew 5 or even our specific passage.

The Claim of Fulfillment (5:17)

From the opening of 5:17, with its sudden and out-of-nowhere "Do not think," we can infer that some had accused Jesus of breaking the Torah or teaching something that deconstructed the Torah.[5] We might pause to speculate what his opponents found so objectionable about him that they could accuse him of abolishing the Torah and the Prophets. In light of what we learn in 5:21–48, where Jesus is seen to be anything but a softy, at the heart of their worry was probably Jesus' willingness to see the entire Torah (and the Prophets) as expressions of the Jesus Creed of loving God and loving others,[6] or the Golden Rule as a variant of the Jesus Creed. The Jesus Creed threatens the legalist and the minimalist, but it expands the Torah to its divine expectations for the one who genuinely loves God and loves others. There's more. It was not that Jesus had an Ethic from Above, Below, or Beyond, but that he had the audacity to think he was the Messiah and taught a Messianic Ethic, reorienting the whole Torah and Prophets. This is what disturbed some of his contemporaries.

In the face of some accusations, Jesus asserts in the strongest of terms that

---

5. For similar language, cf. 9:13; 10:34.
6. Lapide, *Sermon on the Mount*, 15.

his mission ("I have not come") is not to "abolish" the Torah or the Prophets. Notice that his focus is on both—both Moses and Elijah, as the Transfiguration will also show (17:1–13). Instead of abolishing the law, Jesus says his mission is to "fulfill." On this word hangs the meaning of this passage, and the word is used emphatically in Matthew to refer to the salvation-historical, theological, and moral Story of Israel coming to completion in Jesus.

The term *fulfill* relates to Old Testament patterns and predictions coming to realization. Nothing makes this clearer than reading Matthew 1–2, though one can also observe the same at 3:3; 4:1–16; 5:17–48; 8:16–17; 9:13; 10:34–36; 11:10; and 12:16–21. While some have suggested that Jesus "fulfills" by teaching the true meaning of Torah or by "doing what it says," the use of this term "fulfill" in Matthew makes the sense of an eschatological completion the most accurate meaning.[7] In summary: to "fulfill" or "complete" means history has come to its fulfillment in Jesus himself—that is, in his life, death, resurrection, and exaltation and in his teachings.

We must consider the mind-numbing claim here by Jesus: he is claiming that *he fulfills—in a salvation-historical, theological, and moral manner—what the Torah and the Prophets anticipated and predicted and preliminarily taught.* What kind of person makes claims like this? It is one thing to say, as Jesus could have, I can do miracles as mighty as Elijah, or I can predict the future as clearly as did Isaiah, or I can do miracles as astounding as Moses. It's altogether different to claim that he himself *fulfills* the Torah and the Prophets. But that's precisely the claim Jesus makes here. Nothing in history would ever be the same. The Torah had come to its goal. The Torah hereby takes on the face of Jesus. His claim is thoroughly Jewish (Isa 2:1–5; Jer 31:31–34), but of a particular sort: messianic.[8] The first lesson we get in reading the Bible is this one: Look to Jesus as its central Story.

An Elucidation of the Claim (5:18)

The claim by Jesus that he fulfills the Torah and the Prophets might suggest we can be done with the Torah, but Jesus says precisely the opposite. Surprisingly, neither does this passage teach a simple return to the Torah. Our next verse props up the previous one by clarifying just how serious Jesus is when he says "fulfill" and "not ... abolish." He's saying that everything in the Torah (or Prophets) is true, and every bit of it will come to pass *just as it is written.*[9]

---

7. Allison, *Sermon on the Mount*, 59; Hagner, *Matthew 1–13*, 106; France, *Matthew*, 182–83; Turner, *Matthew*, 157–58.

8. Davies, *The Setting of the Sermon*, 109–90.

9. A parallel can be found in Luke 16:17. There are two clauses here that are virtually synonymous and not far from our "until hell freezes over": "until heaven and earth disappear" and "until everything is accomplished." See Hagner, *Matthew 1–13*, 106–8.

But what needs to be observed here is that Jesus is not a Pharisee or a Qumran sectarian, nor is he a later rabbi, each of whom was scrupulous in Torah observance. For Jesus the real Torah is permanent *as Jesus teaches it*, which is the point of 5:21–48 and which illustrates our category of a Messianic Ethic. Still, that Torah and those Prophets are not done away with; they remain in effect (in an even greater way).

The book of Hebrews, not to mention the tensions we find in Paul over the Torah (Rom 7:1–6; 10:4; Gal 3:19–26; 5:1–6), illustrates the tension over what to do with the Torah. In Acts 10–11, in the encounter of the Torah-observant Peter with the God-fearing Gentile Cornelius, we see what "fulfill" looks like for the apostles: it means some radical revisioning without abolishing. Paul's words about accommodating himself to Gentile ways in 1 Corinthians 9:19–23 also illustrate how the apostles "applied" this claim by Jesus. Second lesson in Bible reading: looking to Jesus means following him and through him the Torah.

The Consequences of the Elucidated Claim (5:19)

Jesus' logic is relentlessly practical. If he is the fulfillment, and if in that fulfillment everything is established as true and realized, then morality changes. The clearest way to put this is to say that Jesus thinks that following him means following the Torah. Those who follow him (and his teaching of the Torah) will be called "great" in the kingdom. Anyone who denies his teachings and teaches others not to follow him (and through him the Torah) will be called "least" in the kingdom.

What about the "least" and "great"? Will both enter the kingdom eventually? Are we to see "great" and "least" as two levels of kingdom participation? Some see this distinction (see 18:4; 20:16, 21, 23, 26),[10] but it is more likely that Jesus is using typical Jewish/Hebraic contrasting results for the ones who will enter the kingdom (the doer) vs. the ones who will not enter the kingdom (the nondoer). In other words, "least" in the kingdom is a kind way of saying "suffering eternal judgment."[11] What leads us to this view is the end of the Sermon (7:21–23), where we see that *only* those who do the will of God (as Jesus teaches it) will enter the kingdom. In addition, 8:11–12 says the "subjects [sons] of the kingdom will be thrown outside," so that being in the kingdom and eventually being tossed outside the kingdom are not

---

10. Hagner, *Matthew 1–13*, 108–9.

11. Luz, *Matthew 1–7*, 220, who cites Chromatius and Chrysostom from the early church as well as both Luther and E. Schweizer from modern times. Chrysostom's words: "But when you hear 'least in the kingdom of heaven,' you are to think of *nothing but hell and punishment*" (italics added; from ACCS: *Matthew*, 98). Also Kinghorn, *Wesley on the Sermon*, 134–35.

incompatible ideas for Jesus. Third lesson in Bible reading: following Jesus really means following Jesus, and it matters eternally.

An Elucidation of the Consequences (5:20)

If that statement by Jesus is not clear enough, Jesus makes it more concrete by comparing his followers to existing religious groups. If their righteousness — and here he means "behavior that conforms to the will of God as taught by Jesus" or, as Tom Wright captures it, "your covenant behavior" (KNT) — does not *greatly* surpass[12] that of "the Pharisees and the teachers of the law," they will never *ever* enter the kingdom. The language is as emphatic as the claim is shocking. If you want to pick an example of the pious, you pick the Pharisees, who famously mastered the Torah and all its interpretations and rulings or, like them, the "teachers of the law." Jesus takes such examples — somewhat like taking a Mother Theresa or a John Stott or a Dallas Willard or a Francis Chan — and says, "You've got to be much, much better!"

It is far too easy for Protestants to take the sting from Jesus' words by thinking what Jesus was really saying was not that his followers had to do more, but that they were to trust in the righteousness of Christ while the scribes and Pharisees were trusting in themselves. Or to say the Pharisees were externally righteous only. For this view, "surpasses" is really about *kind* of righteousness and not *degree*.[13] Yes, there's a place for such a concern with externals, and one can find it in some Pharisees and find support in Luke 18:9 – 14 or Romans 10:3, but it is unlikely that we need to think this way here. Others contend that Jesus has in mind not justification but sanctification.

Yes, righteousness emerges out of communion with Jesus and redemption; it is a kingdom righteousness, a kingdom that comes with new covenant power to heal and transform. Yes, this is righteousness under the cross. *But it is a righteousness that is done.* The ethic of this verse is more an Ethic from Above, designed rhetorically to strike the followers with a demand. When we recontextualize it into sanctification, which is where it might fit in our theology, we run the risk of destroying its original rhetorical power. Fourth lesson in Bible reading: we are challenged to be better than nonfollowers. Followers

---

12. The Greek reads *perisseusē ... pleion*, not just *perisseusē*. In other words, "surpass ... greatly." Almost all translations ignore the adverb *pleion* here. But see Luz, *Matthew 1 – 7*, 211, and the discussion in Talbert, *Reading the Sermon on the Mount*, 63 – 65. Righteousness was discussed briefly at 5:6, above.

13. Stott, *Message*, 75. Here are his words: "Christian righteousness far surpasses pharisaic righteousness in kind rather than in degree. It is not so much, shall we say, that Christians succeed in keeping some 240 commandments when the best Pharisees may only have scored 230. No. Christian righteousness is greater than pharisaic righteousness *because it is deeper, being a righteousness of the heart*" (emphasis added). Thus it is a "new heart-righteousness." See also the four points of Quarles, *Sermon on the Mount*, 103.

are marked by a greater righteousness or by more righteousness. (Just what that more will look like can be found in the antitheses of 5:21–48.)

LIVE the Story

Bible Reading

We do not read the Bible aright until we learn to read it as the Story of Israel that comes to completion—fulfillment—in the Story of Jesus Christ. This is the essence of what Paul means by "gospel" in 1 Corinthians 15:1–28, and it is the way the early apostles evangelized when they were telling the gospel: one simply needs to read the sermons in Acts 2; 3;10–11; 13; 14; and 17 to see this.[14] This leads me to say that Matthew 5:17–20 is one of the most pristine expressions of the gospel in the New Testament. Why? Because this passage says overtly and boldly that the Story of Israel is fulfilled in Jesus himself. His life, his teachings, his actions—everything about him completes what was anticipated in the Old Testament. That's the gospel!

From the moment these words were uttered nothing was the same. From that moment Genesis, Exodus, Leviticus, Numbers, Deuteronomy . . . all the way to Malachi (though in Jesus' day the Old Testament ended with 2 Chronicles) were read as texts that in a large canvas and in small brush-strokes pointed toward Jesus. From this point on purely historical readings (what it meant then) will be unsatisfactory; the Story must be read toward Christ the way someone has learned to read a good novel, say Harper Lee's *To Kill a Mockingbird*, or a good short story, say *Parker's Back* by Flannery O'Connor. We read them and then reread them, and the more we know them, the more we read from the ending and not from the beginning. We read the Bible the way we "interpret" a great season for our favorite sports team; we learn to see the first competition as setting the stage for the victory at the end of the season.

Thus, Genesis 1 is not simply about God in heaven, who is called YHWH or Elohim, but about the God and Father of our Lord Jesus Christ; it is about Jesus Christ as God; it is about the Holy Spirit. In other words, we are to read Genesis 1 in a Trinitarian manner now that we know where the "God" of Genesis 1 was headed. And the "image" of God that we find in Adam and Eve is not just about their ability know and to relate to God, nor is it just about the ancient Near Eastern sense of representing the king. Rather, the "image" of Adam and Eve in Genesis 1 is a reflection of Jesus Christ, who is the true and perfect "image" of God (cf. 1 Cor 15:49; 2 Cor 3:18; 4:4; Col 1:15;

14. McKnight, *King Jesus Gospel*.

3:10). In technical terms this is not *eisegesis*, or the reading *into* the texts, but it is a reading of the text in light of the whole Story.

I urge you to be a Bible reader—from Genesis to Revelation. The number of Christians who read the Bible today is not high; in a day when the Bible is more available than ever in history, the Bible is being less read by those who have the Bible in hard and electronic copy. I urge you also to be one who sees the whole Bible through the Story of Jesus, and I urge you to commit to doing what Jesus teaches. A student of mine told me he took an introduction to the Bible class with a "bundle of pastors." The first day the professor asked the class for a show of hands: "How many of you have read the Old Testament?" My student told me no more than five raised their hands—in a class of more than twenty (pastors). Time to commit yourself to reading the whole Bible—front to back.

Ethics

This passage also instructs us how to *live the Story*. Jesus is not offering a lecture in hermeneutics here, though there's plenty of hermeneutics here. Rather, he's explaining how the Bible really works—it comes to completion in him (5:17–20)—in order to tell his followers how to live (5:21–48). Perhaps the words of an early anonymous Jesus-following commentator on the Sermon say it best:

> Christ's commandment contains the law, but the law does not contain Christ's commandment. Therefore whoever fulfills the commandments of Christ implicitly fulfills the commandments of the law.[15]

Take kosher laws. We learn that water-dwelling animals that crawl, like the lobster, are unclean because they don't have fins or scales. Israel followed this commandment (Lev 11:9–12; Deut 14:9–10). A simple "follow the Torah" approach will mean one can't eat such things, but I do and you probably do as well. Are we right? How do we follow what Jesus says here about the fulfilled Torah? I begin with this: kosher, or purity, is now established on a new basis. Jesus is the one who makes clean, and these laws anticipate the purity that is to be found in Jesus.

Furthermore, as these texts are clearly about order and taxonomy and putting things in their proper place, we observe that Jesus has established an entirely new order: he is Lord, his people are his body. Jesus makes clean—and that means those laws are now secondary to him. This is precisely the point made in 15:1–20. It is not what enters the mouth—food—but what comes out of the mouth that makes clean. And what comes out of the mouth

---

15. ACCS: *Matthew*, 101.

comes from the heart, and it is the heart that matters most of all. Jesus wants followers who are purified from the heart out. So, kosher food laws can be observed from a clean heart, but if the heart is clean — by contact with Jesus — then whatever one eats cannot make unclean.

Now I can hear a friend of mine pushing back that kosher food laws do require observance by *messianic Jews* but not by Gentile Christians, and I can agree to that view. But even if one takes that view, one still defines kosher in a new way: Jesus the Messiah makes people clean, and food is but a sign of their messianic purity. This view neither relaxes nor abolishes the Torah but sets it firmly within the hermeneutic of Jesus: kosher is defined by completion in Jesus Christ, and kosher means living a life of loving God and loving others with everything we've got, including food.

I have Jewish friends and I have messianic Jewish friends. I've shared a table with both. Once I was eating breakfast with a well-known Jewish scholar at a buffet. After observing what I was eating, the Jewish scholar asked, "Is there pork in those eggs?" I said, "Yes." I asked him, not knowing his kosher food habits (but I was about to learn), "Do you want me to get you some?" His response: "No. My God cares about what I eat." Matter of fact, no hint of humor. He observed the kosher food laws. Another time I was sharing breakfast with a messianic Jew when the waitress came by and took our order. I asked for a breakfast with some bacon and my messianic friend said, "You're kidding me!" Having recently eaten with my previously mentioned Jewish friend, I said, "My God doesn't care what I eat." He laughed and said back, "My God does. But that's fine."

With my messianic friend I had a wonderful conversation about the gospel — not that I didn't have a wonderful conversation with my rabbi friend. We talked about Christ and about preaching, studying, writing, and attending academic meetings, and about our families and our God. While we differed on the implications of kosher food laws for today, our fellowship was rooted in Christ, not on our kosher food habits. Never did he question if I should be at the table, nor did I question him. He reads the Bible messianically, and so do I. He may have wondered if I should respect his kosher condition by not eating pork, and I may have wondered if the Torah was to be lived differently for messianists than for Gentile Christians. But those were not obstacles to Christ or in our fellowship in Christ.

Extensions

The uncompromising rigor of Jesus in these verses points an accusing finger at a powerful tendency at work in American culture where an increasing number of Christians are posing two kinds of moral standards: one drawn from the Bible/Jesus and one drawn from the Constitution or culture. That is, some say, "I'm personally against abortion but the law now permits it." Or, "I'm personally against homosexuality, but civil unions are now law so I support them." This posture of two moral stances is a *fundamental moral failure*. Yes, as citizens there is the legal or constitutional question, so we are to ask if the law supports or does not support civil unions or the marriages of gays and lesbians, and yes, we are to examine if the law supports or does not support abortion. But what is legal is not the same as what is moral or what is right: the Christian's morals are not determined by whether something is *legal* or *constitutional*, but by what the Story of God in the Bible reveals. A Christian citizen may think civil unions are legally permissible on the basis of legal precedent or legal gaps, but constitutional legality does not determine what is right or wrong, regardless of how much citizens are to respect or live within that law.

The teachings of Jesus are to shape my life, and that means my whole life. I return once again to the Jesus Creed: we are to love God and to love others with "heart, soul, mind, *and strength*" (cf. Deut 6:5; Mark 12:30) — and surely that last term is an embracive term describing all of our resources and externalities. That is, "and strength" would include our political behaviors and actions. If we think the teachings of the gospel are against abortion, we are bound by conscience to support bans on abortion because of what the gospel requires, even if the law permits such. The same applies to so many things, not excluding civil unions, Christian participation in business, the relations of Christians to wartime activities, and divorce, which is one of the topics toward which Jesus turned his gaze in the next passage.

What this passage teaches is that followers of Jesus are called both to teach and to do what Jesus teaches, and through following Jesus they are to do what the Torah and the Prophets reveal. These are the north star for the follower of Jesus, not the US Constitution or the law of the land.

CHAPTER 5

Matthew 5:21-26

 LISTEN to the Story

21"You have heard that it was said to the people long ago, 'You shall not murder, and anyone who murders will be subject to judgment.' 22But I tell you that anyone who is angry with a brother or sister will be subject to judgment. Again, anyone who says to a brother or sister, 'Raca,'[1] is answerable to the court.[2] And anyone who says, 'You fool!' will be in danger of the fire of hell.[3]

23"Therefore, if you are offering your gift at the altar and there remember that your brother or sister has something against you, 24leave your gift there in front of the altar. First go and be reconciled to them; then come and offer your gift.

25"Settle matters quickly with your adversary who is taking you to court. Do it while you are still together on the way, or your adversary may hand you over to the judge, and the judge may hand you over to the officer, and you may be thrown into prison. 26Truly I tell you, you will not get out until you have paid the last penny."

Listening to the text in the Story: Genesis 4; 9:6; Exodus 20:13; Numbers 35:16–34; Deuteronomy 5:17; 19:1–14; Mark 1:41; Ephesians 4:26, 31.

Here begins the first of six "antitheses," a word describing the "you have heard ... *but* I say to you" statements of Jesus.[4] The emphasis here is on

---

1. KNT: "foul and abusive language."
2. TNIV: "Sanhedrin."
3. KNT: "Gehenna."
4. It is worth observing how the six antitheses are formed:
   "You have heard that it was said to the people long ago ..." (5:21).
   "You have heard that it was said ..." (5:27).
   "It has been said ..." (5:31).
   "Again, you have heard that it was said to the people long ago ..." (5:33).
   "You have heard that it was said ..." (5:38).
   "You have heard that it was said ..." (5:43).

Jesus' antithetical relationship to what his Jewish listeners had heard.[5] In each antithesis Jesus quotes Scripture, but Jesus' antithetical relationship is not against the Scripture itself but the interpretation of that Scripture. Jesus actually probes behind the Scripture into the intent of God. Each of these elements is important and so deserves repetition in simple form:[6]

> Jesus quotes from the Bible.
> Jesus interprets, extends, or counters that quotation.
> But his opposition is against how that Scripture has been
>   interpreted.
> Jesus probes behind the original Scripture into God's mind.
> Jesus reveals what that intent is and how his followers are to live.

Thus, it can be said that in these antitheses we are given the original and full intent of God, which both was only partly revealed in Scripture and had been misread by some of Jesus' contemporaries. We have, then, an Ethic from Above. *Jesus reveals a fuller expression of God's will for God's people.*[7] In our specific text the prohibition of murder is the surface expression of a deeper divine intent: God's people aren't to be angry at one another. If one masters one's anger, murder will never occur.

Anger was not taken as seriously in the Old Testament as Jesus takes it here, nor was murder deepened to anger as Jesus does here. It makes sense, then, to see Jesus "deepening" the Torah here. It ought also to be observed that the Jewish world knew considerable variety on what it meant to follow or practice the Torah, and exceptions were made, adjustments occurred (as when financial payment was rendered instead of physical punishment), and circumventions were permitted; and it is said Rabbi Yohanan ben Zakkai

---

The repetition of "to the people long ago" in the first and fourth antitheses cuts the antitheses into two groups. The three-step reduction of formula in the first three is not repeated in the second group of antitheses.

5. David Turner observes that "antitheses" is not the best word since that would imply overt contradiction of the Torah; other terms have been suggested, like "hypertheses" or "epitheses" or "contrasts." See Turner, *Matthew*, 165. Lapide suggests "supertheses"; see Lapide, *Sermon on the Mount*, 46. This all hangs on what Jesus is speaking against; I would contend that if Jesus is speaking against interpretations of the Torah, then the word *antithesis* applies. Stott says it best: "In relation to scribal distortions of the law, the term 'antithesis' rightly describes" what Jesus is teaching, but "in relation to the law itself 'exegesis' would be a more accurate word" (Stott, *Message*, 77).

6. For a more extensive analysis, see G. H. Stassen, "The Fourteen Triads of the Sermon on the Mount (Matthew 5:21–7:12)," *JBL* 122 (2003): 267–308; summarized and graphed in Stassen, *Living the Sermon*. Stassen contends there are three parts to the "antitheses" (and not just two): a citation of a traditional teaching, a diagnosis of a vicious cyle, and—here is his distinction—a "transforming initiative" that maps the way of deliverance.

7. See further Strickland, ed., *Five Views on Law and Gospel*; with appropriate differences and nuances, I side with D. J. Moo's essay in that book (pp. 319–76).

annulled the bitter waters test of Numbers 5.[8] To use the terms of the Jewish world Jesus constructs a "fence around the Torah."[9]

Jesus' statement in 5:21–26 both interacts with and transcends the laws about murder, trials, and revenge found in Numbers 35:16–34 and Deuteronomy 19:1–14. Striking another human with a fatal blow with an iron object, a stone, a wooden object, or a fist, or intentionally shoving or throwing something at a person so that the person dies makes the one so acting a "murderer." That person, properly tried, was to be put to death by the "avenger of blood." If an action that led to death, however, was not intentional, the accused person was not liable for murder and was to be protected from the avenger; this is why there were cities of refuge in the Land. While Jesus will undo retaliation in 5:38–42, in this section he enters into the heart of the "murderer" and condemns the anger and revenge that precipitate murder. Instead of anger, the aim — the transforming initiative — is reconciliation with others.

EXPLAIN the Story

There are three parts to this passage: Jesus' *redefinition of murder* (5:21–22), an exhortation to *reconciliation* (5:23–24), and a *repetition* of the exhortation that results in a warning (5:25–26). The second and third parts vary by offering two different sorts of (exaggerated) examples: interrupting a sacrifice in the temple and finding agreement with an adversary on the way to the court.

Redefining Murder

Jesus quotes Exodus 20:13 or Deuteronomy 5:17: "You have heard that it was said to the people long ago, 'You shall not murder.'" What follows ("and anyone who murders will be subject to judgment") summarizes what is found in a variety of texts, including Numbers 35:16–34 and Deuteronomy 17:8–13; 19:1–14. Some see a connection to Cain and Abel in Genesis 4. In Jesus' context "murder" refers to intentional manslaughter (and not to the sort of death that occurs during warfare), and it was understood almost the same way we would today: it was against God's Torah and against the image of God (Gen 4; 9:6) to murder someone. The laws around the prohibition to murder were designed not to mitigate murder but to protect the innocent and restrain vengeance.

---

8. I take these examples from Garland, *Reading Matthew*, 63.

9. A Jewish expression for clarifying the law: see Aaron M. Gale in *The Jewish Annotated New Testament* (ed. Amy-Jill Levine and Marc Z. Brettler; Oxford: Oxford University Press, 2011), p. 11 notes.

Murder is wrong, but that judgment requires some facts and discernment of intention. Sometimes murder is downgraded to "manslaughter," but Jesus works to reverse the thunder. He probes into what is behind murder, namely, desire, by saying: "But I tell you that anyone who is *angry* with a brother or sister will be subject to judgment" (5:22). Jesus then turns the more general "angry with" to specifics: calling someone "Raca" (an Aramaic word for "empty head" or "fool") and/or accusing someone of being a "Fool!" Jesus here specifies the consequences for each offense: "judgment," "the court" (see also 10:17), and "the fire of hell." One can see these two sets of categories (crime and consequence) in different ways: thus, perhaps there is an escalation of consequence (from judgment to eternal destruction) in accordance with an escalation of crime,[10] but it is more likely that crimes and consequences are synonymous.[11] Jesus knows anger leads to murder, so he prohibits anger and spells out consequences for the "crime of anger." Later Christians made the same connection: "Do not become angry, for anger leads to murder" (*Didache* 3:2).[12]

What grabs us is the shocking disproportion between what we perceive to be the sin (anger) and its consequences (eternal punishment). In the words of R. T. France, "ordinary insults may betray an attitude of contempt which God takes extremely seriously."[13] Perhaps we need to be reminded that Jesus thinks anger leads to "the fire of hell," which translates "Gehenna." Gehenna was the valley south of Jerusalem and, because it had been a place of divine judgment, it became a trope in the Jewish world for the place of divine doom.[14] Examples include 2 Chronicles 28:3, but especially the powerful warning of Jeremiah 19:2–9:

> 2 Chron. 28:3: He [Ahaz] burned sacrifices in the Valley of Ben Hinnom [Gehenna] and sacrificed his children in the fire, engaging in the detestable practices of the nations the LORD had driven out before the Israelites.

> Jer. 19:2–9: ²"… and go out to the Valley of Ben Hinnom, near the entrance of the Potsherd Gate. There proclaim the words I tell you, ³and say, 'Hear the word of the LORD, you kings of Judah and people of Jerusa-

---

10. So Guelich, *Sermon on the Mount*, 187.

11. Keener, *Matthew*, 183–84.

12. Some restrict the anger to anger with fellow believers; this was the view of Hilary and Peter Chrysologus. See ACCS: *Matthew*, 102–3. More below at 5:24.

13. France, *Matthew*, 201.

14. See Davies and Allison, *Matthew*, 1:514–15; see also Dale Allison's exhaustive study in *Resurrecting Jesus: The Earliest Christian Tradition and Its Interpreters* (London: T&T Clark, 2005), 56–100. Although I have myself taken the view in the past that this was Jerusalem's garbage dump, there is no evidence that Gehenna was such in the first century. That evidence is not found until the twelfth century AD.

lem. This is what the LORD Almighty, the God of Israel, says: Listen! I am going to bring a disaster on this place that will make the ears of everyone who hears of it tingle. [4]For they have forsaken me and made this a place of foreign gods; they have burned incense in it to gods that neither they nor their ancestors nor the kings of Judah ever knew, and they have filled this place with the blood of the innocent. [5]They have built the high places of Baal to burn their children in the fire as offerings to Baal — something I did not command or mention, nor did it enter my mind. [6]So beware, the days are coming, declares the LORD, when people will no longer call this place Topheth or the Valley of Ben Hinnom, but the Valley of Slaughter.

[7]" 'In this place I will ruin the plans of Judah and Jerusalem. I will make them fall by the sword before their enemies, at the hands of those who want to kill them, and I will give their carcasses as food to the birds and the wild animals. [8]I will devastate this city and make it an object of horror and scorn; all who pass by will be appalled and will scoff because of all its wounds. [9]I will make them eat the flesh of their sons and daughters, and they will eat one another's flesh because their enemies will press the siege so hard against them to destroy them.' "

Jesus not only dismantles ethical codes at work in his culture, where anger was never on par with murder, but he sets his own ethical code in the context of entrance into the kingdom of God. He threatens his followers with divine judgment for anger. Here we have an Ethic from Beyond established by the Messiah, who reveals God's truth for the kingdom community.

Exhortation to Reconciliation

Because Jesus prohibits anger, he offers counterbehaviors that illustrate what it means to live both beyond anger and in reconciled relations with others. His words are an Ethic from Beyond, that is, the kingdom appearing partially in the now. In 5:23 – 24, Jesus shows that reconciliation with a "brother or sister" (in Matthew the term "brother [and by extension] or sister" may only refer to followers of Jesus; cf. 12:48 – 50)[15] trumps even the sacredness of offering a sacrificial gift in the temple.

Jesus' words are purposefully general: "has *something* against you." But we must observe that Jesus doesn't say in this specific text, "if *you* have something *against someone else*," but if the offended party has something *against you.*[16] Jesus wants his followers to live radically reconciled lives. Pastorally, there is the danger of being overly scrupulous, and this "something" can be petty,

---

15. See France, *Matthew*, 200.
16. He does, however, speak on the opposite issue in 18:15.

trivial, or even controlling. In context, Jesus isn't talking about theological differences or petty human disagreements but anger, the kind of anger that leads to murder. So, in the word "something" we must keep our eyes on the brother or sister who is angry toward us or feels angered by things we have done that offended them; and we need to become aware of our own anger.

There is nothing here that is not a part of Judaism's own teaching, even if the best example comes from the later rabbinic text, *Mishnah Yoma* 8:9:

> This exegesis did R. Eleazar b. Azariah state: "From all your sins shall you be clean before the Lord (Lev. 16:30)—for transgressions between man and the Omnipresent does the Day of Atonement atone. For transgressions between man and his fellow, the Day of Atonement atones, *only if the man will regain the good will of his friend.*"

Jesus emphasizes reconciliation more than what was typical in his world. All of this is wrapped up inside the Jesus Creed and the Golden Rule and will emerge with force in the Lord's Prayer (6:12, 14–15): love means fellowship, and fellowship requires reconciliation. The exaggerated temple scenario, with its instruction to drop the sacrifice right there at the altar, illustrates the importance of living in reconciled relations.

Repetition of Exhortation and a Warning

But Jesus moves reconciliation outside the circle of his followers to include even those with whom one is in a legal dispute (5:25–26) in a scenario of an "adversary" suing a disciple of Jesus. On the way to the court the follower of Jesus is to strive for reconciliation—and here Jesus gives an almost comic, pragmatic example. Instead of trusting matters to the court case, in which case the follower may end up in prison, the follower is to take matters into his (or her) own hands and work for reconciliation—and to do so "quickly" (5:25). Why? Because the judge will have his way and the process of justice may lead to prison. The aim opens the verse: "Settle matters." This expression translates the Greek word *eunoōn*, a term that means "to make friends with," "to be well disposed toward someone," or "to be in agreement with someone." In this context, it could suggest becoming friends with someone, but it is perhaps wiser not to expect too much of this term and to see it as "come to agreeable terms with."[17]

This paragraph illustrates the centrality of reconciliation with others by appealing to an extreme situation: Jesus is for reconciliation, even if it means interrupting sacred actions and legal judgments.

---

17. For an excellent sketch of this term, see C. Spicq, *TLNT*, 2:123–28. See the noun form in Eph. 6:7.

LIVE the Story

Those familiar with the Bible and the teachings of Jesus in the Sermon on the Mount may be those most apt to miss what must have screamed "Can you believe it!" in Jesus' day. In the world of Jesus, especially among the observant types, Moses was *the* man. He was the one through whom God gave the Torah and was held in the highest possible of honors. Jesus, in the antitheses, puts himself not only alongside Moses but *above* Moses. Moses more or less prohibits murder; Jesus flat-out prohibits something deeper and something more transcendent at the level of morality: he prohibits anger. By getting behind murder, Jesus on some level trumps the perceptions of Moses.

We have already discussed the Moses Christology of Matthew, so I don't want to dwell on this any more here, but we dare not miss the fundamental Christology of what Jesus is doing here. He is setting himself up as someone greater than Moses. This is a Messianic Ethic that is at the same time an Ethic from Beyond: the King of the kingdom calls kingdom citizens to live now as if the kingdom had arrived.

While Jesus does not come out and say, "Do not be angry," his words "But … anyone who is angry with a brother or sister" all but lays down a universal prohibition of anger. Three interpretations beckon our allegiance. Some suggest this is a radical and almost utopian, even absolute, prohibition of every and any kind of anger; others suggest it is hyperbolic, and what Jesus has in mind is to get his disciples wedged away from the justification of anger in their culture. Yet a third view could be called a kingdom-perspective view, what I am calling an Ethic from Beyond.

Often enough the Bible counsels against, warns about, or prohibits anger. Thus, one thinks of an Ethic from Above: God says don't be angry. This is where we need to begin. One thinks here of Ecclesiastes 7:9 ("for anger resides in the lap of fools") or Psalm 37:8 ("Refrain from anger and turn from wrath"). The apostle Paul says, "Get rid of all bitterness, rage and anger, brawling and slander, along with every form of malice" (Eph 4:31), and the near parallel (in Col 3:8) says to be rid of "anger, rage, malice, slander, and filthy language from your lips." James says that our "anger does not produce the righteousness that God desires" (Jas 1:20). Taken together, one could easily infer that anger is absolutely prohibited.

But there is the evidence that God himself is sometimes angry (Exod 4:14; Jer 6:11) and that Jesus himself expressed anger (see, e.g., Mark 3:5), and perhaps anger is behind the "You blind fools!" in Matt 23:17 and the cleansing of the temple (Matt 21:12; Mark 11:15; Luke 19:45; John 2:15). Such texts lead others to see in the words of Jesus in our passage an exaggerated or hyperbolic statement, or they see here an Ethic from Below. It is not possible to be free entirely of anger, and there are sometimes when anger is justified, often called "righteous indignation," that creates the difficulty of knowing how to "live" Jesus' words in Matthew 5:22. That is, some would say this is no more than a rhetorical ethic designed to warn.

I disagree. No matter how clear the references are to God's anger or the anger of Jesus, not to mention Paul's own anger (how else to read Gal 3:1), the language of Jesus in Matthew 5:22 is neither easily dismissed nor the context minimized, for in that context Jesus is raising the ante and upping the expectations of his followers. Jesus wants his followers to be different when it comes to anger and murder. So, in light of how the New Testament frames the ethics of Jesus, the best interpretation is what may be called an Ethic from Beyond. The kingdom is both partially realized in the here and now, and the kingdom is also partially yet to come. We live in the "now but not yet." Because the kingdom is in some sense "now"—and that means some of the powers of the kingdom have already been unleashed (think Holy Spirit)—followers of Jesus are to avoid sinful anger, and they are capable of being transformed from anger. In the future kingdom of God, when all is consummated and when heaven comes to earth, anger will vanish because loving fellowship will flourish. The prohibition of anger here is not so much hyperbolic as it is a foretaste of kingdom realities.

Nothing expresses kingdom realities more than reconciled relations. A biblical understanding of love, which lies behind this passage, includes the notions that God is *with us* as the Someone who is *for us*. The core expression of God's love for humans is found in the covenant God made with Abraham, Moses, and David—and then in its complete form through Jesus. That covenant, in the "I will be your God and you will be my people" formula (cf., e.g., Jer 31:33), frames everything needed to be said about reconciled relations. We are to live out that covenant with others, beginning with family and the people of God, but also in connecting ways with everyone we know and meet (so far as is possible).

It is perhaps easier to think here of golden examples, not the least of which would be the Christians of Germany who suffered under Hitler and who found themselves after the war joined by those who served in Hitler's troops. Another example would be the Afrikaner Christians of South Africa with whom Archbishop Desmond Tutu (standing next to Nelson Mandela) worked to form reconciliation as South Africa moved out of apartheid into a genuine expression of what Africans call *ubuntu*, the sense that we become humans by living with other humans in reconciliation. And I think of the extreme example of Tutsis and Hutus as they sought to make peace, where the numbers of atrocities were so great and the legal system so small that courts were formed under trees in local communities as locals sought reconciliation. I think too of the stories that arise when we think of New World slavery, of Jim Crow laws in the South (and less overtly but real in the North), as well as the Great Migration that led to exacerbation of frayed relations between American citizens who were black or white.[18]

Extreme and newsworthy examples, however, aren't the only way Jesus chose to express himself. Thus, I am thinking we would do better to ponder the ordinariness of Jesus' examples: immediately suspending what we are doing to find peace with our own relations. What comes to mind for me are the relations of husbands and wives, the relations of fathers and mothers to children, of sibling relations, and of the relations of neighbors and community members and those with whom we work. It is far too easy to ponder reconciliation of monstrous problems, like those in Rwanda, than it is to ponder a day-to-day pursuit of peace and reconciliation in our own relations. The global issues flow out of local and personal issues.

Here's the nub of the issue: *we must be intentional about reconciliation for it to become a pervasive lifestyle*. This can only begin if we find space and time to ponder, to pray, and to discern where it is that we — let me say "you" — need to pursue reconciliation. We must ponder those with whom we are out of sorts, those who are closest to us with whom we are not living fully reconciled lives, and those who may not even know that we are harboring bitterness and resentment. Reconciliation is not likely to be something that happens to us, as it is something we pursue.

One of my favorite writers is Trevor Hudson, a Methodist minister in Johannesburg, South Africa. I quote now from Trevor's fine study, *Discovering Our Spiritual Identity*, wherein he discloses how his wife pursued reconciliation with him because she wanted it — even when Trevor wasn't aware how out of sorts they were:

> I recall one painful moment in my own marriage. I had just assumed responsibility for my first congregation. Obviously keen to succeed, I worked long, hard hours. Externally things were going well. Attendance was increasing, finances had improved, and a new sanctuary was on the drawing boards. Within my marriage relationship, however, I was not doing well. Often away from home, I was denying the person closest to me the attention, time and energy necessary for real communication and caring. Coming home late one night I found a note at my bedside table.

---

18. The story of the migration north by former slaves and children of slaves has been told by Isabel Wilkerson, *The Warmth of Other Suns: The Epic Story of America's Great Migration* (New York: Random House, 2010).

It read: "Trevor, I love you and want to be married to you. Sometimes I worry though that one day I may not be worried if you don't come home. I miss you and want to reconnect."[19]

Trevor, who uses the expression "acid test" for the Christian's love of those closest to us (in contrast to the easier test of loving the world), said this: "I had failed the acid test."

Perhaps we need to ask ourselves—and I ask myself as you ask yourself: To whom do we need to drop such a note? The hard work is acting on the intention and then living with the tension that is created by the action, but there is no way to create reconciled relations with those around us until we intentionally decide to act on what Jesus summons us to do: "Settle matters quickly." There are no options here: Jesus calls his followers to be people of reconciliation. In fact, he warns his followers of final destruction if they walk away from that path.

19. Trevor Hudson, *Discovering Our Spiritual Identity* (Downers Grove, IL: InterVarsity Press, 2010), 74.

Matthew 5:27-30

 LISTEN to the Story

> ²⁷"You have heard that it was said, 'You shall not commit adultery.'
> ²⁸But I tell you that anyone who looks at a woman lustfully has already
> committed adultery with her in his heart. ²⁹If your right eye causes you to
> stumble,[1] gouge it out and throw it away. It is better for you to lose one
> part of your body than for your whole body to be thrown into hell. ³⁰And
> if your right hand causes you to stumble, cut it off and throw it away. It
> is better for you to lose one part of your body than for your whole body
> to go into hell.
>
> *Listening to the text in the Story*: Genesis 1–2; Exodus 20:14; Leviticus
> 20:10; Deuteronomy 5:18; 22:22; Song of Songs; Jeremiah 3:8–9
> (metaphorical); Hosea 1–3; Mark 12:18–27. *Gospel parallels*: Mat-
> thew 18:8–9; Mark 9:42–47.

On the mountain Jesus sits in the posture of Moses, quotes Moses, and
then deepens Moses. There is a breathtaking audacity about Jesus in this setting: he is giving a new Torah for the new people of God, the community of
Jesus. In our text he utters a new depth for understanding the will of God
when it comes to sexual purity.

Within the Story of the Bible there are two primary reasons for sexual
relations. From the opening page in the Bible (from Gen 1 until the final resurrection, as stated by Jesus in Mark 12:18–27), sexual relations are designed
to produce offspring, and the relations to this end are good and blessed by
God. This *procreative* purpose is complemented by the *pleasures and delights
of physical love*, and surely Song of Songs 7:1–8:7 is one of its most glorious
descriptions. The indirection of the poetry in Song of Songs, which stands
in bold contrast to the vulgarity of contemporary erotic literature, ennobles
sexual relations.

---

1. KNT: "trips you up" (and in v. 30).

But the divinely intended goods of procreation and pleasure seem incapable of harnessing erotic desires in Israel's Story, so there are tales of misdirection and folly, not the least of which tales is Solomon's. In spite of his early yearning for wisdom (2 Chr 1) and his privilege to build the temple (chs. 3–7), Solomon falls into the traps of erotic desire without boundaries (1 Kgs 11:1–13).[2] Solomon was not alone; that is why there needs to be a chapter like Proverbs 5 or 7. Unboundaried desire, male and female, seizes opportunities for scheming and rationalization:

> The eye of the adulterer watches for dusk;
>   he thinks, "No eye will see me,"
>   and he keeps his face concealed. (Job 24:15)

> This is the way of an adulterous woman:
>   She eats and wipes her mouth
>   and says, "I've done nothing wrong." (Prov 30:20)

Adultery became the codeword for religious infidelity because of the depth of the pain in the experience of infidelity (Jer 3:8–9; 9:2; Hos 1–3). Set in contrast to the adulterer is the purity of the faithful, seen in the heartfelt relief in the last chapter of the Song of Songs and in the purity of Christ's purifying love for the church (Eph 5:25b–27; Rev 21:8–27).

EXPLAIN the Story

Our passage quotes the Old Testament (Exod 20:14; Deut 5:18) and abruptly counters with an antithesis, "But I tell you …," which *redefines adultery* at a deeper level. As murder begins with anger, so adultery begins with lust. Following this redefinition, Jesus *demands transformation* by urging his followers metaphorically to remove the source of desire. Jesus does not side with the all-too-common patriarchal, chauvinistic approach to adultery in the ancient world, where adultery was excusable for the husband but not the wife. David Garland cites Aulus Gellius, a second-century AD writer, whose words quote Cato's *On the Dowry*: "If you should take your wife in adultery, you may with impunity put her to death without a trial; but if you should commit adultery or indecency, she must not presume to lay a finger on you, nor does the law allow it."[3]

Redefining Adultery

Adultery in Jesus' world was sexual relations with someone other than one's spouse and, in particular, with someone else's spouse. Thus, one could claim

---

2. Famously omitted by the Chronicler (cf. 2 Chr 9:13–28).

3. See Gellius, *Attic Nights* 10.23.5. Text can be found online at: http://penelope.uchicago.edu/Thayer/E/Roman/Texts/Gellius/10*.html. I found this reference in Garland, *Reading Matthew*, 66.

fidelity to one's spouse if one has had sexual relations only with one's spouse.[4] Also, Jesus opposes adultery and supports Moses' laws about adultery (cf. 5:32; 15:19; 19:9).[5]

But Jesus evidently believes Moses' law is not enough because he thinks sexual relations and purity begin in the heart—or in one's desires. Here's his counter: "But I tell you that anyone who *looks at a woman lustfully* has already committed adultery with her in his heart" (5:28).[6] Adultery is deepened or redefined to the level of desire, a desire fertilized by the gaze or, in the words of Chrysostom, "kindling the furnace within you."[7] Some blamed women for sexual temptations, so the authorities suppressed their freedom of dress and segregated them from men.[8] As Allison observes, "Jesus supplements the law because, while he approves the old law, which condemns the external act as evil, he declares that no less evil is the intention that brings it forth."[9]

But Jesus is not alone in tracing adultery to desire. The Jewish noncanonical text *Testament of Issachar* reads: "I have not had intercourse with any woman other than my wife, nor was I promiscuous by lustful look" (7:2). Even more, the "you shall not covet ... your neighbor's wife" (Exod 20:17) command already connects sexual sins to desire in speaking of coveting. So Jesus stands both on the Torah itself and alongside others in Judaism. It might be asked in passing what is wrong with the lustful look: "Because discipleship is self-denial and a complete bond with Jesus, at no point may the disciple's desire-driven will take over." Why? "Our bond to Jesus Christ permits no desire without love."[10]

There are some details in our passage that deserve closer inspection. First, Jesus says "anyone who looks"; this expression translates *pas ho blepōn*,[11] which is a way of describing the leering (in this case) male. But the Greek

---

4. This text is not, then, referring to the tenth commandment's prohibition of coveting a neighbor's wife (Exod 20:17), even though the same word for desire (here "lustfully") is used.

5. The Mosaic Torah stipulated death for adultery (Deut 22:22), but the only surviving evidence about Jesus on that element of the law comes from the disputed text in John 7:53–8:11. If authentic, that law shows that Jesus suspended the death penalty. It is the absence of the punishment in Jesus' words in Matthew 5 (and 19:18) that indicates that kingdom ethics trade in forgiveness and the transforming power of grace and mercy instead of capital punishment.

6. There is a slight grammatical debate here: does the accusative (*autēn*) mean that the woman is lusted after or the one who lusts? The former is almost certain because it is the man who commits adultery in his heart in the last clause of v. 28; see Quarles, *Sermon on the Mount*, 117–18.

7. In ACCS: *Matthew*, 108.

8. A good example is Tertullian, who wrote an essay on how women should dress: *On the Apparel of Women*. See Garland, *Reading Matthew*, 66–67.

9. Allison, *Sermon on the Mount*, 72.

10. Bonhoeffer, *Discipleship*, 125.

11. A present active participle. Some today see "present tense" and think "ongoing action," but the Greek present participle is designed to speak not of time but of *how the author wants to depict the action*. This is an action that is depicted as vivid, dramatic, and characteristic: "the one who stares" is more accurate than "the one who keeps on staring."

present tense does not suggest the person stares for a long time and that therefore the parting glance is justifiable. That is not the point: it doesn't matter how long the person looks. What matters, second, is the directed intention of his or her staring: "lustfully."[12] Sexual relations begin in the eye.[13] The look-to-desire is about intentionally fostering sexual temptation and arousal through the imagination. Jesus is against sexual fantasizing with an inappropriate person. He knows where it eventually leads, and his brother (Jas 1:15) expounded the process to its destined end: "Then, after desire has conceived, it gives birth to sin; and sin, when it is full-grown, gives birth to death."

The stunning element of Jesus' new ethic is that this sort of lust is equivalent to adultery itself. Since Jesus' intent is rhetorical—that is, he is urging his followers to turn away from lustful stares at the wife of another man—we need to avoid asking whether lust leads to capital punishment in Jesus' kingdom world, for adultery was a capital offense. No, that's taking his words too legalistically. Jesus ramps up his rhetoric in order to force his followers to see the gravity and potential long-term danger of sexually intended staring. This is a Messianic Ethic that reveals an Ethic from Beyond: kingdom realities, in this case sexual purity, begin now.

Whereas the expectation of women wearing head coverings and dressing modestly was male-shaped mores designed to prevent men from leering and being tempted or, which is more likely, to keep women's beauty in line, Jesus sees it otherwise. He lays full responsibility in this text on the male and expects males to be able to control their desires.[14] In other words, a text like the noncanonical *Testament of Reuben* (5:3) finds problems in the wrong place: women "contrive in their hearts against men, then by decking themselves out they lead men's minds astray, by a look they implant their poison, and finally in the act itself they take them captive." Jesus prevents a blame-her-looks or but-she-enticed-me approach. The problem in our text is male desire.

Sexuality has an aesthetic. Gazing and staring at one's spouse is delightful in the Jewish world of Jesus, and nothing proves this more than the Song of Songs. How else could someone describe his wife or her husband in such graphic poetry if one were not in the habit of being ravished by his or her beauty? This text leaves open whether it is possible to be overcome by the beauty of another person without it turning into inappropriate desire, and the history of art agrees. What Jesus sabotages here is not desire but rightful desire spent wrongfully.

---

12. For a sketch of how "lust/desire" was understood in the ancient world, see Keener, *Matthew*, 186.

13. See also Job 31:1; 2 Pet 2:14; 1 John 2:16. Eve's sin in Gen 3:6 is not sexual, though it too began with the eyes.

14. See C. S. Keener, *Paul, Women and Wives: Marriage and Women's Ministry in the Letters of Paul* (Peabody, MA: Hendrickson, 1992), 27–31.

Demanding Transformation

How, then, does Jesus sabotage inappropriate desires? Eliminate what tempts the gaze that prompts lust. Jesus once again uses exaggeration, as he did with dropping one's sacrifice at the altar and making peace while on the road to the judge (5:21–26). This time Jesus' words are even more graphic: gouge out your right eye and chop off your right hand. Why so drastic a measure? "It is better for you to lose one part of your body than for your whole body to be thrown into hell ['Gehenna,' as in KNT]" (5:29; cf. v. 30).

One can understand why Jesus says your "right" hand, but the "right" eye surprises. Perhaps this is only for balance: as with the right hand, so with the right eye. But I suspect there's more involved here. No one disputes that the right hand is the dominant hand for the majority, so that "right" expresses both power and value. Ancients connected the right eye to status. Notice 1 Samuel 11:2: "But Nahash the Ammonite replied, 'I will make a treaty with you only on the condition that I gouge out the right eye of every one of you and so bring disgrace on all Israel.'" Note, too, Zechariah 11:17:

> "Woe to the worthless shepherd,
>   who deserts the flock!
> May the sword strike his arm and his right eye!
>   May his arm be completely withered,
>   his right eye totally blinded!"

A tentative suggestion, then, is that "right eye" means the dominating and empowering eye, which if removed would humiliate and disempower. It is possible that by "right hand" Jesus is referring more particularly to the hand used to masturbate. This text then, with masterful indirection, refers to chopping off the "right hand" because of what it accomplishes.

The word "stumble" brings to expression the nature of the sin: the gazing, fantasizing lust causes the person to fall into sin. There is, of course, a spectrum here: to stumble might mean to trip over a sin, even a peccadillo or a brief spell of sexual fantasy, or the term can refer to the more blatant forms of apostasy and moral corruption, as in sexual addictions and even abandonment of the faith because of sexual desires. Jesus' words belong at the latter end of the spectrum, and one thinks of Matthew 11:6 (cf. 13:21, 57; 18:6; 24:10; 26:33; John 6:61; 16:1), where stumbling refers to rejecting Jesus as Messiah. We are led by this evidence to think that Jesus doesn't have in mind a singular trip-up, where one lusts and thinks hell is the only option, but of someone whose life is wrecked by lust and sexual temptation — though this is not to excuse even a momentary indiscretion.

Once again, Jesus' teachings here matter, and they matter eternally. Recall again his words: "It is better for you to lose one part of your body than for your whole body to be thrown into hell." As in the first antithesis (on murder as anger), so here: ignoring what Jesus says leads to the pit of destruction (see comments on 5:22). Again, this is rhetorical: Jesus goes to the ultimate potential in order to press on his followers the seriousness of the sin. The Ethic from Beyond makes living this possible, while an Ethic from Above creates gravity.

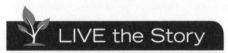

LIVE the Story

Jesus expected his followers to be marked by greater righteousness, that is, by holiness and love. This passage illustrates what Jesus means by "surpassing righteousness" in 5:20 and "perfection" in 5:48. In this passage he expects his followers will exhibit redemption powers in their sexuality. Kingdom realities have already invaded this world, and that means kingdom people begin to exhibit those kingdom realities. In the words of G. E. Ladd, there is still the "not yet," but there is already a "now" of kingdom participation.[15] We stand with Calvin when it comes to the moral compass: Jesus "means that however difficult, arduous, troublesome or painful God's rule may be, we must make no excuse for that, as the righteousness of God should be worth more to us, than all the other things which are chiefly dear and precious."[16] It is true that many have softened the potency of Jesus' words (cf. 5:19), but Jesus' words are meant to be taken seriously for his followers, and we are reminded by 7:21–27 that his followers are expected to follow his teachings.

How to Live the Story of Sexual Redemption

It is wisest for those who find lust difficult to enlist an accountability partner with whom one can be honest and safe to confess. In some church traditions there is such a thing as a confessional booth, while in those without such an arrangement a spiritual advisor, a pastor, or a friend could become the one to whom a person goes for confession and pastoral care. James 5:16 teaches us to confess our sins to one another.[17] Bonhoeffer taught in the context of his underground seminary the importance of confession,[18] and explained that in confession one is approaching not just a fellow Christian but the grace of God

---

15. This "now-but-not-yet kingdom" is the theme of Ladd's *The Presence of the Future*. Ladd has been influential with his theory that the kingdom is "present without consummation."

16. J. Calvin, *A Harmony of the Gospels: Matthew, Mark and Luke* (trans. D. W. Torrance; Grand Rapids: Eerdmans, 1972), 1:118–19.

17. R. J. Foster, *Celebration of Discipline* (rev. ed.; San Francisco: Harper & Row, 1988), 143–57.

18. D. Bonhoeffer, *Life Together* (trans. J. W. Doberstein; New York: Harper, 1954), 108–18; quotation from 109.

mediated through the other Christian. As he put it, "When I go to another believer to confess, I am going to God." He mentioned several breakthroughs that occur when we confess to one another: to community, to the cross, to new life, and to assurance. He urged the believers to pronounce the forgiveness as the word of God's grace to the one who confesses. Bethge records in his biography of Bonhoeffer the surprise when Bonhoeffer himself asked a brother to hear his confession.[19]

Another example of confession can be found in the (almost funny) reports of Lauren Winner, in her *Girl Meets God*, where she details her confessions to a spiritual director who mentored her into a healthier sexual life.[20] If this approach is ineffective, seek professional therapy, knowing that God's Spirit and the kingdom have been unleashed for transformation.

Alongside the discipline of confession are the other spiritual disciplines that are means of transformative grace: Bible reading, listening, prayer, solitude, contemplation, and fasting. This is not to neglect the more ordinary forms of spiritual graces in church worship, singing, sermons, listening to tapes, and attending conferences. A steady diet of "inflow" of God's grace can be transformative for "plucking out the eye" and "cutting off the hand" of inappropriate desire and lust.

This text does not endorse or encourage celibacy, and a topic like celibacy is complicated by both a Christianity committed rigorously to sexual purity as well as a history of convoluted theories of the body, sex, and chastity. Bonhoeffer, we should perhaps note, once asked if this text was to be taken literally or figuratively. We can't answer that question, he replied; "it is precisely the fact that, for us, this basic question is not answered that binds us completely to Jesus' command. Neither option offers us an escape. We are trapped and must obey."[21] He illustrates his typical Ethic from Above in this response.

When it comes to the messed-up view of sexuality in the church, fingers are often pointed at Augustine, but the problems arose a century or two before. Augustine's thinking was buoyed by the struggle to comprehend why God made the body and how to control desire.[22] Still, celibacy is not the issue in this text.

---

19. Bethge, *Dietrich Bonhoeffer*, 465. The person to whom Bonhoeffer confessed was Bethge. See John W. De Gruchy, *Daring, Trusting Spirit: Bonhoeffer's Friend Eberhard Bethge* (Minneapolis: Fortress, 2005), 27, 43, 62–63, 208. My thanks to Katya Covrett for bringing this to my attention.

20. Winner, *Girl Meets God*, 206–15.

21. Bonhoeffer, *Discipleship*, 126.

22. A wide-ranging sketch, and not always favorable to the Christian ethic, can be found in Simon Blackburn, *Lust: The Seven Deadly Sins* (New York: Oxford University Press, 2004). The Roman Catholic view can be seen in John Paul II, *Man and Woman He Created Them: A Theology of the Body* (Boston: Pauline Books and Media, 2006); a recent evangelical approach is Lauren Winner, *Real Sex: The Naked Truth about Chastity* (Grand Rapids: Brazos, 2005).

In the history of interpretation "woman" sometimes became "every woman," "adultery" becomes any kind of unchastity, and "desire" ("lustfully") becomes any inappropriate desire—so that the text in the hand of someone like Tertullian was already beginning to sound like the prohibition of marriage itself.[23]

Luther, who knew the world (and realities) of celibacy, found the ticket to the proper interpretation of this text: "You have no call to pick up your feet and run away, but to stay put, to stand and battle against every kind of temptation like a knight, and with patience to see it through and to triumph."[24] One might be excused for thinking it would simply be easier not to marry (as the disciples noted in 19:10–12), or that it would be more manageable (and devoted) to abandon the society of women and protect oneself in a monastery, and no doubt many did that very thing. But that's not what this text teaches. There is no way for humans to avoid sexual temptation. Jesus teaches control of desire, not suppression of sexuality.

This leads us to the obvious: We are personally responsible for protecting our eyes to be sexually redeemed.[25] We will be tempted, but there is no reason to nurture a temptation or to dally around an image that incites sexual arousal. Years of pastoring and counseling, years of corresponding with his readers, and years of living a life of celibacy led John Stott to make this observation: "Our vivid imagination ... is a precious gift from God.... Imagination enriches the quality of life. But all God's gifts need to be used responsibly; they can readily be degraded or abused."[26]

Sexual arousal can be explained as the neurochemical anticipation of sexual pleasures, and that explanation can help train us to become more pure.[27] The brain is wired for both sexual pleasure as well as for sexual fidelity and rugged faithful commitment. As a result of various forms of contact, from skin-to-skin contact to sexual intercourse, the brain releases dopamine, which is the neurochemical that says, "Wow, this is pleasurable." Dopamine creates brain pathways, tunnels of sexual pleasure if you will, that tell a person to do this again, and those neurochemical passages make it easier to do again; thus, any kind of sexual contact begins to create the desire for more sexual connection with that same person.

In addition to dopamine, the brain releases oxytocin and vasopressin, which tell a woman that the man is hers and the man that the woman is his.

23. On the history of interpretation, see Luz, *Matthew 1–7*, 243–44.

24. Luther, *Sermon on the Mount*, 86.

25. See D. Fitch, *The End of Evangelicalism: Discerning a New Faithfulness for Mission* (Eugene, OR: Cascade, 2011), 88–97.

26. Stott, *Message*, 88.

27. I borrow here from my book *One.Life: Jesus Calls, We Follow* (Grand Rapids: Zondervan, 2010), 128–30.

This kind of bonding is created *every time a human has any kind of sexual experience.* The feeling of "guilt" or "dirtiness" that arises in a human who experiences sex outside the bounds of biblical morals or fidelity is the brain's way of saying, "I'm confused." All of this is to say this: Jesus prohibits illicit sexual encounters, whether physical or fantasy, because God has wired us for sexual fidelity and lifelong rugged commitments of love to one person. Hearts are wired to brains, and brains are wired to commitment.

The focus of the text here is on male responses to females. It is worth reminding ourselves in this media-drenched age where images of women abound that Jesus apparently was pointing his finger at the appropriate gender: males objectify women into sexualized objects. And it is not that the Bible is against the beauty of a woman, and once again one can't read the Song of Songs and not be overcome by the poetic beauty. The problem is not beauty but objectification of a woman and the female body so that it becomes an object of self-satisfying pleasure for the male. We also live in one of the most egalitarian societies in history where women too express their own sexual needs and wants, so it needs to be said that women also objectify males and the male body. Jesus' words in this text prohibit objectification of any sort because he sees the female form and the male form to be fitted for one another only within the bounds of a married relationship.

We conclude with Simon Blackburn's exceptional staccato of comparisons between love and lust:

> Love receives the world's applause. Lust is furtive, ashamed, and embarrassed.
>
> Love pursues the good of the other, with self-control, concern, reason, and patience. Lust pursues its own gratification, headlong, impatient of any control, immune to reason.
>
> Love thrives on candlelight and conversation. Lust is equally happy in a doorway or a taxi, and its conversation is made of animal grunts and cries.
>
> Love is individual: there is only the unique Other, the one doted upon, the single star around whom the lover revolves. Lust takes what comes.
>
> Lovers gaze into each others' eyes. Lust looks sideways, inventing deceits and stratagems and seductions, sizing up opportunities.
>
> Love grows with knowledge and time, courtship, truth, and trust. Lust is a trail of clothing in the hallway, the collision of two football packs.
>
> Love lasts, lust cloys.[28]

---

28. Blackburn, *Lust*, 2. Available at: http://books.google.com/books?id=N0y60xZcSsgC&print sec=frontcover&source=gbs_ViewAPI#v=onepage&q&f=false.

LISTEN to the Story

> [31]"It has been said, 'Anyone who divorces his wife must give her a certificate of divorce.'[1] [32]But I tell you that anyone who divorces his wife, except for sexual immorality, makes her the victim of adultery, and anyone who marries a divorced woman commits adultery."

Listening to the text in the Story: Genesis 1–3; 12; 15; Deuteronomy 24:1–4; Song of Songs; 1 Corinthians 7:1–16; Ephesians 5:21–33.

Divorce confuses the church today because marriage confuses. And marriage confuses the church today because love confuses. Love is understood through the lens of romance, personal fulfillment, self-expansion, sexual satisfaction, and whatever the lasting impressions are in Hollywood's movies, relationship TV specials, and novels and books about marriage, love, and relationships. When someone says they are getting divorced, we are horrified or tongue-tied or say something as trite as "I hope you find someone who makes you happy," or "Not all marriages work out." We often don't know what to say because we don't know what to think, and we don't know what to think because love, marriage, and divorce are confusingly connected.

All of this is to say that the "story" that shapes what we think of divorce in Western culture is as far from the Bible's Story as Dickens's *A Christmas Carol* or Frank Capra's *It's a Wonderful Life* is from the biblical understanding of Christmas. Our commentary series wants to set each passage in the context of the Story of God in the Bible. This means we can't understand divorce until we understand its Storied contours.

Those contours include a number of things. God created humans and divided them into "male and female" as God's own image-bearers (Gen 1:26–27). God made "male and female" to govern this world together on God's behalf, and one way they were to govern was to procreate with one another. Furthermore, God gave Eve to Adam as his 'ēzer kᵉnegdô (NIV

---

1. KNT: "a legal document to prove it."

"helper suitable for him," 2:18) because she was his perfect "companion." Furthermore, Adam and Eve broke their relationship when Eve and Adam chose to eat the fruit, hide from God, and blame one another. Scripture predicts but does not prescribe that Adam and Eve would be at one another's throat— with Adam wanting to control and Eve also wanting to control (3:1 – 16). The charge to human beings as male and female to govern the earth (1:28) would be doubly complicated, God told the primal pair, because of their choice to act like gods (3:14 – 19).

There are examples of married couples in the Bible, including Abraham and Sarah and Moses and Zipporah, but the gloriousness of love and marriage is depicted in the Song of Songs. That book is nothing other than the delightful playfulness of love, relationship, and pleasure. Sadly, Song of Songs is often neglected in books on a "biblical" view of marriage.

Alongside this "story" of relationship, the Bible's Story grounds all love in God's covenant love (Gen 12; 15). My own way of framing this covenant love is to use three prepositions: that God covenants to be *with* us and to be *for* us *unto* full redemption—that is, until we are in the kingdom, are Christlike, and become the holy and loving people of God. This covenant understanding of love means marital love reflects God's love, which means a divorce destroys the reflection of the God who is utterly faithful. Marital love, then, is defined by God's love: our love for our spouse is to be *with* them, to be *for* them, and to be *unto* God's formative purpose for each of us. The three principles of love are thus presence (*with*), advocacy (*for*), and formation (*unto*).

To end the confusion about marriage we have to grasp what love means. I have one more element to add to these three prepositions. The church's faith unfolds to reveal that God is triune. Once we set our teeth into the firm Christian conviction that our God is a One-and-Three God, we are led to the conclusion that the relationship "within" God is a relationship theologians called *perichoresis*. This Greek term describes the mutual indwelling and interpenetration of Father, Son, and Spirit. If this is who God is and what God is, we have another dimension of love. Since God's relationship is "perichoretic" and since our love participates in God's way of loving, then marital love is "perichoretic." That means, above all, that marriage is a relationship of mutual indwelling and interpenetration. Divorce destroys *perichoresis*, our indwelling of one another.

The utter horror Jesus expresses about divorce emerges from the factors sketched above: Adam and Eve's intent, design, and task; the glory of loving relationship; the covenant relationship of God with us as the One who is for us, and how this defines biblical love; and the *perichoresis* of the Trinity. Hauerwas gets it exactly right here: if we come to this text looking for reasons to justify divorce, we miss the whole point. What this text does is to redefine marriage and to anchor it in the new community of Jesus, a community that will make possible both the single life and fidelity.[2] Jesus calls his followers to a better way, to the way of love and marital faithfulness. His Ethic from Beyond contends we can have a surpassing righteousness; his Ethic from Above lays the demand before us. He is the Messiah of this ethic, and he gives a community in which this kind of life is embodied.

We dive now into one of the vexing issues of marriage and divorce. It vexes at the level of understanding what the Bible says. It vexes at the personal level, where divorce emerges out of a relationship fraught with issues, problems, histories, and personalities. And it vexes us at the challenging task of loving people in their marital challenges.

EXPLAIN the Story

This third antithesis in Matthew 5 begins with a text, "It has been said, 'Anyone who divorces his wife must give her a certificate of divorce,'" and Jesus follows with his antithesis. But this time his antithesis reveals his view of the Torah. In his day, the text quoted was understood as a *minimal condition for justified divorce*, but Jesus trumps that interpretation by appealing to the strictness of what Moses himself said: divorce is wrong except for one condition. Because this text is a collection of problems to solve and the discussions are remarkably complex, we will deal with one problem at a time, and we will have to weave in and out of the text, options, historical context, debates, and implications.

The Mosaic Law

Jesus does not quote but instead summarizes Deuteronomy 24:1, and because that text (24:1 – 4) is so important for this passage, the text needs to be quoted in full:

> [1]If a man marries a woman who becomes displeasing to him because he finds something indecent about her, and he writes her a certificate of divorce, gives it to her and sends her from his house, [2]and if after she leaves his house she becomes the wife of another man, [3]and her second husband dislikes her and writes her a certificate of divorce, gives it to her and sends her from his house, or if he dies, [4]then her first husband, who divorced her, is not allowed to marry her again after she has been defiled. That would be detestable in the eyes of the LORD. Do not bring sin upon the land the LORD your God is giving you as an inheritance.

---

2. Hauerwas, *Matthew*, 70.

Permission and Inviolable Union

Divorce was not part of the Creator's design, as Jesus will state up-front in Matthew 19:8–9. Moses *only permitted* divorce because the Israelites had *hard hearts* and didn't want to bear the full burden of God's holy law. In fact, Jesus believes Genesis 1–2 comprehends marriage as an inviolable union created by God—the man and the woman become "one flesh" (19:5–6). For Jesus, marriage is about "with-ness" and the perichoretic indwelling of one another. In addition to this holy union and divorce-as-a-permission, the Mosaic law also prohibited divorce under any circumstances when the union itself was irregular (Deut 22:19, 28–29).

Permission to Permissiveness

But when divorce occurred, in spite of the requirement to surrender the dowry as well as pay off the marriage payment of roughly one year's wages (called a *ketubbah*), Moses' permission had become a license in the hands of some (Jesus calls them "hard-hearted" in 19:8). One prophet who railed against the laxity was Malachi (Mal 2:13–17), who discerned that the holy union of marriage was specifically designed for procreating holy children (2:15). Permissiveness is precisely in question when the Pharisees, who fashioned themselves both as observant and the guardians of Torah observance, ask Jesus: "Is it lawful for a man to divorce his wife *for any and every reason?*" (Matt 19:3).

It should not, however, be supposed that all Jews were lenient as this, for the more conservative Jews opposed permissiveness and had tighter regulations (e.g., the Essenes of Qumran in 11QTemple 57:16–19).[3] But even the rigorous believed divorce was sometimes necessary. Matthew 1:19 makes clear that Joseph, engaged to Mary, felt obligated to divorce Mary on the basis of her pregnancy. For the righteous, sexual interference between husband and wife demanded divorce in order to maintain purity.[4] Rigor, however, was not the problem Jesus faced. Josephus, the Jewish historian, provides an example of laxity with respect to one's marriage covenant in his autobiography:

> At this period I divorced my wife, *being displeased at her behaviour.* She had borne me three children.... Afterwards I married a woman of

---

3. See the discussion of permissions in Quarles, *Sermon on the Mount*, 125–27. Here is the text from 11QTemple 57:16–19: "He may not take a wife from any of the nations. Rather, he must take himself a wife from his father's house—that is, from his father's family. He is not to take another wife in addition to her; no, she alone shall be with him as long as she lives. If she dies, then he may take himself another wife from his father's house, that is, his family."

4. On this, see M. Bockmuehl, *Jewish Law in Gentile Churches: Halakhah and the Beginning of Christian Public Ethics* (Edinburgh: T&T Clark, 2000), 17–21. See also Garland, *Reading Matthew*, 68–69.

Jewish extraction who had settled in Crete. She came of very distinguished parents.[5]

On the basis of Exodus 21:10–11 the most common set of obligations for a husband was to provide food, clothing, and shelter as well as some sense of marital love and intimacy. Thus, Papyrus Yadin 10 records the commitment of a Jewish husband to his wife in these words: "I will feed you and clothe you and I will bring you into my house."[6] Divorce could be granted when one of these conditions was denied, and later rabbis make it clear that "marital love" could be strained to the point of divorce for repulsiveness and cruelty.[7] These are the conditions Jesus is countering in our text.

Divorce Certificate

Moses demanded that the man who divorced his wife (and there is evidence that women could divorce their husbands in the Jewish world as well; see Mark 10:12 and immediately below) *was required to give her a "certificate of divorce"* (Matt 5:31). This certificate, called a *geṭ* in Hebrew,[8] entailed the legality of the dissolution of the marriage and the permission of the woman to remarry. Thus, here is the text from *Mishnah Giṭṭin* 9:3, with italics added:

> The text of the writ of divorce [is as follows]:
> "Lo, you are *permitted* to any man."
> R. Judah says, "Let this be from me your writ of divorce, letter of dismissal, and deed of *liberation*, that you may marry anyone you want."
> The text of a writ of *emancipation* [is as follows]:
> "Lo, you are a *free* girl, lo, you are your own possession."

These legal texts are from the angle of a man divorcing his wife. Contrary to what is often said, one of the texts discovered at Wadi Muraba'at, though just slightly later than the New Testament period, reveals that women too could divorce men—and such texts confirm that a freedom clause was involved. Here are the appropriate lines from a man's and then a woman's divorce settlement:[9]

---

5. *Life*, 426–27. Josephus, too, provides an actual comment on Deut 24:1: "He who desires to be divorced from the wife who is living with him for whatsoever cause—*and with mortals many such may arise*—must certify in writing that he will have no further intercourse with her; for thus will the woman obtain the right to consort with another" (*Ant* 4.253).

6. See also the English translation of Papyrus Yadin 18: http://cojs.org/cojswiki/Papyrus_Yadin_18:_Jewish_Marriage_Contract_in_Greek (accessed 1/11/2013).

7. See *m. Ketubbot* 7:2–10.

8. There is an entire Mishnah tractate about the bill of divorce, called *Giṭṭin*.

9. On this, see Tal Ilan, *Integrating Women into Second Temple History* (Peabody, MA: Hendrickson, 2001), 253–62, with texts in Hebrew and English on pp. 257–59.

On the first day of Marheshwan, year six, at Masada, *I divorce and release* of my own free will, today I Joseph, son of Naqsan....

On the twentieth day of Sivan, year three of the freedom of Israel ... I, Shelamzion, daughter of Joseph Qebshan from Ein Gedi, with you, you Eleazar son of Hananiah, who had been my husband before this time, that *this is for you from me a bill of divorce and release....*

The Context: Permissiveness

Again, the problem is that the *permission* of Moses in Deuteronomy 24 to divorce on the basis of *'erwat dābār* ("something indecent about her") had become too permissive. The later rabbis debated the extent of the *'erwat dābār*, with some making it nearly synonymous with the scriptural texts about sexual sin (adultery) while others found it to be stomping grounds for anything the husband didn't like about the woman. Rabbis sometimes humorously chided the ease of a divorce by suggesting grounds could be found if a woman burned her husband's food. Dale Allison sums up the historical setting with these words: "The impression one gains from ancient Jewish sources is that divorce was relatively easy and was not considered a grave misdeed."[10]

This rather lengthy discussion of context best explains what Jesus means by the words he cites. "Anyone who divorces his wife must give her a certificate of divorce" means for Jesus, "You have heard that it was said that if a man wants to divorce his wife, he must *simply* give her a bill of divorce." Jesus isn't simply citing Moses; he's using words that were used in his day for laxity and permissiveness when it came to a (Torah observant!) man divorcing his wife. What mattered most was not the grounds for the divorce, which is what Moses focused on in his permissions, but the necessity of giving the woman a certificate so she could be set free to remarry.

The View of Jesus

Into that context of Jewish males using the Torah to ground any reason they wanted to give for divorce, Jesus steps in, screeches the discussion to a halt, stands with the conservatives and with Moses—and even goes beyond and deeper than Moses. How so? *Jesus prohibits permissiveness by well-nigh prohibiting divorce altogether.* Matthew makes it clear that Jesus *restricts the legitimate grounds for divorce to no more than what Moses says: "sexual immorality."* But what does that mean? Our second problem.

"Except for Sexual Immorality"

Instead of sorting out all the evidence and instead of cataloguing who believes what and what evidence supports each nuance, I want instead to sketch the

---

10. Davies and Allison, *Matthew*, 1:528.

basics.[11] The Greek word here is *porneia*, which is used elsewhere for sexual immorality in Matthew 15:19 (parallel Mark 7:21); Acts 15:20, 29; 21:25; 1 Corinthians 5:1 (incest); 6:13, 18 (where it means some kind of embodied sin); 7:2; 2 Corinthians 12:21; Galatians 5:19; Ephesians 5:3; Colossians 3:5; 1 Thessalonians 4:3; Revelation 9:21, and in other places in Revelation where physical sins and spiritual adulteries are combined. In the world of Jesus, *porneia* could mean:

1. premarital coitus, but that is not the meaning here
2. incest (as in 1 Cor 5)
3. more generally, sexual sins that destroy a marital covenant

The social context sketched above that focused on permissiveness for some makes the second option less likely, but we should consider the following observations.[12] First, the word *porneia* and the word "commit adultery" (*moichaomai*) are not the same. In Matthew 15:19 the two are distinguished. This might suggest that in *porneia* something more specific is in mind and that what is specific would not be the act of committing adultery. Furthermore, 1 Corinthians 5:1 uses this very term (*porneia*) for incest. One more consideration that for some tips the balance: the word *porneia* is used in Acts 15:20 to describe something Gentile converts were not to do. Most scholars today think the list of four items there—food polluted by idols, *porneia*, strangled meat, and blood—derive from Leviticus 17–18. In that context, *porneia* points to incestuous sins (18:16–18).

To sum this up, there is some evidence to suggest that the exception granted by Jesus in Matthew 5:32 is a very narrow exception; that is, Jesus grants divorce to a man only if his wife has committed incest! In effect, Jesus would then have narrowed *'erwat dābār*, the permissible grounds of divorce, to the most heinous of sexual sins. He has virtually shut the door on divorce in the face of many in his day. Such a rigor comports with how Jesus both understands divorce (only a permission) and understands marriage (an invio-

---

11. Extensive discussions in D. Instone-Brewer, *Divorce and Remarriage in the Bible: The Social and Literary Context* (Grand Rapids: Eerdmans, 2002); idem, *Divorce and Remarriage in the Church: Biblical Solutions for Pastoral Realities* (Downers Grove, IL: InterVarsity Press, 2006); A. Cornes, *Divorce and Remarriage: Biblical Principles and Pastoral Practice* (Grand Rapids: Eerdmans, 1993); C. Keener, ... *And Marries Another: Divorce and Remarriage in the Teaching of the New Testament* (Peabody, MA: Hendrickson, 1991); idem, *Remarriage after Divorce in Today's Church: Three Views* (Grand Rapids: Zondervan, 2006).

12. In one form or another, the "illicit" union/marriage view, or the "incest" view, is held by a variety of scholars. Perhaps most notable is J. Fitzmyer, *To Advance the Gospel* (New York: Crossroad, 1981), 79–111; see also Garland, *Reading Matthew*, 69–70. Guelich, *Sermon on the Mount*, 209–211, advances the view that the exception is from Matthew and pertains to the context of the Gentile mission.

lable, divine union). In effect, Jesus would be teaching that divorce is wrong, and his contemporaries' reading of Deuteronomy 24:1 – 4 is also wrong.

Redactional?

Another problem: the meaning of *porneia* is complicated by the redactional problem. Here are the basic facts: the expression "except for sexual immorality" is found only in Matthew. It is not found in the (probably earlier) Markan parallel at Mark 10:11 – 12, nor is it found in the (probably Q) Lukan parallel at Luke 16:18. Nor is this exception found in Paul's discussion of what Jesus said about divorce in 1 Corinthians 7:10. That this precise expression is found in Matthew alone both of the times he deals with this subject (Matt 5 and 19) gives good grounds to think Matthew added the exception clause as a redactional gloss.

While some might think this means Matthew has tampered with the holy language of Jesus, we need to think harder. If our reading of 5:31 is correct — that Jesus quotes a text that was understood to be the basis for gross permissiveness — and if our reading of 5:32 is correct — that Jesus is all but denying any grounds for divorce because he believes marriage is an inviolable covenant[13] — then it is entirely possible that Jesus originally prohibited divorce in a general manner, but Matthew added the exception clause because he knew Jesus' intent was not to deny the rightness of Deuteronomy 24:1 – 4, but to bring to a halt a widespread permissiveness when it came to divorce.

Sexual Immorality in General?

Not all agree with the incest view. In fact, more think that the word *porneia* cannot be restricted to incestuous relations but refers instead to the more general sense of *sexual sins that break down the marital covenant.* So to the view that *porneia* means sexual behaviors that constitute *adultery*[14] we now turn.

In spite of the attractiveness of connecting the word *porneia* to Leviticus 17 – 18, the word *porneia* does not occur in the Greek translation of that text. More importantly, the word *porneia* often means "adultery." In addition, the contemporary reading of Deuteronomy 24:1 – 4 was along the line of "sexual infidelity" and not the more narrowly defined "incest" mentioned above. And this is how Shammai, if the tradition is accurate about him for the first century, rendered Deuteronomy 24:1 as recorded in *Mishnah Giṭṭin* 9:10:

---

13. Keener, *Matthew*, 190 – 91.

14. This is the consensus view; see Luz, *Matthew 1 – 7*, 253 – 55. On adultery, see 5:27 – 30. Keener, *Matthew*, 189, defines adultery as, and observe the strenuousness of this definition, "unfaithfulness to one's spouse *or accommodating another person's unfaithfulness to that person's spouse*" (italics added).

   A. The House of Shammai say, "A man should divorce his wife only because he has found grounds for it in unchastity,

   B. "since it is said, Because he has found in her indecency in anything (Dt. 24:1)."

   C. And the House of Hillel say, "Even if she spoiled his dish,

   D. "since it is said, Because he has found in her indecency in anything."

   E. R. Aqiba says, "Even if he found someone else prettier than she,

   F. "since it is said, And it shall be if she find no favor in his eyes (Dt. 24:1)."

To summarize a complicated discussion, all of which emerges when pastors and churches are wading into this issue (because someone in the church is filing for divorce): while the narrow sense of *porneia* as incest can be supported by evidence, that evidence is not substantial enough to overturn the rendering of *porneia* as a more general term for sexual behaviors that express infidelity to the marital covenant. Jesus grants divorce for a general reason, "sexual sins," and that means a variety of sexual sins would constitute grounds for divorce.

This brings us back to the apparently redactional addition of "except for sexual immorality." If Jesus is standing against the tradition of permissiveness and his view is essentially that divorce is wrong, then with a more general sense of *porneia*, Matthew may well have added this exception clause because he knew that Jesus was against divorce but, like Moses, knew that God had permitted divorce, though only for sexual sins.[15] In effect, Jesus would be permitting divorce only for sexual sins, which would restrict divorce permissions dramatically. Again, Allison gets this right: Jesus' "purpose was not to lay down the law but to reassert an ideal and make divorce a sin, thereby disturbing the current complacency."[16] It is best to see this, then, as an Ethic from Above that lays before the disciples the expectation that kingdom living entails an Ethic from Beyond—his disciples were not to divorce.

Causes Her to Become an Adulteress

What would have grabbed Jesus' contemporary listeners' attention even more were the words "causes her to become an adulteress" (5:32 TNIV). We natu-

---

15. Some have suggested that *parektos*, "except," instead means "the sexual immorality clause in Deuteronomy 24:1 notwithstanding." That is, Jesus completely undoes the Mosaic legislation that permits divorce. This view of Matt 5:32 is possible, but it is impossible for the *mē epi* clause in 19:9, pushing us to think "except" is the proper translation of *parektos* and *mē epi*. Thus, Jesus truly grants a permission.

16. Davies and Allison, *Matthew*, 1:532. Luz, *Matthew 1–7*, 252–53, disagrees and sees the text as law.

rally ask: How does divorcing a woman make her an adulteress, or how does it make her a "victim of adultery" (NIV 2011)? The answer to this question seems obvious to the historian but deeply disturbs the pastoral situation. The instinctive answer is that a divorce certificate (*get*) included the liberty for the woman to remarry. This generates two problems: first, Jesus does not explicitly say the certificate entails permission to remarry, and more importantly, this means permission to remarry for a divorced woman is rooted in an inference from the text instead of an explicit teaching. So it is.

It is obvious to any reader that divorcing a woman or a man does not make that woman or man an adulterer because to become an adulterer one must somehow engage in sexual relations with someone who is not your spouse. So, what Jesus says—virtually equating divorcing a woman with her subsequent adultery or making her a victim of adultery—logically requires remarriage. This reading of the text, of course, has been opposed by the church in major ways: remarriage has been considered impermissible for much of the history of the church. Some hold to the more strenuous view by saying that since God opposes divorce, any remarriage is adultery.[17] But I'm not convinced the text teaches this. That is, what this text teaches is this: in the case of a permissible divorce, there was a permissible remarriage. This helps explain what follows, our next problem.

Anyone Who Marries the Divorced Woman Commits Adultery

If the woman committed *porneia*, she is an adulteress, and anyone who marries her would be entering a prohibited union. If she was divorced unlawfully, say because her husband just didn't like her, then anyone who marries her is entering forbidden territory because he is making her a "victim of adultery." Why? Because her union with her original husband has not been justifiably broken; she remains "married" to the man though she has been divorced.

In summary, then, Jesus is against divorce. He is for marriage. He believes marriage is a sacred, holy, and inviolable union created by God to make a man and a woman "one flesh." Because he believes this about marriage, he believes divorce is *always contrary to God's creation designs*. But it appears to me that Jesus goes along with the permission Moses granted to sinful Israel in permitting divorce for sexual immorality (*porneia*), and it appears as well that Jesus therefore also permitted remarriage for permissible divorces. But anyone who married an impermissibly divorced woman made that woman commit adultery. Permissible divorces lead to permissible remarriages; but impermissible divorces entail no remarriage.

---

17. "Anonymous" and Theodore of Mopsuestia in ACCS: *Matthew*, 112–13. A fuller defense can be found in Cornes, *Divorce and Remarriage*.

LIVE the Story

The issues are complex and they are often complicated by struggling married people who deserve our understanding. Let's review briefly how this issue is approached in the church today. The Catholic Church has held to a rigorous view because it believes marriage is an ontological union of a man and woman, a sacrament, and cannot be broken except in the rarest of cases (annulment). Divorce is wrong and remarriage is not permitted. Luther is not far from this, though he (unwisely in my view) connected marriage too much to the state.[18] The Orthodox Church has been more accommodating to the sinfulness of humans, while the Protestant churches cross the entire spectrum from radical impermissibility of divorce or remarriage to a casual carelessness of permissibility of both divorce and remarriage. Among evangelicals there seems to be three basic views: the Bible does give permission to divorce but never to remarry; the Bible grants permission to divorce and to remarry, but only for adultery and desertion; and the Bible gives us permission to divorce and to remarry for justifiable reasons. There is no reason to add more options, so to some wisdom about marriage and divorce and remarriage we now turn.

Divorce and remarriage questions are about real persons. Once a friend of mine asked to play golf and said he'd pay—and he said, "Pick your course." So I picked a good course with the kind of fees I rarely pay. As we approached the green on the first hole, he said, "Scot, the reason I asked to play golf was because I have a question." I said back, "Sure," but I was now a bit concerned with where my ball was on the green and whether I had a reasonable putt for a birdie. His question brought me back to the real world with real persons, and it was the only thing we discussed the rest of the day. The question: "Do you believe if I am divorced legitimately that I can remarry legitimately?" What he was asking was whether I, as a teacher of the Bible, believed the Bible taught permissible remarriage. This also meant one of the heavier responsibilities you—my reader—and I bear when we teach the Bible: if our listeners and readers do what we think the Bible teaches, we both need to double our efforts to be "biblical" and to realize that we will in part bear responsibility for our teaching. I recognize this in what I say, and it gives me a pause to consider all over again what I write, and that means I do so with a prayer for God's grace.

Divorce and remarriage questions are also discussed in the context of real people. I am happily married to my grade school, junior high school, and high school sweetheart. Kris and I grew up together. Both of our families have seen divorce—four or five (depending on how you see long-term live-in arrange-

---

18. Luther, *Sermon on the Mount*, 92–98.

ments) of our brothers and sisters are divorced. I have had colleagues who are divorced; I have friends who are divorced. I have known many more who have chosen to remarry than who have chosen to remain "single" (because of a belief that the first union is inviolable). But I do have a friend whose husband divorced her with two young boys many years ago, and she chose to pray for the restoration of her marriage and has waited beyond waiting years for that to happen. I have known people who have divorced recklessly and those who have divorced reluctantly; I have known people who virtually ran away from marriages with someone they shouldn't have run away with — and I've seen one such couple find repentance and a flourishing ministry. You know these situations too, and they are the realities out of which these questions have to be discussed and decisions discerned.

Divorce and remarriage decisions are not to be left to the individuals but require both pastoral leadership and ecclesial discernment. Just broaching this point creates enough problems on its own, but the following discussion will seek to work this point out.

First, *churches and pastors and followers of Jesus are challenged by these words to recommit themselves to the covenant nature of love and to marriage as a sacred union blessed and established by God.* Too many Christians are divorced, are divorcing, and get married knowing divorce will always be an option. So I would urge churches to ramp up their teachings on the nature of covenant love and of the sacredness of marriage. Churches must have the courage to teach that divorce is never the will of God, and that divorce is only permitted because of the hard-heartedness of humans. These are the words of Jesus, and we do not have the option of toning them down (5:17–20) or pretending they don't exist. John Stott has pastorally sensitive words of wisdom: "whenever somebody asks to speak with me about divorce, I have now for some years steadfastly refused to do so. I have the rule never to speak with anybody about divorce, until I have first spoken with him (or her) about two other subjects, namely marriage and reconciliation."[19]

Second, *we have an obligation as followers of Jesus of holding in balance the twin nonnegotiable virtues of mercy and righteousness.* When we are confronted with a marriage that is failing, we are to be merciful, to listen, to probe, to "live with and through" those persons, and to do so in a way that reflects the Jesus Creed of loving God and others with everything we've got. This does not mean tolerance. Instead, a nonnegotiable is righteousness, probably the single most important virtue of the Sermon on the Mount. Righteousness, once again, is a term describing behaviors and conditions that reflect doing

---

19. Stott, *Message*, 98.

God's will. That will, according to Jesus our Lord, is that divorce is wrong. We are to hold fellow followers of Jesus to that standard. There is no question that the church has an awful time holding mercy and righteousness in balance. Some churches are demonstratively merciful, to the degree that divorce is condoned, overlooked, and even casually dismissed. Other churches are so rigorous in their commitment that they fail to show any mercy toward those who have gotten themselves into pits of desperation.

I have one word of advice here: every time a pastoral situation arises in which a person states they are thinking about divorce, it is important for the follower of Jesus to remind the struggling spouses that divorce is not God's will. My experience is that this causes discomfort for all in the room, so it becomes the unspoken assumption, and as long as it's unspoken it will easily drift into the unspoken acceptance. Still, the pastoral situation requires compassion and mercy on the part of the follower of Jesus. We are called to listen, to empathize, to probe, and to walk with a person whose relationships is breaking up in such a way that the person knows we love them, are with them, and want God's will for them.

Third, *no pastor, no leader, and no church should hold out a rigorous view of marriage, divorce, or remarriage without providing the resources, time, personal attention, and help that such a rigorous view entails.* If you believe in one of the most traditional views—namely, that divorce is always wrong and remarriage not permissible—then you have an obligation not only to teach that view but also to support the persons who are entangled in marriage problems and potential divorce, and those rendered alone by divorce. Perhaps the most glaring contradiction of the more rigorous teachings about divorce and remarriage is the total absence of support, love, and ongoing attention required for those who suffer.

Fourth, *the fundamental disposition and orientation of pastors, churches, and all followers of Jesus should be toward reconciliation of the husband and wife.* Pastors, counselors, and friends quickly learn from the husband and the wife what the precipitating issues are, and once those are learned, there are clear areas where each person will need to go to work *because the goal is reconciliation.* Churches cannot permit themselves to fall into the "listen" and then "we'll see how things work out for them" approach. It is too benign, it is too hands-off, it is too passive, and it simply isn't gospel shaped. The gospel summons us to become peacemakers and agents of reconciliation because of the power of the unleashed Spirit and the potency of a life of loving self-denial for the good of the other. Jesus teaches an Ethic from Beyond, and as followers of this Messianic Ethic we are in touch with the Lord who calls us to surpassing righteousness. Once we come to terms with what covenant love is, and I have defined it as "being with, for, and unto," we are encouraged to get each couple to begin thinking of what they can do "for" the other person. To ask, "What is best for my husband or my wife?" By what is "best" here we mean for those who follow Jesus down the long road of the sacred union of marriage.

Fifth, *I now want to step into this line of thinking with how I understand Matthew 5:31–32.* I have argued, even if not extensively, that Jesus' intent was to affirm the inviolable nature of marriage, and to make that point clear he simply stated that divorce was wrong. I have also suggested that Matthew "added" the exception clause, but that his addition was implicit already in what Jesus was saying. Jesus did not want divorce, and he said that in a context of permissiveness. That's not what God wants for his followers. But if *porneia* occurs, divorce is permissible and remarriage justifiable. But this is not what is to happen for his followers. The problem is that it does because, even if Jesus in Matthew 19:1–9 will push back to the intent of the Creator in Genesis 1—2, we are not yet in Eden or Paradise. In a cracked world, even the followers of Jesus will commit sins that destroy a marriage.

This leads us to the most contested point of all: *the grounds for divorce obviously expand within the pages of the New Testament.* Even if we are not accurate in thinking that Matthew added the exception clause to make explicit what Jesus implied, there is one ground of permission with Jesus: *porneia.* I take *porneia* to refer to sexual behaviors that ruin the marital covenant. But the apostle Paul, knowing full well what Jesus taught, *added another exception* to permissible divorce. For him, desertion by an unbelieving spouse constituted grounds for divorce and therefore, implicitly but within the bounds of all perceptions of the Jewish divorce certifications, permitted remarriage for the Christian who had been deserted.

I believe we can learn from this what constitutes love and marriage as well as what constitutes grounds for divorce. Let me rephrase this in my own categories: if covenant love is commitment to be "with someone and for someone as someone who is working unto divine ends," then marriages are destroyed when one partner refuses to be "with" the spouse or who becomes someone who is "against" that spouse. When a man obviously fails to be the husband that covenant love demands, or when a wife obviously fails to be the wife that covenant love demands, grounds for divorce may be present *because the covenant is being destroyed.*

This contention of what covenant love is and of what destroying it means leads directly now to the issue of spousal abuse. Remember what Exodus said about the expectations of a husband for his wife—food, clothing, shelter, and covenant love. Physical abuse, emotional abuse, and psychological abuse are actions that destroy the marital covenant as understood in the Bible. Let's not treat Jesus' words (or add to them Paul's words) and think that *every possible ground for divorce has been covered by Jesus or Paul* and, if abuse can't be found within *porneia* or desertion, then abuse isn't a legitimate ground for divorce. Abuse destroys what it means to have shelter because the house is no longer safe; abuse is a legitimate reason for divorce. Furthermore, our text in the Sermon on the Mount should never be used to protect aggressive males or be used to justify abuse of a wife.

But I want to stop right here for a moment because this entire discussion creates tension with what Jesus is actually teaching in this text. We are discussing legitimate grounds for divorce, and that is an important discussion, but Jesus wanted us to know that divorce is wrong. Jesus is saying "No!" to divorce, and we want to ask, "But what about in this case?" We need to keep in mind what Jesus is teaching: the sacredness and permanency of the marital covenant. But, yes, with that reminder once again in place, we have to admit the hard-heartedness even of followers of Jesus and recognize that grounds for divorce will be pushed to the fore and churches and Christians will have to render discerning decisions.

So now a sixth point: *divorce decisions are to be rendered not by the state (as Luther too easily suggested) but by discerning Christian leaders and churches.* Aside from the incredibly ineffective issue we have in Western churches — namely, that if we don't like a particular church, we can go somewhere else — I believe no follower of Jesus ought to pursue a divorce in the legal system without the official permission of that person's church and its leaders. I make no apology for this. Followers of Jesus are a fellowship; we are responsible to one another and accountable to one another; Jesus is our Lord and his teachings our rule. The only responsible place for a decision to be made is in the context of a local church and its wise leadership.

Seventh, *remarriage is both permissible and not necessary.* I hang my hat on the hook of evidence that is implicit in the words of Jesus in 5:31 – 32: permissible divorces made possible permissible remarriages. While a divorced woman in the first century was much more vulnerable economically and socially, not to mention spiritually and physically, than in our Western affluent world, and therefore remarriage was a much higher priority, there are noble examples of many today who have chosen the harder path of respecting their original sacred union and, out of fear of God, have chosen not to remarry. Not remarrying is a noble choice. But for many that choice will be nearly impossible and so remarriage will be pursued. Our advice: wait and wait. Our second piece of advice: listen to the wisdom of those who love you and those who are your leaders. We are not talking about the infallibility of the church or of the absolute control of the church, but we are talking about the importance for followers of Jesus to live out of a fellowship with others that blesses and mentors weighty decisions in life.

Eighth, *what about remarriage of the guilty partner?* I have not used the expression "guilty partner" up to now, but it deserves its time on the table. Our supposition is that a marriage is sometimes destroyed by the actions of one person, more often than not the act of adultery. The act is sinful, and the act may well have destroyed the marriage, and the guilty partner here is responsible. The question that emerges in nearly every church and pastoral office I know of is this one: Can the guilty partner ever remarry? There are some who believe we are to remain rigorous in this matter and prohibit the guilty partner from ever remarrying. But I wonder if this commitment to righteousness fits with the biblical teaching on repentance and forgiveness. While the guilty partner ought to undergo a serious church evaluation and then an ongoing process of counseling and guidance with discernments rendered all along, I believe a guilty person can find genuine repentance and receive forgiveness from God. Not all will agree with the next step, and this discernment is always to be rendered by the leaders and local church context — and never simply by the individual Christian — but once repentance is discerned and forgiveness granted, the guilty partner can, under the guidance of a local church, begin to pursue remarriage.

Back now to the golf course. My golfing friend, as I learned while we played, had done about as much as anyone can to reconcile. So he kept pressing me on a simple logical point: if divorce is permissible, is remarriage permissible? As you can tell from what I have written above, which fleshes out more than what I said that day, I advised him on the basis of how I understood the Bible that yes, his permissible divorce could lead to a permissible remarriage. Two years later he got remarried, and he has thanked me for the conversation a number of times.

God help us!

LISTEN to the Story

33"Again, you have heard that it was said to the people long ago, 'Do not break your oath, but fulfill to the Lord the vows you have made.' 34But I tell you, do not swear an oath at all: either by heaven, for it is God's throne; 35or by the earth, for it is his footstool; or by Jerusalem, for it is the city of the Great King. 36And do not swear by your head, for you cannot make even one hair white or black. 37All you need to say is simply 'Yes,' or 'No';[1] anything beyond this comes from the evil one."

Listen to the text in the Story: Exodus 20:7; Leviticus 19:12; Numbers 30:3–15; Deuteronomy 23:21–22; Matthew 23:16–22; James 5:12; 11Q19 (Temple) 53:11–54:7; *Mishnah Nedarim* 1:3.

As marriage is inviolable, so honesty in words should be invariable. Jesus' concerns here are theoretical: words were being mapped on an honesty or obligation scale by the magnitude of the source of their vow, and Jesus' counters the scaling of words by requiring truth. Again, Jesus is using an Ethic from Beyond in a Messianic Ethic framework. Because messianic, kingdom people are honest, they do not need oaths.

There are a few historical items behind the practicing of scaling words. To begin with, an oath or vow draws on a history of Israel's experience in the courtroom and with judicial obligations. In the courtroom and in public, there is the command to be honest. Scaling words was influenced by another item: the prohibition of using the name of God carelessly. The most complete form of this prohibition is found in Leviticus 19:12: "Do not swear falsely by my name and so profane the name of your God. I am the LORD." The sacredness of God's name led to the practice in Judaism of substituting words for God's name. At this point Jesus enters into this history: the various substitutions for God's name were not as sacred as God's name, and that led to scaling one's words. Four substitutions appear in our antithesis (heaven,

---

1. KNT: "say yes when you mean yes, and no when you mean no."

earth, Jerusalem, head). Jesus found scales connected to various descriptions of God to be inconsistent with the sacredness of God's name and how kingdom people were to live.[2]

King Jesus presses deeper by summarizing words probably taken from Deuteronomy 23:21–23 (or even Psalm 50:14).

> If you make a vow to the LORD your God, do not be slow to pay it, for the LORD your God will certainly demand it of you and you will be guilty of sin. But if you refrain from making a vow, you will not be guilty. Whatever your lips utter you must be sure to do, because you made your vow freely to the LORD your God with your own mouth. (Deut 23:21–23)

> Sacrifice thank offerings to God,
>   fulfill your vows to the Most High. (Ps 50:14)

At the heart of the Ten Commandments is an Israelite's honesty about one's neighbor (Exod 20:16). At the heart of the Bible's ethic is telling the truth. Honesty mattered then and it matters now. Nearly two-thirds of America's youth admit they've lied to a parent, teacher, or someone else in the last three months; about 60 percent admit they've lied to a friend or peer in the last three months; about a third admit they've cheated on a test in the last three months.[3] As a professor at a Christian college for more than fifteen years, I have seen an increase in wandering eyes during quizzes and exams. We now (have to?) have sophisticated programs that compare student papers to Internet sources and other student papers, but even when students know their papers will be run through this program, they choose to swipe and plagiarize rather than write the paper in their own honest prose.

From the beginning honesty was the assumption for human interactions. Without that assumption trust breaks down culture into chaos. The serpent dishonestly reframed the words of God in the garden of Eden, and Adam didn't tell the whole truth to God (Gen 3). Abraham lied about Sarah (cf. 12:10–20); Jacob tricked Esau with twisted words (27:1–40) but was tricked in turn (29:1–30); the brothers of Joseph lied to their father about Joseph (37:12–36) … and it goes on and sadly on. Against such verbal trickery, the Bible constantly commands honesty.

In framing honest statements in courts, Israelites took oaths that made

---

2. There are some additional rulings. An example can be found in Numbers 30:3–15, where a woman's vowed words are examined in the situation of her phase in life: before marriage, married, widowed, and divorced. The implication is that a woman's vow can be overturned by her father and husband. Notably, Jesus' words provide no opportunity for such patriarchalism because he demands honesty in all verbal exchanges, whether words from a woman or a man.

3. See Josh McDowell, *Right from Wrong* (Nashville: Word, 1994), 11–22.

their statements legally obligating because they implored the presence of God in the commitment—*but this only happened because verbal trickery was too common*. As Matthew 23:16–22 shows, those oaths became the source for scaling honesty in words—those connected to the highest level were most honest while words uttered without a connection were less honest. This pernicious tendency is the source of Jesus' stark and simple demand for kingdom people: invariable honesty.

The heart of the demand of honesty is the fidelity of God to his covenant oath. "I will be your God and you will be my people," the covenant words often repeated in one form or another in the Old Testament, express a covenant oath of loyalty by God to his people that he will be with them and for them, and he will make them into kingdom people. Honesty, then, is grounded in the covenant God made with Israel.

EXPLAIN the Story

Jesus summarizes what can be found in the following passages: Exodus 20:7; Leviticus 6:3–5; 19:12; Numbers 30:2–15; Deuteronomy 23:21–23; Psalms 24:4; 50:14; and Ecclesiastes 5:4. Perhaps his words combine Leviticus 19:12 with Deuteronomy 23:23. Jesus' first expression—"Do not break your oath"—could be about swearing falsely or more likely about breaking an oath; the second expression—"fulfill to the Lord the vows [oaths] you have made"—entails a person before God alone. It could appear that Jesus is touching on laws about two kinds of verbal promises, namely, oaths and vows—the first about verbal commitments to another person or party, and the second about dedicating something to God. It seems that all of Matthew 5:33 is about *oaths* and not partly about oaths (5:33a) and partly about vows (5:33b, NIV).[4] This would make the NIV's use of "vow" inaccurate. Put in the simplest of terms, Jesus is saying "don't break your oaths" (negative) and "fulfill your oaths" (positive). The vocabulary clearly indicates that oaths are in view.[5]

What Jesus points out from this teaching of Moses is that Israelites were obligated to keep their oaths, but it is "oathing" that grabs Jesus' attention because oaths assume a world in which honesty must be promised—implying that honesty is not always present.

---

4. Notice that if "but fulfill to the Lord the vows you made" derives explicitly from Ps 50:14, where the word "vows" (*euchas*) becomes "oaths" (*orkous*), the explicit change from *euchas* to *orkous* probably means Jesus is talking about oaths (not vows). But, since these two terms overlap, we need to avoid dogmatism. See Davies and Allison, *Matthew*, 1:534.

5. Guelich, *Sermon on the Mount*, 212–14; A. Gross, "Oaths and Vows," *EDEJ*, 1005–6.

Jesus' Total Prohibition

The problem was that honesty was being fiddled with because some rendered words less than honest by scaling oaths (and vows) and by multiplying occasions for which oaths were to be used. Philo complains about this: "There are some who ... have an evil habit of swearing incessantly and thoughtlessly about ordinary matters" (*Decalogue* 92). To counter this multiplication and scaling, Jesus registers a total and unequivocal prohibition. The finality of Jesus' words deserves emphasis because Matthew's word that precedes his sketch of how they were scaling oaths is *holōs*: "do not swear an oath *at all.*"

Luther is but one example of someone who thought "at all" meant only in one's private world.[6] Any reading of the text, though, reveals that oaths were fundamentally a legal, courtroom, public issue and not just a private matter. Jesus' total prohibition is stronger than anything found in the Jewish world of his day, and this fits into what we are calling the Ethic from Beyond. What Jesus reveals is God's will, but it stretches us beyond what we think we can accomplish.

Most of the early Christians, including James (Jas 5:12) took this saying literally and abided by it. The major shift in how to live out this word of Jesus occurred with Constantine, making oaths to Christian emperors a common practice.[7] The exceptions from the Middle Ages on were few: the Cathari, Waldensians, and the various forms of Anabaptists.

Banning Oaths

Jesus here mentions four kinds of scaled oaths: those "by heaven," those "by the earth," those "by Jerusalem," and those "by your head." In light of 23:16–22, oaths became the opportunity to scale one's obligations to what one said. A good example of how scaling worked is found in the *Mishnah Šebuʿot* 4:13. The words in italics are the source of one's oath, but this text begins with exemptions from one's words. Yet once an oath is given, the person becomes more accountable:[8]

> [If] he had sent through his slave [to impose the oath on the witnesses],
> or if the defendant had said to them, "I impose an oath on you, that if you know testimony concerning him, you come and give evidence concerning him,"
> they are exempt.

---

6. Luther, *Sermon on the Mount*, 99. The simple fact is that "at all" means just that. Far wiser to see this as exaggerated rhetoric in a particular context of scaling obligations than to tamper with what the words actually mean.

7. Luz, *Matthew 1–7*, 266.

8. For an exceptional discussion of disagreement over this issue, with R. Aqiba agreeing more or less with Jesus, see *m. Nedarim* 1; see also *m. Sanhedrin* 3:2.

Next comes the ramping of accountability once an oath is stated:
unless they hear [the oath] from the mouth of the plaintiff,
"I impose an oath on you," (2) "I command you," (3) "I bind you," — lo,
these are liable.

Now we get the explicit sources of the oath:
"By heaven and earth," lo, these are exempt.
(1) "By [the name of] Alef-dalet [Adonai]" or (2) "Yud-he [Yahweh]," (3)
"By the Almighty," (4) "By Hosts," (5) "By him who is merciful and gracious,"
(6) "By him who is long-suffering and abundant in mercy," or by any other
euphemism —
lo, these are liable.

But some rabbis would later call into question this approach to oaths and
vows, and *Mishnah Nedarim* 1:1 makes the case Jesus himself makes by saying
we are obligated to our commitments: "All substitutes for [language used to
express] (1) vows are equivalent to vows, and for (2) bans (herem) are equivalent to bans, and for (3) oaths are equivalent to oaths, and for (4) Nazirite
vows are equivalent to Nazirite vows." And Philo, a near contemporary to
Jesus, makes it clear that all oath-taking implicated a person before God:
"For an oath is an appeal to God as a witness on matters in dispute, and to
call Him as a witness to a lie is the height of profanity" (*Decalogue* 86). The
Essenes were rigorous about avoiding oaths. One who claimed to know them,
Josephus, offers a wonderful complement to the integrity of their words: "Any
word of theirs has more force than an oath; swearing they avoid, regarding it
as worse than perjury, for they say that one who is not believed without an
appeal to God stands condemned already" (*Jewish War* 2.135).[9]

Any oath-taking (or swearing) in God's name put an Israelite in jeopardy
of taking the name of God in vain. So as not to infringe on that possibility,
what developed was called *kinnuyim*, substitutionary words for God, that protected a person from profaning the name. Jesus deals in theology: since God
is omnipresent, none of these substitutions — heaven, throne, etc. — escapes
direct connection with God. An oath is an oath (demanding keeping it), and
an oath isn't an oath if God is not involved (implying that God is at work
regardless of how the oath itself is framed). Swearing by "heaven" is not less
than swearing by God because heaven "is God's throne." Swearing by "earth"
is not lower than heaven because "it is [God's] footstool." Swearing by Jerusalem is not less than either heaven or earth because "it is the city of the Great
King." And swearing by one's head, well, "you cannot make one hair white or
black" — and God can, so he's in charge even of your head! You might think

---

9. But they did flex on this in requiring oaths to enter into the sect (1QS 5:8).

that Jesus is speaking here of omni*science*, but it is wiser to see an appeal here both to God's omni*presence*. God is King over all; any oath that touches anything under God makes a person accountable for the words used.

Kingdom Honesty

The Bible permitted oaths, but Jesus calls the whole thing to a final stop. Why? In a world where oaths were seen as disconnected from God or where they permitted one to scale one's obligation to what one promised, Jesus (Messianic Ethic) steps in to say kingdom people (Ethic from Beyond) are so honest there is no need for any oaths. They always tell the truth because they indwell the kingdom now.

The legitimacy of oaths is thus challenged by Jesus with these words: "All you need to say is simply 'Yes,' or 'No.'" While 5:33 merely instructed Israelites always to perform their oaths, Jesus goes beyond that instruction. His language is designed to push into the deepest levels of verbal communications: one is to be invariably honest, and when everyone is invariably honest, we will have a kingdom world wherein oaths will not be needed. This is exactly how James uses these words of Jesus at James 5:12.[10] His people do not need any buttressing words or any oaths that scale human words from lower to higher levels of obligation. They will be known as truth-tellers; like the Essenes.

Jesus concludes with nothing less than an insult: "Anything beyond this comes from the evil one." James will later say it slightly differently: "Otherwise you will be condemned" (Jas 5:12). Jesus could be appealing to the devious nature of the serpent's words in the garden of Eden, or he could be appealing to the general Jewish belief that the evil one is a liar, or he could be thinking more abstractly ("from evil"). It is impossible to know with confidence which of these options Jesus intended; what does matter is that kingdom people tell the truth.

 LIVE the Story

The questions that come to my attention on a routine basis when teaching or listening to students are these: What would you do if someone came to your door and asked if Anne Frank was in your home? Or, what if a follower of Jesus were in your basement in hiding and a persecutor looking for that person asked you if you were hiding that person? Or, was Bonhoeffer right in pushing the boundaries of honesty in the conspiracy against Hitler?

---

10. S. McKnight, *The Letter of James* (NICNT; Grand Rapids: Eerdmans, 2011), 423–29. The Greek has "yes yes" and "no no", and the duplication serves to emphasize. We could translate, "Let your agreement be simply with Yes." The use of No No or Yes Yes is not an alternative oath, as can be seen in *2 Enoch* 49:1, which appears to be dependent on either our antithesis or Jas 5:12.

Truth in Relation to Ultimate Realities

In November and December 1943, while in Tegel prison, Dietrich Bonhoeffer, who had himself participated in deception in the conspiracy, composed an essay called, "What Does It Mean to Tell the Truth?"[11] He creates a scenario: a child whose teacher asks him (or her) if his (or her) father is a drunk. Bonhoeffer believes the teacher has inappropriately invaded morally private territory. Truth, he contends, is relational and connected to the ultimate truth of God's revelation in Christ. It would be wrong for the Christian to tell a truth for the sake of mapping words solely on a scale of correspondence to experienced realities. Instead, the appropriate words are to be found for that particular setting and should be measured by the gospel of Christ.

This approach Bonhoeffer calls "living truth," and it requires "attentive discernment of the relevant contents and limits that the real itself specifies for one's utterance in order to make it a truthful one." The child, by saying no to the teacher, "contains more truth … than if the child had revealed the father's weakness before the class." Therefore, for Bonhoeffer there can be a "necessary deception of the enemy in war." So his theory of when our word becomes true works out to three lines:

> by recognizing who calls on me to speak and what authorizes me to speak
> by recognizing the place in which I stand
> by putting the subject I am speaking about into this context

We ask: Even if we recognize the unbearable difference between our theoretical discussion of truth-telling and Bonhoeffer's staring abominable evils in the face, does Bonhoeffer's proposal of discerning truth on the basis of relations and realities contradict the words of Jesus? We are also required to ask if Jesus' words are adequate for such a situation. We are asking if Jesus' Ethic from Beyond is to succumb to an Ethic from Below in light of the crushing fallenness of creation.

Ambiguities and Clarity

Ulrich Luz puts into words the wake that has remained turbulent since the day Jesus uttered his total prohibition of oaths and the reduction of his followers' words to utter simple honesty: "As is the case with other categorical demands of Jesus, there is also something unrealistic about this one. Jesus gives no more

---

11. D. Bonhoeffer, ""What Does It Mean to Tell the Truth?" in *Conspiracy and Imprisonment: 1940–1945* (Dietrich Bonhoeffer Works 16; ed. M. S. Brocker; trans. L. E. Dahill; Minneapolis: Fortress, 2006), 601–8. All citations are from these pages.

thought to what kind of problematic consequences would result from his absolute prohibition of oaths than he does with his demand to reject violence or with his prohibition of divorce."[12] Hagner follows this line of thinking in these words: "It is a mistake, however, to take a biblicistic approach to this passage that would disallow Christians from taking an oath, say in a court of justice. The issue is nothing less than and nothing more than truthfulness."[13]

Such words have a way of being both pragmatically realistic and at the same time tone down what Jesus said. The irony is obvious: it was precisely public oaths that got Jesus' concern going, and it was precisely public oaths that Jesus flat-out forbade for his followers. Any kind of "application" of this antithesis that permits legal oaths undoes the very point Jesus is making. The rhetoric of Jesus envisions a world where oaths are not needed, and he summons his followers to live in that kind of world (an Ethic from Beyond). The Ethic from Below being used in Jesus' day had dissolved the need for honesty, so Jesus ramps up the demand to kingdom proportions.

Let's be clear here: *Jesus is talking about legal oaths* and *Jesus is against legal oaths*. This passage isn't simply a clever way of asking, "We should all be honest, shouldn't we?" As if he is saying, "The world would be a better place if we all told the truth." But to make this point, he chose a narrow slice of life, namely, a legal oath. No, our zeal to "apply" fails us here. Jesus is talking about oaths, legally binding oaths. That's what he quoted from Moses, that's what he ridicules in his four kinds of oaths, and that's what he prohibits at the end of the passage.

But he is not talking just about legal oaths. Jesus wants utter honesty from his followers, and he illustrates a world where utter honesty has been compromised by speaking about oaths. So the way to read this passage is this: *because he values honesty so much, he uses a concrete example of a world that establishes dishonesty*. Jesus wants a world of utter honesty, and that would mean, among other things, nonparticipation in the use of oaths. We live this text into our world when we live with utter honesty and work against systems where dishonesty has become systemic.

Those Who Use Oaths, Including God

But perhaps it's not that simple. So we need to ponder the ideas that come to mind if we want to live this passage anew in our world. Behind Christian nervousness about making this antithesis of Jesus a new rule for Christian living, as is seen in those who refuse to take legal oaths, is the ambiguity of the

---

12. Luz, *Matthew 1–7*, 264. See also his sketch of the history of interpretation (266–69).
13. Hagner, *Matthew 1–13*, 129. See the discussion of this in Quarles, *Sermon on the Mount*, 143–44.

Bible itself on this issue. We can begin with the folly of oaths in the gospel of Matthew: Herod (14:7, 9) and Peter (26:74) reveal the problem. Oaths put one into foolish situations. But God makes oaths (Gen 22:16–18; Exod 6:8; Isa 45:23; Luke 1:73; Acts 2:30), and Abraham makes an oath (Gen 14:22). Perhaps we can push these aside because they are pre-Jesus' words here. But Paul appeals to God as his witness (Rom 1:9; 2 Cor 1:23; Gal 1:20; Phil 1:8), which is exactly what an oath was, often enough that one would have to say he has at some level gone against what appears to be the intent of our antithesis, and an angel from God seems to do the same (Rev 10:6).

But let's come back to Jesus. When he was charged under oath to identify himself, he refused to speak (Matt 26:62–64). Was this because of kingdom honesty? I think so. What Jesus is teaching here is not the absolute prohibition of all oaths, for then he'd be against God's ways of dealing with our redemption, but against legal oaths that reflect distancing God from what we do in scaling our obligations. He calls his followers into kingdom realities.

Not in Court

Luther overtly mismanaged this text when he turned it into its exact opposite. That is, Luther said it is okay to use oaths in public (legal courts) but not permissible for Christians in their private world. His two-kingdom ethical theory thus played itself out in a way that undid exactly what Jesus was doing. Jesus is here *reforming* public life *because one's private world is properly ordered*. Nor will it do, as so many try to make it do, to say that Jesus is hyperbolically contending for overall honesty but a little oath is simply unimportant. What Jesus is doing in this saying is extending kingdom ethics from the private life of the disciple into the legal world into which they enter. As they seek reconciliation in legal situations (cf. 5:25–26), so they form honest habits that extend into legal situations (5:33–37).

Nor, as Allison suggests, is this simply an ideal toward which we are to strive, though I agree that an ideal is at work here. Rather, this is nothing less than Jesus' kingdom subversion of a legal code that encoded subtle distancing from God as well as scales of obligation to one's words. Jesus' is against such things, and so he flatly prohibits his followers from using oaths (which are by nature legal, public performative utterances). God is with us in everything we do, so we are to be honest in all we do.

A Permission Now Taken Back

What Jesus is saying, then, is that oaths, like divorce, were a *permission* because of the corruption of humans. Jesus is against the permission because he has come to transform humans into kingdom people. For Jesus, participation in the oath system of Judaism (or today) is to become complicit in systemic distancing from God's omnipresence and in the scaling of obligation to one's words. Since kingdom people are honest, they do not need to participate in oaths or scaling of one's obligations.

Probing Our Complicities

We live this text out when we begin to see how complicit we are in legal systems that encode ethics out of sync with the kingdom ethic of Jesus. We live this text out when we learn the simplicity of honesty, when we learn that our yes really does mean yes and our no really does mean no, and when we learn that our yes obligates us and that our no obligates us. I would argue, then, that followers of Jesus are to tell a judge who requests an oath that they are bound by Jesus not to use oaths because their words are honest.

Notice the order: it is because the kingdom is a world of utter honesty, hence an Ethic from Beyond, that followers of Jesus choose not to participate in a system, like oaths, where dishonesty becomes systemic. Again, he is sketching a world in which utter honesty rules. The text teaches, then, that eschatological honesty should rule in the words of his followers in the now.

Simple Honesty

But, yes, the last verse of our passage permits us to widen the scope of the passage to see that followers of Jesus are called to live with utter honesty. Simple honesty emerges in concrete ordinary events and not just when we are asked to swear on a Bible in a courtroom ("Do you swear to tell the whole truth and nothing but the truth?" "I swear."). I was for more than a decade a codirector with Jim Panther of a summer baseball camp, which created the daily wonder of the sort of weather we might have. Jim was a marvel of simple honesty when it came to camp times and work habits, and what I saw was that he worked against systems that didn't always value "money paid for work done."

We wrote on our camp brochure that camp ended at 3:00 p.m. Some days it was so hot that ending fifteen minutes early seemed almost unstoppable — but not Jim, and so not with me or our kids. The kids could go hide in a dugout or leave, but we kept teaching and pitching and hitting and instructing until 3:00 p.m. — every day, every week, for more than a decade. I can't remember that we ever quit early, and the reason why is that camp ended at 3:00 p.m.

A second reason was this: parents paid for a week in our camp. The first year a parent decided to take his son out of camp after three days (it was scorching hot that week), and came to us after camp that day and said, "I don't think Ben will be at camp the rest of the week; the heat has just been too much." Jim immediately said, "We'll refund your money for the two days Ben misses." Jim that night wrote out a check to Ben's parents, and we mailed it to the parents the next day. That note of simple honesty pervaded our camp for the next decade. I remember mailing a check to a mother because her son missed a day of camp. That night she called me and said, "Why? I assumed if my son missed camp, we lost the money for that day." I said, "You paid for five days, your son played four days, so we will refund your money for the day he missed." Honestly, she was a bit stunned by our simple honesty, but I think she was stunned because our world's system far too often works the other way.

CHAPTER 9

Matthew 5:38 – 42

 ## LISTEN to the Story

> [38]"You have heard that it was said, 'Eye for eye, and tooth for tooth.' [39]But I tell you, do not resist an evil person. If anyone slaps you on the right cheek, turn to them the other cheek also. [40]And if anyone wants to sue you and take your shirt, hand over your coat as well. [41]If anyone forces you to go one mile, go with them two miles. [42]Give to the one who asks you, and do not turn away from the one who wants to borrow from you."

> *Listen to the text in the Story*: Exodus 21:23 – 25; Leviticus 24:19 – 20; Deuteronomy 19:21; Obadiah 15.

Where to begin? With justice. Justice is the core of the world's system of appropriate and justifiable relations among people. Behind every attempt to define justice is a standard. In the United States that standard is the US Constitution, in England it is the Magna Carta, in Germany it is the *Grundgesetz*. A society's legal standard creates a certain kind of society: the Germans call their society a *Rechtsstaat* — a society ruled by law. The same applies to England and to the United States, where we say we have the "rule of law." "Justice," then, is used for *conditions* and *behaviors* that conform to the standards or the laws at work in a particular society.

But where do we get the standard so a society can be ruled by law? There is a social history and a theological answer. The social history answer is that, say, the USA got its laws from England, not to neglect important voices like those of Thomas Paine, Benjamin Franklin, Thomas Jefferson, or James Madison; and England got its laws from Europe, and Europe from Rome and Greece. This will lead us to admit that all of the Western countries owe their basic legal systems to early codes like the *Nomos* of Solon and *The Digest of Justinian*. The prominent laws of a given society are the laws that have worked well in this history, and they are more or less the *will of a society or the will of its lawmakers*.[1]

---

1. For an informed and jaunty sketch of this history, see W. I. Miller, *Eye for an Eye* (New York: Cambridge University Press, 2006).

Ancient Israelites had the Torah of Moses, but with one major difference from our law codes: it was claimed that the Torah of Moses had a divine origin. This claim transformed Israel's sense of justice because it became conditions and behaviors that conformed *to the will of God.* While the social history answer seeks to explain a given set of laws in light of its predecessors, a theological approach finds divine revelation. That revelation is expressed in Exodus, Leviticus, and Deuteronomy, and those laws were then worked out in rulings down the ages in Judaism in what was eventually called *halakhot.* So the Story of Israel, within which one can find the central role of the "story of the Torah," has its own story of how justice is formed and reformed, shaped and reshaped. In other words, the Torah story is one of formation and adaptation, and these adaptations (later rulings of interpretation) were sometimes perceived as divine.

In both the social and theological worlds, a staple of law is *commensurable punishment.* Punishments are to be equal to the crime. In Latin this is called *lex talionis,* or the law of retribution. A fundamental expression of this is found in Exodus 21:23–25:

> But if there is serious injury, you are to take life for life, eye for eye, tooth for tooth, hand for hand, foot for foot, burn for burn, wound for wound, bruise for bruise.

This *lex talionis* is expressed more theoretically in Leviticus 24:19–20:

> Anyone who injures their neighbor is to be *injured in the same manner:* fracture for fracture, eye for eye, tooth for tooth. *The one who has inflicted the injury must suffer the same injury.*

A third expression in Deuteronomy 19:21 is much like Exodus 21 but a bit more succinct:

> Show no pity: life for life, eye for eye, tooth for tooth, hand for hand, foot for foot.

The impact of these three expressions of law is clear: justice requires retribution. Notice the words "show *no* pity," and "if there is … you *are* to take …," and "*anyone* who injures … *is* to be injured.…" But retribution is limited, but equal to, the original injury. This principle of equal retribution curbs violence and prevents vengeance from spinning out of control.

A good example of reckless violence in the Bible is Lamech in Genesis 4:23–24. Samson in Judges 16:28 relishes victory over his enemy when he transforms blindness into the death of many. But settling on the Old Testament as offering the *lex talionis* only to restrict revenge misses a major theme: retribution is *demanded* in these texts. The *lex talionis* leads to two fundamentals of law: required retribution and equal retribution. By making it law, punishment is moved out of the private sphere into the sphere of the public forum. For Israel, behind the *lex talionis* stands a God who himself takes vengeance (cf. Ezek 16:59; Obad 15).

Jesus steps into this legal history.[2] What he teaches in this fifth antithesis is both a revelation of God's intent and a "constitution" for the kingdom society. This text is a Messianic Ethic for the messianic community and an Ethic from Beyond. Instead of the requirement of retribution, Jesus reveals that grace, love, and forgiveness can reverse the dangers of retribution and, even more, create an alternative society.

EXPLAIN the Story

Unlike the previous two antitheses, where Jesus summarized one or more passages, this time he simply quotes Scripture. Still, there is no way to know which text he is quoting because the same precise words are found at Exodus 21:24; Leviticus 24:20; and Deuteronomy 19:21, and we will also need to take looks at texts like Genesis 9:6; Exodus 21:28–32; Leviticus 19:18; Numbers 35:31–32; Deuteronomy 25:11–12; 32:35; Judges 1:6–7; 2 Samuel 4:9–12; 1 Kings 20:39, 42; Esther 7:10; Job 2:4; Psalms 9–10; Proverbs 20:22; 24:29; 25:21–22; and Daniel 6:19–24. Jesus quotes the Torah and then counters an understanding of Torah with his own kingdom ethics, his Ethic from Beyond. Anyone who heard Jesus would have asked, "Who does he think he is?" That is, we see again his Messianic Ethic.

Lex Talionis

Israel's law on retaliation included both capital punishment ("life for life") and corporal punishment ("tooth for tooth"). It is not entirely clear if ancient Israelites distinguished manslaughter (unintentional) from murder (intentional) as carefully as we do in Western law (cf. Exod 21:18–19; Num 35:22–23; Deut 19:5). The principle here is not just "life" but the taking of a "human life," and it required the retribution of capital sentence. The death of another person's animal only required a commensurate animal's life (cf. Lev 24:17–21). As well, a feature of Israel's *talion* law is that it is egalitarian: man or woman, young or old, rich or poor — each is subject to retribution while some Mesopotamian cultures scaled the retribution according to one's status.[3]

The requirement of equal retribution was at times transformed into

---

2. J. F. Davis, *Lex Talionis in Early Judaism and the Exhortation of Jesus in Matthew 5.38–42* (JSNTMS 281; London/New York: T&T Clark/Continuum, 2005).

3. W. H. C. Propp, *Exodus 19–40* (AB 2A; New York: Doubleday, 2006), 228.

financial compensation. At Numbers 35:31 we read, "Do not accept a ransom [a fine] for the life of a murderer." The prohibition of a "ransom" for the taking of a life implies that a ransom was paid for other crimes. Fines are clearly taught by later rabbis for at least the "tooth for a tooth" law. Thus, *Mishnah Baba Qamma* 8:1 says: "He who injures his fellow is liable to [compensate] him on five counts: injury, pain, medical costs, loss of income, and indignity." This leads to how much one is worth, and here is the ruling: "If one has blinded his eye, cut off his hand, broken his leg, they regard him as a slave up for sale in the market and make an estimate of how much he was worth beforehand [when whole], and how much he is now worth." The *lex talionis* is still required but converted into financial value. The potentially barbaric nature of the *talion* led many to convert punishment into fines. But rendering the retribution into financial compensation does not go as far as Jesus went.

Jesus' Kingdom Vision: Nonresistant Love

The *lex talionis* was not just about curbing violence; it was an emphatic *requirement* of justice. Deuteronomy 19:21 says, "Show no pity." The "no pity" clause is not just for cases of murder but for the entire system: "life for life, eye for eye, tooth for tooth, hand for hand, foot for foot." A crime required a just retribution.

There is no way around explaining what Jesus is saying in our text: *Jesus overtly ends the Mosaic command to "show no pity" in the appropriation of the* lex talionis *and in its place orders his followers to be merciful.* Jesus' words take the *lex talionis* to a different place: that law was concerned with the requirement of equal retribution while Jesus undermines the requirement and reshapes how his followers are to respond to perpetrators. Jesus' words are: "But I tell you, do not resist an evil person." Or, as Tom Wright has it, "don't use violence to resist evil!" (KNT). Bonhoeffer draws us to Jesus' kingdom society: "Jesus releases his community from the political and legal order, from the national form of the people of Israel, and makes it into what it truly is, namely, the community of the faithful that is not bound by political or national ties."[4]

Jesus uses a term that indicates "nonresistance" (*antistēnai*), but the specifics of this word take on concrete variations in the lines that follow and caution us to build our beliefs on the specifics instead of on our philosophy. His examples reveal that "do not resist" is as much a positive action of love as it is a negative posture. It could be translated, "Be ready for an act of grace." Jesus' words also "resist" Moses' words: the older framework was one of resisting injustice by requiring equal retribution, but Jesus denounces resistance. It is too easy to stand up and give a big clap for Jesus and his innovation. The

---

4. Bonhoeffer, *Discipleship*, 132.

facts are that Jesus is not alone in his Jewish world in this teaching, and there are precedents in the Old Testament itself (Lev 19:18; Prov 20:22; 24:29). He is, then, drawing on a latent theme in the Bible and in his Jewish world, and there are similar ideas in the wider Mediterranean world.[5]

It is not clear *why* Jesus teaches this. It may be that he saw the *lex talionis* as a permission granted because of the sinfulness of Israel. Such an approach is not consciously expressed here, as it is in the divorce teaching of Jesus, but by implication has something to commend it. Jesus is teaching a kingdom ethic, and the kingdom will not trade in retribution because people will live justly, lovingly, and peacefully with one another. Bringing that kingdom reality into the present is what the kingdom ethic of Jesus is all about. Hence, one could infer from his Ethic from Beyond that the entire legal apparatus was only a permission from God rather than the intent of God for his true people. I'm inclined to accept this interpretation but not to grant it logical priority. In addition to this reading, is there not an inkling of resignation here, as if Jesus were saying, "Look, guys, you can do nothing about it so you might as well go limp in the face of their power"? And neither does Jesus seem to be using this as a strategy, as if he were saying, "The really good way to get their goat or to get them on our side is to cooperate."

Rather, Jesus' ethic here, like so much of his Messianic Ethic, is shaped by the Jesus Creed of loving God and loving others. Those who love will love even those who dish out injustices. A person shaped by the Jesus Creed responds to injustice not with retaliation and vengeance but with grace, compassion, and abundant mercy in such a way that it reverses injustice. In other words, Jesus' followers dwell in an alternative society that protests systemic injustice and embodies an alternative love-shaped justice. No one said this better than Bonhoeffer, whose final end embodied it: "Evil will become powerless when it finds no opposing object, no resistance, but, instead, is willingly borne and suffered. Evil meets an opponent for which it is not a match."[6]

Jesus defines the one who treats others unjustly with this expression: "an evil person." The word used here (*ponēros*) is the same word used in 5:37: "from the evil one." Whether or not that text or this text is referring to the Evil One, i.e., Satan (cf. 12:45; 13:19), is less important than seeing the character of those who deal in injustice (20:15). He refers to those who sin (7:11; 12:34 – 35; 13:38; 15:19), who break shalom, who are unloving, and who violate the codes of the Torah.[7] But this term "evil" could be a code word for those who "belong to the other group," those who don't follow Jesus or who are

---

5. Luz, *Matthew 1 – 7*, 273 nn. 26 – 29.

6. Bonhoeffer, *Discipleship*, 133.

7. France, *Matthew*, 220.

Gentiles (cf. 5:45; 7:17–18; 13:49; 18:32; 22:10; 25:26). Thus, though perhaps a little on the speculative side, the term could be referring to "Romans."

But Jesus' point is not so much to *label* the other person as "evil" but to reveal to his followers that messianic people respond to the "other" with nonresistant, life-transforming love. In fact, Jesus prepares for the next antithesis by showing that in his Ethic from Beyond, the "evil person" becomes the "neighbor."

Examples of Jesus' Kingdom Vision of Nonresistance

Jesus' four examples of how to behave "nonresistantly" to "evil" persons emerge from the concrete experience of subjection to Rome. The four examples, and they may be in descending order of severity of offense, concern being insulted, being sued in court, being conscripted to support the Roman military, and being asked to help others with money.[8] In each instance Jesus advocates grace beyond retribution and expectation. He does not advocate passivity but active generosity that deconstructs the system because of the presence of the kingdom. Surrendering one's rights for the good of the other manifests the Jesus Creed and its variant, the Golden Rule of 7:12.

Reading this antithesis in light of the Story of God in the Bible, with its concentration on Jesus as the center of the Story, cannot help but find parallels in Isaiah 50's servant description.[9] Most notably, Isaiah 50:6–8:

> I offered my back to those who beat me,
>   my cheeks to those who pulled out my beard;
> I did not hide my face
>   from mocking and spitting.
> Because the Sovereign LORD helps me,
>   I will not be disgraced.
> Therefore have I set my face like flint,
>   and I know I will not be put to shame.
> He who vindicates me is near.
>   Who then will bring charges against me?
>   Let us face each other!
> Who is my accuser?
>   Let him confront me!

---

8. Hence, Guelich's translation, "*You shall not oppose an evil person in court,*" while contextually sensitive, misses the concreteness of Jesus' own illustrations. See his *Sermon on the Mount*, 219–20. To keep this "in court" theme, he presses 5:38–39 into the mold of Deut 19:16–21 (unsuccessfully). One is hard-pressed to get each of the concrete instances of nonresistance into a courtroom setting, and it might be argued that only one of them plausibly belongs in that context — "if anyone wants to sue you ..." — and Jesus contends to act before that even happens. The Q parallel in Luke 6:29–30 is even less courtroomish, and the order varies slightly.

9. See Davies and Allison, *Matthew*, 1:544.

"If anyone slaps you …": For a person to be slapped on the right cheek apparently assumes being hit by a person facing them with a backhanded slap (or a left-handed person striking a person with an open hand). The backhanded slap is a gross insult to the dignity of a person. This principle of the later rabbinic rulings probably reflects the social customs at work in first-century Galilee, and here is the principle: "Everything is in accord with one's station [status]." This means, "if he smacked him, he pays him *two* hundred zuz." But, the text continues, "if it is with the back of the hand, he pays him *four* hundred zuz" (*Mishnah Baba Qamma* 8:6, italics added). Instead of striking back, which would be both justifiable and equal retribution and a part of Moses' "no mercy" law, Jesus creates an almost laughable scene of grace: "turn to them the other cheek also." This is how Jesus did respond (Matt 26:67).

"If anyone wants to sue you …": Jesus subverts and parodies a legal setting and a social custom. Males wore two levels of clothing: an outer cloak and an inner garment, roughly a coat and shirt. In the event someone seeks to sue a follower of Jesus in court, and the reasons aren't stated, and they sue for one's shirt (undergarment), Jesus urges his followers to go further and give them the robe as well. But the social custom is more particular here, as it was in the previous example: a person's robe was used both as a cover and a sleeping blanket, but it was prohibited to take such from an Israelite for any length of time (cf. Exod 22:26 – 27; Deut 24:12 – 13). So the person suing goes for what is legal (a shirt), but Jesus goes further by urging his followers to relinquish their rights to a robe. This would deprive the person of standard comforts and provision. What Jesus says, at face value, is to strip in front of the person as a means of exhibiting radical distance from social custom. Jesus experienced this too (cf. Matt 27:35).

"If anyone forces you to go one mile …": Once again, a social custom is at work. Roman soldiers had the legal rights to requisition occupied people into compulsory work to aid the Roman military. So we are to imagine a Roman soldier approaching one of Jesus' followers, demanding transportation for a mile; Jesus' radical go-beyond-their-expectations response is to help for a second mile. This approach to a Roman demand, so unlike the violent-minded Zealots, subverts the powerful. This may all have been parodied later by Jesus when he entered Jerusalem on a mule with his followers throwing down their robes—all of this mocking the Roman victory march.[10]

"The one who asks you …": Jesus urges his followers to give to those beggars who ask for something, and there is no indication here of exacting payment back or even at interest.

---

10. An instance connected to Jesus is Matt 27:32; Mark 15:21.

"The one who wants to borrow from you …": Once again, in parallel fashion, Jesus urges his followers not to demand back what one loans to another. The operative category is avoiding the world of the court and of retribution or payment for offenses. Jesus subverts that system by creating a system of grace, compassion, and love because he seeks to create a culture of generosity. He operates in a kingdom world and reveals an Ethic from Beyond.

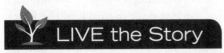

LIVE the Story

Our antithesis on the *lex talionis* is a watershed when it comes to how to live out the Sermon on the Mount. Luther contended famously that the problem here is the failure to "to distinguish properly between the secular and the spiritual, between the kingdom of Christ and the kingdom of the world."[11] Some of the saddest lines I have ever read by a Christian, let alone one of Luther's status, are these:

> [In speaking of "holy martyrs" …] When they were called to arms even by infidel emperors and lords, they went to war. In all good conscience they slashed and killed, in this respect there was no difference between Christians and heathen. Yet they did not sin against this text. For they were not doing this as Christians, for their own persons, but as obedient members and subjects, under obligation to a secular person and authority. But in areas where you are free and without any obligation to such a secular authority, you have a different rule, since you are a different person.[12]

Utter nonsense. Another Lutheran responds: "But this distinction between a private person and bearer of an office as normative for my behavior is foreign to Jesus.… 'Private' and 'official' spheres are all completely subject to Jesus' command. The word of Jesus claimed them undividedly." Is this realistic? Of course Jesus knows the reality of sin and "Jesus calls evil evil and that is just why he speaks to his disciples in this way."[13] This command, as Bonhoeffer routinely observes, is anchored in the cross that Jesus himself bore. This is why Bonhoeffer can also say, "Only those who there, in the cross of Jesus, find faith in the victory over evil can obey his command."[14]

One of the main thrusts of the ethic of Jesus is the radicalization of an ethic so that we live consistently, from the so-called "private" to the "public" spheres. There is for Jesus no distinction between a secular life and spiritual

---

11. Luther, *Sermon on the Mount*, 105.
12. Ibid., 110.
13. Bonhoeffer, *Discipleship*, 134–35.
14. Ibid., 136.

life: we are always to follow him. His ethic is an Ethic from Beyond. But others, in words not so wrongheaded as Luther's, have continued Luther's personal vs. public or spiritual vs. secular distinction when it comes to ethics.[15]

Thus, Peter Craigie, himself a Mennonite, writes: "Contrast the different spirit in the ... teaching of Jesus, *though the context there has to do with personal behavior and attitudes and not with the courts of law*."[16] Oddly, the *lex talionis* antithesis is a public (not private) framework, and that is what Jesus is stopping. Although he is exploring rather than expressing his view dogmatically, Dale Allison approaches this Lutheran view when he says Jesus is "speaking about interpersonal relations and declaring that it is illegitimate for his followers to apply the *lex talionis* to their private problems."[17] And I would add: "and to their public problems as well." Along the same line Charles Quarles can somehow manage to convince himself of this: "No evidence suggests that Jesus intended to contradict the *lex talionis* of the Mosaic law."[18] Let the word be as rugged as it really is; its ruggedness carries its rhetorical power to call his disciples into the kingdom where retaliation will end.

The question that confronts any serious reading of the Sermon on the Mount is this: Would Jesus have seen a difference between a kingdom ethic for his followers in their so-called private life but a different ethic in public? I doubt it. Why? Because Jesus' Messianic Ethic, an ethic for his community of followers, is an Ethic from Above and Beyond. The question every reader of the Sermon must ask is this: *Does that world begin now, or does it begin now in private but not in public, or does it begin now for his followers in both private and to the degree possible in the public realm as well?*

Show No Mercy

Perhaps the most neglected element in interpreting this text is what is said in Deuteronomy 19:21: "*Show no pity*: life for life, eye for eye, tooth for tooth, hand for hand, foot for foot" (italics added). The judicial posture in the Torah for the *lex talionis* was this: retribution was not an option. Israelites soon converted the equal retribution dimension of this law into financial fines, but justice was *required*, and the requirement was "show no pity" even if the punishment was converted into economic value. What a person has done wrong needs to be undone by doing that same wrong back to them in order to balance the social scale of justice.

But Jesus' posture is the opposite, and it cannot be seen as a form of

---

15. Calvin's form of the two-realms thinking (Christ vs. Caesar) is not as severe as Luther's; see Calvin, *Harmony of the Gospels*, 1:193 – 95; Hagner, *Matthew 1 – 13*, 131 – 32; Turner, *Matthew*, 174.

16. P. Craigie, *The Book of Deuteronomy* (Grand Rapids: Eerdmans, 1976), 270 n. 21.

17. Allison, *Sermon on the Mount*, 93.

18. Quarles, *Sermon on the Mount*, 146.

exaggeration. His revolutionary preface, in effect, to the *lex talionis* was: "Show mercy." While he doesn't say this explicitly when he quotes the Old Testament, his own words that form the antithesis are clearly a variant of "show mercy": "Do not resist an evil person." Instead of prosecution and instead of exacting retribution to redress the imbalance of justice, Jesus forms another way: *show mercy and unravel the system of retribution that pervades our society.*

The Orthodox Jewish commentator on the Sermon on the Mount, Pinchas Lapide, toward the end of his book that develops what he calls a theo-politics of loving small steps, finds in these words of Jesus six pillars that can help each of us reshape our culture from hate toward love: (1) Jesus is a realist who knows a world of evil; (2) Jesus has a faith that humans can change; (3) Jesus humanizes haters and their hatred; (4) Jesus calls us to imitate God; (5) Jesus knows this is a battle to fight; and (6) this theo-politics moves in small steps:

> *Away* from conflict, *toward* empathy;
> *Away* from confrontation, *toward* cooperation;
> *Away* from dogmatic monologue, *toward* a dialogue of equals.[19]

Going even further, Glen Stassen, ethics professor at Fuller Seminary, proposes ten steps in just peacemaking. They are worth proposing here because they show how the ethic of Jesus can foster peace on a global scale: (1) support nonviolent action; (2) take independent initiatives to reduce threat; (3) use cooperative conflict resolution; (4) acknowledge responsibility for conflict and injustice; seek repentance and forgiveness; (5) promote democracy, human rights, and religious liberty; (6) foster just and sustainable economic development; (7) work with emerging cooperative forces in the international system; (8) strengthen the United Nations and international organizations; (9) reduce offensive weapons and weapons trade; (10) encourage grassroots peacemaking groups and voluntary associations.[20]

Pacifism?

It is hard for me to square any Christian military posture toward "our enemies" — the kind of label unworthy for the follower of Jesus — with what Jesus both performed in his last week and what he teaches here (as well as at Matt 26:52). Prior to Constantine, apart from a few exceptions, Christians refused to participate in the military.[21] No theologian or leader supported participation in the military. Their nonparticipation was no ethic of resigna-

---

19. Lapide, *Sermon on the Mount*, 127.
20. Stassen and Gushee, *Kingdom Ethics*, 170–73.
21. For an excellent sourcebook, see R. J. Sider, ed., *The Early Church on Killing* (Grand Rapids: Baker Academic, 2012).

tion to Rome's might but an ethic of resistance in the form of creating an alternative political society, the church. Beside their obvious denunciation of the pervasive presence of idols and false religions in that military, the earliest followers of Jesus did not enter the military because they believingly thought Jesus meant business in the passage under discussion. The issue for the pre-Constantine church was killing those made in God's image.

They would have known that Jesus' posture was the exact opposite of the Zealots, who believed God's will for the Land could come through violence. Jesus spoke both into that viewpoint and against it when he summoned his followers to be peacemakers (5:9).[22] The apostles tell us how Jesus' words were understood, and they read Jesus' words in a much more literal way than do many today. Thus, 1 Peter 2:21 reveals a radical nonviolent form of resistance: "To this you were called, because Christ suffered for you, leaving you an example, that you should follow in his steps." And Paul in Romans 12:21 speaks about the outcome of such a posture toward those who act unjustly: "Do not be overcome by evil, but overcome evil with good."

One of the themes of the Sermon is refusing complicity with a system that assumes corruption. Jesus urges his followers to end their complicity. So the "just-war theory" breaks down the words of Jesus because it too is a blatant compromise and is overtly complicit in the ways of violence. Both Augustine and Calvin, who each helped shape the just-war theory, admitted that Jesus is against revenge at the *personal* level. That admission undermines their just-war theory. Jesus knows of no distinction between what he wants his followers to do and what society should do. Society may be corrupt, but his posture is to resist corruption by forming an alternative kingdom community rather than become complicit in our fallen world. Jesus' Messianic Ethic from Beyond may create ambivalence and even a feeling of anarchy over against the state, but the response of the followers of Jesus to such is not to capitulate or to moderate but to follow the Crucified One.

Pacifism isn't quietism or withdrawal or inactivity, and it isn't simple submission. Pacifism's root is connected to the peacemaking beatitude, rooted in love and expressed when the follower of Jesus actively *seeks* peace. Pacifism isn't a lack of interest or noninvolvement, but the hard work of seeking peace. Pacifism is nonviolent resistance, not nonresistance. What Jesus teaches his followers to do illustrates the sort of pacifism he advocates: turn the other cheek, surrender even more clothing, go the extra mile, lend and do

---

22. See the comments and bibliography at 5:9. Also Luz, *Matthew 1 – 7*, 277 – 78, who mentions the Waldensians, St. Francis, the followers of Wycliffe, Erasmus, the Anabaptists, Quakers, Tolstoy, Albert Schweitzer, and the now-growing Christian pacifists. He observes that "they are in agreement with the overwhelming witness of the ancient church."

not charge interest or require a payment back. Hardly the stuff of the inactive. These acts subvert the Roman system.

The dominating idea here is that following Jesus matters above everything else. My own posture is one of pacifism, and here is the logic that I find compelling:

> I cannot kill a non-Christian, for whom Christ has died and to whom I am called to preach the gospel, for the state; that would be rendering to Caesar what is God's and deconstruct the kingdom mission.
>
> I cannot kill a fellow Christian for the state; that would be rendering to Caesar what is God's. My first allegiance is to the King and to his kingdom people.
>
> I am called to cooperate with the state to the degree it is consistent with the kingdom; I cannot in good conscience cooperate with the state when it is inconsistent with the kingdom; that would be to render to Caesar what is God's.
>
> I cannot ask in the first instance if this is practicable. I am to ask in the first instance what it means to follow Jesus.

The Jesus Creed, which forms the bedrock for Jesus' statement about the *lex talionis*, is radical beyond calculation: it calls us to love both the neighbor and the enemy. Love or violence are the two options.

The cross reveals how God himself deals with injustice and violence; by absorbing and bearing it away, the sin is removed and the mask of injustice stripped away to reveal injustice. It was through the cross that Jesus was vindicated in resurrection and exaltation, and that same promise is given to his followers in Mark 8:34–9:1.

What Happens with Virtue Ethics?

One's posture when it comes to the way Jesus did ethics matters immensely in reading the Sermon. In particular, while not as bald-faced as one finds in Luther, virtue ethicists ground Jesus' Sermon in character formation. In other words, sometimes what Jesus *says* is not what we are to *do*; rather, he is casting forth a moral vision, using what Talbert calls a "verbal icon" through which we are to see the world differently by becoming new people. I agree: the issue is which virtue is being formed.

Our passage then becomes a classic location for virtue ethics and the Anabaptist or kingdom vision to part ways. "There may be occasions when love of one's neighbor trumps one's commitment to non-retaliation," Talbert observes.[23] When? "Confronted by an evildoer, the disciple, whose character

---

23. Talbert, *Reading the Sermon on the Mount*, 92.

incorporates both love of the neighbor and non-retaliation but privileges the former as more basic, would likely respond if necessary to defend, protect, and vindicate the neighbor." He then asks what Jesus would have taught had the good Samaritan come upon the traveling man as he was being beaten and robbed. Would he have refrained from violence, or would he have taken physical steps to stop the violence? Talbert contends confidently, on the basis of virtue ethics, that Jesus would have cuffed the men, chased them away, and tended to the abused man. Talbert observes that it is from such considerations that the just-war theory emerges.

This is a species of mitigating the words of Jesus, for the kingdom character of the Crucified/Resurrected One knew a different way. I contend that it is hard to know how to respond when what Jesus says is not what is to be done, but instead *what Jesus would have said* or what Jesus *means on the basis of a hierarchy of values,* values that are not mentioned in this text. Now we cannot expect Jesus to construct a casuistry of options and actions, but the point of Jesus here is to *avoid violence, absorb injustice,* and *live in light of what the kingdom is like* in spite of what the world is like now. Had Jesus followed Talbert's advice, he would have encouraged Peter to use the sword in Gethsemane. He didn't, and so we shouldn't.

What about the Old Testament and War?

Let us ask ourselves this question in a more pointed way: Was *Jesus* not aware of the Old Testament war and *lex talionis* narratives when he said what he said in this (and the next) text? Indeed he was, which again is precisely the point: he did, and he still said what he said. Yes, one can justify war by appealing to the Old Testament. It's all set out in gory detail with divine justification. But this begs the question of how to read the Bible.

What the Bible's Story does is this: it takes us from Moses to Christ and says, "Now, follow Jesus." It doesn't place Christ as an equal alongside Moses or Elijah, which was Peter's temptation in Matthew 17. No, it says, "Listen to him!" Jesus is the one to whom we listen, and that means the *lex talionis* at work in the Torah and which prompted Israel's wars has been set into a new cruciform reality. The wars of Israel say nothing to the follower of Jesus about how to deal with enemies. Again, "Listen to him" are the words of the Father to Peter and to us.

Maddeningly Impractical

Pacifists have been criticized as maddeningly impractical. "How," many ask, "can such a posture by followers of Jesus be realistic in our world?" Some have quipped in clever rhetoric that the problem with Tolstoy's and Ghandi's idealism was not that they didn't live it out but that they didn't live in the 1930s and 1940s in Germany. I find the quip disrespectful of the radical lifestyle of each. Both would have been executed by Hitler, which is just the point. Unrealistic? The early Bonhoeffer talks back: "It is the great mistake of a false Protestant ethic to assume that loving Christ can be the same as loving one's native country, or friendship or profession, that the better righteousness and justitia civilis are the same."[24]

Realism reveals the problem: Why would a follower of Jesus be driven by what is "realistic"? Luther drove this viewpoint to an absurdity when he said, "Personal safety and private property would be impossible, and finally the social order would collapse."[25] Perhaps collapsing the system was inherent to the kingdom vision Jesus had! But by driving these texts over the wedge of the public vs. the private or Christ vs. Caesar, Luther doesn't solve this problem he finds. The impracticality of these verses is not resolved in the Lutheran false dichotomy of Caesar vs. Christ. In fact, discipleship is crushed.

The words of Jesus stand up on the page of the Bible we are reading. They stare at us in their rugged vision. The end of the Sermon makes it clear that Jesus expects his followers to take up his words and live them out regardless of the cost. I know of no alternative. Take them or leave them, is what I say to myself.

I've been asked time and time again these two questions: Do you think the entire country should demilitarize? (What the country does is the country's business. As a citizen I advocate following Jesus.) What about a person who invades your home? (I'd use force to the point of not murdering him.) These two questions get wrapped up in this question: Isn't this incredibly naïve or maddeningly impractical? No and Yes. No, this is not naïve. This is kingdom behavior in the here and now. Yes, this is impractical because Jesus doesn't spell things out. Perhaps that is Jesus' point. Dale Allison's expression emerges once again: Jesus summons us here to live in our world with the kingdom's "moral imagination." Those expressions of Allison's are not so much impractical as they are countercultural. And that, reader, is the point of the Sermon on the Mount over and over. The kingdom is amazingly practical.

Amazingly Practical

Perhaps you have a story to tell of resisting violence with grace or mercy or love or kindness. Those who have experienced such do have a story to tell. One of the most active nonviolent resisters today is a young man in Western Australia named Jarrod McKenna, and he wrote the following story in

---

24. Bonhoeffer, *Discipleship*, 144.
25. Luther, *Sermon on the Mount*, 107.

response to a question I asked him: "How did you get to where you are today in your commitment to nonviolent resistance?" If this story doesn't show the power of creative nonviolent resistance, I don't know what does.[26]

MUGGED by Jesus
By Jarrod McKenna

I was eighteen. It was my first year in University, studying Fine Arts. I was coming back on the train and I had been reading Martin Luther King Jr. for the first time. I got off at Warwick train station. I was walking over the overpass bridge away from the train station and in my typical ADD dreamland state, I thought of Dr. King's talk of the nonviolent resistance of the early Christians. I had hardly noticed the big guy in a dark tracksuit with his sleeves rolled up walking toward me.

Still a couple of meters off, he loudly grunted something at me. I missed what he said. A little shocked to have Jarrod's dream world interrupted, I quickly tried to piece together what he had said ... I definitely heard the word "money." Thinking he asked for a few bucks to catch the train, I got my wallet out.

Bad move.

Lunging at me with his fist clenched and other hand reaching for something in his pocket, he yelled, "Give me your money!" (He actually said a sentence along these lines only with words you can't say in front of your mum in the mix.) At that point a number of things went through my head (including some other words you can't say in front of your mum).

A number of things flashed through my head that years later Walter Wink would put into words for me with such clarity:

> *The Split option.* [Flight] The only thing about running was that I was wearing my backpack with all my art equipment in it. If I ran, this would make my getaway at best a fast waddle. Not to mention ... he's huge! (Not hard compared to my towering 5.7 ft stature).

> *The Hit option.* [Fight] Only (as I mentioned earlier) ... he's huge! Maybe I could get one cheap shot and if he wants to have kids, he'll have to adopt. More likely, I take a shot at him, then he's unaffected, like a machine in a Terminator movie, then transforms me into a red puddle formerly known as Jarrod.

---

26. Jarrod sent this to me 2/23/2011. I have slightly reduced it with Jarrod's permission.

I joke about it now, but there was nothing funny at the time. If you've ever been mugged or held up or threatened violently, you know the shock can be numbing. What next flashed through my head short-circuited my panic and crazy split-second plans of "split" or "hit." The words of Jesus that Martin Luther King Jr. had been experimenting with: "You have heard that it was said, 'Eye for eye, and tooth for tooth.' But I tell you. . . ."

The flash of those words in my imagination felt like warm oil over my head with a tangible sense of this is how God has related to me. For the first time in the situation I felt grounded. I had already gotten out my wallet, so I reached in and gave him what I had, which was only ten dollars; you'd think he'd have known better than to choose an art student as his victim.

I'm still not sure why, but I didn't simply hand over the money, I stuck out my hand and said, "I'm Jarrod."

Wide-eyed and with mouth open, he grabbed my hand and grunted, "James!"

Surprised and confused I said, "No, Jarrod."

To which he with a surprise to match mine said, "No. I'm James."

"Oh," I said.

There was an awkward pause. This was by far the weirdest passing of the peace I'd been involved with.

I noticed his arm. The bruising ran all along it, interrupted only by the scarring that rivaled a pincushion. James's arm was offered to me like an icon in an Orthodox worship service to contemplate the depth of his pain and all the desperate attempts to escape it. He couldn't have been more than a couple of years older than me. The next thing that hit me was the stench. Like stale urine mixed with cigarettes. As we stood on the bridge suspended above the freeway, James launched into his life story at a pace to rival the cars passing below.

His words seemed to overtake each other, then cut each other off. He said he was sorry to be doing this to me, that he was in a bad way. He'd been doing really well, he was on the naltrexene program and getting off the stuff, but then his mum kicked him out of home again and now he was back on the streets.

I asked him to come back to my house and eat and have a shower, get a change of clothes. I'd try to find him a new place to stay.

Another awkward pause.

Then, through the middle of us both on the bridge darted a young woman in another black tracksuit, with a bag under her arm, yelling,

"Go! Go! We gotta go!" At the time I didn't know if she'd been hassled by security guards at the train station or if she had stolen the bag, but it was clear that she knew James and she wanted to get out of there, fast.

"Wait, James, before you go ..." I shuffled in my backpack past my art gear and textbooks to reach in and grab the little New Testament I always carried with me. "It's got my name and number in it if you ever change your mind about a place to stay."

For the first time since I was staring at this big guy's fist, it got ugly again. James got right up in my face and started yelling:

"What do I want a Bible for—I'm going to hell!"

His face contorted with an anger that had an intensity that explained his arm. Without even thinking, I found myself saying, "James, we're all going to hell. That's why Jesus came." Now, I know that statement rates low on the theological "wow" scale (and maybe embarrassingly high on the theological cringe factor), but it's what I said. What happened next, I think, was one of the weirdest experiences of my life. This big guy who, only moments earlier was ready to beat me up (if not worse), just started crying. I'm not talking one tear sad movie crying. He burst out crying. Like a little kid does. Suddenly this pain that was so visible in his anger, on his scarred arms and in his situation, seemed to burst like a floodgate at the news of God's love for him.

As this big guy stood there crying, I honestly didn't know what to do. In the same way that my response had put him off balance, James's tears now totally threw me. I just stood there while his head hung, his shoulders heaved and he wept.

James didn't say anything more to me. He snorted to try to stop the snot and tears, and then he grabbed the Bible and started running.

After a few paces he turned, looked me in the eye, waved the Bible at me and nodded. Then he kept running.

I stood a long moment on the bridge, stunned. Then I picked up my bag, a bit dazed and continued along the overpass. As I neared the end of the bridge I saw [his female accomplice] jump into an already crowded beaten up maroon VK Holden Commodore sedan. As she got in she yelled over the music to the others, "I got a bag."

James run up and as he got in the car he yelled over the music, "I ... I got a Bible!?!" They piled in and drove off, and I walked right past my bus stop.

I just kept walking.

James taught me that there is nothing that shows the world what

God is like more clearly than when we love our enemies. Despite the reality that throughout the New Testament the cross is not only how God saves us, it is how we witness to that salvation. I'm aware that "enemy love" still scandalizes many a fundamentalist and liberal alike. Who wants a Savior who loves the enemies we want to kill? Who wants to witness to the God whose love falls like rain on the just and the unjust alike? Who wants a God who longs to heal those who have hurt us so they hurt no more? Who wants a Christ who comes to us in the pain we want to run from?

CHAPTER 10

Matthew 5:43 – 48

 LISTEN to the Story

43"You have heard that it was said, 'Love your neighbor and hate your enemy.' 44But I tell you, love your enemies and pray for those who persecute you, 45that you may be children of your Father in heaven. He causes his sun to rise on the evil and the good, and sends rain on the righteous and the unrighteous. 46If you love those who love you, what reward will you get? Are not even the tax collectors doing that? 47And if you greet only your own people, what are you doing more than others? Do not even pagans do that? 48Be perfect, therefore, as your heavenly Father is perfect."

Listening to the text in the Story: Leviticus 19:18; Matthew 22:34 – 40; Luke 10:27; Galatians 5:14; Romans 12:19; 13:9; James 2:8.

One can dip into any number of moments in the Story of Jesus and observe that Leviticus 19:18, the second half of what I call the "Jesus Creed," played a formative role for Jesus. Thus, when Jesus was asked which of the (613) commandments was the greatest, his response was the combination of the Shema (Deut 6:4 – 9) with love of neighbor (Lev 19:18). But the questioner wanted more, so he pressed Jesus with a question: "Who is my neighbor?" Jesus responded by illustrating that love for God must be attended by love for the (wounded/dying) neighbor (Luke 10:25 – 37).

But the law was not limited to the 613. Alongside them, at readied attention, stood innumerable *halakhic* rulings, like the list of forty items that constituted "work" so that one would know how to keep the Sabbath, one of the 613. This discussion in Matthew 15:1 – 20 about hand purity reflects an additional ruling that needed to be observed in order to be considered observant. Jesus calls these *halakhic* rulings "heavy ... burdens" (23:4), and Peter observes that the weight of the Torah had become burdensome (Acts 15:10).

In that context Jesus stepped in to provide nothing short of a radical hermeneutical guide for proper observance of the Torah: love God and love others. This hermeneutic of Jesus, which Matthew will tell us later is the double hook from which hang all the Torah and the Prophets (22:34–40), is not a criticism of the Torah itself but of what the Torah had become: fertile ground for multiplying commandments. Jesus' reduction of the 613 (plus rulings) to two—love God, love neighbor—gave his disciples a divine guide for life.

That radical hermeneutic is given a new life by Jesus in our passage (5:43–48) to put forward one of the most radical of Jesus' moral directives: "love your enemies." The Story of Israel tended in differing directions when it came to Gentiles (*gôyim*).[1] Sometimes they were distanced from the holy community and labeled as "others" (Gen 10; 17:20; 1 Sam 8:5, 20), idolaters (Deut 12:30; 1 Kgs 11:1–4; Isa 44), and unclean/inferior (temple restriction; cf. Josephus, *Jewish War* 1.152, 354), and they were to be avoided (cf. Deut 7; Ezra 9). But alongside "othering," some urged Jews to see that the Gentiles were neighbors to be treated with civility (cf. Philo, *Life of Moses* 1:23–24; Josephus, *Antiquities* 2:412–16), and they were a future part of God's all-embracing kingdom (Sir 36:11–17; *Sibylline Oracles* 5:493–500). Sometimes the distancing got fierce and they became "enemies." Thus, the *Kittim*, a code word for the Romans, of the Dead Sea Scrolls were part of the historical context for Jesus. I give but one example, from the opening column in the famous "War Scroll" between the Essenes of Qumran and the Kittim (1QM 1:9–11):

> On the day when the Kittim fall there shall be a battle and horrible carnage before the God of Israel, for it is a day appointed by Him from ancient times as a battle of annihilation for the Sons of Darkness. On that day the congregation of the gods and the Congregation of men shall engage one another, resulting in great carnage. The Sons of Light and the forces of Darkness shall fight together to show the strength of God with the roar of a great multitude and the shout of gods and men; a day of disaster.

Jews knew who they were; they were God's elect people. Because they were the elect, they knew where other people stood, and the Gentiles were those "others"; whether they were sinners, neighbors, or enemies in the face of Rome, they were still others. Those who thought of Gentiles as enemies were about to be turned inside out in the kingdom game Jesus played. He was about to reveal an Ethic from (so far) Beyond that it would boggle some of his audience.

---

1. G. Gilbert, "Gentiles, Jewish Attitudes toward," *EDEJ*, 670–73.

EXPLAIN the Story

This passage is the summary antithesis that brings into crystallization the essential feature of the ethic of Jesus: the centrality of love. Matthew 5:17–20 established the categories: Jesus' ethic flows out of the Torah and the Prophets without setting either aside; yet his ethic also deepens and sharpens both Torah and Prophets. His deepening and sharpening were in the direction of loving God and loving others; hence, the surpassing righteousness of 5:20 is a kaleidoscope revealing in separate views the Jesus Creed of loving God and loving others, being "perfect" in 5:48, and the Golden Rule of 7:12.

The present passage cites an explicit Old Testament text (Lev 19:18) and then adds something implied by some (not all) of Jesus' contemporaries: "and hate your enemy." Following this "thesis," Jesus forms an antithesis: first, he gives his prescribed behavior (5:44—love your enemies, pray for your persecutors); second, he grounds the love-your-enemy command in the universal love of God for all humans (5:45). Third, Jesus interrogates his followers by pushing back against an ethnic-family-only kind of love. That sort of biased love makes them no different than the tax collectors and Gentiles (5:46–47). Finally, he offers a summary statement: "Be perfect." But this summary makes sense only by perceiving the logic of 5:44–45: as God cares for all, so they are to love all; as God is perfect, so they are to be perfect (5:48).

The Misunderstood Love-of-Neighbor Command

There is no evidence from the Jewish world that anyone quoted—verbatim quotation—Leviticus 19:18 from the time of Moses to the time of Jesus. But Jesus intentionally and provocatively clasped their (neglected) Torah ("love your neighbor")[2] to their disposition toward others ("hate your enemy"). This is deconstruction. Leviticus 19:18 was elevated to cardinal, principal status by Jesus, and the verse became fundamental to the ethic of Paul and James as well as to John and to a lesser degree Peter.[3]

Where Jesus got "and hate your enemy" is unclear, and perhaps David Garland is right in minimizing it a bit by contending it means "place the

---

2. The word "neighbor" means one's fellow human being with whom one has some kind of relationship: next-door neighbor, fellow townsperson, person in the adjacent village, government official who works in your community, etc. But the term was usually exclusively viewed as one's fellow Jewish "compatriot." Hence, "neighbor" often lacked any sense of diversity. This is where Jesus alters the meaning of the term.

3. Davies and Allison, *Matthew*, 1:551–52, who say, "Despite all the parallels just listed, the succinct, arresting imperative, 'Love your enemies,' is undoubtedly the invention of Jesus' own mind, and it stands out as fresh and unforgettable."

neighbor first and the enemy second."[4] Perhaps, but it is more important to observe that hating your enemy was not typical of Judaism at the time of Jesus.[5] "Hate your enemy" is not found in the Old Testament, though there are glimpses of such an idea. Thus, one thinks of Psalm 139:21–22:

> Do I not hate those who hate you, LORD,
>   and abhor those who are in rebellion against you?
> I have nothing but hatred for them;
>   I count them my enemies.

Here is fertile ground for those so inclined to connect "love your [Israelite] neighbor" with "hate your enemy." If this is the text, or others like it, Jesus is once again summarizing Scriptures rather than quoting a particular one. Instead of quoting a text, many think Jesus here is contesting a group of fiercely zealous Jews of his day, the Qumran-dwelling Essenes. More than one text discovered among the Dead Sea Scrolls contains injunctions to hate the enemies, and that means the Romans. This set of lines tells the whole story:

> He is to teach them both to love all the Children of Light — each
> commensurate with his rightful place in the council of God — and to hate
> all the Children of Darkness, each commensurate with his guilt and the
> vengeance due him from God (1QS 1:9–11).

But one doesn't have to go to the Qumran dwellers to find the prejudicial love or ethnic bias that one finds in Jesus' opening "thesis." Loving those we like and hating those we don't like is as common as skin.

In other words, the term "neighbor" had taken on skin itself. As the scribe asked, "Who is my neighbor?" and as the Jewish culture embodied such distinctions in the temple courts in Jerusalem, so "neighbor" was seen by some to be "Jews of my ilk." While some would see "neighbor" to be any Jew, others would have restricted "neighbor" to "Jews of my particular sort," and one thinks here of Pharisees and Zealots and Essenes. Jews weren't and aren't alone in this endeavor.

The Understood Love-of-Enemy Command

Here's where Jesus was, then: "neighbor" was the Jewish neighbor, the "enemy" was Rome, and the "enemy" was dishing out persecution. Jesus counters with "love your enemies and pray for those who persecute you" (5:44). Hence the parallelism of Jesus' lines is addressing more or less the same command:

---

4. Garland, *Reading Matthew*, 76–77.
5. Lapide, *Sermon on the Mount*, 85–95.

Love your **enemy**
Pray for **those who persecute you.**[6]

The enemy is the persecutor; loving means at least praying for that person.

This passage hinges on the meaning of "love." Briefly we remind ourselves what was said above on 5:31 – 32. Love must be defined by how God loves. From God's behaviors we learn that love is a "rugged commitment to be *with* someone as someone who is *for* that person's good and to love them *unto* God's formative purpose." The eternal relations within the Trinity, commonly called the *perichoresis,* or mutual indwelling and interpenetration, form the eternal foundations for love, and God's covenant relationship and commitment to Israel reveals that God is one who enters into relationship (presence) as the God who is for Israel's good.

With that as our understanding of love, what Jesus says takes on a far more radical meaning. Jesus commands his followers to commit themselves to be *with* their enemies, which involves proximity and attentiveness, and to be the sort of person who longs *for* and works *for* the good of the enemy. Because love cannot be reduced to "toleration," working for the good of another, including one's enemies, means striving for them *to become the sort of person God wants them to be.* If love and praying are parallel expressions, and if love means what we have described, then praying for those who persecute is not a cute formula designed to get us over the hump of bad feelings or resentment but the concrete behavior of going to God in the hope of reconciliation, love, justice, peace, and a kingdom society.

The radicality of Jesus' words is matched by their frequency of both quotation and allusion in the early church. Jesus himself forgives enemy-persecutors at the cross (Luke 23:34); Stephen does the same (Acts 7:60); Paul counsels the same response (Rom 12:14; 1 Cor 4:12 – 13; 1 Thess 5:15); and Peter, in the midst of the fire of suffering, urges his readers to follow Jesus (1 Pet 3:9). One has to think here of the *Martyrdom of Polycarp* and also Polycarp's letter *To the Philippians* 12:3, which has more than a notable connection to our antithesis:

> Pray for all the saints. *Pray* also *for* kings and powers and rulers, and for those who *persecute* and hate you, and for the *enemies* of the cross, in order that your fruit may be evident among all people, that you may be *perfect* in him. (italics added)

---

6. Notice Luke 6:27 – 28: "Love your enemies, do good to those who hate you, bless those who curse you, pray for those who mistreat you." And 6:35: "But love your enemies, do good to them, and lend to them without expecting to get anything back. Then your reward will be great, and you will be children of the Most High, because he is kind to the ungrateful and wicked."

Jesus' words were not considered clever by his followers; they were seen as a challenging demand, an Ethic from Beyond that mapped a new future for kingdom people.

Love of Enemy's Ultimate Ground

As the seventh beatitude promised his listeners that they would be the "children of God" for their peacemaking (5:9), so Jesus promises his followers they will be "children of your Father" if they act lovingly toward their enemies (5:45). The connection reveals Jesus' kingdom is marked by shalom: to love and pray for the enemy is the first step toward shalom.

Notice the reward Jesus has in mind: "that you may be children of your Father in heaven." If we take Luke 6:35 or Matthew 5:9 into consideration, "that" seems to indicate the consequence or the reward for love and prayer. Verses 46 – 47 clinch the case because Jesus himself shows he's thinking in terms of reward, and this idea leads us to see here an Ethic from Above. By using reward language, Jesus is telling us what God ultimately thinks.

Reward theology, which is found throughout Matthew's gospel,[7] can make Protestants nervous because it can suggest works righteousness, but the Jewish context, where "reward" and "merit" are the way Jesus' contemporaries customarily spoke — in rhetorical terms — of both the motive and benefit of salvation because they also spoke of sin as "debt," is far less squeamish about using the idea of reward.[8] Thus, I am inclined to think "that" is the reward, expressed as a promise. Put slightly differently, this is the rhetoric of motivation instead of a theology of merit. This idea, that we are to live in a way that reflects who God is, fills the pages of the New Testament (see 1 John 4:7 – 12).

God's love — seen in sun and rain — is showered on all humans, both "the evil and the good" or "the righteous and the unrighteous," which stands for the "observant" and "nonobservant."

Interrogation

Prejudicial love is no barometer of one's moral life. Prejudicial love is only a way of loving ourselves. To love enemies breaks through the self barrier into divine space. Each of the antitheses reflects what Jesus meant by surpassing righteousness in 5:20, but this one perhaps even more than the others.

Jesus trades in conventional stereotypes, the sort of stereotype that has become both politically incorrect in our world but also potentially damaging to the social status of others. The Gospels indicate that Jesus was a friend of

---

7. See 5:12, 46; 6:1 – 2, 5, 16; 10:41 – 42; 20:8.
8. On this, Anderson, *Sin: A History*.

tax collectors (Matt 11:19) and concerned with Gentiles (21:43; 28:19); thus, his behavior indicates that his rhetoric here is not prejudicial but an acceptable trope. His conventions connect prejudicial love with "tax collectors," the famous "tax farmer" known for abuse, and "pagans," who are used by Jesus as a way of showing one more time how ungodly people can be. These stereotypes function to highlight the unacceptable form of behavior one finds among those who consider themselves to be loving and godly. We are drawn back to the rhetorical plot of 5:43: those who claim to believe in the Bible's words to love their neighbor are all too often those who hate humans, and now Jesus shows that too many see love in ethnically exclusive terms. To love humans is to love all humans.

Summary Command

"Be perfect, therefore, as your heavenly Father is perfect," which completes 5:43–47 and is not simply a summary of 5:21–47, has suffered at the hands of its readers and interpreters and preachers, and it has flourished at the hands of the same. The ending of the chapter all hinges on one word—*perfect*.

Here are some of the options in the history of the church.[9] I begin with Luther, who sees in the word "perfection" not the rigors of the priests, monks, bishop, and pope, but in right doctrine shaping right behaviors, which means an "entire, whole, and undivided love."[10] Calvin sees "sheer and free generosity" and "exceptional goodness." He further observes that it "comes out better in Luke's words, *Be ye merciful....*"[11] Guelich focuses on a sense of "wholeness" as one's "qualitative standing before God and others," but this is neither moral nor legal perfection. In the end, for Guelich this is mostly about a restored and reconciled relationship with God.[12] Ulrich Luz observes two dimensions to "perfection": unity of the heart and total obedience, one subjective and the other objective.[13] Hagner writes: "they are to be like their Father in loving their enemies."[14] Keener observes "full allegiance to God's will in the Mosaic law as Jesus has interpreted it."[15] Strecker understands it as "the human realization of the totality of Jesus' instructions and hence identical with the demanded righteousness (5:20)" and "agape and righteousness" together.[16] N. T. Wright writes of "a character formed by overflowing

---

9. Luz, *Matthew 1–7*, 290–91, for a brief sketch.
10. Luther, *Sermon on the Mount*, 129.
11. Calvin, *Harmony of the Gospels*, 1:200.
12. Guelich, *Sermon on the Mount*, 255.
13. Luz, *Matthew 1–7*, 289–90.
14. Hagner, *Matthew 1–13*, 135. So also Stott, *Message*, 122; Talbert, *Reading the Sermon on the Mount*, 96–98.
15. Keener, *Matthew*, 205.
16. Strecker, *Sermon on the Mount*, 94.

generous love."[17] We could stop here and say a consensus is emerging that "perfect" is essentially love of others, but this needs to be established by evidence, not just a listing of major interpreters.

We begin with the word *perfect*. The Greek word *teleios*, in general, means "completion, perfect, mature, adult, full development." Jesus probably didn't speak Greek on this occasion, if he ever did, so we are tempted to reconstruct which Hebrew or Aramaic word Jesus would have used, and most land on *šālēm* or *tāmîm*, in which case the term would have meant "unblemished" or "whole."[18] Neither the term in general nor the reconstructed background end the questions about the meaning of the term.

Other passages help, so we turn to the rich young ruler episode (Matt 19:16–30). Jesus challenges the man by listing God's expectations, and the list Jesus uses conforms substantively with the antitheses of 5:21–48. Jesus refers to murder, adultery, divorce, swearing, turning the other cheek, loving your enemies, and then perfection. Matthew 19:16–22 refers to murder, adultery, *stealing*, bearing false witness (cf. swearing in Matt 5), *honoring parents*, loving your neighbor, and the call to perfection. This leads to the suggestion that "perfection" at least means something like "completely obedient to God (as especially revealed in the Torah)." The notion, then, is not the rigor of sinlessness but the rigor of utter devotion.

But commitment to the fullness of God's Torah does not quite satisfy most readers of 5:48 since there seems to be more involved. Perhaps the most neglected feature in probing the meaning of "perfect" is the word "as" (in "*as* your heavenly Father is perfect"). The word "as" connects "perfect" to God, revealing that ethics are derived from the character of God. There is yet another consideration: Luke 6:36 has "Be *merciful*, just as your Father is merciful." While it might be tempting to think Luke softened the word "perfect" to "merciful," I suggest that it is precisely here that we get the decisive clue as to what Matthew's text actually means, and it importantly connects to the flow of the paragraph in Matthew. A careful reading of 5:48 as the summary for 5:43–47, which focused on love or mercy for one's enemies because of God's love for all, cracks the rock open to find the diamond. The "perfect" of God in this text is his love for all. Thus, Jesus is urging his followers to be "perfect in love" or to "love completely" in the sense that they are to love not only fellow Jewish neighbors but also enemy neighbors. Jesus urged his disciples to love all because God loves all (5:45). Put together, then, an expanded paraphrase looks like this:

---

17. Wright, *After You Believe*, 109 (all in italics in original).
18. Gale, in *The Jewish Annotated New Testament*, at 5:48 (p. 12).

Be *perfect*, that is, love both your fellow Jewish neighbors and the Roman enemies in your midst ... as your Father makes the sun to rise and the rain to fall on all humans — Jews and Romans — so you are to be perfect in love *as* your Father is perfect in love.

The word "perfect," we conclude with the emerging consensus above, means "to love all humans, Jews and Romans, as neighbors."[19] This view of perfection lines up with Jesus' own hermeneutical approach to the Torah. He says in Matthew 22:34 – 40 that the Torah (and the Prophets) hang on two commands — to love God and to love one's neighbor as oneself. Perfection is to be the person who treats everyone as the neighbor, and this fulfills the entirety of God's will. This too is surpassing righteousness (5:17 – 20).

 LIVE the Story

Enemy love is not a command with a purpose — Jesus nowhere tells *why we are to love the enemy*. This not Jesus' strategy for conquering; it is not pragmatic. Nor is enemy love natural. This command, instead, confronts us with the one who is Lord and confronts from a world that is not yet ours: the kingdom. So asking about practicalities and practicability both miss the point. The Ethic from Beyond almost never bows to practicality.

There is only one approach to living the words of this text. *It begins when we confess who is our enemy* and *it ends when we learn to love them as our neighbor.* Until we name our enemies, we can't live these words of Jesus. Until we invite them into our home, or treat them as our neighbor, or love them as we love ourselves, we do not live these words. Until we regard them, dwell with them, and embrace them as God regards, dwells with, and embraces them, we cannot live these words of Jesus.

So we have to begin with this question: *Who is your enemy?*

I want now to dig under the surface of our claim to love our enemies, and in doing this digging I want to replicate for us what Jesus did for his contemporaries. You may remember that I suggested "love your neighbor" was used to justify "hating your enemies." In Jesus' world "enemies" were the Romans and "neighbors" were sympathetic Jews. They loved their neighbors in such a way that it expressed nonlove for the Romans.

We do the same thing today: many of us love our neighbors in such a way that it is at the same time a powerful damnation of others, and we do this

---

19. This view was common in the early church, as can be seen in Chromatius in ACCS: *Matthew*, 122.

damnation in the socially acceptable form of exclusion, denunciation, and libel. So here we go, and I would urge you to spend some time pondering alone right now, asking yourself the honest question who your enemy is.

We've all got enemies. I want to suggest America's enemy is the Muslim countries, and Christians have joined in. Evangelicalism's enemy is mainline Protestant liberals and Roman Catholics, and to a lesser degree, Eastern Orthodox. The enemy of the white person is the black person, and the enemy of the black person is the brown person. The enemy of the Christian Republican is the Democrat, and the enemy of the Christian Democrat is the Republican. The enemy of the morally conservative Christian is the homosexual. And I'm not even beginning to touch on particular enemies—the people you see daily, bump into on street corners in your community, see as you drive through your neighborhood—but those are enemies too. Those folks may be your real enemies, those who get your blood boiling and who get your emotions akilter, and those ... yes, those whom Jesus calls you to respond to in a radical new society called "kingdom". The Ethic from Beyond calls you beyond your comfort zone.

The question we must ask now is this: *How are you turning your enemies into your neighbors?* The implication of this enemy love passage is the elimination of enemies and the creation of a society marked by shalom because the kingdom is shalom. Jesus' fundamental strategy for enemies was to make them our neighbors, and the concrete form of Jesus' enemy love was to invite them to his table—so that at the table of Jesus we find typical "enemies" like tax collectors and sinners. One of the women who accompanied Jesus in his missional work was Joanna, wife of Chuza, the manager of Herod's household (Luke 8:1–4)—about as close to Rome as one could get in the Jewish world of Jesus. She not only shared the table, but she also shared the ministry with Jesus. And Jesus healed the Roman centurion's servant (Matt 8:5–13). In other words, Jesus reached out to those perceived to be Jewish "enemies." *What are you doing to make your enemies your neighbors?*

She Sat in the Back Right Corner

She sat in the back right corner of my class. Her name was "Mussaret." I was unsure what to think, if I tell the truth. She wore the hijab every day to class. She rarely spoke in class, and then only if asked, and what she had to say was intelligent and informed. About midway through the Jesus of Nazareth class I gave a long test on the facts of the Gospels, and her score was the highest in the class. On another assignment, on the theme of conversion in the Gospels, she wrote an exceptional paper. She then wrote one of the finest papers I ever got at North Park on Jesus' own self-perception. We had barely spoken beyond the customary "good mornings" and "hellos." So I asked her one time at the doorway as she left class if she could come by office to chat, but only if she wanted to. I told her I wanted to get to know her. I was concerned she might see this as marking her out as someone different, but she smiled back at me and said, "I'd love to. I have so many questions."

Mussaret came into my office before class one day and, after I stumbled out a few words, she said, "I'm a believer. My family doesn't know it. When I'm at home, I love to hide in my bedroom and read the Bible. When my parents ask me what I'm reading, I tell them 'Assignments for class.' But I want you to know that I love Jesus, I pray at the mosque to the God of Jesus, and while I look like a Muslim, I'm a follower of Jesus."

The conversation did not go in the direction I anticipated. I was a bit stunned, so we talked for thirty minutes about the Bible, about questions she had about the Christian faith — how to explain the Trinity — and then she and I walked to class together. I would not have known this about her had I not asked her to come to my office.

After class one day, when she was the last to leave, I asked her why she hid out to read her Bible. She said, "If my mother or father find out I'm a follower of Jesus, they'll send me to the Middle East to marry a true Muslim man and I'll never see America again. My mom told me that last week."

Can We Be Friends?

For three and a half years, two to three times a month, sometimes in the summer at a coffee shop near my home, I met with a young college student to talk life. He came into my office one day and said this: "I read your blog about homosexuality." Then he said nothing, so I tried to ease into the conversation by saying, "What did you think?" His response was this: "I'm a homosexual. It's a struggle for me." I expressed empathy with the best of my (not all that natural) powers, and then he said this, "Can we be friends?"

I said, "Of course."

He then told me how he had "discovered" he was gay, how he did everything he could — prayer, counseling, and the like — to get rid of it, but nothing was working. He admitted to a few casual relations that went too far, and then said again, "But we can be friends, right?" I said, "Yes, we can be friends. You are my neighbor."

For nearly four years we met. The subject of his homosexuality never came up again, and that was all right with me as long as it was all right with him. Occasionally he'd say something about his "struggle" or allude to it, but we met to talk about classes, about my own writing, about his desire to be a public schoolteacher, about his family, and about my family. When he graduated, he came up to me in his gown, hugged me, and said, "Thanks. You've been my friend."

I have never wondered why his question was asked—his question was: "Can we be friends?"

It's about Neighborliness

Enemy love is not a magic formula. It's not a trick. It's a posture toward every human being we meet. We are challenged in this passage to discern who it is whom we treat as enemies—those we claim to love but don't, those who never sit at table with us, those we label and libel—and to convert enemies into neighbors by simply extending love to them. Love is to treat others as we treat ourselves, and it is the rugged commitment to be with someone as someone who is for them in order to foster Christlikeness.

We can't do this by saying we will do it or saying we believe it, but by extending in concrete actions the love of God for all to others. We need to ask who our enemies are and get busy converting them into our neighbors. We will discover God is already there.

CHAPTER 11

Matthew 6:1–4

 ## LISTEN to the Story

¹"Be careful not to practice your righteousness[1] in front of others to be seen by them.[2] If you do, you will have no reward from your Father in heaven.

² "So when you give to the needy, do not announce it with trumpets, as the hypocrites[3] do in the synagogues and on the streets, to be honored by others. Truly I tell you, they have received their reward in full. ³But when you give to the needy, do not let your left hand know what your right hand is doing, ⁴so that your giving may be in secret. Then your Father, who sees what is done in secret, will reward you."

Listening to the text in the Story: Exodus 20:1–17; Leviticus 19; Deuteronomy 15

In some ways this passage forces the Bible's behaviors through the sieve of motivation. Thus, whether one looks at the Ten Commandments and the Book of the Covenant (Exod 20:1–17; Deut 5:1–21 and Exod 20:22–23:33), the tabernacle laws (Exod 25–31; 35–40), the Holiness Code or, perhaps better, the laws of Leviticus (Leviticus) and the various laws of Deuteronomy (Deut 12–26), Jesus' words drive his followers to see that they are to seek the pleasure of God and not the approval of others. Jesus calls his followers to direct engagement, much as Martin Buber did in *I and Thou*.

Direct engagement with God flows from the central theme of the Bible: Yahweh, the God of Israel, is the one and only God. This God has entered into a covenant relationship with Israel in order to bless the world through Israel, and this God ransomed Israel from slavery in Egypt, gave Israel its mode of being, led Israel to the Land, and sustained, protected, disciplined,

---

1. KNT: "practice your piety."
2. KNT: "mind you don't do it with an eye on the audience!"
3. KNT: "That's what people do when they're just play-acting."

and restored Israel. In Israel's Story, God is preeminent. Observance of the Torah is to be done before God. God-centered obedience glorifies God by making God preeminent.

But humans want to usurp the place of God, making themselves the center of the Story. This happens at two levels in our passage: on the one hand, humans have a proclivity to usurp the place of God by sitting in judgment on one another, which is why humans seek the approval of others; on the other hand, we seek the approval of others instead of the pleasure of God in our behaviors because, as it often turns out, they will give us what we want (whereas God gives us what is good and right).

EXPLAIN the Story

Matthew 6:1–18 contains three illustrations—almsgiving, prayer, and fasting. They comically and incisively illustrate the principles of Matthew 6:1. Thus, Matthew 6:1 is a thesis statement for how specific Torah-observance behaviors are to be done. The fundamental elements of 6:1's thesis look like this:

> God the Father engages you directly; you are to engage directly.
> God the Father knows what you are doing.
> God the Father is the judge; humans are not the judge.
> So do your acts of righteousness before God, not before others.
> Do these acts to be approved by God, not by humans.

Jesus develops these elements in 6:2–18. Each of the three illustrations has a tidy organization. We will observe that the Lord's Prayer (6:9–15) interrupts the flow, the theme—it concerns Gentiles and not hypocrites—and the organization (more of that in the commentary on 6:9–15). The organization of 6:1–18, excluding the Lord's Prayer, looks like this:

	Almsgiving	Prayer	Fasting
The observance	6:2a	6:5a	6:16a
Prohibition	6:2b	6:5b	6:16b
Intent	6:2c	6:5c	6:16c
Amen ... reward	6:2d	6:5d	6:16d
Alternative observance	6:3–4a	6:6a	6:17–18a
Father's reward	6:4b	6:6b	6:18b

Now for the almsgiving passage in 6:2–4:

The observance (6:2a):

"So when you give to the needy …"

Prohibition (6:2b):

"do not announce it with trumpets, as the hypocrites do in the synagogues and on the streets …"

Intent (6:2c):

"to be honored by others. "

Amen … reward (6:2d):

"Truly I tell you, they have received their reward in full."

Alternative observance (6:3–4a):

"But when you give to the needy, do not let your left hand know what your right hand is doing, so that your giving may be in secret."

Father's reward (6:4b):

"Then your Father, who sees what is done in secret, will reward you."

This structure provides focus: each passage concerns an observance, human intention, and a shift from human approval to divine approval. Each of the three pious acts (almsgiving, prayer, fasting) makes concrete the fundamental thematic statement of 6:1. To get the three pious acts right, we have to get the thematic statement right.

Thematic Statement (6:1)

Jesus' warning in "Be careful," a term he uses in addressing the Pharisees (16:6, 11, 12) and the wayward (7:15; 10:17), concerns "righteousness" (*dikaiosynē*). This term, which in Hebrew would have been ṣᵉdāqâ, can refer either to behaviors that conform to the Torah or to the paradigmatic act of the Torah at that time, giving alms.[4] In 6:1 "righteousness" refers to pious deeds that express Torah observance.

The warning is not to do these acts of righteousness "in front of others to be seen by them." Taken literally, or better, taken flat-footedly, Jesus would be saying that no pious deed could ever been done in public. But how then would one pray for one's family at Passover? Instead, Jesus here digs into *motivation* and *intention*,

---

4. This is why some Greek manuscripts, like L and Family 13, have "almsgiving" (*eleēmosynē*) instead of "righteousness" (*dikaiosynē*).

and what he says is as Jewish[5] as it is antihypocritical. Jesus pounds the hammer down on hypocrisy.[6] His instructions are designed not to create scrupulosity but to criticize the ostentatious behaviors of those who do things to be seen — like the Pharisees and teachers of the law (see Matt 23) — and to urge his followers to engage God and others directly. No one can improve on Chrysostom:[7]

> Alms may be given in the presence of others primarily to be seen by them, or
> They may be given in the presence of others but not to be seen, or
> They may be openly given in order to be seen but still not seen, or
> They may be given quietly and still seen.

Hence Jesus' next words: "If you do, you will have no reward from your Father in heaven." Jesus is not attracted to the most common form of ethical motivation in the Western world: altruism, or doing good things because of their intrinsic merit. Rather, this text operates with an Ethic from Above (Messiah Jesus reveals God's will) wrapped inside an Ethic from Beyond (the final judgment ushering in the kingdom). Modern ethical theorists often look down their nose at Jesus because he speaks of rewards, but a more biblical ethic faithfully pushes back. Since God is inherently meritorious as the all-glorious Perfect One, seeking reward from God is actually seeking something because of its inherent worth.

But such an approach fails to walk on the ground of Jesus. His appeal is not to the inherent goodness of an action but to God, what God says, and to God's people being listeners.[8] The reward involves living in God's world in God's way, and such living brings glory to God and blessing and eternal life. Jesus motivates his followers to do good things on the basis of reward often (cf. 5:12, 46; 10:41 – 42; 20:8). We need to remind ourselves again that reward language emerges from a world in which sin was seen as demerit and an observant act was seen as a merit. This is not works righteousness but framing moral behaviors before a God who is judge.[9]

The Observance (6:2a)

"So when you give to the needy. . . ." The first concrete kind of "righteousness" is almsgiving. The Torah itself ordered Israelites to care for the poor in the

---

5. See Rom 2:28 – 29, where Paul uses "inwardly," but it is the same words as found in Matthew 6:4 ("in secret"). And the *Letter of Aristeas* has: "Practice righteousness before all men, being mindful of God" (168). A good collection of later texts is Luz, *Matthew 1 – 7*, 300 – 301.

6. For a humanitarian study of this theme, W. I. Miller, *Faking It* (New York: Cambridge University Press, 2003).

7. ACCS: *Matthew*, 123.

8. McKnight, *Blue Parakeet*, 83 – 112.

9. Two important studies are E. P. Sanders, *Paul and Palestinian Judaism* (Philadelphia: Fortress, 1977), 107 – 47; Anderson, *Sin: A History*.

laws of gleaning (Lev 19:9 – 10), the Sabbath rules about harvesting (Exod 23:11), and the year of canceling debts (Deut 15). Prophets pound away at Israelite leaders for injustice toward the poor (Isa 3:14 – 15; Amos 8:4 – 6). A later text by Jesus ben Sirach virtually equates almsgiving with sacrifice (Sir 3:30). Following the New Testament period, the rabbis created piety around three nodes: Torah study, prayer, and almsgiving, and almsgiving was seen as the substitute of sacrifice once the temple was destroyed (cf. *Mishnah 'Abot* 1:2).[10] Almsgiving, at least in the minds of many, had become at the time of Jesus the singular act of piety. Schürer's famous work observes:

> A distinction was made between the weekly money-chest [*quppa*, goods and clothing], from which the local poor were supported regularly once a week, and the "plate" [*tamhuy*, food like bread, beans, and fruit], from which any needy person (especially strangers) could obtain a daily portion.

And a rule developed:

> Whoever had food for two meals was to take nothing from the "plate," and whoever had food for fourteen meals, nothing from the money-chest.[11]

Prohibition (6:2b)

Jesus: "do not announce it with trumpets, as the hypocrites do in the synagogues and on the streets." Interpretations boil down to two: blowing trumpets is either a physical activity (a trumpet blowing aloud or the shofar chest in the temple noisily clanging when someone's coins hit them as they entered the chest), or it is a figurative expression for acts done to be noticed by others. The former preaches, the latter is almost certainly accurate — not the least of which reasons is that Jesus' own words locate the almsgiving in synagogues and on streets and not in the temple (where trumpets were blown and the shofar chests were found).[12] Jesus hereby prohibits giving alms in a way that draws attention to the giver.

Jesus contrasts the right behavior of his disciples with the behavior of the "hypocrites." In the gospel of Matthew this term refers both to those whose behaviors were out of sync with the heart as well as to those behaviors that followed the false teaching of the Pharisees and teachers of the law; in addition,

---

10. See Kyong-Jin Lee, "Almsgiving," *EDEJ*, 324 – 25.

11. E. Schürer, *A History of the Jewish People in the Age of Jesus Christ (175 B.C – A.D. 135)* (rev. G. Vermes et al.; Edinburgh: T&T Clark, 1979), 2:437. For a full discussion, see J. Jeremias, *Jerusalem in the Time of Jesus* (Philadelphia: Fortress, 1975), 126 – 34.

12. See Davies and Allison, *Matthew*, 1:579; Turner, *Matthew*, 183.

there can be an element of self-deception on the part of the hypocrite. One simply needs to read Matthew 23 to see why the Pharisees and teachers of the law were accused of hypocrisy, and not all of it has to do with the inner versus outer inconsistency.[13] The word "hypocrite" refers often in the Greek world to the masked actor, and it is not impossible that Jesus picked up this word from the actors and actresses on the stage of Sepphoris's theater.[14] The form of deceit in our text appears to be both self-deceit and the attempt to deceive others.

Intent (6:2c)

The intent of the feigned behavior rises to the surface in each section in this passage. Thus, "to be honored" (6:2c) stands alongside "to be seen by others" (6:5c) and "to show others they are fasting" (6:16c). A world of revelation is at work in these intent statements. The act itself is not the problem, nor even its visibility, but instead the act itself is transformed into hypocrisy and self-preoccupation when the intent is attraction to oneself.

Amen ... Reward (6:2d)

These words, repeated in each paragraph, are damning words and are a form of incisive ironic indirection like the "least in the kingdom" in 5:19. Their reward will be what humans give the ostentatious givers in synagogues and on street corners.

Alternative Observance (6:3–4a)

Jesus both critiques and constructs. He goes once again to a metaphor: "But when you give to the needy, do not let your left hand know what your right hand is doing, so that your giving may be in secret." There is a variety of interpretations, with the left hand being the weaker and the right hand being the stronger, but most likely the metaphor refers to direct engagement with the one in need (or the God who commands compassion).[15]

How then does one give "in secret"? Luther's words get to the point of Jesus well: it is about "singleness of heart" and means that "the heart is not ostentatious or desirous of gaining honor and reputation from it, but is moved to contribute freely regardless of whether it makes an impression and gains the praise of the people or whether everyone despises and profanes it."[16] Per-

---

13. The best study on this is David E. Garland, *The Intention of Matthew 23* (Leiden: Brill, 1979), 91–123. See also Garland, *Reading Matthew*, 78.

14. On this, see R. A. Batey, *Jesus and the Forgotten City* (Grand Rapids: Baker, 2000), 83–103.

15. Allison, *Sermon on the Mount*, 110, which differs somewhat from his commentary (Davies and Allison, *Matthew*, 1:583); Luz, *Matthew 1–7*, 300.

16. Luther, *Sermon on the Mount*, 136.

haps the finest commentary on giving in secret is Matthew 25:31 – 46, where disciples are surprised at the judgment because they weren't aware that their actions were directed at Jesus.

Father's Reward (6:4b):

The final end of Jesus' combination of an Ethic from Above and Beyond is God's blessing: "Then your Father, who sees what is done in secret, will reward you." Perhaps the stunning words here are that God "sees what is done in secret." As Calvin puts it, "The theater of God is in the hidden corners."[17] We can infer that this "reward" is the same as the "blessing" of Matthew 5:3 – 12, the joy of entering into relationship with God that both sustains life, regardless of its conditions, and unleashes flourishing relationships.

 LIVE the Story

The essence of the principle for piety that Jesus develops has to do with the one before whom we stand when we do righteousness. Do we stand before others or do we stand before God? To develop a before-God-alone approach to piety we must become more introspective, asking "Why am I doing this?" and "Who is watching me?" We also need to ask about our pleasures: "What is it about this religious deed that brings me pleasure?"

The Language of Reward

C. S. Lewis chased the criticism of appealing to rewards in Christian ethics into the hinterlands in these memorable words:

> Indeed, if we consider the unblushing promises of reward and the staggering nature of rewards promised in the Gospels, it would seem that Our Lord finds our desires not too strong, but too weak. We are half-hearted creatures, fooling about with drink and sex and ambition when infinite joy is offered us, like an ignorant child who wants to go on making mud pies in a slum because he cannot imagine what is meant by the offer of a holiday at the sea. We are far too easily pleased.
>
> We must not be troubled by unbelievers when they say that this promise of reward makes the Christian life a mercenary affair. There are different kinds of rewards. There is the reward which has no natural connection with the things you do to earn it and it is quite foreign to the desires that ought to accompany those things. Money is not the natural reward of love; that is why we call a man a mercenary if he marries a woman for the

---

17. Calvin, *Harmony of the Gospels*, 1:202.

sake of her money. But marriage is the proper reward for a real lover, and he is not mercenary for desiring it.... The proper rewards are not simply tacked on to the activity itself in consummation. There is also a third case, which is more complicated. An enjoyment of Greek poetry is certainly a proper ... reward for learning Greek; but only those who have reached the stage of enjoying Greek poetry can tell from their own experience that this is so ... enjoyment creeps in upon the mere drudgery, and nobody could point to a day or an hour when the one ceased and the other began. But it is just insofar as he approaches the reward that he becomes able to desire it for its own sake; indeed, the power of so desiring it is itself a preliminary reward....

Now, if we are made for heaven, the desire for our proper place will be already in us.[18]

There is an important caution we must use in talking about rewards because it can suggest to some that we earn our way into the kingdom of God. But what the Jewish context above has shown, and what Lewis then develops, is that only a flat-footedness leads us to works righteousness when we see the word "reward." A fuller theology, one that balances the rhetoric of motivation, a theology of grace and demand, as well as a recognition of the thirst within us to live out what God is doing in us, leads us to a renewed embrace of the rhetoric of reward.

Thoughts on Hypocrisy

There is nothing peculiar about Judaism when it comes to hypocrisy, and Jesus' warnings to his contemporaries deserve our hearing today. There lurks in each of us a desire to be congratulated for our religious deeds. Social approval, whether it comes from an entire community (your local church) or from the religious authority (a pastor), *because it is religious*, functions as divine approval. As disapproval can be deeply wounding to a church member, so approval can be just as deeply rewarding. We must not forget the ecclesial power of disapproval and approval. While psychologists are teaching us that approval forms a healthy ego and a strong self-image, Jesus warns us of the danger of seeking the approval of others because of its intoxicating and self-deceiving powers.

What Jesus has in mind is not simply fakery, as if hypocrisy could be reduced to the alarming contrast of who we are and how we want to be seen. What Jesus aims at is the self-deceit that weaves itself into the fabric of a person's spirituality in which there is not only a notice-me approach, but also an

18. C. S. Lewis, *The Weight of Glory, and Other Addresses* (New York: HarperCollins, 2000), 26–27, 28, 29.

inability to know that the problem is present. This sense of hypocrisy ought to warn us. This is why spiritual directors or close friends or leaders need to be attentive to the codes of our actions.

Jesus is infallible and we are not. In fact, we are particularly fallible, and our judgment of when someone is hypocritical in their piety should be subjected to severe constraints. Not only that, but we need to work at seeing the good in the other instead of developing a cynical approach to the pious deeds of others. What may bother you, say someone's dancing in the worship team that you find to be showy, may be a genuine expression of piety—not unlike David's dancing in public before the Lord—and we may simply be off base in our judgment.

Jesus wants honesty and self-awareness of our own fallibility and our own selfish desires. Telling the truth about such things is participation in the goodness of the gospel. Contrast that with this story. A friend of mine combed through the recent archives of a library and in going through one set of files found some particularly unflattering observations about some Christian leaders. The most recent report is that many of those files have since been removed into a set of private files known only to … well, whomever that archivist decides to make them known. The sad reality here is that there is a tandem relation of leaders not wanting their sorrier traits known to others and an archivist who is complicit in such squelching of information. What is happening here embodies what hypocrisy is all about: the nurturance of image, the protection of image, the use of power to protect that image, and the refusal to live in the light.

But hypocrisy, that cruel combination of publicly motivated actions that are out of sync with our inner realities and the self-deceit that masks that reality from the person doing the deeds, is real, and it is the pastoral and loving task to point it out and to help people get through it and over it. We are to be more merciful than just, as James 2:13 reminds us, but we are to be firm and to be a blessing of development when we are called to this pastoral task.

A Theologian's Story

Stanley Hauerwas, who tells his own story in *Hannah's Child*,[19] is a titan for American theologians. His books on ethics and the relation of church and state, not to mention the opportunity to give the celebrated Gifford Lectures, along with his colossal status for many of his former students, have each contributed to his "fame" as a theologian. On top of this Hauerwas has stubbornly argued for an Anabaptist theology in so many areas that I had developed an image of the man's life that made me think I knew how tranquil his life must have been.

---

19. Titled after his mother: *Hannah's Child: A Theologian's Memoir.*

Far from it. Hauerwas's first wife was mentally ill and created chaos in his home. Hauerwas somehow managed to double down on his work, concentrate with powers that would have been incapable for most of us—and I say this as one who comes from a wonderfully tranquil home—and show tender care and nurture for his son Adam. What amazed me as I read his life story is that, though I know some of his students and plenty more who admire him and read all his books, no one I know had ever said a word about the daily strife of his life. And here's my point: few of us could have gone through those kinds of decades in life, in the heat of our developing academic years without saying something aloud about how hard life was. It is precisely here that the words of Jesus strike home in our own souls: it is often challenging to keep our good deeds to ourselves.[20]

On Giving

Danger lurks when we conclude that Jesus is against public piety, since 5:13–16 has taught that others are to see our good deeds and those good deeds will lead to their glorifying God. Furthermore, Jesus went to the synagogue and read Scripture there, and those are public deeds; Jesus also went to temple and celebrated the feasts of Israel, and those too were done in public. He praised the widow who gave all she had, and for him to praise her he had to see her. So these statements do not prohibit public deeds but warn about the temptation to use publicity of our deeds as a form of gaining approval from our religious community. The ideal, then, is to do things that have to be done publicly in such a way that we focus on God and are not driven by public congratulations.

We do this in a variety of ways, and not all of them by ringing the collection plate, writing our names in ALL CAPS on the offering envelope, announcing how much we give, or enjoying being congratulated for what we have given. So, a few pieces of advice. One thing that has to cease among Christians is the appeal to an audience to give with the promise of getting something. Second, we need to cease appealing to the vanity of people when we solicit funds for some noble cause. Third in line is appealing to give, or simply giving, in order to gain a tax break. What we can encourage is that people do every pious action as close to the border of secrecy as possible. The more we give in private, whether it is writing a check to World Vision or donating canned goods to a relief shelter, the more we will focus on the person in need. Perhaps another way of saying it is that the more secretive we

---

20. The postmoderns among us will now point to the irony of Hauerwas's silence now broadcast in a memoir; I would come back that he told this story because he thought it could be of help to others.

become, the more we are like lights, the more like a city on a hill that cannot be hidden (5:14–16).

What are some signs that we need to back off and go more private with our giving? The first sign of a person having a motivation problem is grumbling when his or her actions aren't noticed or congratulated. The second sign is envy and jealousy when others gain credit and they don't. A third sign is irritation or volatile emotions when one doesn't get one's wishes—on, say, the choice of a pastor—in spite of how much one has given to that church. And a fourth sign of mismanaged motivations is counting heads or numbers when one is asked to do a religious deed like teaching a Sunday School class.

CHAPTER 12

Matthew 6:5-6

 LISTEN to the Story

> 5"And when you pray, do not be like the hypocrites, for they love to pray standing in the synagogues and on the street corners to be seen by others. Truly I tell you, they have received their reward in full. 6But when you pray, go into your room, close the door and pray to your Father, who is unseen. Then your Father, who sees what is done in secret, will reward you."

Listening to the text in the Story: The Psalms. Deuteronomy 6:4–8 (with 11:13–21; Num 15:37–41; these three texts combine to form the full Shema said by orthodox Jews daily to this day); the *Amidah.*[1]

Prayer is as human as eating, and every ancient culture has its prayers. Whatever a contemporary philosopher of religion or a brain scientist might want to make of prayer, whether explaining it away as a form of manipulation of the gods or some relic of an ancient dimension of the brain, the fact remains that prayer is part of human existence.

Especially so when it comes to the ancient Israelites. God conversed with Adam and Eve in the garden of Eden, the idyllic form of prayer (Gen 3:8). But prayer begins in the Bible with God's speaking to humans to communicate with them (1:28–30; 2:16–17). Human prayer is a response to God's word to humans. Because humans take the fullness of experience to God, prayer connects to everything. Thus, one form of prayer emerges from sacrifice, another from worship, another from intercession, another from petition and pleading, and yet another to managing a home or loving one's husband or nurturing one's children.

Prayer was and is both a spontaneous act and a recitative act. Israelites *recited prayers* as a routine form of piety at prescribed hours of prayer (Ps

---

1. The *Amidah*, also called *Ha-Tepillah* or *Shemoneh Esreh*, is a traditional prayer recited by Jews two or three times per day. It is not easy to know what form it had in the first century. The prayer can be found by googling "The Amidah."

55:17; Dan 6:10; Acts 3:1). Two kinds of prayers are noteworthy. First, Jews prayed and in many cases memorized the Psalms.[2] Second, Jews developed customary prayers, the most notable of which appears to be the *Amidah*, or the Eighteen Benedictions,[3] which was accompanied by the recitation of the Shema and the Ten Commandments.[4]

These recited prayers had one other noteworthy dimension: Jews prayed three times per day. When? Before going to bed (vespers or compline today), when they arose (lauds or morning prayer today), and at the time of the afternoon sacrifice (midday prayer today), roughly at 3:00 p.m. That means they prayed wherever they were at the hour of prayer, but it so happens that some hypocrites planned where to be at the hour of prayer—that is, they planned to be conspicuous at the time of prayer.

Jesus' teaching in Matthew 6:5–6 is about that kind of prayer, the publicly recited prayer at (roughly) specific times in the day,[5] not about spontaneous prayers one uttered in the everyday bustle of life. Jesus zeros in on publicly recited prayers said by observant Jews in public places and excoriates the habit of praying publicly in order to be observed by others. The vast majority of Western Christians, and here we mean Roman Catholics, Eastern Orthodox, and Protestants, do not practice the hours of prayer. Furthermore, this text is taken even further from our world by the fact that few Christians pray publicly in a church setting. More pray in small groups and in Bible studies, so as we approach this text, perhaps we can keep our minds on such settings as well.

EXPLAIN the Story

As with the organization of the almsgiving passage (6:2–4), so with the prayer passage:

The observance (6:5a):

"And when you pray…"

Prohibition (6:5b):

"do not be like the hypocrites …"

---

2. P. D. Miller, *They Cried to the Lord: The Form and Theology of Biblical Prayer* (Minneapolis: Fortress, 1994); W. Brueggemann, *The Psalms and the Life of Faith* (Minneapolis: Fortress, 1995). For prayers in Judaism, see M. Riley et al., *Prayer from Alexander to Constantine: A Critical Anthology* (London: Routledge, 1997).

3. Here is one modern English version: http://tzion.org/articles/EighteenBenedictions.htm.

4. S. McKnight, *Praying with the Church: Following Jesus Daily, Hourly, Today* (Brewster, MA: Paraclete, 2006).

5. See *m. Berakot* 1:1–2.

Intent (6:5c):

"for they love to pray standing in the synagogues and on the street corners to be seen by others."

Amen ... reward (6:5d):

"Truly I tell you, they have received their reward in full."

Alternative observance (6:6a):

"But when you pray, go into your room, close the door and pray to your Father, who is unseen."

Father's reward (6:6b):

"Then your Father, who sees what is done in secret, will reward you."

The Observance (6:5a)

"And when you pray...." One could translate this "when*ever* you pray," but that nicety aside, Jesus focuses on how the religiously observant prayed in public places. A friend of mine was with a well-known author on prayer when they both entered a quick-food store. Smack-dab in the middle of the store her friend's watch made a dinging sound and her friend said, "We've got to stop and say our prayers. It's time for afternoon prayers." My friend's response was, "Here? In the store? Why not when we get to the car?" And these words came back: "Because it's the time for prayer and we will pray." So they did.

The person praying was Phyllis Tickle.[6] My friend's response would have been mine and perhaps yours, but those responses are at the other end of the spectrum of the hypocrites of Jesus' day. Growing up in a world where the dinging of the alarm in their minds meant stopping whatever they were doing, facing Jerusalem and praying, these observant Jews decided to use the custom to the advantage of their reputation. (Phyllis didn't. She was letting her light shine.)

Prohibition (6:5b)

"Do not be like the hypocrites...." We discussed the word "hypocrite" at 6:2. The hypocrites think folks perceive them as pious when the person with insight observes blatant pretense and self-promotion. What Jesus wants is utter concentration. A story: not that long ago Kris and I received an incredible invitation to participate in the Easter breakfast at the White House. I will avoid the whole story and go toward the end: the moment of our being buzzed at the door on Pennsylvania Avenue to leave was the first time I thought about

---

6. See esp. her *The Divine Hours* (New York: Doubleday, 2000–2001).

the other areas of my life. I hadn't thought about our home, my writing projects, students, classes, or the school; I hadn't daydreamed about playing golf or traveling. I realized I had been 100 percent consumed by our time in the East Room, and as we walked away Kris and I chatted about what it was like. We could remember in startling detail everything that happened. I use this as an analogy to something far greater: in the presence of God we should give ourselves in utter devotion to communicate with our Father. Nothing else matters.

Intent (6:5c)

"For they love to pray standing in the synagogues and on the street corners to be seen by others." The kind of prayer Jesus has in mind now becomes clear to his audience and readers, for the *Amidah* was to be said standing. The hypocrites seek conspicuous places the way contemporaries purchase items with labels (someone say UGG aloud) that draw attention to what we want folks to think of us. Hypocrites like places connected to worship and publicity. Synagogues were *the* place of prayer for Jews, and for that reason perhaps the most typical word in the Greek-speaking world used for synagogues was *proseuchē*, or "house of prayer."[7]

There is nothing wrong with praying in a synagogue or reading Scripture aloud in a synagogue (Luke 4:16 – 20). Nor is there anything inherently wrong praying in a place as public as a street corner. What is wrong here is praying in order "to be seen by others." Jesus focuses on intent. Instead of talking to God, as Adam and Eve did in the garden as a form of fellowship and worship and petition or as David does in the Psalms, hypocrites prayed to be seen.

Amen ... Reward (6:5d)

"Truly I tell you, they have received their reward in full." These words are powerfully judgmental: to say they have their reward in full is to say they will have no reward from God. They got the good they wanted, but what they wanted was not good.

Alternative Observance (6:6a)

"But when you pray, go into your room, close the door and pray to your Father, who is unseen." As with blowing trumpets, so with closing doors and praying in closets: they are hyperbolic for privacy. Jesus prayed publicly (e.g., Matt 6:7 – 13; 11:25 – 27; John 17). The language of Jesus is graphic if not comic: as the hypocrites sought the most public of places, so Jesus urges his

---

7. There is an exceptional article on "Synagogues" in *EDEJ*, 1260 – 71. For an ancient text calling the synagogue a *proseuchē*, see Josephus, *Life* 277 – 98.

followers to find the most private of places. The word "room" can be translated "closet, inner room, or pantry." To live this out does not mean we have to construct an inner closet in our homes to which we retire in utter privacy. Rather, we take Hannah, Daniel, and Cornelius as our examples (1 Sam 1:13–17; Dan 6:10; Acts 10:1–4) and add to them Jesus' withdrawals in order to focus on prayer (see Matt 26:36–37; Mark 1:35).

Father's Reward (6:6b)

"Then your Father, who sees what is done in secret, will reward you." Jesus believes in the omniscience and omnipresence of his Father and knows the Father knows the unseen places of one's home. The hypocrites and the judges of hypocrites and the public may not see the person who prays in a home closet, but the Father does—and that's before whom all our pious deeds are to be done (6:1).

LIVE the Story

Years ago a friend gave me a copy of a little book called *A Guide to Ecclesiastical Birdwatching.*[8] It was a set of short chapters with a drawing of a kind of "bird" in the church that could be satirized. In that it was done humorously and not overly seriously, it has served a good purpose: to hold our foibles up to evaluation in order to make us more self-conscious of our sins.

So we begin with some fun. I want to play off of *Ecclesiastical Birdwatching* and apply it to how people pray in church. There is a bird in church we can name *Pious Paddy*. When he prays, everyone knows he's serious and pious because he says Lahwwed and Gawwed and Geez-uussssssssssh.

Then over there sits *Repetitious Rollie*, who can't quite take the impiety of silence, so he says either "our heavenly Father" or "and Lord" between every sentence, and sometimes between clauses and by the time he's done he's really Father-ed and Lord-ified his prayers.

Next to Repetitious Rollie is his buddy *Focused Frederick*, who somewhere got the idea that the word "just," as in "we just thank you, Lord," doesn't mean "only" and doesn't limit what he's saying but instead expresses just how focused he is in prayer requests.

Sitting all alone in the front, and known for his intelligence, is *Highfalutin' Harold*, whose prayers are loaded up theologically, and sometimes he even uses the word "eschatological" or "soteriological," and sometimes says "our exegesis has grounded us in a biblicism and theology that makes you proud."

---

8. LeRoy Koopman, *A Guide to Ecclesiastical Birdwatching* (Glendale, CA: Regal/GL Publications, 1973).

Born and bred in the 60s, *Informal Isabel* and *Authentic Adam* have a style of public prayer noted by saying whatever is on their minds and in their hearts, irreverent or not. Isabel once prayed, "I'm so frickin' mad about poverty, God ..." and after Adam amen'd her, he upped the ante a bit with his own prayer: "God, I'm with Isabel, 'Like what the hell's going on in Rwanda?!'" They enjoyed the provocation but blanketed themselves with the good Christian idea that prayer that is not honest and authentic is not real prayer. "Like David" is one of their defenses.

At the other end of their pew is *Cliché Clarissa*, who somehow has accumulated a storehouse of Christian expressions for each of her prayers, like finishing off her individual requests with "and we'll be careful to give you thanks," or beginning her prayers with "And Lord, bless the missionaries and the starving children of this world."

Quotatious Quentin, friend of Highfalutin' Harold, likes to quote books and authors and Bible verses when he prays. One time he said, "As Richard Foster taught us, 'We today yearn for prayer and hide from prayer.'" He lifted his voice a bit on the "and" to give it that bilateral problem. He continued, "But Jesus knew what Richard Foster would say, so he taught us 'For your Father knows the thing you have need of before you ask him,' as my translation reads." [He is known for his use of the KJV and NKJV because of their quotatious powers.]

Some preachers, too, have a preacher's habit. Like *Summarizing Stefan*, who sums up his sermons in the first two minutes of his postsermon prayer, or like *Preaching Peter*, who doesn't make a good transition from his sermon to his closing prayer and rams home his points one more time in his prayer. We close with *Sendoff Sam*, who has developed the Old Testament habit—at least he thinks it's Old Testament—of loading up his prayer at the end. Some people load up front, but he loads at the end. One time he finished his sermon something like this, and it was hard to get it all down but I did my best: " ... in the glorious and majestic and everlasting and beautiful and everlovin' and glorious [he goes on so long sometimes he repeats words] name of our One and Only Lord, Savior, your Son and our Savior, the Lord Christ Messiah and God of our fathers, to whom be glory and majesty and honor forever and ever ... in the matchless, unconquerable, victorious, glorious name of Geee-zuss. Amen. Amen. Amen."

It is much easier to satirize than to instruct, and so we move into some practical suggestions for living the story of this text in our world.

But How?

I want to make two suggestions about what we can do, and these two are the ones that have helped me the most in public prayers. One of the finest lessons

I ever learned about prayer was never said but was acted. Murray Harris, one of my seminary professors, was known as much for his preclass prayers as he was for the brilliance of his lectures. While Murray's prayers were eloquent, soaked in a theological understanding of Scripture, and bathed in personal piety, what some of us observed was how he began his prayers. First, he gathered himself physically with his head down, said, "Let us pray," and then . . . in an almost uncomfortable duration of silence, waited and out of that collection of his thoughts, his reverence, and his disposition toward God, he prayed. I learned public prayer ought to begin with a time of collecting our thoughts in silence as we prepare ourselves to approach God. (Of course, the same applies to private prayer.)

Second, I believe public prayers ought to be both spontaneous and recited and in both forms the pray-er needs to pray slowly (and loudly) enough to be understood by everyone. Slowing down has a way of concentrating our attention, while rattling off a recited or written prayer has a way of turning something into rote or routine. Pausing to collect our thoughts and speaking slowly in prayers are the best patterns I know to praying in public in a way that we are speaking to God.

I end with Luther's pastoral words for us: "In the morning and in the evening, at table and whenever he [or she] has time, every individual should speak a benediction or the Our Father or the Creed or a psalm."[9]

---

9. Luther, *Sermon on the Mount*, 139.

CHAPTER 13

Matthew 6:7 – 15

 LISTEN to the Story

7"And when you pray, do not keep on babbling like pagans,[1] for they think they will be heard because of their many words. 8Do not be like them, for your Father knows what you need before you ask him.

9"This, then, is how you should pray:

" 'Our Father in heaven,
hallowed be your name,
10your kingdom come,
your will be done,
    on earth as it is in heaven.
11Give us today our daily bread.
12And forgive us our debts,
    as we also have forgiven our debtors.
13And lead us not into temptation,
    but deliver us from the evil one.'[2]

14For if you forgive other people when they sin against you, your heavenly Father will also forgive you. 15But if you do not forgive others their sins, your Father will not forgive your sins."

Listening to the text in the Story: Exodus 32; 1 Kings 18:16 – 46; Isaiah 44:6 – 20; also Deuteronomy 6:4 – 8; the Psalms.

You may well be preparing to preach or teach this passage and so may feel as I do. Thus, I will ask your question: How does one say anything fresh about the Lord's Prayer? The first thing to say is this: Don't try to say something new because you'll be wrong. The second thing to say is this: Let traditional significance shape what you say. And third is this: Say what it says. Its value is its heritage, and its heritage will guide you.

---

1. KNT: "don't pile up a jumbled heap of words!"
2. KNT: "Don't bring us into the great trial, but rescue us from evil."

Observe that Matthew 6:7–15 is an intrusion into what is otherwise a tightly organized section. If you regard 6:1 as the theme verse and then look at the units on almsgiving (6:2–4), prayer (6:5–6), skip the next unit (6:7–15), and then fasting (6:16–18), you will easily observe an almost obsessive organization of those sections. Matthew 6:7–15 doesn't fit in two ways: first, thematically, it isn't concerned with acts of piety done by Jewish "hypocrites" to impress others but with long-winded, gassy prayers *by Gentiles* designed to manipulate God into answering; second, grammatically and syntactically 6:7–8 isn't like 6:2–4, 5–6, or 16–18, but varies significantly. Along this line, 6:9–13, the Lord's Prayer itself, has no similar type of positive instruction in the other sections of 6:1–18; moreover, 6:14–15 is yet another intrusion—a parenthetical set of lines that form a "commentary" on 6:12. In our day, an author would have put 6:14–15 into a footnote at the end of 6:12.

Our section, then, draws on the contrast between pagan piety and God's design. The theology of the pagans involves a god who can be manipulated, against which view Jesus teaches a God who *already* knows and can be trusted. This unit draws out Israel's strict monotheism (Exod 20:3–5; Deut 6:4–8) and the Story of Israel in their interaction with pagan gods, including the golden calf episode in Exodus 32 and Elijah's challenge of the Baalim on Mount Carmel in 1 Kings 18 as well as the standard trope against idolatry in the prophets (e.g., Isa 44:6–20). Furthermore, what Jesus teaches here expresses again the ongoing Jewish denunciation of pagan gods and religious practices (e.g., 1 Macc 2).[3]

God, the one and only true God, who loves Israel as a father loves his children, forms the foundation of the theology of the Lord's Prayer. But the content of the prayer is shaped by hope: this is preeminently a prayer that expresses a longing for God's promises for Israel and the earth to come true. It mirrors the Magnificat of Mary (Luke 1:46–55) and the Benedictus of Zechariah (1:67–79), but instead of announcing the dawn of the kingdom, this prayer teaches the disciples to orient prayers toward the dawn of that kingdom. As the Son of the Father, Jesus shows the disciples *how he himself prays to the Father.* Using this prayer, then, is one way of entering into the perichoretic, or inner-relational life, of the Trinity: this prayer reveals how God communicates with God.

---

3. For an excellent source on Hellenstic and Roman religions, see E. Ferguson, *Backgrounds of Early Christianity* (3rd ed.; Grand Rapids: Eerdmans, 2003), 148–317.

EXPLAIN the Story

There are two natural parts: the setting (6:7–8) and the response (6:9–15).

The Setting (6:7–8)

The NIV's "*when* you pray" is identical to "*when* you give to the needy" (6:2), "*when* you pray" (6:5), and "*when* you fast" (6:16), but "when" does not bring to the surface that the Greek construction in 6:7 varies from the Greek in 6:2, 5, 16.[4] One way of translating this in a way that reflects the Greek variation from the pattern in 6:2, 5, 16 would be to translate it as "In your praying...." Such a translation tips the reader off to the variation and prevents one from thinking there are actually four identical sections in 6:1–18.

Jesus has Gentiles in mind with their piling up of the names of their gods.[5] Sometimes the Gentiles seemed to be hoping a god would be awake or listening—and it is not wrong here to humanize these gods because that his how they come off in texts like *The Iliad* and *The Odyssey*. Catullus wrote a poem about the goddess Diana; the fourth line from the end perfectly illustrates the problem Jesus sees in Gentile prayers (put in italics):

Under **Diana's** protection,
we pure girls, and boys:
we pure boys, and girls,
we sing of Diana.
O, daughter of Latona,
greatest child of great Jove,
whose mother gave birth
near the Delian olive,
mistress of mountains
and the green groves,
the secret glades,
and the sounding streams:
you, called Juno Lucina
in childbirth's pains,
you, called all-powerful Trivia

---

4. Instead of an indefinite temporal clause with the subjunctive (introduced by *hotan*), 6:7 has a subordinating (perhaps temporal) participle (*proseuchomenoi*).

5. As an example, in Lucius Apuleius's famous novel, *The Golden Ass*, a prayer begins to "O Queen of heaven" and then proceeds to wonder which god is being addressed: "if you are Dame Ceres ... or Celestial Venus" (Apuleius, *Golden Ass [Metamorphoses]* 11.2 [ch. 47]). In Philostratus, *Life of Apollonius of Tyana*, the emperor Domitian imprisoned a man for failing to mention that he, Domitian, was son of Athene (7.24).

and Luna, of counterfeit daylight.
Your monthly passage
measures the course of the year,
you fill the rustic farmer's
roof with good crops.
*Take whatever sacred name
pleases you*, be a sweet help
to the people of Rome,
as you have been of old.[6]

Jesus' observation about Gentile prayer is common in Judaism: "do not keep on babbling like pagans."[7] The Greek word behind our "babble" is a bit of a mystery when it comes to its origins, but that Greek word (*battalogeō*) creates the impression of mindless babbling.[8] At the end of this verse the words "many words" (*polylogia*) is used, and it permits us to combine it with "babble" to see Jesus' criticism directed at a nonstop prattling in the presence of God. Jesus focuses on *intent*. The pagan intent is the belief that if they are long-winded or pray long enough or if they show their sincerity by going on and on, God will hear them. Pushing Gentile anxiety in prayer was the offendability and capriciousness of the gods. Jesus teaches the goodness and love of God, here speaking of God's loving care of all (5:43–48) and calling God "Father."

Contrary to pagan perceptions of who God is, Jesus' Father knows needs before God's people ask. Perhaps this idea is from one of the predictions about the new heavens and the new earth from Isaiah 65:24:

Before they call I will answer;
    while they are still speaking I will hear.

This does not say the Father knows what they will ask before they ask but that the Father knows their needs before they make them known. Jesus' intent is not to discourage his followers from petitioning the Father but from thinking they can manipulate or cajole God. This means that the major intent of the Lord's Prayer is to reveal a short prayer in contradiction to the long prayers of the pagans. Few prayers say so much in such few words, but good examples of "short" prayers can be found in the Psalms, none perhaps more notable than Psalm 23.

---

6. From: www.poetryintranslation.com/PITBR/Latin/Catullus.htm#_Toc531846759.

7. The "keep on" is an unsuccessful attempt to translate the combination of the present participle (*proseuchomenoi*) alongside the aorist subjunctive (*battalogēsēte*). There is too much time emphasis in the "keep on." I suggest "In your praying, do not babble like the Gentiles."

8. See Davies and Allison, *Matthew*, 1:587–88.

The Response (6:9 – 15)

Gentiles, because of what they believe about God, are defective in their prayers. Jesus knows God as Father and as good, kind, and benevolent and as holy and just. That theology empowers him to teach his followers to approach God in confidence. Prayer is not informing God of something unknown but drawing oneself in the divine life of the Trinity and into the very mission of God in this world — this God loves us and invites us into his presence with our petitions.

Tradition has observed that the Lord's Prayer is broken into two parts: You petitions and We petitions — those directed at God and those directed for others. The Jesus Creed sharpens this tradition of seeing the Lord's Prayer in two parts. With the Jesus Creed, the Lord took the Jewish *Shema*, rooted in Deuteronomy 6:4 – 8, and added Leviticus 19:18. Thus, his fundamental creed is *to love God* and *to love others as ourselves.* Jesus hereby adds a horizontal dimension to the Shema to supplement the vertical.

The same sort of addition happens in the Lord's Prayer. Many scholars observe that the Lord's Prayer has notable connections to a Jewish prayer now called *Qaddish*, to which Jesus added concerns *for others.* I provide a common translation of *Qaddish*, though we cannot be sure about its precise form in the first century, and I have italicized words that show similarities to the Lord's Prayer.

> *Magnified and sanctified be His great name* in the world which He created according to *His will.*
>
> And may He establish *His kingdom during your life and during your days, and during the life of all the house of Israel, speedily and in the near future*, and say Amen.
>
> Response: May His great *Name* be blessed forever and ever.
>
> *Blessed, praised and glorified, exalted, extolled and honored, adored and lauded by the Name* of the Holy One, blessed be He, beyond all blessings and hymns, praises and songs that are uttered in the world, and say Amen.

The parallels are notable, and they can't be ignored. We have every reason to think the Lord's Prayer builds on and modifies the *Qaddish*, with one notable difference: instead of the prayer/creed being focused solely on the vertical, *the horizontal is added.* The Lord's Prayer adapts the *Qaddish's* focus on God (the You petitions) and *adds without parallel in the Qaddish* the We petitions. True piety for Jesus transcends our relationship with God and becomes relation to both God and others. True piety is about loving God and loving others, and this works into prayer: prayer is about praying for God's glory *and* for blessings for others. Those who love God yearn for his Name to be sanctified, his kingdom to come, and his will to be done. Those who love others yearn for their daily bread, their reciprocal forgiveness, their growth in holiness, and their deliverance from the evil one.

Introduction (6:9a)

The introduction to the Lord's Prayer, when compared with Luke's version, introduces us to the world of Jewish prayer at the time of Jesus. Matthew's text reads: "This, then, is how you should pray."

Matthew's "this" and "how" translate *houtōs*, an adverb. One could translate, "Pray thusly." That is, the Lord's Prayer is *how* the disciples are to pray, and this would throw emphasis on the brevity and directness of the Lord's Prayer in contrast to the length of Gentile prayers. The Lord's Prayer is a model of *how* to pray; some infer that the Lord's Prayer is not a set of words to be recited.[9] Such a view ignores the plain meaning of Luke's text. Here is Luke 11:1–2.[10]

> One day Jesus was praying in a certain place. When he finished, one of his disciples said to him, "Lord, teach us to pray, just as John taught his disciples."
>
> He said to them, "When you pray, say. . . ."[11]

The disciples approach Jesus and ask him to teach them to pray, and they ask to be taught the way John taught his disciples to pray. But the next words clarify what they are requesting and make the request much more concrete. Jesus says to them, and now I translate more literally to bring out the nuances of the Greek text, "When*ever* you pray, *recite* this." Jesus' words show that he is thinking they are asking for a set prayer—something very Jewish to do—and he gives them just that. Then he says they are to pray this prayer when*ever* they (perhaps only as a group but probably whenever any of them prays) pray. And the word "say" can be translated "recite."

These verses, then, don't teach so much *how* to pray *but what to say whenever they pray.* Jesus taps into the great Jewish prayer tradition of memorized prayers and gives a new template of prayer,[12] but the kind of template that is

---

9. So Calvin, *Harmony of the Gospels*, 1:205; Wesley in Kinghorn, *Wesley on the Sermon*, 157. Also Guelich, *Sermon on the Mount*, 308; France, *Matthew*, 241, who calls it "the Pattern Prayer."

10. Variation between Matthew's and Luke's versions of the Lord's Prayer does not prove the prayer was not recited, any more than variation in other set prayers in Judaism, like the *Amidah*, shows they weren't recited. Variations reveal both a fixed prayer but willingness to shorten or lengthen according to context. There is no good evidence that the followers of Jesus *didn't* recite this prayer, and the entire history of the church counts in favor of reciting it.

11. *Didache* 8:2–3 says to pray the Lord's Prayer three times a day *and uses the words of Matthew:* "pray thus." This becomes our earliest commentary on the Lord's Prayer as given in Matthew and indicates, as I've said, the use of the Lord's Prayer as recited prayer.

12. Davies and Allison, *Matthew*, 1:599–600. Thus, I stand here with Luther, *Sermon on the Mount*, 145.

recited over and over as a form of spiritual formation. We have the book of Psalms because these were prayers deemed worthy of recitation in public, and we have the Lord's Prayer as another instance of recited prayer.

What is for me the clincher in this issue: the church has always recited the Lord's Prayer. The recitation of the Lord's Prayer among Catholics, the Orthodox, the Protestants (the Reformers emphasized the Lord's Prayer as template and as recited), and among all Christians occurred until the informality of prayers became the rule in the twentieth century for some groups of Christians. It's time for many of us to regain what we dropped. Informality has had its day; it's time for some formality too.

Our Father (6:9b)

Those who love God know God as Father. Jesus includes the disciples and excludes the hypocrites and Gentiles in the model prayer by saying "our" (making it a public prayer). By calling God "Father"[13] Jesus focuses on his own relationship—he is Son—and the kind of relationship he wants his followers to have (John 10:30). But the first comes first: our "sonship," or "familial relation with God as Father," derives from and participates in the Son's relationship to the Father. We are not equal children but sons and daughters *through* and *in* the Son's filial relation with the Father (cf. Matt 5:45; Gal 3:26; 1 John 5:1).

Long ago Joachim Jeremias explained at length that calling God "Father" was profoundly important to Jesus and should be connected to justification and adoption in Pauline theology.[14] The heart of the message of the term *Abba* meant something like "Daddy," partaking as it did in the intimacy of the Jewish family. Jeremias was right to point to the intimacy dimension of the term. But he also pushed harder to suggest that this was not only innovative and unique on the part of Jesus but transcended Jewish religion, and on this scholarship has firmly pronounced Jeremias mistaken. Calling God "Father" (*Abba*) is not unique to Jesus,[15] and neither is it a revelation of a religious profundity that Judaism had not yet comprehended (what can be more intimate than Hosea 1–2 or 11:1–4?).

Instead of its being *unique*, "Father" is *characteristic* of Jesus but would not have been at all offensive in Judaism. All of Jesus' prayers, except his cry of dereliction (Mark 15:34), begin with "Father" (e.g., Matt 11:25–26; John

---

13. S. McKnight, *A New Vision for Israel: The Teachings of Jesus in National Context* (Grand Rapids: Eerdmans, 1999), 49–65; Dunn, *Jesus Remembered*, 711–18.

14. J. Jeremias, *The Prayers of Jesus* (London: SCM, 1967), 11–65; idem, *The Central Message of the New Testament* (London: SCM, 1965).

15. Thus, see Old Testament texts like Pss 68:5; 103:13–14; Isa 63:15–16; Jer 31:9, 20, the famous *avinu malkeinu* ("Our Father, our King") lines in classic Jewish prayers, like *Ahabah Rabah* and *The Litany for the New Year*, and texts like 4Q372 fragment 1:16.

17). The term "Father" brings together at least two attributes of God: his intimate love for his children as well as his sovereign power, which is evoked with "in heaven." To call God "Father" in prayer is to receive that love, to know his power, and to seek to embody his will, which are expressed in the You petitions of the Lord's Prayer.

The Name (6:9c)

Those who love God long for God to be honored. The "name" of God is often referred to as the sacred tetragrammaton (the holy four letters), often spelled YHWH and sometimes as Yahweh. Many Christians are sensitive to Jewish scruples, so they write the unpronounceable YHWH. This name is said to derive from God's conversation with Moses in Exodus 3:13–15. There are interesting variants on the Name in the New Testament, including both a focus on the name of Jesus (Yeshua; Phil 2:9) and the Trinitarian formula (Matt 28:18–20). Anything said of YHWH can be said of Jesus, or of the Trinitarian God, but YHWH remains the Old Testament name for God.[16] In the "lexicon" of the Bible and ancient Judaism, the "name" represents the person and that person's character. Not using the Name is not simply about protective speech but is about God—to honor God's Name is to honor God, the God who is so impeccably perfect that language is to be given full consideration when speaking to and about God.

Nothing in the Old Testament prohibits pronouncing the sacred Name, though the strict warning about "misusing" it in the Ten Commandments (Exod 20:7) led to restrictions. One sure way of never taking God's name in vain is never to use it, and not saying the Name was Jewish custom at the time of Jesus. The Lord's Prayer is a good indicator that Jesus joined his fellow Jews in not uttering the sacred Name. Jesus routinely uses language that reveals respect for God through indirect mention (as in "the Mighty One" at Mark 14:62),[17] and he seems also to have substituted "the Name" (*HaShem*) for the sacred Name when speaking (Matt 23:39).

It is customary, and I have said this myself, to say that Jesus exhorts his followers to "hallow" the Name in how they live, but this is not accurate: the first three petitions are aimed at God in prayer.[18] Thus, Jesus here petitions *God to*

---

16. See my *New Vision for Israel*, 27–30, with correction from Pennington in the next note.

17. On kingdom of *heaven* see esp. J. T. Pennington, *Heaven and Earth in the Gospel of Matthew* (Grand Rapids: Baker Academic, 2009), 13–37.

18. The third person singular imperative is used, in passive form, to read: "May your Name *be* hallowed," instead of a second person singular imperative, which would have been "(You) hallow your Name." Perhaps the third person is used out of reverence, which the passive voice could also indicate, or perhaps the third person does open it up more for human inclusion and responsibility. I'm inclined toward the former view. There is, of course, moral implication for the one who so addresses God, but had Jesus wanted this to be a moral imperative, he could have said it directly, as in "May your people hallow your Name."

hallow God's Name.[19] To be sure, if God acts to honor God's Name, then surely the followers of Jesus will too, but this text actually speaks of a divine action and in this evokes a common theme in the prophets. Note Ezekiel's words:

> Therefore say to the house of Israel, Thus says the Lord GOD: It is not for your sake, O house of Israel, that I am about to act, but for the sake of my holy name, which you have profaned among the nations to which you came. (Ezek 36:22 NRSV)

> … when I have brought them back from the peoples and gathered them from their enemies' lands, and through them have displayed my holiness in the sight of many nations. Then they shall know that I am the LORD their God because I sent them into exile among the nations, and then gathered them into their own land. I will leave none of them behind. (Ezek 39:27–28 NRSV)

The word "hallow" translates the Greek word *hagiasthētō*, which means to honor, sanctify, set apart, and treat with the highest of respect. In this context, since it refers to divine (not human) action, this petition is a prayer that God will act in a way that glorifies himself (cf. John 12:28). What Jesus has in mind is clear: he wants God to act to bring in the kingdom in order to display God's rule. Humans, particularly Israelites or the Romans occupying the Land, defile and profane the name of God in sinful living (Lev 18:21).[20] Again, focusing on how *we* profane God's name is not the point of Jesus' words; this petition is not a veiled act by the pray-er to get more Torah observance, nor is it a side glance at others to become more obedient. This is a petition for God to act.

The opposite is our cold, shallow choice not to desire or pray for God's glorious name to be established above all names. This, then, is more about *our hopes, our desires, our affections, and our aches* than it is about what we are doing or not doing in the realm of behaviors. Again, this request casts light on what we most want to be raised on high—God's name or something else? The petition is about priorities and a request for revival.

Pastors, theologians, and writers reflect on the significance of beginning the Lord's Prayer with this petition to hallow the name as the model for prayer; that is, all prayer should begin with God. However sound theologically, there is a difference between beginning with God and teaching us always to begin with God. Jesus does begin with God, but he is not teaching that here.

---

19. So Guelich, *Sermon on the Mount*, 289; Hagner, *Matthew 1–13*, 148. But see Luz, *Matthew 1–7*, 317–18; France, *Matthew*, 246, focuses on the human dimension.

20. Martin Luther, *An Exposition of the Lord's Prayer for Simple Laymen* (Luther's Works 42: *Devotional Writings*, v. 1; Philadelphia: Fortress, 1969), 27–37.

The Kingdom and Will of God (6:10)

What Jesus meant by "kingdom" has a long history. Some focus on the time element. One group of scholars, teaching what is often called "consistent" eschatology, focuses on the kingdom as on the verge of arrival at the time of Jesus. That is, Jesus believed the kingdom was about to arrive. Two elements are at work in this view: that kingdom would entail a total restoration of creation and the redemption of Israel; also at work here is the view that Jesus was at least in some sense mistaken.[21]

Resistance to this interpretation surfaced in the English scholar C. H. Dodd. His tiny book *The Parables of Jesus*[22] was the beginning of his exposition of the eschatology of Jesus under the lens of what is now called "realized" eschatology because for Dodd the kingdom was already present in Jesus. What remained was only the apocalyptic completion of history.

Between these poles of eschatology, one emphasizing imminent arrival of the kingdom and the other its "already" manifestation, lies a host of scholars in what is probably the consensus of scholars today: the kingdom of God for Jesus is both present and future. It is present but without consummation; it is both now and not yet. This view is often called "inaugurated" eschatology. The most influential presentation of this view for the more evangelical audience was George Eldon Ladd.[23]

Ladd defined the kingdom as dynamically active in Jesus (see Matt 4:17; 12:28). He was pressed hard in his day by dispensationalists, who more or less saw the kingdom as millennium/heaven; in response Ladd probably exaggerated both the abstract and "dynamic" nature of the kingdom. Consequently, for some of his followers "kingdom" gets close to personal salvation and the experience of surrendering one's life to God as King.[24] Now, surely submission is inherent to kingdom language, but when it is reduced to the personal experience of surrender, we are mistaking what "kingdom" meant in Jesus' world. Ladd did not teach such simplicities.

But I want to suggest a way of thinking about the kingdom that modifies inaugurated eschatology, though I cannot defend that view at length here. A first-century Jew would have at least had the following ideas in mind whenever the word "kingdom" was mentioned, and all of this rolls out of the Old Testament expectations for God's future:[25] *God* as King, and for Jesus this mutates

---

21. This view is classically connected with Albert Schweitzer, *The Quest of the Historical Jesus* (ed. J. Bowden: Minneapolis: Fortress, 2001).

22. C. H. Dodd, *The Parables of Jesus* (London: Religious Book Club, 1942).

23. Ladd, *The Presence of the Future.*

24. A good example is R. T. Kendall, *The Sermon on the Mount* (Minneapolis: Chosen, 2011).

25. Beasley-Murray, *Jesus and the Kingdom of God*; McKnight, *King Jesus Gospel*, 93–100; idem, *One.Life*, 27–34.

into the *Davidic* hope with himself as the *messianic* King; an Israelite *society* governed by the Davidic Messiah; a society or a people marked by *peace, holiness, love,* and *wisdom* in the *land* of Israel; a people governed by the *Torah* of Moses, but now once again mutated by Jesus into *his teachings*; and finally, since the kingdom would be the final realization of prophetic hopes, the kingdom would also be marked by *new creation, new power, new obedience, and the healing of all sicknesses and diseases.* The essential society-shaped, or people-shaped, form of the kingdom must be recovered, and this means the kingdom cannot be divorced from the church. So for Jesus "kingdom" would have meant the society of God's people flourishing in this world under Christ as the King.

The second petition of the Lord's Prayer, then, expresses, as found in the *Qaddish* and expressed by Simeon (Luke 2:25) and Joseph of Arimathea (Mark 15:43), the Jewish ache for God's society to be fully established on earth. The vision of Revelation 21 is what Jesus has in mind. The highest form of loving God is longing for what most glorifies God. The Story of God in the Bible is the Story that God is Creator, Lord, and Redeemer, and that God's plan for history is for it all to be summed up with Christ as Lord and with God ruling over the entire world.

The first and second petitions of the Lord's Prayer are fundamentally gospel aches: they ache for the full Story to become complete where God is All in All. But this ache is not just for the global, cosmic, and universal reign of God. Since the kingdom is already making itself present, and since we are called to live now in light of that future consummation, each and every act of love, peace, justice, and wisdom that we do enters into that final kingdom reality. But again, this petition is about God's acting and not about our moral behaviors. A beautiful, poetic and prophetic announcement of what Jesus is saying can be found in Isaiah 52:7–10:

> [7]How beautiful on the mountains
>   are the feet of those who bring good news,
> who proclaim peace,
>   who bring good tidings,
>   who proclaim salvation,
> who say to Zion,
>   "Your God reigns!"
> [8]Listen! Your watchmen lift up their voices;
>   together they shout for joy.
> When the LORD returns to Zion,
>   they will see it with their own eyes.
> [9]Burst into songs of joy together,
>   you ruins of Jerusalem,

for the LORD has comforted his people,
  he has redeemed Jerusalem.
[10]The LORD will lay bare his holy arm
  in the sight of all the nations,
and all the ends of the earth will see
  the salvation of our God.

The second petition of the Lord's Prayer unfolds into a third. Some have thought Matthew himself defined "your kingdom come" by adding the explanation: "your will be done." Its absence in the Lukan version of the Lord's Prayer adds support to such a view, but when one is pushed to demonstrate that Matthew added the line, the evidence gets flimsier. Whatever its pedigree, "your will be done" is both an eloquent explanation of "your kingdom come" as well as a slight variant. The kingdom emphasizes a social order and a cosmic redemption, while "will" emphasizes the redemptive and moral intent of God for this world and for God's people (see 7:21; 12:50; 18:14; 21:31; 26:42). Again, this is a prayer for God to act.

"On earth as it is in heaven" is fundamental to the entire Lord's Prayer as well as all of early Christian eschatology.[26] Jesus clearly has no desire, as was the case in Platonic and the wider reaches of much of Greek and Roman thought, to move through this life with as little hassle and suffering as possible. The release of souls from this embodied life into a celestial disembodied existence is not a biblical notion. The opposite is the case with Jesus and for the entire Bible.

A simple tracing of the word "heaven" and "new heavens and a new earth" in the New Testament shows that the final ending is found in Revelation 20–22. There it is not about our going up into the sky or into a disembodied state in heaven but of heaven coming down to earth. The final state according to Revelation 20–22 is on earth. *That is why the Lord's prayer says, "on earth as it is in heaven."* God's redemptive power aims at realizing the heavenly condition on earth. It follows, then, that "kingdom of heaven" entails the idea that the earthly kingdom will be like the heavenly kingdom; that is, it will be a perfect manifestation of God's will.

The Bread (6:11)

The Lord's Prayer now shifts into a second part: from the You petitions to the We petitions. This second half finds itself in asking God for bread, for forgiveness, and for a moral life that flows out of a God whose name is to be

---

26. See here N. T. Wright, *Surprised by Hope: Rethinking Heaven, the Resurrection, and the Mission of the Church* (New York: HarperOne, 2008).

hallowed, a kingdom whose desire is uppermost and a divine will that shapes all we do.

It can be put baldly: *we do not know exactly what "daily bread" means.*[27] For some this wrecks what we have always known to be true, but "our daily bread" uses a Greek term that is used but one time in the ancient literature. Dale Allison, a master in the history of interpretation, says "daily" is "an unresolved puzzle."[28] After observing that the third-century scholar Origen said that perhaps the Evangelists invented the word themselves, Allison begins to list and sort out the options: it could mean "needful" or "needed,"[29] or "for the current day" (which is what Luke seems to suggest when he adds "each day" in Luke 11:3), or the Eucharist ("supersubstantial"; a majority of the church fathers read it this way; Matt 26:26), or spiritual sustenance (John 6, which can be narrowed as Luther did to the Word of God),[30] or Jesus himself (6:48); it could also mean the kind of bread served in the kingdom (Luke 14:15), or the bread of "the coming [final] day."[31]

Allison himself leads a number of interpreters when he opts for the "coming day" view, observing that it has ancient support in both patristic writings and early translations of the Bible. That interpretation is rooted in the hope of the eschatological manna (Exod 16; Num 21:5), and the eschatological themes of the first three petitions would then come in to support such a view: eschatological manna for the eschaton.

Do we need to limit our views to one? Allison, for instance, sees it as a blur of daily provision, the eschatological banquet, and the Eucharist, which anticipates that banquet.[32] It is wisest to ask what Jesus would have meant, what Matthew's own horizon could have comprehended, and then to give some freedom to reading this text in light of the Story of God. What appears to be in view is prayer for daily provisions. In support of this view is that the second half of the Lord's Prayer is concerned with the normal needs of humans. But because the first three petitions focus on the consummation of history, perhaps the bread petition is about the so-called eschatological or kingdom manna. But again, both in the Sermon on the Mount and elsewhere in the Gospels there are indications of routine needs being met (6:25–34),

---

27. Luz, *Matthew 1–7*, 319–22. Already with Jerome we read of debates on the meaning of the term translated "daily" (*epiousios*): see Jerome, *Matthew*, 88–89.

28. Allison, *Sermon on the Mount*, 125.

29. Strecker, *Sermon on the Mount*, 117–18.

30. Luther, *Exposition of the Lord's Prayer*, 52–53. Later Luther narrows this to Jesus himself, dispensed through Word and sacrament.

31. The etymology of this rare term favors this last view: "coming day." *The Gospel of the Nazarenes*, a second-century Jewish Christian text, uses the word *mahar*, which means "of tomorrow."

32. Allison, *Sermon on the Mount*, 127.

and this leads me to think Jesus was thinking of ordinary bread for ordinary days,[33] even if his listeners thought the divine provision was partaking in the bounty of kingdom redemption.[34] I doubt that that Eucharist is in view.

The sweep of the Gospels, not to mention 6:25–34, where Jesus points a long finger at consumerism and preoccupation with money and possessions, suggests that when Jesus says, "Give us today our daily bread," the word *today* suggests we are not to worry about tomorrow or about storing up food but to trust God for what we need that day. We perhaps need to remind ourselves that the followers of Jesus were not wealthy with pantries and refrigerators filled with food.

The Forgiveness (6:12) and a Clarifying Commentary (6:14–15)

Forgiveness is difficult at the personal and pastoral level, and the twofold reason is because Jesus was so forceful about its necessity for his followers and we find forgiveness so demanding and difficult. We attend to the words of 6:12 as well as the commentary on those words in 6:14–15, words probably added by Matthew on the basis of Mark 11:25–26.[35]

We begin with the obvious: what Jesus says strikes the Christian as backward and conditional, and we are tempted to fill in the blanks. But what Jesus says in 6:12 as a petition to God is what Jesus says elsewhere in 7:1–5 and in 18:21–35. What Jesus forcefully focuses on his kingdom vision for his followers can be summarized in these two lines, and they summarize both 6:12 and 6:14–15:

We are to forgive others.
If we don't forgive others, God won't forgive us.

Verse 12 is a prayer request: forgive us our sins *as* we have forgiven those who have sinned against us. In other words, the appeal to God for forgiveness is rooted in our forgiving others. For most of us this seems backward because it seems to make God's forgiveness conditioned on our forgiving others. But that's what Jesus says! Matthew 6:14–15, which interrupts the flow from 6:13 to 6:16–18 (but 6:7–13 is an interruption already, and 6:14–15 interrupts further), repeats this. It is likely that Matthew added this as a footnote, or a clarifying comment, by grabbing Mark 11:25–26. Forgiveness from God and our forgiving others are tied together by Jesus. This jars our Christian sensibilities, but that is precisely why Jesus says it as he does: we need to hear

---

33. Calvin, *Harmony of the Gospels*, 1:209–10; Guelich, *Sermon on the Mount*, 293, 312; France, *Matthew*, 247–49; Keener, *Matthew*, 220–22.

34. Hagner, *Matthew 1–13*, 150.

35. The words are not connected to the Lord's Prayer in Luke 11:1–4.

how connected our forgiveness and God's forgiveness are—not so we will go about trying to earn our forgiveness by forgiving others but so we will see the utter importance of being people who forgive.

In our faith we are taught that the *real* #1 is God has forgiven us, so the *real* order, and implied by Jesus, is this:

1. God has graciously forgiven us (of much greater sin/s).
2. Therefore, we are to forgive others to extend God's grace.
3. If we don't forgive others, we show we are not forgiven.
4. Forgiven people forgive others.
5. But our forgiveness does not earn God's forgiveness.

These five points can be taken as a rough-and-ready sketch of the process of how God's gracious forgiveness finds a moral compass of forgiveness in the life of the follower of Jesus without compromising the priority of grace; I am confident it is consistent with the kingdom vision of Jesus, and it is confirmed by Matthew 18:23–35.

We are bound in any teaching on forgiveness to speak to the seeming conditionality of how forgiveness works, and this can be taken as a footnote to #1 in the paragraph immediately above. This is where this prayer partakes in Jesus' Ethic from Above, forcing us to see God's demand, and an Ethic from Beyond, showing that new creation is already at work. In the Bible God is good, gracious, loving, and forgiving; God offers forgiveness. *But Jesus' intent in this passage is not to frame a forgiveness ethic in the deeper forgiveness by God. Instead, Jesus' aim is to demand forgiveness of his followers and threaten them with God's judgment if they don't become forgiving people.* His theory, then, is that forgiveness is reciprocal.[36]

Jesus is teaching a kingdom perspective on how to deal with those who have sinned against us. Since the kingdom is a world of reconciliation, kingdom people are to forgive. He doesn't need the above five points to make his case. He reduces the five points in order to sharpen the rhetoric of his concern. He's staring into the face of fellow Israelites who don't know the grace of enemy love and who want to appeal too quickly to the *lex talionis* or who want to become judges like God (7:1–5; cf. Jas 4:11–12). Moreover, that same audience needed to hear that forgiveness is the way kingdom living works. Those who genuinely love others forgive. Those who don't are not kingdom people.

Back now to the fifth petition of the Lord's Prayer. The petition to forgive finds its first-century life in the kingdom vision of Jesus to become forgiving people. So important to Jesus is forgiving others that he teaches his followers to ask God for forgiveness for themselves and others *because we are grace-receiving*

---

36. France, *Matthew*, 249–51.

and grace-giving people. Such an appeal to one's own virtues, righteousness, and morality is consistent with a long string of prayers in the Psalms, and though the language may grate against our grace-shaped nerves, that language never expunges the priority of God's grace. These words are designed to sharpen the edge of the need to forgive others, beginning with the Roman enemies. Jesus teaches his followers to ask God to forgive their "debts," and this metaphor "debt" is interpreted in the surrounding verses and parallel.

> Matthew 6:12 uses "debts."
> Matthew 6:14–15 uses "sin/trespasses."
> Luke 11:4 uses "sins."

We've already mentioned this, but it needs to be said again. In the world of Judaism there were two major ways to express the implications of sins and trespasses: burdens and debts.[37] If sin incurred a burden, a person wanted it lifted. Forgiveness in that world is the removal of a burden. The second way to express what incurred from sin was a debt. This opened a new linguistic game for how forgiveness worked: for the debtor, what one needed was cancellation of the debt or credits to compensate the debt. This kind of debt language, which was perfectly common to Jews of Jesus' day, also produced a way of expressing good moral deeds: they were seen as merits or credits.

Again, this does not mean Judaism was a works-based religion but that it chose to express sins and the removal of sin in that kind of language. Jesus, too, expressed himself in this kind of language, and he does not thereby imply a works-based religion. So, while we are prone to critique Judaism as a works religion because of its debt-merit language, we are prone also to relieve Jesus of such a charge when he speaks of heaven as a reward (which is debt-merit language that correlates one's "reward" from God to one's behaviors). We need to be more honest. Jesus talked like his contemporaries.

> Rejoice and be glad, for your reward is great in heaven (5:12).
> ... for then you have no reward from your Father in heaven (6:1; cf. vv. 2, 5, 16).
> When evening came, the owner of the vineyard said to his foreman, "Call the workers and pay them their wages, beginning with the last ones hired and going on to the first" (20:8).

As we release Jesus from the charge, so we ought to release Judaism from the accusation. What perhaps pokes us in the eye in this issue is that Judaism

---

37. The best discussion of the various images of sin in the Bible is J. Goldingay, "Your Iniquities Have Made a Separation between You and Your God," in *Atonement Today* (ed. J. Goldingay; London: SPCK, 1995), 39–53, who explores nine terms for sin in the Old Testament.

doesn't have a prayer seeking for God's forgiveness that is as conditional as the Lord's Prayer.[38] I'm not saying that Judaism didn't have pockets of works-shaped religion, but so also does Christianity. What goes alongside any kind of compensatory language in the Bible is a God who is gracious, who acts first to establish covenant, who redeems and transforms and restores, who in that covenant redemptive model exhorts the people of God to live obediently, and then who rewards them for their behaviors.

The Temptation and the Evil One (6:13)

At one level, the sixth petition seems preposterous. Does Jesus really mean we are to ask God to pave the road of life in such a way that we are never tempted? I wonder how many millions of Christians have prayed this sixth petition without ever thinking of the shocking nature of its words if taken at face value. Interpreters tend to assume this request hinges on the meaning of two words: the meaning of "temptation" and the meaning of "the evil one."

What does it mean to ask God not to lead us into "temptation"? Since the word *peirasmos*, used here, means either "test, trial" or "temptation," one could also render it, "Lead me not into the test, or the trial." The word itself doesn't decide for us but context does, and this leads to the question of why God would test/tempt, or even more, *could* God tempt/test. While it is possible that God could test, which is the whole point of the wilderness wanderings of Israel and was recently the experience of Jesus (Matt 4:1 – 11), both Jewish and Christian tradition affirm both the utter goodness of God as well as the impossibility for the good God to be complicit in evil. This is clearly taught in James 1:13: "For God cannot be tempted by evil, nor does he tempt anyone."

This means the word "temptation" must mean "test" if God is the one "leading." But this is where "deliver" rescues us, for the word "lead" gains clarity in the next verb, *rhysai*, "to rescue," which means to deliver both from and out of or to preserve (see, e.g., Matt 27:43; Luke 1:74; Rom 7:24; Col 1:13; 1 Thess 1:10; 2 Thess 3:2; 2 Tim 3:11; 2 Pet 2:7, 9). As a result, this petition is not so much about God's not leading us into testing or about God's leading us into temptation, but about God's protecting and rescuing us from temptation (or testing). In fact, this approach encourages us to read this temptation as a request not to endure what Jesus endured in his test in Matthew 4:1 – 11. In this case, then, "lead us not into temptation" could be understood as an equivalent to the apostle Paul's famous line in 1 Corinthians 10:13:

---

38. Both *Ha-Tepillah* and *Avinu Melkenu* plead for forgiveness from God but do not condition forgiveness on our forgiving others. But, as Allison cites the texts (*Sermon on the Mount*, 128), there is connection between God's forgiveness and our forgiving others at Sir 28:2; *m. Yoma* 8:9; *b. Šabbat* 15b; *Roš Haššanah* 17a. And he also cites Col 3:13.

> No temptation has overtaken you except what is common to man-
> kind. And God is faithful; he will not let you be tempted beyond what
> you can bear. But when you are tempted, he will also provide a way out
> so that you can endure it.

Thus, this request is about preservation from sin in temptation.

But using the seventh to interpret the sixth petition does not resolve the
meaning of "temptation." Does it mean moral "temptations"[39] or divine tests
(Gen 22:1–19) or the eschatological[40] "test" or "tribulation"? Many scholars
today, not the least of whom is Raymond Brown, contend that the Lord's
Prayer is thoroughly eschatological—that it is a prayer shaped entirely by the
prospect of an imminent arrival of the fullness of the kingdom.[41] It is hard to
gainsay such a reading of history for it is part of the earliest Christians' way
of thinking; but when one reads history like this, the eschatological dimension—because it becomes so all-pervasive—seems to diminish. I'm inclined
to think that temptation/test and the evil one are, like bread and sins, ordinary
dimensions of ordinary life for those who follow Jesus.[42]

This leads us to "evil one" or to "evil." Is "deliver us from evil" referring to
deliverance from sin in general, or is this about Satan, the evil one?[43] In the
gospel of Matthew, *ho ponēros* can refer to the evil one (see 5:37; 13:19, 38)
and in another prayer of Jesus this expression refers to Satan (John 17:15),[44]
but the evidence is not as clear as some think. For example, in 2 Timothy
4:18 Paul prays that the Lord will "rescue" (same word) him from every "evil"
attack, and *Didache* 10:5 prays the church may be saved from evil—and this
in contrast to love. Evidence then can be brought in to support both views.

These two petitions, at the safest level, are about aching that one's fellow
followers of Jesus will live morally holy and loving lives and will be rescued
through trust in God from temptations and from evil or the wiles of the Evil
One. What Peter says in 1 Peter 5:8 confirms this interpretation: "Be alert and
of sober mind. Your enemy the devil prowls around like a roaring lion looking
for someone to devour."

A brief note on the doxology. Readers of most editions of the Bible will
find a note that the best and earliest manuscripts do not have the commonly
recited doxology at the end of the Lord's Prayer: "For thine is the kingdom,

---

39. Calvin, *Harmony of the Gospels*, 1:213.

40. Davies and Allison, *Matthew*, 1:612–14.

41. R. E. Brown, "The Pater Noster as an Eschatological Prayer," in his *New Testament Essays* (Garden City, NY: Image, 1968), 265–320.

42. With Luz, *Matthew 1–7*, 322; Keener, *Matthew*, 223–24.

43. *Apo tou ponērou* is neuter in the general sense but masculine in the Evil One sense.

44. So Guelich, *Sermon on the Mount*, 314. See also Luke 22:28–32. But there is counterevi-
dence as well: see Luke 6:45; Rom 12:9.

and the power, and the glory, forever. Amen" (KJV). Neither does Luke's version of the Lord's Prayer in Luke 11:1–4 have a doxology. Those words appear to have been formed on the basis of 1 Chronicles 29:11–13 by someone later than Jesus and the writing of the gospel of Matthew; the doxology was added to the Lord's Prayer in public prayer, and then was gradually added to the text of the New Testament itself. We recite them today because the public recitation of the Lord's Prayer seems incomplete without such an ending.

 LIVE the Story

Whenever we talk about prayer, major questions arise, even if this is not the context in which to attempt answers to them. And since I've extended my limits already in a more extensive commentary on the passage, I'm already running short of space. But still, we ask, why pray? Does prayer make a difference, and if so, how?[45] Is God changeable?[46] How should we pray, and is there a better way to pray? It is too simplistic to propose, as Luther once did, that prayer does not enter into some form of an interactive relationship with God. Thus, he writes:

> The reason He commands it [prayer] is, of course, not in order to have us make our prayers an instruction to Him as to what He ought to give us, but in order to have us acknowledge and confess that He is already bestowing many blessings upon us and that He can and will give us still more.[47]

Undoubtedly this is true, but it is inadequate as a basis for our theology of prayer. The biblical facts are clear: God's changeability, not the least of which is to withdraw judgment upon repentance, is more often part of the biblical narrative than the rather rare comment that God is unchangeable, which pertains to God's utter faithfulness to promises. Good examples include Exodus 32:14; Psalm 106:45; Amos 7:3–6; Joel 2:13–14; and Jonah 4:2. Other biblical facts are also clear, though it is not often clear how we ought to bring them into a cohesive and compelling order: humans are in some sense free, with the stronger position believing in libertarian free will, while at the other end we have some form of compatibilism. As Calvin expresses this compatibilist view, which is undergirded by a view not unlike the citation from Luther

---

45. T. Tiessen, *Providence and Prayer: How Does God Work in Our World?* (Downers Grove, IL: InterVarsity Press, 2000), with an exceptional chart on pp. 363–64 that sorts out the options.

46. For an excellent sketch of this topic, see D. Lamb, *God Behaving Badly* (Downers Grove, IL: InterVarsity Press, 2011), 135–52.

47. Luther, *Exposition of the Lord's Prayer*, 144.

above: "Keep hold of both points, then: our prayers are anticipated by Him in His freedom, yet, what we ask we gain by prayer."[48]

I affirm what Tiessen calls the redemptive intervention model, in which God's overall plan is established and known to God while granting freedom within that plan. In this model, prayer changes things, and I believe the biblical models of prayer, from Abraham to David to Elijah to Isaiah to Jesus to Paul and the early churches, affirm this interactive model in which prayer sometimes alters the path of history within the overall plan of God *in response to the prayers of God's people*. The upload from this theoretical sketch is that our yearning and our aching for God's name to be hallowed, for God's kingdom to come, and for others to experience the blessing of God can prompt God to actions that satisfy those yearnings and aches.

The Lord's Prayer as Our Prayer

Perhaps the most neglected feature of the Lord's Prayer in the Sermon is that the long-winded prayers of the Gentiles form the foil for Jesus' prayer. In other words, the Lord's Prayer is a short and to-the-point prayer over against long prayers. Short prayers are good prayers. But again we need circumspection: there are lengthy prayers in the Bible that are commended, and Jesus prayed all night on occasions. The shortness of the Lord's Prayer, then, is not an instruction that all prayers on all occasions must be short, but that the long and gassy prayers of the Gentiles do not enter into the presence of God as does the Lord's Prayer.

The Lord's Prayer marks God's people. In the context of the Lord's Prayer in the Sermon and at Luke 11:1–4, its possible presence in 2 Timothy 4:18, but even more in *Didache* 8, the Lord's Prayer both formed and became a prayer that marked off the followers of Jesus from other groups in Judaism and the broader Roman world. Luke 11:1 informs us on the context of the Lord's Prayer. As Jews of Jesus' day had *Ha-Tepillah* (recited two to three times per day according to tradition), and as John's disciples had their prayer (Luke 11:1), so the Lord's Prayer is the distinctive prayer for the followers of Jesus.

This leads to the focus of this section: the Lord's Prayer is meant to be recited *whenever* the follower of Jesus prays.[49] This observation derives from the grammar of Luke 11:2: *whenever you pray, say this* [or, *recite this*]. What this means in the Jewish world is that *at the set hours of prayer*, which are almost certainly morning, midafternoon, and evening, the followers of Jesus either added the Lord's Prayer to *Ha-Tepillah*, or they replaced *Ha-Tepillah* with the Lord's Prayer. We are not to think every whisper of a prayer had to

---

48. Calvin, *Harmony of the Gospels*, 1:204.
49. For my own journey into set prayers at set times, see my *Praying with the Church*.

be accompanied with a Lord's Prayer. The facts are that the first-century Jew lived in a world where piety was marked by pausing three times a day (cf. Ps 55:17; Dan 6:10; Matt 6:5–6; Acts 3:1) and saying one's prayers, adding to them one's personal prayer requests.

Anyone who has been to Israel or been among the Orthodox Jews, or who has experience with a Muslim community, knows that set times for set prayers is an old, old tradition. It was pervasive among the Jewish community in the first century. To this day monastic communities pray at set times, and Kris and I have been the accidental beneficiaries of such prayer times. Once we entered a basilica in Norcia in order to cool off from the searing heat of Umbria only to discover a concert of prayer as the Benedictine monks chanted their morning prayers—in Latin of course! This experience of set times and set prayers is growing among many Protestant Christians in the world today, the sales of Phyllis Tickle's three-volume *Divine Hours* confirming this movement. A simple form of set time and set prayers is the recitation of the Jesus Creed as well as the Lord's Prayer, followed up by one's own personal prayers. The most typical times for such prayers are upon awaking, at noontime, and in the evening after dinner.

Before we put the second foot in the water, however, it must be observed that praying recited prayers is only one part of prayer. Alongside recited prayers, and our Bible's Psalter involves the use of set prayers, are personal prayers, spontaneous prayers, breath prayers, and meditative prayers done whenever and wherever we find ourselves. This too is how the Psalter arose: those were personal prayers raised to the level of set prayers.

For some it is tempting to use only set prayers, while for others it is almost a solemn requirement to use only spontaneous prayers. We need both, and in my *Praying with the Church* book I use an image from an experience in Italy. In Assisi Kris and I eventually found the famous Portiuncola church of Saint Francis, the small church that Francis restored shortly after his conversion. Today one can see that small chapel but, remarkably, it is in the middle of a large basilica—and these two "churches" illustrate two kinds of prayer. We are to pray our personal and spontaneous prayers in our own little Portiuncola while we are also encouraged to join the large assembly in the basilica as we pray set prayers at set times *with* the church.

The *Didache*, a Jewish Christian document, informs us that the Christians were instructed to pray the Lord's Prayer "three times a day" (*Did.* 8:3). This fits with the Jewish custom of three set times of prayer per day. Now turned toward us, this early Christian tradition found in Luke 11:2 as well as the *Didache* is not good advice but commandment: Jesus expected his followers to use this prayer daily. The early Christians used this prayer daily. The church prayer tradition has always used this prayer daily. We would do well to get back in sync with our Lord's instructions and the tradition of the church. I say this as one who grew up being taught and then believing that set prayers were for sissies, or to put it more piously, set prayers were nothing more than "vain repetition." This attitude is profoundly unbiblical and directly contrary to what Jesus taught and the church has always practiced.

Dale Allison has marshaled evidence in favor of the view that the Lord's Prayer is an *example* or a *model* rather than a set prayer, even if the earliest evidence, as noted above, counters that later evidence. Here are two examples from Allison's sketch.[50] Origen saw the Lord's Prayer as a form or an outline, and Isaac of Nineveh said that those who say we should "recite the prayer ... in all our prayers using the same wording and keeping the exact order of the words, rather than their sense, such a person is very deficient in his understanding." John Gill, the Baptist theologian, said the variants between the two Lord's Prayer accounts reveal that it was not a set prayer. But the examples of adding to the Lord's Prayer probably reveal the opposing viewpoint: namely, once one recited the Lord's Prayer, one then added personal prayer petitions, which also conforms to how some Jews used the *Ha-Tepillah*.

Allison's final examples also illustrate the recitation of the Lord's Prayer. Ambrose urged it be prayed only one time per day, while Cyril of Jerusalem shows its prominence in the Sunday liturgies. John Calvin, who did not think it had to be recited, is nonetheless right in the effects: the Lord's Prayer is our teacher and from it we learn the art of prayer. "So no-one," Calvin observed, "will learn to pray aright whose lips and heart are not schooled by the heavenly Teacher."[51] The Lord's Prayer is designed to control our prayers and provides the substance of our prayers.

Yes, the Lord's Prayer is our teacher; and the Lord's Prayer teaches us what we are to yearn for. Yet how can the Lord's Prayer accomplish such lofty goals—and learning how to pray aright is a lofty thing indeed—if we don't memorize it and recite it and let its words work their way into our heart and bones? Perhaps some have learned another way, but the age-old church way is the way of memorizing and reciting—daily—as a way of learning to pray with our Lord and as our Lord. This is perhaps why Luther, who himself had an aversion toward anything pedantic or pompous, said: "Hence it is a very good practice, especially for the common man and for children and servants in the household, to pray the entire Lord's Prayer every day, morning and evening and at table, and otherwise, too, as a way of presenting all sorts of general needs to God."[52]

---

50. Allison, *Sermon on the Mount*, 132–33.
51. Calvin, *Harmony of the Gospels*, 1:205.
52. Luther, *Exposition of the Lord's Prayer*, 145.

Prayer as Aching and Yearning

In the Lord's Prayer our desires are reordered into the ways of God and the ways of the kingdom. For seventeen years I taught college students a course called "Jesus of Nazareth." We begin each class period by reciting the Jesus Creed, and we end each class period by reciting the Lord's Prayer. I cannot tell you the number of times I have repeated, just after our recitation of the Lord's Prayer, how appropriate a line or two is for what we discussed that day. In other words, I stand with those who see in the Lord's Prayer an essential guide to the message and mission of Jesus. It falls short, of course, of being a compendium to Christian theology, though some have with ingenuity, if not downright manipulation, tried to wring all of Christian theology from this prayer. That won't do, but it will do to emphasize that his prayer expresses the heart of Jesus' kingdom vision. The Lord's Prayer teaches us to pray, not to theologize, but there is a theology at work in the Lord's Prayer, and that theology is the essence of Jesus' vision.

As such, it reorders our desires. We learn in the recitation, memorization, and repetition of this prayer to yearn for God's glory and for God's name to be held in highest honor, and we learn to long for God's kingdom (not ours) and for God's will (not ours) to be done. Then we learn to yearn and ache for the good of others. We yearn that each person will have sufficient food, that each person will find reconciliation with God through forgiveness of sins, and that each person will be protected and preserved by God's grace from the snares of temptations and the grasps of evil (or the evil one). When we are done, our desires have been reordered to God and to others, and in having those desires we find ourselves as God made us to be: beings designed to have proper loves, that is, love for God and love for others.

Is Calling God "Father" Patriarchal?

I want to end this sketch of the Lord's Prayer with an excursus on a debated topic. Charles Talbert, in a brief but insightful discussion of this question,[53] contends that language has two primary connotations: one relational and one political. In the first, a label — in this case calling God "Father" — describes a relationship. That is, God relates to us as a father relates to one of his children, and we are children as children relate to their parents or to a parent. In the second, one uses language to project onto the canvas of the cosmos one's beliefs, or one's cosmological world imposes language on the way we talk. Thus, to say God is a father is to project God as a father in the political landscape of the world, or we use "father" because, like fathers in this world, we get to impose power on others the way fathers impose on children.

---

53. Talbert, *Reading the Sermon on the Mount*, 112–15.

But Talbert contends biblical language does not work politically, or else goddess language would have emerged from matriarchal cultures. But it didn't; it emerged from patriarchal cultures. Thus, the political approach to the biblical language for God isn't helpful. Talbert further argues that a relational view of language transcends sexuality in the Bible, for God is often described in maternal images, not the least being that God can cry out like a woman in travail (Isa 42:14). He then suggests that God is called "father" in the Bible because of Israel's experience of God and because Jesus taught us to. Neither of these elements has anything to do with making God male or a sexual being.

Talbert has adequately discussed the language of the Bible and mined the sources to show that the language was not sexist in the way many talk today, but he has only gone halfway round the track. The issue is as much today as it was then. That is, "father" today evokes a kind of paternalism or male authority that creates problems in understanding what God is like in the Bible. We are in need of sensitivity training here, and I would urge us to spend more time explaining both what fatherhood meant in that ancient world, where intimacy and authority were combined but where authority could be unquestioned, and what fatherhood evokes today, where once again authority can be unquestioned and abusive.

I don't think any term—and family language is at the heart of the biblical vision of God—will escape the problems of abuse. Instead, the teacher of Scripture is called to teach what the Bible says, apply it ruthlessly against abuses, and at the same time embody a godly fatherliness (or motherliness) so that children can both see the Bible's vision and experience the love and intimacy of the family—from fathers and mothers. This approach, in other words, calls into question many cheap and authoritarian views of parenting in our world and draws us to reform society on the basis of what God is like. So I would urge us to double our efforts to restore what "father" means and embody it in our world so that the day will come when the term "father" will never evoke abuse or authoritarian behaviors.

CHAPTER 14

Matthew 6:16–18

16"When you fast, do not look somber as the hypocrites[1] do, for they disfigure their faces to show others they are fasting. Truly I tell you, they have received their reward in full. 17But when you fast, put oil on your head and wash your face,[2] 18so that it will not be obvious to others that you are fasting, but only to your Father, who is unseen; and your Father, who sees what is done in secret, will reward you."

Listening to the text in the Story: Leviticus 16:29–31; 23:26–32; Psalm 35:13–14; Isaiah 58.

Fasting has a colorful history both in the Story of the Bible and in the Story of the church after the apostles, and some of that history can be found in the sharp criticisms of Luther.[3] But the colorful history of fasting in the church has substantively reshaped what we find in the Bible.[4] The most influential understanding of fasting today is the *instrumental* theory. In the simplest of terms, this theory teaches that we fast *in order to gain some benefit*. The most commonly promised benefits are spiritual growth, suppression of sins, improved health, and a much better chance of answers to our prayers. Some even contend that many Christians haven't realized higher levels of spirituality because they do not fast. This more instrumental view is a fixed part of the church tradition, including Calvin, who said:

> [Fasting] pleases Him up to a point, as long as it is directed to an end beyond itself, namely, to prompt us to abstinence, to subject the lasciviousness of the flesh, to incense us to a desire for prayer, to testify to our repentance, whenever we are moved by the judgment of God.[5]

---

1. KNT: "play-actors."
2. KNT: "tidy your hair and beard the way you normally do."
3. Luther, *Sermon on the Mount*, 155–66, esp. 157. After listing the various fasts, he concludes: "Now, if you put all this fasting together on one pile, it is not worth a heller."
4. A classic short treatment is Foster, *Celebration of Discipline*, 47–61.
5. Calvin, *Harmony of the Gospels*, 1:215.

But instrumental fasting is all but impossible to find in the pages of the Bible and is rarely reflected in ancient Judaism or the rabbis.[6] Instead of an instrumental approach, the genius of the Bible is its focus on the whole-body *response* of a human being to grievous, severe conditions. Fasting means a human being refrains from food or water, or both, for a limited period of time *in response to some sacred, grievous moment.* Such sacred or grievous moments include death, the threat of war, sin, our neediness, or our fear of God's judgment. These kinds of events expose God as judge, God as the giver and taker of life, and God as the one before whom we live.

John Wesley, who himself fasted rigorously and about whom criticisms were made for his rigor, said it this way: the "natural incentive for fasting … [is for those] who are under deep affliction, overwhelmed with sorrow for sin, and filled with a strong anxiety about the wrath of God."[7] To say this once again, the focus of the Bible on fasting is *not on what we get* from fasting or on motivating people to fast in order to acquire something, but instead lands squarely *on responding to sacred moments in life.*[8] Fasting enters into how God interprets, experiences, understands, and explains significant events. Fasting, in fact, enters into God's pathos, or into what God thinks and feels about death, sin, war, violence, and injustice.

If we listen to the Bible's Story and pay attention to the emergence of fasting, we discover three major ideas: fasting is connected to Yom Kippur, the Day of Atonement, as the Israelite prepared for confession, atonement, and forgiveness (Lev 16:29–31; 23:26–32). Fasting also includes a spontaneous response to a grievous event, as when David interceded and prayed for the healing of his enemies (Ps 35:11–16). In Isaiah 58 the prophet connects the true fast to doing justice, caring for the poor, and providing food for the hungry.

Our passage in the Sermon on the Mount draws from the custom of fasting at a specific time as well as from the spontaneous, voluntary response to a grievous moment (like David). Overall, then, fasting is how Israel responded when God's glory was dishonored, when God's will was thwarted, when God's people suffered defeat, or when one of God's people experienced sickness, tragedy, or death. God's people, in effect then, took up the posture of God toward grievous events when they fasted.

By the time of Jesus, fasting had become a biweekly act of piety for many observant Jews. Nowhere in the Old Testament are Israelites told to fast twice

---

6. Thus, *m. Taʿanit* 1:2–7 then in the Talmud at *b. Taʿanit* 12b; also at *b. Baba Meṣiʿa* 85a. See G. F. Moore, *Judaism in the First Centuries of the Christian Era, The Age of the Tannaim* (3 vols.; Cambridge, MA: Harvard University Press, 1932), 2.55–69, 257–66.

7. Kinghorn, *Wesley on the Sermon,* 181. For his practical advice, see pp. 191–95.

8. See S. McKnight, *Fasting* (The Ancient Practices Series; Nashville: Nelson, 2009).

a week, but by the time of Jesus fasting every Monday and Thursday was common piety:[9]

> The Pharisee stood by himself and prayed: "God, I thank you that I am not like other people — robbers, evildoers, adulterers — or even like this tax collector. *I fast twice a week* and give a tenth of all I get." (Luke 18:11 – 12, italics added)

This biweekly fasting discipline was so ingrained that Jesus was called into question because his followers did not fast as, or when, the Pharisees did (Mark 2:18 – 22). In response, Jesus indicated that his disciples, though they might not be fasting while he was present, would fast in the future.[10] An early Christian text (*Did.* 8.1) indicates that some of Jesus' followers fasted twice a week, though they did so on Wednesday and Friday to distinguish themselves from the Jews, who fasted on Monday and Thursday. This custom of regularly scheduled, or stationary, fasting became not only a fixed feature of the church's spiritual disciplines but the dominant mode of fasting. Examination of the history of fasting in the postapostolic church, however, reveals that the earliest impulses for stationary fasting were grieving responses to sin and human unworthiness before the Eucharist.

EXPLAIN the Story

Jesus sketches before the eyes (through graphic verbal images) and ears what following him entails and so provides an "ethic of the kingdom," what we are calling an Ethic from Beyond. He expects his disciples *to practice* what he teaches, and he warns those who don't want to practice what he teaches about God's judgment (Matt 7:13 – 27). At the heart of the Sermon is a section on spiritual disciplines because Jesus expects his disciples to practice charity, praying, and fasting. Jesus, however, doesn't command almsgiving, prayer, or fasting but assumes them. The central issue that provokes Jesus is an act done to be noticed as pious and to gain a reputation. Disciplines are done with eye, heart, mind, and soul focused on God. Fasting had been abused at least since the days of Isaiah 58. Zechariah, too, asked, "When you fasted ... was it really for me [God] that you fasted?" (Zech 7:5).[11]

---

9. Suetonius, *Augustus* 76, tells us that Augustus compared his own sparing eating habits favorably over against the fasting practices of the Jews. See: www.gutenberg.org/files/6400/6400.txt.

10. Instances include Acts 13:2 – 3; 14:23.

11. From the OT Apocrypha, Jesus ben Sirach (Sir 34:31; in Greek, 34:26) writes: "So if one fasts for his sins, and goes again and does the same things, who will listen to his prayer? And what has he gained by humbling himself?" See *T. Asher* 2.5 – 10. For further information, Moore, *Judaism in the First Centuries*, 2:55 – 69 (public piety), 257 – 66 (private piety); R. Banks, "Fasting," *DJG*, 233 – 34.

Matthew 6:16–18 continues with the structural outline given in 6:1, and in our new paragraph he plugs fasting into the structure we observed at 6:1–4:

The observance (6:16a):

"When you fast ..."

Prohibition (6:16b):

"do not look somber as the hypocrites do..."

Intent (6:16c):

"for they disfigure their faces to show others they are fasting."

Amen ... reward (6:16d):

"Truly I tell you, they have received their reward in full."

Alternative observance (6:17–18a):

"But when you fast, put oil on your head and wash your face, so that it will not be obvious to others that you are fasting, but only to your Father, who is unseen ..."

Father's reward (6:18b):

"and your Father, who sees what is done in secret, will reward you."

The Observance (6:16a)

"When"—or perhaps even more accurately "whenever"—the disciples fast, they are to avoid looking somber and instead anoint the head with oil (6:17). But what is involved when someone in Jesus' day fasted? A good example is found in the later Mishnah, *Ta'anit* 1:3–7, where fasting is a response to a drought and the text clarifies what the people are permitted to do on those days: "They eat and drink once it gets dark. And they are permitted to work, bathe, anoint, put on a sandal, and have sexual relations." The common fast in Judaism was from the evening meal to the next evening meal—skipping food at breakfast and midday. It wasn't heroic but demanded enough for discomfort.

The Prohibition (6:16b)

Jesus tells his followers not to "look somber" like the hypocrites, and he partly explains what this means when he adds that the hypocrites "disfigure their faces." Jesus describes some kind of gloomy disposition, as is apparent in the faces of the disciples on the road to Emmaus (Luke 24:17). Their gloominess is *intentional* because the term "disfigure"[12] evokes the intentional masking or contorting of a face in some manner—perhaps the way small children put on a face when they are informed of something they don't want to happen. One could think of using dust or ashes on the top of one's head as a sign of grief, or it is also possible that "disfigure" is a metaphor. Perhaps Jesus is thinking of even more, like donning sackcloth or even rending one's garments to show one's grief.[13]

Intent (6:16c)

The element of intention is central to Jesus' point. Grief is fine; sullenness is fine; gloom is fine—but to display them intentionally is wrong. The hypocrites disfigure themselves in order "to show others they are fasting." As Calvin put it, they were "playing to the gallery."[14] They convert the act of fasting into performance. Instead of participating in God's perspective on something over which one ought to be sorrowful and instead of entering into the grief of a sacred moment, the hypocrites (see comment on 6:1) turn a sacred occasion into theatrical performance to draw attention to their own piety. This passage provides us with a sharp understanding of "hypocrisy" as the intentional manipulation of a sacred moment into a moment of self-adulation.[15] Fasting is designed to show grief about someone or something else but here morphs tragically into a public display of the ego.

Amen ... Reward (6:16d)

Jesus' terse evaluation is damning: "Truly I tell you, they have their reward" (6:16). Clearly cutting humans into two categories here, as he does elsewhere in this Sermon (cf. 5:3–12, 13–16; 7:13–27), Jesus informs his followers (or would-be followers) that hypocritical behavior is how "they" (the hypocrites) behave, but with his followers behaviors are to be different. Furthermore, the public praise the hypocrites gain from their pious behaviors is as far as it will go: God is not in that adulation and stands as a judge over against that behavior. Jesus' words "they have received their reward in full" is a powerful understatement, and one finds a similar understatement in the word "least" in 5:19. Those who convert piety into performance are the least; those who fast properly are the "great" (5:19).

---

12. Greek *aphanizō* means "to make unrecognizable through change in appearance" (BDAG, 154). There is a play on words here in what can be called a "delicious irony" (France, *Matthew*, 255): "disfigure" and "show" translate words that sound alike (*aphanizō* and *phainō*). For more discussion, see Betz, *Sermon on the Mount*, 420–21.

13. See Dan 9:3; Jonah 3:5.

14. Calvin, *Harmony of the Gospels*, 1:214.

15. The Greek term *hypocritēs* emerges from theater. See BDAG, 1038. A suggestive study here is Batey, *Jesus and the Forgotten City*, 83–103.

Alternative Observance (6:17 – 18a)

Instead of transforming a spiritual act into an opportunity to be congratulated, Jesus summons them to bury what they do and to sink their pious deeds so deeply into the heart and soul that they become unaware of what others think or see. Jesus may well be turning the act of fasting inside out in a comic act of exaggeration: the quintessential act of grief in the Jewish world (fasting) becomes an act of celebration. How so? He tells them to "put oil on your head and wash your face" (6:17). As we find in Psalms 23:5 and 104:15, oil on the head or face is a sign of gladness and joy, and this might mean Jesus encourages them to dress up for a party.

But perhaps this view overstates the evidence. It is just as likely that Jesus is urging his followers to do what is common for everyday hygiene: application of oil to the hair and a face or body wash in a bath or *mikveh* or even a stream or lake, which would be customary for the followers of Jesus near the Sea of Galilee, are normal daily behaviors (see 2 Sam 12:20; 14:2). One might argue that Jesus urges his followers to deceive their observers into thinking the disciples are not in fact fasting when they are. Such a nettle does not appear in the path or need to be navigated if one prefers, as many have, to see "put oil on your head and wash your face" as only an effective figure of speech. That is, Jesus means nothing more than avoid making your fasting public, whatever that might involve. This is the emphasis of Jesus in verse 18: "so that it will not be obvious to others that you are fasting."

Father's Reward (6:18b)

Jesus turns his disciples away from the way of the hypocrite and toward God alone. He doesn't provide a trick or a technique for how that might be accomplished. Instead, he narrows his scope, as he often does, to the orientation of the heart. We live in a world of evaluations, assessments, and measurements, but Jesus turns his gaze deeper because he knows that what is measurable can be faked. His focus is that his followers are to focus their deeds on the God who rewards direct engagement.

Moderns, as we said in the previous passage, balk at Jesus' overt emphasis on rewards, but for those who care to think about this more deeply, Jesus escapes modern sensibilities and fussiness about the superiority of abstract altruism. For Jesus God matters (Ethic from Above, Messianic Ethic), and doing things for God's final approval (Ethic from Beyond) is all that matters. Religious deeds are not done according to Jesus because of their abstract quality of goodness but because God, who alone is good, summons his people to share in his goodness by extending it to others.

Jesus can urge followers to love their neighbor as themselves (22:39) just as he can teach the Golden Rule that we should use our own desires as the measure of how we treat others (7:12). One might construe such moral instructions to be selfish, but this too is a mistake. As Allison observes, the Sermon "does not overestimate human nature but confronts it in its self-centered reality with fear and hope."[16] For Jesus, doing something with an eye toward God's approval transcends both altruism and selfishness.

LIVE the Story

Fasting has been abused in the history of the church just as it was abused by the hypocrites and before them by Isaiah's audience—as people used it to enhance their reputations. Thus, Christians have added to that temptation by extending it into a manipulative device by which the fasting person believes he or she can pressure God into doing what he or she wants. There is much to learn from Jesus' teaching about fasting in its Jewish context,[17] and there is much to learn from the temptations to abuse and manipulate fasting. Perhaps we need to reinvigorate fasting as a Christian response to life's sacred moments and to probe when, why, and how fasting has for so many become a negligible dimension of Christian praxis.

Bonhoeffer follows a long line of Christians who have an instrumental theory of fasting and who think rigor and austerity are fundamental to genuine discipleship, but he warns: "The only purpose of such practices [as fasting] is to make disciples more willing and more joyous in following the designated path and doing the works required of them." His words come today as a reminder of how easy we have made it: "Satiated flesh is unwilling to pray and is unfit for self-sacrificing service."[18] But Bonhoeffer reminds us again of a fuller sense of what all this means as a Christian: the daily death of the old self can only come through faith in a King Jesus who lived, died, was buried, and was raised to be exalted to the right hand of God. Yet, the church's tradition aside, fasting is largely irrelevant to most Protestants today, though it remains a fixed part of the calendar and ideal spiritual practice in church traditions.

There is more to what Jesus says about fasting than what is found here. One passage that deserves attention is Mark 2:18 – 22, where fasting is a response to kingdom hope. Jesus declares that his disciples will fast as a way of yearning for God's glory, for God's kingdom, for God's justice, and for God's peace.[19]

---

16. Allison, *Sermon on the Mount*, 137.
17. Keener, *Matthew*, 226 – 28.
18. Bonhoeffer, *Discipleship*, 158.
19. See John Piper, *A Hunger for God: Desiring God through Fasting and Prayer* (Wheaton, IL: Crossway, 1997); Kent Berghuis, *Christian Fasting: A Theological Approach* (Richardson, TX: Biblical Studies Press, 2007).

The Christian is the person who has absorbed the Story of God in Jesus Christ, and that gospel Story teaches us that God's grace comes to us in a way that redounds to the glory of Jesus Christ — not to ourselves. One might even say that Jesus' own fasting (4:1 – 11) perfects any fasting we might do, and our task is simply to participate in his fasting the way we participate in his life, death, and resurrection. Because our life participates in his, any attempt to draw attention to our own piety dishonors Christ. So what can we learn from what Jesus says about fasting?

First, we need to bury our disciplines deeply into the heart to do them for the right reason: to engage with God for the good of others. Motive is what matters to Jesus. Different individuals will approach this differently: some will refuse to tell others they are fasting, some will have to mask their own pain (fasting can be a challenge physically), while yet others will be able to discuss it openly without the temptation to congratulate themselves. But probably each of us needs to be conscious of our desire for a good reputation.

The colorful language of Martin Luther can hardly be improved. Fasting, he observed, had become "a device for having people look at them, talk about them, admire them, and say in astonishment: 'Oh, what wonderful saints these people are! They do not live like the other, ordinary people. They go around in gray coats, with their heads hanging down and a sour, pale expression on their faces. If such people do not get to heaven, what will become of the rest of us?' "[20] John Chrysostom knew of Christians who, though not fasting themselves, wore the garments of those who were fasting in order to exonerate themselves.[21] Every time we fast we need to check ourselves.

Second, the lack of emphasis on the promises that come to the one fasting — Jesus only promises "reward" — means we need to avoid motivating people to fast by what they might gain. The obsession some have with marketing fasting because of its many blessings can be called "benefititis," the inflammation of material and spiritual blessings that come to the one who fasts. There are no guarantees because fasting is not a mechanical device we ply in order to get something. Fasting responds to sacred and grievous moments, and sometimes we get what we hoped for, but it is not because we fasted — and showed to God how serious we were — but because God, in his grace, showered us with blessings.

Third, fasting is not the same thing as abstinence. To abstain is to select one item, say chocolate, the Internet, Twitter, Facebook, the movies, or a vacation in the heat during the winter, and to cut it out of one's life as a spiritual act of discipline. Fasting is the voluntary choice not to eat at all (or not eat or

---

20. Luther, *Sermon on the Mount*, 155.
21. In ACCS: *Matthew*, 140 – 41.

drink) for a specific period in response to something. One isn't "fasting" when one chooses to abstain from the Internet. (I know, people call this fasting, but it cheapens the meaning of fasting as it also cheapens the significance of sacred, grievous moments in life.)

Fourth, because my wife, Kris, is a psychologist and because we have had friends' children with severe cases of anorexia nervosa (and I have taught a few college students with that condition), I urge anyone who teaches about fasting to minimize its significance for teenagers, young adults, and anyone who struggles with eating disorders and body image. This is precisely what Jesus is talking about: he urged his followers to fast for the right reasons and not to fast if they had the wrong motives, and young adults who fast in order to lose weight are not genuinely fasting—they are starving themselves.[22] It is unwise for pastors, parents, and youth pastors to excite youth into fasting, then, for both spiritual and developmental reasons.

Fifth, it is noticeable that Jesus does not evoke fasting heroes—like Moses or Elijah (or even himself), who fasted for long periods. It is too noticeable that we do. One such fasting hero is the Roman Catholic monk Adalbert de Vogüé, whose book *To Love Fasting* tells the story of his romantic lifetime of fasting—and it's a good book and a good story—but few of us are monks and few of us need to begin fasting every day for the rest of our lives. The emphasis in the Bible is that fasting is a *response* to sacred moments, like death, or the realization of sinfulness, or the fear of death, danger, or disaster, or the new medical report of a potentially fatal disease.

The routine or stationary fast of one or two days a week simply isn't the way the Bible describes fasting, even if the church has thrown its weight in that direction. The stationary fast has a place in the church, *as long as it learns to orient itself toward the grievous condition or sacred moments and avoids concentrating on what we can gain from it.* And the routine calendrical fasting—such as during Lent or in preparation for Advent—have clear biblical precedent in the Day of Atonement fast, but that fast was not depicted as heroic. It was expected to be done by all Israelites as a way of facing sin and looking to God.

Sixth, at work in the Bible's teaching on fasting is an anthropology: that we are an organic unity and not dualisms. We are body, soul, and spirit and not bodies with a spirit or soul dwelling in us. The former sees us as an organic unity, while the latter sees us as having an inferior part (body) and a superior part (soul, spirit). Fasting in the Bible is the organic, unified response of a whole person to a sacred moment. We can provoke more biblical fasting simply by teaching a more organic sense of who we are.

---

22. See Joan Jacobs Brumberg, *Fasting Girls* (rev. ed.; New York: Vintage, 2000).

Finally, we can help the church become more biblical by responding to sacred, grievous moments—like 9/11, a hurricane's devastation, or a fire tearing across a California hillside—by calling Christians to fast in response to the devastation and as a way of entering into the grief of God. Instead of promising blessings and benefits, we can call attention to the grievous moments of our lives, our church, and our communities and urging God's people to fast. Time will tie our bodies to our mind, soul, spirit, and heart.

Matthew 6:19–24

 LISTEN to the Story

¹⁹"Do not store up for yourselves treasures on earth, where moths and vermin destroy, and where thieves break in and steal. ²⁰But store up for yourselves treasures in heaven, where moth and rust do not destroy, and where thieves do not break in and steal. ²¹For where your treasure is, there your heart will be also.[1]

²²"The eye is the lamp of the body. If your eyes are healthy,[2] your whole body will be full of light. ²³But if your eyes are unhealthy,[3] your whole body will be full of darkness. If then the light within you is darkness, how great is that darkness![4]

²⁴"No one can serve two masters. Either you will hate the one and love the other, or you will be devoted to the one and despise the other. You cannot serve both God and money."

Listening to the text in the Story: Exodus 20:3; Leviticus 19:9; 23:22; 24:19; 25; Deuteronomy 24:19; 28; Amos; Haggai 1.

More than one billion people in the world live on less than one dollar per day; about three billion live on less than two dollars per day. Between 12 and 20 percent of Americans live below what we call our poverty line. With those simple facts on your mind, I'd like you to get up from reading this book and observe what you have, what is accessible to you, and what you and I take for granted. I'm sitting in my personal library: a heater next to me, a workable computer I own, thousands of books within twenty or thirty feet. If I want water, I can get it; if I prefer coffee, I can get that—espresso machine, bean grinder, milk frother. If I want a snack, I have a pantry full of food. If I need lunch, I see what's available in the refrigerator. The house is warm or, in the summer, cooled by air conditioning. I do not worry what to wear, for I have a

---

1. KNT: "Show me your treasure, and I'll show you where your heart is."
2. KNT: "honest and clear."
3. KNT: "evil."
4. KNT: "darkness doesn't come any darker than that."

dresser and a closet full of clothing. I do not worry about safety as my house is sturdy, and we have had funds available for repairs and reconstruction. Our community is policed and safe.

The Jesus we follow seems to have had nothing. He lived in a dry, hot, and dusty world. What food he ate he received by fishing, by farming, or by donations. The summers were long and filled with famine-causing heat; the houses in places like Capernaum were made of black basalt and were sturdy but hardly cool enough to make life comfortable. To cool off people waded into the Sea of Galilee. He lived on little; he lived from the generosity of others; he undoubtedly knew some hunger and thirst.

Jesus saw homes every day, from Sepphoris (just north of Nazareth) to Tiberias all the way around to the cities of the Decapolis, where wealthier Jews or Romans had villas and plenty of food and entertainment. He undoubtedly knew of the heated Roman baths Herod had built at Masada and other locations. He knew what it was to have little and to dwell with those who had even less while others around him basked in luxury and filled their mouths with delicacies. In Jesus' Bible were passages about the Jubilee, and he evoked that very theme in his opening sermon in Luke 4:16–30. His vision tapped into the Jubilee, the gleanings, and the prophetic words — and he embodied a carefree, trust-in-God kind of economic vision. He demanded simplicity because he lived it; he expected care for the poor because he had experienced it.

The irony of wealthy followers of Jesus cannot be ignored.

In the history of the church a number of Christians have stood up and said, "Enough is enough!" and called the church to its knees about its participation in wealth and opulence while those around them were suffering in poverty and hunger. Some of them were extremists, like Saint Anthony of the Desert, Saint Francis of Assisi, and in our own day Shane Claiborne of Philadelphia. Their extremism reminds us of the call to simplicity by Jesus. Others write themselves into a pitch about our extravagances and comforts, and I think here of both the ancient church's Clement of Alexandria's famous *Who Is the Rich Man?* and Ronald Sider's *Rich Christians in an Age of Hunger: Moving from Affluence to Generosity.*[5]

Back to Jesus again, who knew the obedience-leads-to-material-blessings tradition of Deuteronomy 28 and who had contemporaries who no doubt embraced that very tradition, especially if they were wealthy. When Jesus stood up to warn his followers about attachment to or accumulation of possessions, he stood in a long line of biblical laws and prophetic announcements about idolatry, the danger of accumulation, justice, and the need to distribute

---

5. R. J. Sider, *Rich Christians in an Age of Hunger: Moving from Affluence to Generosity* (Dallas: Word, 1997).

one's excess in order to care for those who had little.[6] Like the ancient prophets, Jesus' teaching in our passages isn't simply about the ideal society, and neither is it an economic theory; this is about worship and idolatry. What Jesus had to say to his followers who were seeking to embody the kingdom vision of Jesus has even more to say to the affluence of Christians in the West. Jesus' message can be reduced to these ideas: Live simply. Possessions are mysteriously idolatrous. Trust God.

EXPLAIN the Story

In 6:19 Jesus begins a new set of instructions; the connection to what precedes is far from clear as he moves from three spiritual disciplines (6:1–18) to the idea of lordship and possessions (6:19–34). Dale Allison explains this as a shift to "social obligations."[7] Luther calls it "Sir Greed,"[8] but Calvin, correctly I think, reminds us "that we have here a series of short utterances, not a continuing address."[9] As any synopsis of the Gospels shows, Matthew's three sayings in 6:19–24 are found in three different locations in Luke (see Luke 12:33–34; 11:34–35; 16:13).

However one explains the shift, or however far one extends the next section (I connect 6:19 through 6:34), 6:19–24 contains three separable but similar units that use concrete images/metaphors to teach one simple message on the necessity of disciples disentangling themselves from possessions: treasures (6:19–21), the single eye (6:22–23), and serving two masters (6:24). And then in 6:25–34 Jesus uses images of God's care for creation to instill trust in him for provisions. Instead of seeing a logical progression in 6:19–24, which would assume these were given in rapid succession by Jesus, it might be wiser for us to see these as three images communicating a similar idea. Each unit contains a thesis statement (6:19a, 22a, 24a, 25) followed by two observations (6:19b–20, 22b–23b, 24b-c, and 26, 28–30) and a concluding summary (6:21, 23c-d, 24d, 31–34).

Treasures (6:19–21)
The treasure image unit has three elements: a prohibition (6:19), a positive command (6:20), and the reason (6:21). The follower of Jesus—that is, the one who is committed both to Jesus and to his kingdom vision and who lets that vision frame all of life, is prohibited from storing up treasures. The word

---

6. See appropriate texts in Keener, *Matthew*, 228–34.
7. Allison, *Sermon on the Mount*, 138.
8. Luther, *Sermon on the Mount*, 166.
9. Calvin, *Harmony of the Gospels*, 1:217.

"treasures" here surely involves possessions, but it is not the same as possessions. Instead, it refers to the accumulation of things as a focus of joy. It refers to the spirit of acquisitiveness or the desire to acquire.

Jesus' point is that these things are temporary,[10] a point trenchantly painted by James (James 5:1–6), and no one reading this book hasn't had something that has worn out (jeans, shoes, a car, a lawnmower, a computer). Joe Kapolyo, a Zambian, tells of taking out an endowment policy that would have matured at 45,000 kwacha, enough to buy a retirement home, but five years later a schoolteacher was making 110,000 kwacha.[11] The brevity of the life of things can become a sacrament of the eternal if we but look into the depth of how transitory our things are. In fact, Luther says the "great idol Mammon" has anointed "three trustees — rust, moths, and thieves" — that ought to remind us of the temporality of possessions.[12]

In contrast, the disciple is commanded to store up treasures that last, and here "treasures" moves from things we value that are temporal to things we value that are moral and eternal. Jesus uses typical merit language when he uses "treasures."

> For behold, the days are coming, and the books will be opened in which are written the sins of all those who have sinned, and moreover, also the treasuries in which are brought together the righteousness of all those who have proved themselves to be righteous. (*2 Bar.* 24:1)

> Our rabbis taught: It is related of King Monobaz [first-century king of Adiabene, who was accused by his brothers of squandering possessions, said to them:] ... "My fathers stored up below and I am storing above.... My fathers stored in a place which can be tampered with, but I have stored in a place which cannot be tampered with.... My fathers gathered treasures of money, but I have gathered treasures of souls.... My

---

10. The words used are "where moths and vermin destroy" (NIV). Many translations have "moth and rust." For discussion, see Davies and Allison, *Matthew*, 1:629–30; Hagner, *Matthew 1–13*, 157. The Greek term *brōsis* means "eating" or even "decay," but the issue is what is doing the eating/decaying, and many think James 5:2–3's use of "corrosion" (a different Greek term, *ios*) tells us what is doing the eating/decaying. But this term *brōsis* might mean a living organism (cf. Isa 51:8; Mal 3:11), like a grasshopper, a worm, or, as in the NIV, a more general idea like "vermin." If the two doing the destroying are creatures instead of natural aging, then what is being eaten/decayed is probably clothing or food, in which case the "treasures" are clothing or food. This image is then doubled with the image of thieves breaking through the walls; most of the area in Galilee had homes built of stone, but also some of wood and earth (mud bricks). On this K. Galor, "Domestic Architecture," in C. Hezser, ed., *The Oxford Handbook of Jewish Daily Life in Roman Palestine* (New York: Oxford University Press, 2010), 420–39.

11. Kapolyo, "Matthew," 1123.

12. Luther, *Sermon on the Mount*, 168. He mocks the great idol Mammon: "The best guards and courtiers he can assemble are moths and rust" (169).

fathers gathered for this world, but I have gathered for the future world."
(*b. Baba Batra* 11a)

This means we are led to ask what lasts, and what lasts is love (see 1 Cor 13). We can begin to focus on the eternal if we live to *love* God and others (the Jesus Creed), if we pursue *justice* as the way we are called to love others as God's creations, if we live out a life that drives for *peace* as how loving people treat one another, and if we strive for *wisdom* instead of just knowledge or bounty. Jesus commonly urges his followers to live in the light of life after death, or the age to come (his Ethic from Beyond): Matt 5:3–12, 19–20, 22, 29–30; 6:10; 7:13–14, 21–27. A concrete expression of treasures that last is how Martin Luther King Jr., after winning the Nobel Peace Prize, donated his considerable financial award to the cause of human freedom.[13]

Jesus' grounding argument is that what we value—our treasures, which are measured by where and on what we spend our energies—indicates where our heart, or the center of our passion, is. I think of Joseph of Arimathea, who, though rich *and* a disciple (27:57), had a treasure centered on Jesus. The rich young ruler had treasures centered on possessions and not on caring for the poor (19:16–30), and the disciples who left family and economic/ social security to follow Jesus (4:18–22; 8:18–22; 9:9–13) illustrate Jesus' point about treasures. The story about Zacchaeus illustrates our passage (Luke 19:1–10).

The Eye of the Body (6:22–23)

These two verses express something through an ancient image. Notice that it says the "eye is the lamp of the body." Lamps give off light. In this image, Jesus says the eye is *something through which light passes* onto objects. Such a view of how humans could see was widespread in the ancient world, and there were two theories: the "intromission" and "extramission" theory of light.[14] That is, did the eye permit light to enter the body (intromission), or did it send light out from inside the body (extramission)? In both views the eye is a window. Nearly four centuries later Augustine used the extramission theory of vision when he said that "rays shine through the eyes and touch whatever they see."[15] Jesus too assumes the extramission theory of light in this saying that the eye,

---

13. Michael Joseph Brown, "Matthew," *True to Our Native Land: An African American New Testament Commentary* (ed. B. K. Blount et al.; Minneapolis: Fortress, 2007), 94.

14. Allison, *Sermon on the Mount*, 142–45; idem, "The Eye Is the Lamp of the Body (Matthew 6:22–23 = Luke 11:34–36)," *NTS* 33 (1987): 61–83. Guelich leans toward the extramission theory (Guelich, *Sermon on the Mount*, 329–32). France (*Matthew*, 260–61) opts for a more general idea: eye and light and body need one another. Quarles seeks to undo the whole approach of Allison; Quarles, *Sermon on the Mount*, 244–46.

15. *The Trinity* 9.3.3.

like a lamp, permits light to exit the body. He uses that perception to probe into the condition of one's heart, to probe whether it was light or darkness. Hence, "the eye is [a window for] the lamp of [inside] the body."

But what point is Jesus making? Allison thinks it's about the inner light of God's work of grace that flows into compassion and generosity,[16] but Calvin saw in this image an appeal to the mind's capacity to control the emotions.[17] Guelich thinks pointing toward specific ethical concerns like generosity over-cooks the image; it's about being in the light or in the darkness (cf. 4:15–17, 23).[18] But France and Hagner, closer to Allison, conclude we are to see in the "evil eye" (cf. *m. 'Abot* 2:12, 15; 5:16, 22) a stinginess contrasted with generosity.[19] Each of these illustrates the specifics; the evidence isn't clear enough to know firmly.

Next Jesus says: "If your eyes are healthy [perhaps 'generous'], your whole body is full of light." But this might suggest the eye is a window through which light passes into the body, morally purifying the inner person. Dale Allison, who is at least partly responsible for uncovering the ancient theory for how eyes did their seeing, contends that *a sound or healthy eye indicates a light within*, and he also distinguishes from the source (light) and the organ through which light passes (eye). Verse 23 confirms Allison's point: "If then the light within you is darkness, how great is that darkness!" Jesus' focus is on the inner person: Is it full of light or full of darkness? The use of light versus darkness is a rhetorical way for Jesus to contrast two options in life: a good source (light) versus a bad source (darkness), and the good life of deeds (healthy eye) versus the immoral life of no deeds (unhealthy eye)—in other words, the way of God and the way of evil.[20] This saying, then, is not unlike what Jesus says about good trees and good fruit in 7:15–20; 12:33–34; 15:18–20.

But what perhaps surprises us here is that the words used for "healthy" (*haplous*) and "unhealthy" (*ponēros*) are words often used for "generous" and "stingy."[21] Words that appear to be rather innocent take on a more pointed economic flavor. The economic hints of these images make more clear why "healthy" and "unhealthy" are connected to the previous one ("treasure" in 6:21) and the following one ("God and money" in 6:24): the image about the lamp and the eye is a moral image for how one responds to the needy with compassion.

---

16. See also Betz, *Sermon on the Mount*, 449–51.
17. Calvin, *Harmony of the Gospels*, 1:217–18.
18. Guelich, *Sermon on the Mount*, 365–67.
19. Hagner, *Matthew 1–13*, 158; France, *Matthew*, 261–62.
20. Guelich, *Sermon on the Mount*, 331–32.
21. Cf. Deut 15:9; Prov 22:9, and esp. for us Matt 20:15.

Two Masters (6:24)

Jesus says, "No one can serve two masters," and his words apply the first commandment to the idol of possessions (Exod 20:3). That commandment was rooted in the distinct affirmation of ancient Israel's faith: there is only one God, YHWH (Deut 6:4). One's affections are for either one or the other. Jesus pushes the disciple to his major point: there are two masters; one master is God and the other master is "mammon" (NIV "money), or possessions.[22] Luther has put it graphically: "as Mammon's master, a man must make him [Mammon] lie at his feet; but he must be subject to no one and have no master except the Word of God."[23] Aaron M. Gale, in *The Jewish Annotated New Testament*, makes an important observation about the irony of this term: the term was "originally derived from '*aman*,' 'trust, reliance,' meaning 'that in which [other than God] one places one's trust."[24]

Ordinary life is not this simple, of course, for many have faced the decision whether they are to abandon a good job in which they have had ample time to serve God and to work in churches in order to pursue some less lucrative ministry, or hang on to that job and not do that ministry. But Jesus here isn't into the nuance or the ambiguity of decision. Instead, he offers a woodcut of two options: either you run on the treadmill of money or you live for God. His Ethic from Beyond and Above drives him to confront the disciple with decision.

LIVE the Story

If we return to the introduction to this section, we are reminded again of the kind of life Jesus lived and the enormous differences we now live—and by "we" I'm assuming a comparative affluence in contrast to what he knew. How do we, the affluent, follow Jesus, the poor man?

Hermeneutics of Possessions

I begin with a point of hermeneutics, one that could take books and books to explore. Following Jesus doesn't mean slavish imitation, as if we were to

---

22. Davies and Allison, *Matthew*, 1:643. On Jesus and possessions, McKnight, *New Vision for Israel*, 187–93; M. Hengel, *Property and Riches in the Early Church: Aspects of a Social History of Early Christianity* (trans. J. Bowden; Philadelphia: Fortress, 1974); C. Blomberg, *Neither Poverty Nor Riches: A Biblical Theology of Material Possessions* (Grand Rapids: Eerdmans, 1999); S. E. Wheeler, *Wealth as Peril and Obligation: The New Testament on Possessions* (Grand Rapids: Eerdmans, 1995). See also A. Sivertsev, "The Household Economy," J. Pastor, "Trade, Commerce, and Consumption," and G. Hamel, "Poverty and Charity," in C. Hezser, ed., *Oxford Handbook of Jewish Daily Life*, 229–45, 297–307, 308–34.

23. Luther, *Sermon on the Mount*, 192.

24. *The Jewish Annotated New Testament*, at 6:24 (p. 14).

say, "If Jesus wore sandals, so should we." Sophisticated and sensitive hermeneutics—not designed to rationalize our behavior or lifestyle but seriously intended to explore how we live out the teachings of Jesus in completely different circumstances, not unlike the way Paul took the gospel into Gentile lands (1 Cor 9:19–23)—requires both challenging our world but also adapting and adopting Jesus' vision to our world. I hold it, then, as an axiom—or else I'd stop writing right now—that our calling is to follow Jesus *in our context* rather than to retrieve and re-create his context in our world. What he says about possessions in our text is of direct value in ours; he is not asking us to replicate first-century Galilee but to live out *his* kingdom vision in *our* world.

This Does Not Deny the Value of Work and Profit

John Wesley recognized that Jesus' words could fire up people into behaviors that were irresponsible, and so he made it clear what "Do not store up" *did not mean*: it did not mean we shouldn't pay taxes or pay off loans; it does not prohibit providing the means of sustenance; it does not prohibit labor that provides for our families; and it does not prohibit occasionally storing up in order to accomplish what God has called us to accomplish.[25] Wesley's observations draw us back to the first point about hermeneutics: we must learn to use this text in context, and that means wisely and not recklessly. Jesus said these words as an itinerant who was provided for by those who did labor with profit and were able to care for him and his followers (Matt 10:9–15; Luke 8:1–3). The danger for him and his followers was the lure of riches, wealth, and possessions.

The Essence: Simplicity

Craig Keener helps us live out this text in the direction of simplicity; he makes three points:[26] (1) If disciples really trust God, they will live as if treasures in heaven really matter; (2) those whose perspective is distorted by materialism are blinded to God's truth; and (3) one either loves God or money, and those who think they can love both are idolaters. How should we live this out? I make one suggestion: *Jesus summons us to simplify our lifestyle to focus on the kingdom.*

Eschatological Orientation

A friend of mine is writing a commentary in this series, and he happened to be assigned to a book shaped much more by eschatology than this one. (By "eschatology" I mean what most mean by that term: what will happen in

---

25. Kinghorn, *Wesley on the Sermon*, 205–7.
26. Keener, *Matthew*, 230–34.

the new heavens and new earth.) As I was reading his section, I began to ask myself personal questions like these: How do I live in such a way that my life is shaped by Jesus' and the earliest Christians' perspective on the future? Am I absorbed with an Ethic from Beyond? Is my life too absorbed with the here and now?

The first thing that came to mind is that we need to *think about that future more often*. I confess I don't. My mind is tied too much to the here and now and not enough to God's future kingdom. To be sure, that kingdom in the future will shape how we live now, but there is a yearning for the kingdom at work in Jesus' prayer (6:9–13) and in the early Christians; we can recover that yearning in part *simply by spending more time pondering what God has told us about that future*. Praying the Lord's Prayer often can do this for us, as can routine reflection on the eschatological consummation texts of the New Testament. I like to focus on 1 Corinthians 15:20–28, where God will be all in all; on Philippians 2:6–11, where everyone will bow in worship before Jesus Christ; and on Revelation 21–22, where we have a grand vision of the new Jerusalem, pure fellowship with God and others, where Jesus is at the center of everything (as Jerusalem's temple was in the first century), and where the bustle of life seems to be endless delight in love, justice, peace, and wisdom.

Pondering that future, I am suggesting, brings us to see what God most wants for us now as followers of Jesus. To see that kingdom as it is, and we gain only glimpses now, drives us to see that what matters and what doesn't matter are more and more of what we've got and want but less and less hassle so we can be freed up to focus on the kingdom of love, peace, justice, and wisdom.

Simplification

This makes me think that simplification is the natural response to a kingdom vision. In that kingdom we won't be hoarding or storing up treasures but instead living in the bounty of God's gracious provision so we can enjoy what he wants for us: to serve God and to serve others. This sort of vision, an ethic shaped by knowing what the future will be, does indeed trade in a motivation by reward. Again, some are bothered by this, but Dale Allison tosses cold water all over that concern: "For [Jesus] the issue was not whether there would or should be reward. For him the issue was: whose reward matters—man's or God's?"[27]

But Allison, probing the centrality and incalculable nature of love, probes further by suggesting that Jesus' ethical vision is not amenable to the scales and balances of calculating one's merits. He points to 6:3; 20:1–16; 25:31–46

---

27. Davies and Allison, *Matthew*, 1:634.

as a reminder. So, while we may live for the reward of that kingdom, not as a way of getting more but as a way of being closer to God, we don't do so in some kind of crass calculations of what we are doing in light of what we will get. But neither is this altruism: *at the heart of Jesus' ethical vision is a motivation to live before God and in light of God's revealed future*; that is, it is an Ethic from Above and Beyond.

This drives us toward simplicity and focus, toward voluntary acts of cutting back and even stepping into poverty instead of accumulating possessions. It is not that we need to abandon the city to dwell in the desert with Saint Anthony or in the ghettos with those who are so called, but, as Ronald Sider and others constantly remind us, *if the kingdom vision of Jesus doesn't reshape our approach to possessions, then we are not living out the kingdom vision*. If we are living to the end of our means (and here I'm speaking to the affluent West, and excluding the unemployed) and have little for the poor, if we are extending our budgets and giving only from what is left over, and if we have not cut back on how we live, then we are not embracing the kingdom vision of Jesus.

The call, I am suggesting, is toward simplicity and not toward intentional, radical poverty. Jesus constantly benefited from the wealth and possessions of others (read, e.g., Luke 8:1–3, or consider that he dined in the homes of others), and that means he wasn't against wealth so much as against hoarding, nor was he against possessions so much as for those who had them to use in service to others.

Mammonolatry
Long ago Ralph Martin wrote a short sketch of what the New Testament says about money. I summarize it in his warning about *mammonolatry*.[28] Money has a way of freezing our hands and feet and stiffening our hearts; it has a way of becoming, like Gollum's ring, something we cannot do without and that becomes the focus of our attention. Jesus knew the danger of money. Ralph Martin defines it this way:

> This sin may be defined as the spirit of grasping greed and acquisitiveness, the insatiable longing for more of material possessions and a consequent lack of contentment and absence of trust in God our Father who has promised to supply all needful things to His children (Matthew 6:32).

This is why, Martin observed, Jesus personifies "mammon" in this text. He makes it a god alongside the one true God and says, "Take your pick, and you only get to pick one." Then Martin says, as if he is writing a commentary

---

28. R. P. Martin, *Worship in the Early Church* (Grand Rapids: Eerdmans, 1975), 80–86. I quote from pp. 82, 84.

on Matthew 6:19–24: "The acid test is not what we say, but what we do; not what we promise in words, but what we actually give in money."

Martin went on to explore some principles of Christian stewardship, focusing especially on 2 Corinthians 8–9, by which he meant giving money to God through the local church and through various ministries. Here are his points. It all begins with God's gracious gifts to us, made visibly clear in the incarnation and in the depth of humiliation by the Son of God; the most important offering we make is ourselves; our giving is to be prompted by God's grace but should be voluntary, eager, cheerful, and sacrificial; we are to give according our ability and to encourage equality; we are to be scrupulously honest; and a sincere care for others breeds a bond of love between givers and the recipients, all of which leads to the praise of God.

Martin is right on: because money wants to be a god, Jesus calls us to an entirely different agenda in this world as we seek to embody the kingdom now, because of what we see it will be like in the new heavens and new earth.

Simplicity, then, is learning to lean forward toward the kingdom in all we do, whatever it might be that God calls us to do.

At Northern Seminary recently, in a class devoted to the gospel in the book of Revelation, I mentioned the powerful, sometimes violent, bizarre, and grotesque imagery in Revelation. I explained that we need not make one-to-one correspondences between imagery and God's intended realities. In my explanation I made an analogy to the brilliant author Flannery O'Connor, who used some of the most bizarre and violent imagery of any American writer.[29] One of my students, Ashley, suddenly came alive, as if the analogy gave her a handle on how to read Revelation. Had we had more time, we could have gone on and on about Flannery and her use of what is often called "Southern grotesque" imagery, but the one dimension of her life I would have wanted to dwell on (which has nothing to do with Revelation!) was her simplicity. She lived on a farm in an out-of-the-way place in Georgia, and she and her mother tended some animals, including peacocks. She worked in a simple study in a simple home on a budget that permitted both of them to get by.

This was the way for her to express her devout, God-fearing faith. And part of that life was bearing with the awful pain of lupus that took this gifted writer's life far too early. Lorraine V. Murray's life of Flannery O'Connor[30] tells the story of a correspondence with T. R. Spivey, who asked her about how to experience God's grace. Flannery wrote: "You have to practice self-denial." Murray continues: "For her that meant immersing herself in writing: 'I never

---

29. Flannery O'Connor, *Collected Works* (New York: Library of America, 1988).

30. Lorraine V. Murray, *The Abbess of Andalusia: Flannery O'Connor's Spiritual Journey* (Charlotte, NC: Saint Benedict Press, 2009), quoting from p. 188, italics added.

completely forget myself except when I am writing.'" Murray's next words reveal Flannery's simplicity: "She also practiced self-denial by giving money to charity rather than spending it on herself. Flannery had money to give *only because, like a true monastic, she did not require much to live on*—not because she had a great surplus of cash."

Murray recounts how little she made from her books, how little the family farm brought in as income, and how she—by now a well-known author— would travel (in pain, often mentioned in her letters with humor) to speak at colleges for the small fee so she could pay bills. She once received more than a normal amount for speaking, and she used it to buy her mother a refrigerator. She checked out books from libraries so as not to spend more money, and she once earned an $8,000 grant—which would have been two years for most, but she announced she could make that last five years.

I wonder if we need to immerse ourselves more in the stories of people like Flannery O'Connor, who, out of their devotion to Christ, lived on less so they could live a fuller life of love for others.

LISTEN to the Story

> [25]"Therefore I tell you, do not worry about your life, what you will eat or drink; or about your body, what you will wear. Is not life more than food, and the body more than clothes? [26]Look at the birds of the air; they do not sow or reap or store away in barns, and yet your heavenly Father feeds them. Are you not much more valuable than they? [27]Can any one of you by worrying add a single hour to your life?[1]
>
> [28]"And why do you worry about clothes? See how the flowers of the field grow. They do not labor or spin. [29]Yet I tell you that not even Solomon in all his splendor[2] was dressed like one of these. [30]If that is how God clothes the grass of the field, which is here today and tomorrow is thrown into the fire,[3] will he not much more clothe you — you of little faith? [31]So do not worry, saying, 'What shall we eat?' or 'What shall we drink?' or 'What shall we wear?' [32]For the pagans run after all these things, and your heavenly Father knows that you need them. [33]But seek first his kingdom and his righteousness,[4] and all these things will be given to you as well. [34]Therefore do not worry about tomorrow, for tomorrow will worry about itself. Each day has enough trouble of its own."[5]

Listening to the text in the Story: Genesis 1 – 2; Exodus 16; Psalm 19; Matthew 10:9 – 15; 1 Peter 5:7.

God is the Creator and Sustainer. Too often we believe like theists (a personal God) and act like deists (a distant, impersonal, noninteractive, uninvolved god). We say we believe in God, trust in God, and are sustained by God; but in our actions we do everything for ourselves, trusting in ourselves and anxious about the providence of God, which unravels our theism. We

---

1. KNT: "fifteen inches to your height."
2. KNT: "finery."
3. KNT: "on the bonfire tomorrow."
4. KNT: "make your top priority God's kingdom and his way of life."
5. KNT: "One day's trouble at a time is quite enough."

believe that God not only gives life but *is life itself,* and that belief means that every breath we take and every moment of life we live comes from and is sustained by the creator God. Without venturing into pantheism (all is God) or a softer version in panentheism (God is in all), the Christian faith affirms that all of life in the entire cosmos is from God and is sustained by God. God, then, is actively at work in all of life.

This is why the ancient Israelites prayed to God for provisions and thanked God for the provisions they had. This is why the entire framework of blessings and curses (Lev 26; Deut 28) finds its way so deeply in the Bible's understanding of how life works: since God is Creator, and since God is responsible for sustenance, the presence and absence of provisions are acts of God.

This is not to say there is a one-to-one correlation of obedience and provision because God's world is more flexible and complex than this. As Job teaches us, sometimes God withholds blessing in order to test. As the exiles in Babylon reveal, sometimes God's entire people suffer because of the sins of its leaders even when some have been faithful. And as prophets like Amos and Haggai warn, sometimes the poor suffer because the powerful exploit and oppress. An abundance of possessions can create anxiety, as Hillel once said ("the more property, the more care" [*m. 'Abot* 2:7]), while their absence can also create anxiety.

Deep in the heart of the biblical Story is the conviction that the creator God provides. Nothing makes this more manifest than the famous manna and quail story of Exodus 16 and God's sustaining of Elisha (2 Kings 4:42–44), two depictions of God's provision outdone only by Jesus' feeding miracles (Matt 14:13–21; 15:32–39; John 6:5–13) and by the Eucharist itself (Matt 26:17–30). This deep source of provision in the God who cares (cf. Lev 25:18–24; 1 Pet 5:7) summons us to trust God for provision in Jesus' ministry.

For sale on the wall in nearly every Christian bookstore and then found sometimes on the walls of Christian homes is a picture of an old man or an old woman bowing in thanks over a small loaf of bread. This posture of thanks reminds us that God cares and provides. A careful reading of our text in the context of Jesus' own radical itinerant ministry prompts us to think that our full pantries and refrigerators are playing a different game than the one Jesus and his followers played. *These are words for radicals about a radical lifestyle of trusting God for the ordinaries of life while devoting oneself unreservedly toward the kingdom mission.* This leads us to think of the Nazirite vow (Num 6:1–21), of the rugged (not romantic) realities of Psalm 23, and of John the Baptist's minimalist diet in the wilderness (Matt 3:4). This passage is designed to make us feel uncomfortable about our lifestyle.

EXPLAIN the Story

Jesus continues with the themes of 6:19 – 24: the danger of possessions and their capacity to become idols that demolish faithfulness and mission. The good treasure, the sound/generous eye, and the one true master will morph in 6:25 – 34[6] to be trusting God for provision in order to focus life on the kingdom and righteousness (6:33). Matthew (or Jesus) ties our passage to the previous one as if to say, if you have to choose which God you will serve, if you are to have a sound/generous eye, and if you are to store up treasures that last, then you will not worry about provisions, will trust God, and will pursue the kingdom and righteousness.

The untidy structure of our passage looks like this:

1. Prohibition, with questions (6:25)
2. Illustration 1: birds, with questions (6:26 – 27)
3. Illustration 2: flowers, with questions (6:28 – 30)
4. Prohibition repeated (6:31)
5. Two reasons for prohibition: pagans and providence (6:32)
6. Counteraction (6:33)
7. Prohibition repeated, with wisdom argument (6:34)

As can be seen from the outline, three times Jesus prohibits anxiety over provisions. He provides three reasons not to have that kind of anxiety: pagans do such things, God in his providence cares, and each day has its own problems, so let tomorrow take care of itself. This is an Ethic from Below, a rare approach of Jesus in the Sermon.

This passage requires that we remind ourselves to whom Jesus is speaking: his disciples. He is addressing not the poor as a result of a famine but instead disciples who have more or less what they need; in fact, when he sent them out later, he told them not to secure provisions or protection for their mission trips (cf. 9:35 – 10:14, 40 – 42). During that mission trip they would be taken care of by those who responded to the kingdom vision and praxis. Jesus himself was an itinerant who did not have provisions or even safety (8:18 – 22), but he trusted his Father to provide; he is now urging his disciples to follow him in that trust. At the heart of the Lord's Prayer is the petition for daily bread (6:11), and that request sets the context for our passage.

Prohibition, with Questions (6:25)

Anxiety is a barometer of one's God: those with anxiety about "life" worship Mammon, while those without anxiety worship the providing God. Teachings

---

6. Matthew 6:25 – 34 is more or less found in the parallel at Luke 12:22 – 31, except Matt 6:34 has no parallel.

like these, of course, fall hard on the emotions of those who are more prone to worry than those who are careless, while the same words of Jesus are easily absorbed by shirkers. Jesus' words are misunderstood by both: some of us need to learn to trust while others need to be more concerned in a proper way.

I suspect we need to consider this as rhetoric and not psychology; Jesus forces his disciples to get their priorities right. The term "worry," which appears in this passage six times (6:25, 27, 28, 31, 34 [2x]), translates the Greek verb *merimnaō* and describes, when used negatively,[7] internal disturbance at the emotional and psychological level that disrupts life. Guelich sees in this term "an anxious endeavor to secure one's needs."[8] This term "worry" needs to be connected to the disposition of fear and little faith in verse 30.

Martha provides a living example in Luke 10:41, where this word is accompanied by another one, *thorybazō*, which describes agitation, disorder, and disturbance. In this text Jesus seeks to create tranquil Marys out of anxious Marthas, and it appears that Paul's words in Philippians 4:6 are a variant on Jesus' words.

Two Illustrations, with Questions (6:26–30)

From nature one can learn the lessons of divine providence, and some of us need to be reminded of this because we can look and not see a world alive with God's presence. Natural theology, which is a form and extension of wisdom and an Ethic from Below, is a world unto itself. Beginning in some important ways with Aristotle but much more fully developed by the Aristotelian Roman Catholic theologians, like Aquinas, it has now taken on intense debates with arcane footnotes. Sometimes we can get lost in the philosophical discussion, and it is then that we need to come in contact with traditions like the Eastern Orthodox tradition, where the world is aflame with the presence of God. So Father Alexander Schmemann writes: "All that exists is God's gift to man, and it all exists to make God known to man, to make man's life communion with God."[9] The eye of faith can see in nature what Jesus saw: the providential care of the Father. Jesus' favored form of "natural" theology was to tell parables.

Guelich reminds us that Jesus' words here deal with eschatological providence: "Jesus sees creation in light of the presence of the new age," and only "in light of the new age, the coming of the Kingdom, does Jesus assure his own that the Father in heaven will act on their behalf."[10] This eschatological orientation transforms Jesus' teachings here from mere wisdom into mere

---

7. It is used positively, as in "cares for," in 1 Cor 7:32–34; 12:25; Phil 2:20.

8. Guelich, *Sermon on the Mount*, 369.

9. A. Schmemann, *For the Life of the World: Sacraments and Orthodoxy* (Crestwood, NY: St Vladimir's Seminary Press, 2000), 14.

10. Guelich, *Sermon on the Mount*, 370.

kingdom, from mere provisions into mere blessings, or from an Ethic from Below to an Ethic from Beyond. The "Beyond" reshapes the "Below."

Birds[11] live from day to day, taking what they find and finding enough. Hence, they don't manifest the anxiety of sowing and reaping and storing away for later. The Father provides for them and always has (Ps 147:9; Matt 10:29). Once again, Jesus probes his disciples with two questions: a theological question about the inherently greater value of disciples over birds and a pragmatic question about the utter uselessness for adding an hour to life by worrying.[12]

Next to birds Jesus sees divine providence at work in the many colorful Galilean flowers, which do not "labor" or "spin" (as in creating fabric) but are beautiful—even more beautiful than Solomon at the top of his game. Jesus probes again. He argues from the lesser (birds, flowers) to the greater (humans) and argues that if God provides for the lesser, surely he will provide for the greater. But we dare not miss the value Jesus places on humans. Hear the words of Chrysostom: "The force of the emphasis is on 'you' to indicate covertly how great is the value set upon your personal existence and the concern God shows for you in particular."[13]

Those who are unwilling to see the hand of God in providence and trust the caring Father for the necessities of life are called "you of little faith," a term in Matthew for faith failure, that is, those living between faithful discipleship and unbelief (8:26; 14:31; 16:8; 17:20).

Prohibition Repeated (6:31)

Jesus repeatedly prohibits anxiety. Ancient education knew the value of repetition, and an ancient Greek line went like this: *meletē to pan* ("practice/repetition is everything").[14] But this repetition is not so much educative as it is rhetorical: he repeats, like using a drill, in order to probe deeper.

Two Reasons: Pagans and Providence (6:32)

A rhetorically forceful argument for a Jew was to say that a given behavior was Gentile or pagan, and Jesus has already done this in the Sermon (6:7–8). But Jesus' words are not just rhetorical; for him the pagans were the Romans who were found just north of Nazareth, in Sepphoris (where wine, women,

---

11. Luke has "ravens" (*korakas*), an unclean bird (Lev 11:15; Deut 14:14). Matthew has the more general term for "birds" (*peteina*). On learning from the birds, see J. R. W. Stott, *The Birds Our Teachers: Essays in Orni-Theology* (Wheaton, IL: Harold Shaw, 1999).

12. The word for "hour" (πῆχυν) is thought by some to mean adding height to one's stature; the evidence supports a reference to time, hence "hour." See Davies and Allison, *Matthew*, 1:652–53.

13. ACCS: *Matthew*, 145.

14. I learned this in college from my Greek professor and have no idea of its source.

song, theater, and opulence were the way of life) or Tiberias (in full view from Capernaum and from the traditional location of this Sermon). They provided a living example of what the disciple was not to be.

Even more, and again unlike the Roman pagan who did not trust in Israel's God, Jesus informs his followers that "your heavenly Father knows you need" things for your life, such as something to eat and drink and something to wear. Here he appeals to providence at the level of God's omniscience and benevolence: God both knows what you need and God will provide what you need.

Counteraction (6:33)

Jesus' strategy for the disciple is to pursue two things: God's kingdom[15] and righteousness. Are they near synonyms? Both of these terms are central terms for Jesus, and we have already discussed both (at 5:3 and 5:6). The "kingdom" is Jesus' shorthand expression for the Story of Israel's hope for this world coming to completion in Jesus, and it takes place as the society that does God's will under King Jesus is empowered by God's redemptive work. As such, it partakes in the Story of Jesus—his life, death, burial, resurrection, and exaltation as King and Judge—and those who enter that Story through repentance, faith, and baptism are those who will enter into that kingdom reality.

When Jesus says "righteousness," he is using a common term in the Jewish world: it describes God's will, and those who are "righteous" are those who do that will. It means behavioral conformity to God's will, now made known in Jesus. It is central to the Messianic Ethic. Both "kingdom" and "righteousness" are about God's will: the first focused on the Story now realized and the second on that kingdom's ethics. We should connect these two terms as we pray for God's kingdom and God's will to be done on earth as in heaven in the Lord's Prayer.

For kingdom and righteousness the disciple of Jesus is to "seek" or "pursue." The idea is to focus on, to want, to plot, and to act in a way that keeps one aimed at the goal—and I'm thinking of how Olympic athletes (like Allyson Felix) aim their entire life toward the gold medal. It is not unlike Jesus' image that the one who follows him and looks back is not fit for the kingdom (cf. Luke 9:57–62). This word of Jesus isn't legalism ramped up to the highest level, but confrontation with the messianic King, who offers his citizens the way to live the gospel-drenched life of the kingdom.

---

15. Matthew normally has "kingdom *of heaven/s*" but here has kingdom "of God," something he has five times. On this subject see Pennington, *Heaven and Earth in the Gospel of Matthew*. Pennington contends that "heaven" and "heavenly" are not reverential circumlocutions but instead a kind of rhetorical counterforce: heaven stands over against earth.

How do we "seek" the kingdom and righteousness? Luther's strategy is this: "believing in Christ and practicing and applying the Gospel, to which faith clings," and "this involves growing and being strengthened at heart through preaching, listening, reading, singing, meditating, and every other possible way."[16] Dallas Willard is well-known for his "VIM" strategy in spiritual formation: we need a *vision*, and this needs to prompt in us *intention* to accomplish that vision, and then we need to discover the proper *means* to get there. Willard's focus is on the spiritual disciplines, which are not directly addressed here by Jesus, but his "seek" encompasses what Willard means by VIM.[17] I would add to Willard's VIM a more intentional focusing on spiritual formation as living out the Story of Jesus by absorbing that Story and practicing the disciplines, like Bible reading, Eucharist, and church calendar, that keep our eyes fixed on the Story of Jesus.[18]

Prohibition Repeated, with Wisdom (6:34)

Again, Jesus prohibits anxiety or "worry." But this time he uses "tomorrow," which becomes the basis for a bit of wisdom: "for tomorrow will worry about itself." This is not a light dismissal but a theological perception that kingdom and righteousness require full attention each day. Tomorrow can wait; for those who let this theological vision shape their life, there will be provision. Furthermore, Jesus offers more ordinary wisdom as a reason for concentrating on the kingdom mission of Jesus: "Each day has enough trouble of its own." But this ordinary wisdom, this Ethic from Below, is anchored in observing the providence of a loving Father.

LIVE the Story

But, and I hear this often when teaching this passage to college students, "What about the poor?" The problem has been expressed well by Ulrich Luz, who batters his readers with the standard criticisms of Jesus' vision in unforgettable words:

> It is said that every "starving sparrow" contradicts Jesus, not to mention every famine and every war; that the text gives the appearance of being extremely simpleminded; that it acts as if there were no economic problems, only ethical ones, and that it is a good symbol of the economic naïveté that has characterized Christianity in the course of its history; that

---

16. Luther, *Sermon on the Mount*, 204.
17. Willard, *Renovation of the Heart*, 85 – 91.
18. McKnight, *King Jesus Gospel*, 146 – 60.

it is applicable only in the special situation of the unmarried Jesus living with friends in sunny Galilee; that it is also ethically problematic, since it speaks of work "in the most disdainful terms" and appears to encourage laziness.[19]

In spite of the heated rhetoric and the often compassionate aims of the criticism, this text is not about those concerns. These charges may strike deeply into the heart of many Christian readings of this text, but they fail to connect to the real world of Jesus and what he is teaching in his context. Let us begin with this: *Jesus assumes a world in this teaching in which his followers, while they will not have a bounty, will have enough for sustenance.* His teachings here assume the ordinary provisions for life, and he instructs his followers about how to live in that kind of world.

What Jesus is saying, then, is not insensitive to many who pray for food and starve to death. He would say something else to that condition. France mistakenly states that in this passage Jesus "seems to envisage the world as it should be rather than the world as it is."[20] No, it needs to be emphasized, Jesus is not dreaming of some far-off world that does not yet exist; rather, he is seeing the world through the eyes of a first-century Galilean *whose followers have access to provisions.* This is not a dreamy Ethic from Beyond, but a God-drenched, prayer-infested, and obedience-shaped Ethic from Below. That stance alone explains the entire focus of this passage. To think Jesus offers here a strategy for the starving fails every time; any criticism that attacks him on that score fails as well.

Nor will it do to listen to this text, observe that God normally provides provisions through others (as in 10:9–14), and then say that the reason some don't have provisions is because of the greed or insensitivity of others. Again, we cannot ask Jesus to tackle all problems every time he issues a press release about possessions and provisions. He was not an economist. He's talking to first-century Galilean disciples who have access to provisions in their Galilean context. Or, we could say Jesus is speaking to mission-sent disciples with access to others who will provide for them (as is often the case in the world today), and in that context he urges them to trust God and not to focus on securing their provisions against the future.

On Mission

Learning to read passages in a realistic context can help relieve some of the tensions those texts create for us. I suggest, then, that we learn to hop over

---

19. Luz, *Matthew 1–7*, 341.
20. France, *Matthew*, 266.

these critical tremors that come our way, and I have myself experienced this text's tremors in the face of class after class of young college students wondering how in the world Jesus could say such things when there are people who are starving. I don't say this insensitively toward those who suffer, but instead I say this with an eye out for those who are called by God to some mission and who need to trust God for what God is calling them to do.

There are, then, a few points we need to keep in mind when we seek to live out this Story today. We need to trust God as the creator and sustainer of all of life. We need to embrace the mission that God has given us, and "my mission" is as a husband and father, as well as professor and preacher and author. We need to dwell in the confidence that the kingdom is reaching from the future into the present world and that God promises to bless those who are indwelling that kingdom. This is not to say that each of us will always have all that we want or even what we need; rather, we must see Jesus' teachings as they were meant to be seen: assuming the reality and availability of provisions, Jesus calls us to strike out and trust God for what we need.

As a child I grew up in a church that was big on missionaries. Every year we had a conference for missionaries, and every year we were treated to the regaling stories of conversions and the witness to the provision of God. As a seminary student I read Edith Schaeffer's *L'Abri*, a book that told time and time again of how the Lord had provided for the Schaeffer family, and sometimes in the most uncanny of ways.[21] There is no reason to think God doesn't still provide for those sent on mission. More importantly, those called will learn to trust God.

Attitude

But there is something in this text about life today that transcends the one sent on mission. Jesus is probing into the heart of his followers to ask them if they value life more than kingdom and righteousness. Perhaps the best way to think about this is that *Jesus doesn't call us to be care-less about provisions but to be care-free.* Some folks find in this text an opportunity to be lazy, or an opportunity to give away everything in a reckless or unwise manner. Jesus isn't encouraging his disciples to be reckless. Instead, he's calling them to follow him and to see that following him, or (in our text) seeking first the kingdom and righteousness, reshapes what we value most.

Money matters; without it we can't do most things that a capitalist world requires. Provisions matter; without food or drink or clothing we don't survive. But "matter" is not the same as "worship." Our central ache or yearning or seeking is to be for God, for God's kingdom, and for God's righteousness. Those things do "matter," but the kingdom matters even more.

---

21. Edith Schaeffer, *L'Abri* (Wheaton, IL: Crossway, 1992).

Ron Sider asked the question of what is the secret to a carefree existence that lives out what Jesus teaches here.[22] It begins, he wrote, when we really do believe and live out that God, the God of all, is our loving, creating, sustaining Father. Then he urged us to see that we are called to live under Jesus as our Lord. But he knew that such a life meant sacrifice and not just a mental attitude toward things: the summons not to be anxious was a summons both to trust and to entrust a life of solidarity with others, from our church to global needs, to the caring Father. This is where Sider makes one of his most famous comments ever: "What 99 percent of North Americans need to hear 99 percent of the time is this: 'Give to everyone who begs from you,' and 'sell your possessions.'"

This is real. It gets ordinary. Every day. I was speaking at Fuller Theological Seminary in their chapel, and I spoke on the "Parable from Hell" (Luke 16:19–31). The point of my talk was that we want to know who will go to heaven and how long hell will last, but Jesus used hell language not to satisfy our curiosity but to urge us to see the Lazaruses at our gate. When I was done, Kara Powell, a wonderful professor at Fuller, and I had coffee. On our way to the local coffee shop she told me how her daughter had become wonderfully sensitive to the poor. As a result, they all had some McDonald's coupons with them so if they saw someone in need they could help.

Then it happened. As Kara and I left the coffee shop to sit outside to chat, a beggar asked for something. Kara, knowing that beggar's style, sat down, and we chatted. On our way back to Fuller the man was still there, and she said words I will not forget: "Hi, I'm Kara. What's your name? I'd like to help you with these two coupons. Will you use this to buy some food?" It is easier to walk by than to help. It is easier to save than to give. The disciple of Jesus is called to see those in need and do something about it. It begins when we ask their name. Kara illustrated for me what it means to relax our grip on securing our provisions and to live a carefree existence of following Jesus into kingdom conditions.

The Birds, Our Teachers

John Stott was not only one of the finest Christian leaders and expositors of the Bible in the twentieth century, but he was also a rabid bird-watcher and photographer. All those years of watching birds led him to see all sorts of lessons about life in the birds. In his book *The Birds Our Teachers*, Stott found eleven lessons about life:

> From the ravens, we learn faith.
> From the migration of storks, repentance.
> From the head of owls, facing both ways.

---

22. Sider, *Rich Christians in an Age of Hunger*, 102–5. Quotations are from this section.

From the value of sparrows, self-esteem.
From the drinking of pigeons, gratitude.
From the metabolism of hummingbirds, work.
From the soaring of eagles, freedom.
From the territory of (English) robins, space.
From the wings of a hen, shelter.
From the song of larks, joy.
From the breeding cycle of all birds, love.

This will be perhaps enough concrete detail to trigger your own thinking about birds, but let me add two. From a neighbor's blue parakeet, a story I tell in my book *The Blue Parakeet*,[23] I learned the fastidious and nervous habits of our sparrows and how it took time for them to welcome a stranger. And from a male mallard on a roadside one day who had just lost his bride when a car struck her, I saw commitment. The male had put himself in serious jeopardy to care for his "wife" as she expired.

Indeed, the birds can be our teachers. One can peer into the hand of God in this world as well by examining flowers (and we are fond of decorative grasses, mums, and the varieties of perennials we plant), as did Jesus, but what he calls us to do here is not so much to be bird-watchers or gardeners but to be sensitive enough to stop and listen and see the hand of God at work in this world, and from that to learn that God is a loving Father who cares for us.

---

23. McKnight, *Blue Parakeet*, 22 – 25.

CHAPTER 17

Matthew 7:1–5

 LISTEN to the Story

¹"Do not judge, or you too will be judged. ²For in the same way you judge others, you will be judged, and with the measure you use, it will be measured to you.

³"Why do you look at the speck of sawdust in your brother's [TNIV: 'someone else's'] eye and pay no attention to the plank in your own eye? ⁴How can you say to your brother [TNIV: omits 'to your brother'], 'Let me take the speck out of your eye,' when all the time there is a plank in your own eye? ⁵You hypocrite, first take the plank out of your own eye, and then you will see clearly to remove the speck from your brother's [TNIV: 'the other person's'] eye."

Listening to the text in the Story: Judges; 2 Samuel 12:1–5; Matthew 18:23–35; Romans 2:1; James 2:13; 4:11–12; 5:9.

The tension of this text is unavoidable. From Genesis 1 to Revelation 22 God issues one command after another. On top of those commands are prophetic evaluations of the sins of the people who failed to live responsibly within the terms of the covenant God had made with humans. In other words, we who seek to indwell the Bible's Story are indwelling *the omniscient perspective of the divine's narration*. When we read, say, Judges, Zechariah, the gospel of Luke, Acts, 2 Corinthians, 1 John, or Revelation, we are led to hear *what God thinks of what humans are doing*. It is impossible for us to indwell this Story *and not assume that narrative's perspective*. Again, that perspective is God's perspective. It is not *our* perspective; it is *God's* perspective. It is God's perspective *on us*, not *our* perspective on *others*.

Bible readers, especially pastors (and commenters on blogs), inevitably *begin to think like God about ourselves and others*. Mark Allan Powell discovered that pastors and preachers tend to identify with Jesus (and God) when they read the Bible, while lay folks almost always identify with characters in the text instead of with Jesus or God.[1] So perhaps the primary readers of this book—pastors,

---

1. M. A. Powell, *What Do They Hear? Bridging the Gap between Pulpit and Pew* (Nashville: Abingdon, 2007).

teachers — will need to be reminded that the danger I have been speaking about here is a pastoral and didactic posture rather than the posture of laypeople. Those most familiar with the Bible are tempted to think they are God!

Perhaps so, and even if not, standing in for God was a problem for those whom Jesus is addressing. It is likely that Bible readers, because they absorb God's perspective in Bible reading, *will become judges*. In spite of the strong warnings in the Bible about not being judges, we often find ourselves judging others. So we need to hear what James 4:11 – 12 says to us:

> Brothers and sisters, do not slander one another. Anyone who speaks against a brother or sister or judges them speaks against the law and judges it. When you judge the law, you are not keeping it, but sitting in judgment on it. There is only one Lawgiver and Judge, the one who is able to save and destroy. But you — who are you to judge your neighbor?

This text (and we should not forget Romans 14 as a similar text) provides an early window into what Jesus was getting at when he said, "Do not judge." James warns his readers that when they begin to judge (condemn) others, they are assuming the posture of God, not the posture of humans. In assuming that posture, they have usurped the role of God and begun to be the ones who determine what is right and wrong, and who is right and who is wrong.

Once again: it is nearly impossible for most Bible readers not to enter into the divine perspective of the narrative of the Bible. Yet, and here is the point, learning to enter into that Story's perspective does not make us God, as David himself had to learn (2 Sam 12:1 – 5). We may know what God thinks, but we are not God. Instead, we need to hear from God and to be responsive to and responsible for that perspective in our world.

This leads to what might be the cutting edge of learning how to read this passage most accurately: we must learn to distinguish moral discernment from personal condemnation.[2] This distinction — the ability to know what is good from what is bad and to be able to discern the difference versus the posture of condemning another person — enables us to see what Jesus prohibits in this passage. The flipside of this posture of condemnation is love, humility, mercy, and forgiveness (see 18:23 – 35). In other words, a Jesus Creed – driven disciple does not sit in judgment but acts with mercy toward others. John Wesley said this well: "The judging that Jesus condemns here is thinking about another person in a way that is contrary to love."[3]

But there is more here than a Jesus version of "Don't judge a man until you've walked a mile in his sandals." The Sermon on the Mount frames a

---

2. See also Kapolyo, "Matthew," 1123 – 24.
3. Kinghorn, *Wesley on the Sermon*, 247.

kingdom ethic, an Ethic from Beyond. In Israel's history there were judges (who unfolded into kings and justices), but in the kingdom *of God*, God alone is Judge; human judges will not be needed because kingdom citizens live under the Messiah King and do the will of God. Jesus' disciples are being summoned to live in that kind of world among themselves as they seek to embody in the here and now that future kingdom. Instead of a society marked by condemnation, they are to form a society marked by humility, love for neighbor and enemy, and mutual reconciliation.

EXPLAIN the Story

Our section's central theme in 7:1 is expressed as a prohibition-with-warning, and everything that follows grounds and elucidates that single prohibition: "Do not judge, or you too will be judged." In moving to 7:2 we find verse 1 slightly extended since it more or less repeats what we find there. Then in 7:3–4 Jesus interrogates his followers by revealing that they deconstruct themselves in judging others. Jesus closes with his kingdom alternative: take care of yourself first (7:5).

Prohibition with Warning (7:1)

Everything in our passage depends on defining the term "judge" (*krinō*), but unfortunately, that word doesn't help us because it is sufficiently expansive to cover moral discernment (knowing good from bad; cf. Luke 12:57; John 7:24; Acts 4:19), lawsuits (Matt 5:40; John 7:51), governmental direction (Matt19:28), and final damnation by God (Luke 19:22; John 3:17–18; 5:22; 12:48). The difficulty is determining which is in mind, and we get nowhere if we don't admit that Jesus rendered strong moral judgment of others (Matt 6:1–18; 7:13–27) and that he compelled his disciples to know the difference between what is good and what is bad—in fact, the whole Sermon is just that.

Within the spectrum of the term *krinō* there is something prohibited. It makes most sense to interpret that as assuming the posture of God in condemning a person. If so, 7:1 is not a prohibition of rendering judgment or discernment about good and bad. Perhaps we can simplify it to this: we are to conclude "that is wrong" and "that is good," but we must not pronounce "you are condemned by God." The Ethic from Beyond shapes a society for reconciliation instead of damnation. Kingdom people are called to love, not to act the part of God. Thus, judging others "is the forbidden evaluation of other persons. It corrodes simple love."[4]

---

4. Bonhoeffer, *Discipleship*, 171.

Hence, I suggest the best translation—in context—is: "Do not condemn or you too will be condemned [by God at the judgment]."[5] Without this nuanced difference between discernment and condemnation, we run the risk of (1) becoming mute on moral judgment or (2) missing the powerful warning about assuming we are God.

Extension (7:2)

This verse both repeats and slightly extends what is found in the prohibition of verse 1. Two words are now used: "judge" and "measure," and they are to be synthesized because they are typical Jewish parallelism (saying one thing with two words). The standard that the condemner uses will be the standard God uses against the condemner; this was found elsewhere in the Jewish world (e.g., Rom 2:1, 3).[6] Since no human lives up to his or her own standard, that standard deconstructs a human's attempt to play God with others. God will be the final judge because God alone is the Judge (cf. Rom 14:10; 1 Cor 4:5; Jas 4:11–12).

Interrogation (7:3–4)

Jesus creates an image that is both comic and deadly serious. To point out the deconstructive potential of assuming the posture of God Jesus forms the image of a human who has a big ol' plank in his eye sitting in judgment over someone who has but a speck in her eye. The plank is a comic image, like the camel in 19:24 or the straining of gnats in 23:24, except that the discovery of our own sins is so blatantly humiliating. We sometimes assume the posture of God against other humans; then, when the light begins to shine on our own sins, we are convicted of the sin and stand before God in the hope of mercy and grace. Jesus' plank versus speck could simply be an exaggerated way of saying what Paul says in Romans 2:1: "because you who pass judgment [krinō] do the same things." In other words, the point may be not that we have worse sins than others but that we have sins too.

Alternative to Condemning (7:5)

This paragraph ends where one might not have thought. To avoid the powerful indictment of being called "you hypocrite," we must clean up our own act by removing the plank of our own sins. Then we will see clearly enough (1) not to

---

5. Allison, *Sermon on the Mount*, 152; Hagner, *Matthew 1–13*, 169. One sees that in the parallel passage in Luke 6:37, "Do not condemn [*katadikazō*], and you will not be condemned," follows an identical parallel to Matthew's "Do not judge...." Guelich thinks 7:1 illustrates the opposite of forgiving others; see Guelich, *Sermon on the Mount*, 374. Some Anabaptists find grounds for the Christian not taking up the office of a judge; see Luz, *Matthew 1–7*, 351.

6. Talbert, *Reading the Sermon on the Mount*, 132–33.

posture ourselves as God but instead (2) in mercy to seek to help the other who has but a peccadillo that could be removed. Moral discernment is necessary for the disciple; it shows that genuine love and friendship, to borrow from Aristotle's *Nicomachean Ethics* as well as from Jesus' words in Matthew 18:15–20 about church discipline, mean commitment to moral progress with one another; and it shows that once we get ourselves properly postured under God, we can join others in mutual sanctification and growth as kingdom followers of Jesus.

What Jesus does here is complex: he creates self-awareness leading to self-judgment; this leads to humility, which in turn leads to repentance and sanctification; this leads to the kind of humility that treats other sinners with mercy (cf. Gal. 6:1; Jas 2:13); it creates a kingdom society shaped not by condemnation but humility, love, and forgiveness.[7]

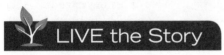

LIVE the Story

Followers of Jesus take up his vision and put the kingdom into play in the here and now. Instead of waiting for the age to come to actualize God's will, Jesus' disciples pray that the kingdom may happen now (6:10). There is a long history of a struggle with kings in Israel's Story: what began as a theocracy with local judges (see Judges) up through Samuel became, reluctantly for God, a monarchy in which God appointed kings (from Saul on).

But the vision of God, as Tom Wright has so well expounded in a steady stream of books, including *Simply Jesus* and *How God Became King*, is that God would someday once again reign himself, this time through his Davidic Son, the Messiah King. In that day there would be no need for someone to condemn. Instead, as a community marked by love, peace, justice, and reconciliation, disciples would not resort to judgment but would pursue mutual sanctification and fellowship. Jesus is not offering here in 7:1–5 a society of blanket tolerance or moral indifference; instead, he is reaching forward into the age to come and pulling it back into the present for his followers. It is an Ethic from Beyond.

Proclivity

Humans have a proclivity to judge, and they have that proclivity especially if they know God's will for society and have a zeal for God's glory. But Jesus urges us to posture ourselves as God's citizens in the kingdom, not as God. That

---

7. McKnight, *New Vision for Israel*, 224–27. A connection of not judging and forgiveness is found in *1 Clement* 13:2 ("forgive, that it may be forgiven you. As you do, so it will be done to you"), and by Polycarp in *Philippians* 2:3 ("forgive and it will be forgiven you ... the amount you dispense will be the amount you receive in return").

posture leads us first to examine ourselves; only after we have duly inspected ourselves through the searching guidance of the Spirit of God, confessed our sins, and made peace with God, can we see the sins of others in such a way that we strive with them to live together in love, justice, and peace. So instead of caving into the proclivity to be gods, as was the case with humans from Adam and Eve to the Essenes and the Pharisees and to modern-day Christian critics, we are called to love God and love our neighbors as ourselves.

It's about a self-awareness and an other-awareness shaped by a God-awareness. Jesus urges us to cease being condemners by first examining ourselves. To be sure, when we peer into our own hearts, we will have sufficient cause—even laughably ridiculous cause—to see our own sin and be humbled before God. That will lead us to an other-awareness that our fellow disciples and humans are like us, sinners in need of mercy, grace, forgiveness, and patience. This reversal of the proclivity to be gods creates on our part a tenderness in our perception of the sins of others.

Tendency

Christians tend to be harder on fellow Christians than on others, and this can sometimes breed suspicion of one another and judgmentalism. The Pharisees were most provoked by Jesus because, as it turns out to the historian, he was closer to them than to the Sadducees, Zealots, and Essenes. So in our day we find more family squabbles within denominations and local churches than with other faiths or other denominations. Calvin saw in the words "Do not judge" a tendency to become overly curious about the sins of others (including those closest to us) that needed to be checked and handed over to God—who alone is the Judge.

Besides damning our own too easily, we also tend to distort things: what is central becomes decentralized and what is inessential becomes the focus of our attention. Jesus addressed this when he said to some of his contemporaries in 23:23–24 something similar to what he said in 7:1–5:

> Woe to you, teachers of the law and Pharisees, you hypocrites! You give a tenth of your spices—mint, dill and cumin. But you have neglected the more important matters of the law—justice, mercy and faithfulness. You should have practiced the latter, without neglecting the former. You blind guides! You strain out a gnat but swallow a camel.

Even today we tend to be censorious of other Christians for the most insignificant of things, especially if they are not in our "group," and we fail to see important failures on our own part. What happens to this tendency when we come down from the throne, stop acting the part of God, and learn to see ourselves as recipients of God's grace and forgiveness—the sort of grace we are then called to extend to others?

Michael Cheshire tells a story of encountering a man with notoriously public sin, and it taught him about being judgmental and extending grace:[8]

> I didn't plan to care about Ted Haggard. After all, I have access to Google and a Bible. I heard about what he did and knew it was wrong. I saw the clips from the news and the HBO documentary about his life after his fall. I honestly felt bad for him but figured it was his own undoing. When the topic came up with others I know in ministry, we would feign sadness, but inside we couldn't care less. One close friend said he would understand it more if Ted had just sinned with a woman. I agreed with him at the time. It's amazing how much more mercy I give to people who struggle with sins I understand. The further their sin is from my own personal struggles, the more judgmental and callous I become. I'm not proud of that. It's just where I was at that time in my walk. But that all changed in one short afternoon.

Michael encountered the harsh judgmentalism of Christians toward other Christians in a conversation with a non-Christian who said he could not be a Christian because they eat their own. Michael absorbed that statement, and it began to work on him:

> I began to distance myself from my previously harsh statements and tried to understand what Ted and his family must have been through. When I brought up the topic to other men and women I love and respect, the very mention of Haggard's name made our conversations toxic. Their reactions were visceral.... So I felt I needed to meet Ted for myself. So I had my assistant track him down for a lunch appointment. I live outside Denver and he was living in Colorado Springs, a little over an hour away. Perfect!
>
> In less than five minutes of talking with Ted, I realized a horrible truth—I liked him. He was brutally honest about his failures. He was excited that the only people who would talk to him now were the truly broken and hurt.... I met his wonderful wife, Gayle. She is a terrific teacher of grace and one of my heroes. When I grow up, I want to be Gayle Haggard. And so I became close friends with Ted Haggard.
>
> But then the funniest thing started happening to me. Some Christians I hung out with told me they would distance themselves from me if

8. Michael Cheshire, "Going to Hell with Ted Haggard," from *Christianity Today* online: www.christianitytoday.com/le/2012/december-online-only/going-to-hell-with-ted-haggard.html.

I continued reaching out to Ted. Several people in my church said they would leave. Really? Does he have leprosy? Will he infect me? We are friends. We aren't dating! But in the end, I was told that my voice as a pastor and author would be tarnished if I continued to spend time with him. I found this sickening. Not just because people can be so small, but because I have a firsthand account from Ted and Gayle of how they lost many friends they had known for years. Much of it is pretty coldblooded. Now the "Christian machine" was trying to take away their new friends.

It would do some Christians good to stay home one weekend and watch the entire DVD collection of HBO's *Band of Brothers*. Marinate in it. Take notes. Write down words like *loyalty*, *friendship*, and *sacrifice*. Understand the phrase: never leave a fallen man behind.

In many ways I have not been aggressive enough with the application of the gospel. My concept of grace needed to mature, to grow muscles, teeth, and bad breath.

If we need to learn that we are not the judge, that God extends us grace, and that the experience of grace leads us to extend grace to others, there's something else to learn too.

Moral Discernment and Mutual Edification

Many in our day climb under the moral shade of Matthew 7:1 to take the supposed high road in saying, "I'm not the judge." Those who take this supposed high road may be missing the whole point of Jesus' words: sin is sin, and one cannot follow Jesus and turn a blind eye to sin. What Jesus is calling us to here is not the absence of moral discernment. After all, he concludes our passage with the permission to help with the moral failings of others, and then he turns around in the very next verse (7:6) and refers to some people as "dogs"!

Instead, he is calling us not to assume the condemning role of God. We are to discern things morally, after we have inspected ourselves, and we are to speak the truth about sins. The New Testament is filled with authors who had to utter strong words about sins. These are not damnations but discernments. I take James as an example. Read James 3:1 through 4:12 and you will see a brother of Jesus who both calls sin sin and then calls us not to be judges. This is the tension of 7:1-5 that has led to squishy moral theology in the church and culture.

An Ethic from Beyond transcends judgmentalism by pursuing both sanctification and reconciliation. As Jesus had to rebuke his followers when they failed (see 14:22-33), so he also forgave them and called them back to the path of discipleship. So we are to do the same: when we fail, we confess our sins; then we get back up and follow Jesus. Close to the heart of obeying this passage is a willingness to be people of introspection and confession. The church has always taught us to confess our sins, both before God and before one another, and the routine practice of confession makes us aware of our own sins and merciful to those of our brothers and sisters in the kingdom. But this does not make us mute; it makes us humbly seek to grow together in love for God and one another, to grow in holiness and justice, and to become a society marked by authentic honesty and genuine growth in both personal and ecclesial spiritual formation.[9]

A meme of our culture today is that Christians are judgmental. Two recent studies have revealed that many don't like the church or Christians because they perceive them as judgmental.[10] Before I proceed to strip some of this criticism bare, we need to confess our sin of standing in judgment on others at times. Having said that, however, we need to point out the major issue: much of the "Christians are judgmental" meme never gets beyond the simple observation that Christians, because they are Christians and read the Bible and seek to practice it, think some things are wrong—like adultery and divorce and homosexuality and gossip and greed and Green Bay Packers (sorry, but I was groping for another "g"). It is one thing to be judgmental; it is entirely different to say greed is wrong or that sexual sins are wrong, and saying so is not judgmentalism. Some, I am arguing, of the accusation is simply an intolerance for those who think something is wrong (that many in our culture think is none of their business).

Perhaps the best example of how to live out the words of Jesus in Matthew 7:1–5 can be found in John 7:53–8:11, a text that is probably not original to the gospel of John but which may well be a solid remembrance of what Jesus one time did. I close with that text:

> Then they all went home, but Jesus went to the Mount of Olives.
>
> At dawn he appeared again in the temple courts, where all the people gathered around him, and he sat down to teach them. The teachers of the law and the Pharisees brought in a woman caught in adultery. They made her stand before the group and said to Jesus, "Teacher, this woman was caught in the act of adultery. In the Law Moses commanded us to stone such women. Now what do you say?" They were using this question as a trap, in order to have a basis for accusing him.
>
> But Jesus bent down and started to write on the ground with his fin-

---

9. T. F. Latini, *The Church and the Crisis of Community: A Practical Theology of Small-Group Ministry* (Grand Rapids: Eerdmans, 2011), 106–17.

10. G. Lyons and D. Kinnaman, *Unchristian: What a New Generation Really Thinks about Christianity . . . and Why It Matters* (Grand Rapids: Baker, 2007); D. Kimball, *They Like Jesus but Not the Church: Insights from Emerging Generations* (Grand Rapids: Zondervan, 2007).

ger. When they kept on questioning him, he straightened up and said to them, "Let any one of you who is without sin be the first to throw a stone at her." Again he stooped down and wrote on the ground.

At this, those who heard began to go away one at a time, the older ones first, until only Jesus was left, with the woman still standing there. Jesus straightened up and asked her, "Woman, where are they? Has no one condemned you?"

"No one, sir," she said.

"Then neither do I condemn you," Jesus declared. "Go now and leave your life of sin."

Maybe what Jesus wrote on the ground was: "Do not judge." Maybe he wrote: "Grace works wonders."

CHAPTER 18

Matthew 7:6

 LISTEN to the Story

> [6]"Do not give dogs what is sacred; do not throw your pearls to pigs. If you do, they may trample them under their feet, and turn and tear you to pieces."

Listening to the text in the Story: Exodus 19; 24; Leviticus; 1 Kings 2:1–9:9; Isaiah 6; Ezra 9–10; Revelation 4–5; 20–22.

Mormons have holy underwear, Catholic priests can't throw away consecrated wine, Anglicans can't walk by the communion table without genuflecting, and it seems low church evangelicals have nothing physical that evokes that sense of the sacred. Yet the Israelites had a temple open to almost no one, and Jesus informs his followers that there is something so "sacred" they are to be exceedingly careful to whom they divulge it. Just what that "sacred" might be is discussed below, but what needs immediate attention is that the Bible's Story affirms over and over the division between the sacred and the common. God is holy; his people are to be holy; those not in God's people are unholy. God's people are to know and honor the difference.

Three factors seem to work against our appreciation of the sacred/secular divide. First, the wall separating Gentiles from Jews was broken down by the gospel about Jesus Christ (Eph 2:11–18), and we *all* now have direct access God (Heb 4:14–16; 9:1–10:18). Democratized access to God benefits us all, but some go too far. Second, the Reformation teaching on the priesthood of all believers alongside Luther's brilliant teaching that everyone's job is a vocation paved the way for a modern-day diminution of the sacredness of a pastoral calling versus a "secular" calling. Finally, our post–Thomas Paine's Western world's embracing of the "rights of man" have been converted by some into entitlement for all into the realms of what was previously sacred. When many today mix the above three into postmodernity's irreverent soup, we are not surprised that many hesitate at the door of words like those of Jesus in Matthew 7:6.

But for Jesus there was a sacred versus secular divide because he lived in a world where the temple's sacredness permeated the consciousness of all of his followers. So we dare not forget that when Jesus said, "Do not give dogs what is *sacred*," none of his followers thought it inappropriate to see some things as profoundly sacred. That raises the question of what Jesus meant by "sacred."

EXPLAIN the Story

How does 7:6 fit in its context? Some have suggested connections between 7:1–5 and 7:6, or between 7:1–5 and 7:11 or 7:12, but such explanatory connections struggle to be convincing.[1] We *can* put these lines together in a variety of ways, but none seems compelling. I stand with Don Hagner: "This verse appears to be a detached independent logion [saying] apparently unrelated to the preceding."[2]

Matthew 7:6 is a classic "chiasm."[3] Chiasms say one or two things and then repeat those same items in reverse order. Thus, "ABBA" is a chiasm. Here's how it works in Matthew 7:6:

> A Do not give dogs what is sacred;
>   B do not throw your pearls to pigs.
>   B′ If you do, they may trample them under their feet,
> A′ and turn and tear you to pieces.

The important download for interpretation here is that the "pigs" and "trample" belong together, while the "turn and tear" and "dogs" belong together. Some have made valiant attempts to explain the ferocity of pigs because they think A′ describes the behavior of pigs, while a chiastic reading of it leads us to see that line describing dogs, who were mostly wild and ravenous.

The animals chosen by Jesus were among the most despised; thus, to speak of other humans in such derogatory terms reveals the utter seriousness of Jesus. Dogs and pigs have no sense of value, so dogs will rip apart a precious item and pigs will trample on items of immense worth. Jesus is labeling those

---

1. Davies and Allison (*Matthew*, 1:672) see 7:6 counteracting potential misuses of 7:1–5. Guelich (*Sermon on the Mount*, 376–77) sees a connection to the salt of 5:13 and the sixth and seventh petitions of the Lord's Prayer (6:13). Keener (*Matthew*, 244) offers this: 7:1–5 says don't prejudge; 7:6 says don't force the gospel on others. Turner (*Matthew*, 210): disciples are to be neither inquisitors (7:1–5) nor simpletons (7:6). John Stott (*Message*, 174–75) sees the whole of 7:1–27 shaped by various relationships.
2. Hagner, *Matthew 1–13*, 171.
3. N. W. Lund, *Chiasmus in the New Testament: A Study in the Form and Function of Chiastic Structures* (Peabody, MA: Hendrickson, 1992), 32.

who despise the kingdom (also at 7:21–23; 13:24–30, 36–43; 15:26–27; 18:17). The chiastic organization leads us to see "sacred" and "pearls" as synonyms and therefore provokes two questions for Bible readers: What is this "sacred" or "pearl"? What is Jesus teaching his followers *not* to do?

There is a splendid history on what "sacred" means. It begins with the Jewishness of what Jesus said. "Do not give dogs what is sacred" had an original connection to sacrificial meat or to leaven. Thus, Leviticus 22:10 reads: "No one outside a priest's family may eat the sacred offering."[4] The later rabbis said something quite like this statement by Jesus: "For they do not redeem Holy Things to feed them to the dogs" (*m. Temurah* 6:5). Jesus has obviously adapted a typical expression and applied it to his own sense of the sacred.

What might that be? The traditional understanding is that this refers to saving one's gospeling energies for those who will listen and not wasting one's energies on those who will not listen.[5] Since "pearl" is used in Matthew 13:45–46 for the supreme possession of the kingdom, and since Jesus elsewhere demands that his missionaries wipe the dust off their feet on communities that do not respond to the kingdom (10:14), we can safely say that "sacred" and "pearl" refer to the gospel. But others have pushed further to see esoteric or insider teachings of the church, which is not unusual for those who are a minority or persecuted. Hence, silence, or insider-only talk, might be the preferred approach to speaking (cf. 13:36–52). Yet others suggest the sacred is the Eucharist; since it is only for those who believe, the Eucharist is closed to outsiders (*Did.* 9.5).

The traditional view has a more refined meaning, recently stated briefly anew by Tom Wright,[6] and it is the more accurate one. As "dogs" and "pigs" were terms used so widely by Jews of Gentiles (cf. 15:26–27) and all of Jesus' hearers would have made that connection immediately, and as Jesus urged his disciples (for the time being anyway) not to preach the gospel of the kingdom to the Gentiles (10:5–6; cf. 24:14; 28:19–20) and to be circumspect (10:16), so here: this is a simple prohibition of taking the gospel and the kingdom vision to the Gentile world until after the resurrection, the Great Commission, the ascension, and Pentecost, which unleashed the Gentile mission—a

---

4. Exod 29:33; Lev 2:3; 22:6–7, 10–16; Num 18:8–19. At Qumran a text, called 4QMMT394 (Halakhic Letter) in which dogs are prohibited from the "holy camp" because they are known to eat bones and meat (see fragment 8, 4.8–10).

5. Luther, *Sermon on the Mount*, 225–28. Luther's concerns are the schismatics and the Catholics. Calvin (*Harmony of the Gospels*, 1:227–28) was concerned with foul scorners of the gospel. Stott (*Message*, 182) focuses on those who have decisively and defiantly rejected the gospel. This view was held by Augustine as well: ACCS: *Matthew*, 148.

6. Wright, *Matthew for Everyone*, 1:70–71.

theme that unfolds in Matthew's gospel.[7] For the time being Jesus wants his followers to "gospel" the Jews of Galilee and Judea even if at times gospeling will spill over to the Gentiles during his lifetime. Deliberate expansion to Gentiles will come later.

LIVE the Story

Sometimes in our zeal to "apply" a text, we fail to read the text in its context. And more often than we may all care to admit, our frustrations over how to apply a text can be completely resolved with a more accurate interpretation. The fuss that has been created over what "sacred" and (its oft-neglected twin) "pearls" might mean can be silenced if we admit that the best reading of this text is that Jesus was telling his disciples in metaphorical terms what he would say again in more direct terms when he sent them out: do not (yet) evangelize the Gentiles; they aren't ready for it; it's time for our fellow Jews right now (10:5–6).

Begin Close to Home

At one level, of course, history has completely uprooted this saying because from Matthew 28:19–20, Acts 10–11, and Paul's mission, the gospel has gone out to the Gentiles. The church today is a Gentile church far more than a Jewish church. As we have interpreted Matthew 7:6, then, it has been "fulfilled" or run its course and it now belongs to a period of history—the two to three years of Jesus' public ministry prior to Pentecost.

But on another level the point Jesus was making may obtain meaning for us in a new way: we could learn to focus our gospeling energies on those closest to us, on those who are in our orbit with whom we have natural connections, and to leave the worldwide preaching of the gospel to those who have that calling. Perhaps more of us need to gospel our families, our neighbors, and those in our community more than we are.

This does not prohibit gospeling in Africa, Asia, South America, or Australia, but it does remind us that the approach of the apostle Paul is one that can be replicated: he was a zealous missionary, but he always began on his home turf, at the synagogue with his fellow Jews. Jesus too began with his own people. But we do perhaps need the reminder that this saying pertains to a specific time in history—to the time when Jesus was gospeling the Jews prior to his crucifixion, resurrection, ascension, and Pentecost. That period will never occur again.

---

7. It begins with Abraham in the genealogy of 1:1–17, shows up in the Gentile magi of 2:1–12, comes to the surface in Jesus' ministry in Galilee (4:12–16). Along the way there are hints and glimpses, but it comes to full expression only with the Great Commission of 28:16–20.

Hold Sacred Things with Care

But this text is telling us something about the sacred trust of the gospel. The gospel is sacred. In this Story of Jesus the mysteries of God are now disclosed to us, and in the privilege of knowing it and telling others of it we are in possession of ultimate truths. We are to honor what we have by treasuring it, we convey it to others with the most profound of speech acts, we are to study it because in it we come to know and be known by God, and we are to learn to talk about it only in ways that honor the glories that it holds. Yet we are charged by God to tell others about Jesus, the kingdom, and the gospel.

While some seem to enjoy the biting response of rejection when they speak of the gospel and may even take a sense of pride in "suffering for Jesus," I am not persuaded our task is as much about being offensive as being wise and using our gospel energies appropriately. I learned in high school that taking my Bible into the locker room can be a good way to become an object of ridicule, and speaking up—which I did—is just another opportunity for ridicule, and I learned at that time that there's a time to speak and a time to be silent.

What Jesus has in mind here is not fear about speaking but *profound respect for the gloriousness of the gospel, a desire to honor God, and an approach to gospeling that does the most service to Christ.* In other words, we need to ask if speaking up in a given situation will honor or vilify Christ, and then to act accordingly. There is no reason to venture forward if we discern confidently that this will yield nothing but an opportunity for someone to take a shot in public at God and the church. Instead, we need to learn from such discernments to spend our time on those who listen. What this text teaches us is that we have to learn when to speak and when to walk away, and sometimes walking away is the most gospel-honoring thing we can do.

LISTEN to the Story

> [7]"Ask and it will be given to you; seek and you will find; knock and the door will be opened to you. [8]For everyone who asks receives; the one who seeks finds; and to the one who knocks, the door will be opened.
>
> [9]"Which of you, if your son asks for bread, will give him a stone? [10]Or if he asks for a fish, will give him a snake? [11]If you, then, though you are evil, know how to give good gifts to your children, how much more will your Father in heaven give good gifts to those who ask him!"

Listening to the text in the Story: Psalm 37:4; 84:11; Jeremiah 29:13–14; John 16:23–24; James 1:3–5, 16–17.

Most of us at some point in our Christian journey were taught Matthew 7:7 as a progression: first, **A**sk, then **S**eek, and finally **K**nock. The cleverness of seeing A-S-K in the first word seemed to make the interpretation right. Of course, the complicating factor is that in Greek this clever little mnemonic device doesn't exist (although it's close: *A-Z-K*).

Furthermore, many of us were taught that the three verbs (ask, seek, knock) were *present* imperatives, which means we are to persist and not give up, and if we kept on asking, kept on seeking, and kept on knocking, God would hear us.[1] If we are not careful with this persistence theme, we create a God who seems to be either tired or busy, or perhaps uninterested, but persistence might stir his attention. Some appeal to Luke 11:5–8 (the knocker at midnight) or to Luke 18:1–8 (the persistent widow) to prop up the persistence view of our verses. Then along comes the preacher or author who tells us that any view that teaches God responds to persistence demeans God's glory and character, and so we get stuck with these texts, wondering what they might mean—and so this text pushes us to think hard again about what prayer is: Does it really make a difference? Does God change the course of history because we pray, or

---

1. Seeing persistence here is common; thus, see Luther, *Sermon on the Mount*, 234; Hagner, *Matthew 1–13*, 174. Hagner cites Clement as seeing persistence here.

don't pray? Does persistence pay off? Is God sovereign? Why does God answer prayer—for his own glory or to form an interactive relationship with us?

This makes us wonder about what prayer was like in the world of Jesus.[2] We perhaps need to remind ourselves that Israel was a praying nation. One of its favorite books, if we judge by the number of quotations in the New Testament, was the book of Psalms, a prayer book. The back of my Greek New Testament contains a list of passages alluded to or cited from the Old Testament. The book of Psalms has ten columns of passages cited in the New Testament, while no other book has more than five other than Isaiah, which has seven. It has been said that the average Jew had the entire book of Psalms memorized.

A personal experience with the monastic traditions taught me that some have always memorized the book of Psalms (in Latin, of course!) in order to recite it weekly in the daily office of prayers. As I mentioned earlier, Kris and I stumbled into an Italian basilica, sat down in the last row to cool off, only to be a treated to a Benedictine concert of prayer. The monks were chanting Psalm 119, which they knew by heart, as part of a weekly routine of chanting the entire Psalter from memory! Israel was a praying nation, and one central element of their prayers, and you can find these sorts of prayers throughout the Psalms, was petitions. The Israelites learned at an early age that part of praying was asking God for what one needed (e.g., Ps 55), and petitionary prayer forms the heart of everyone who learns to pray the way Jesus taught us in this Sermon (Matt 6:9–13).[3]

But petitionary prayer always faces a few problems, not the least being whether God, the God of the cosmos and beyond, really cares about my personal petitions. Jesus' teachings here are shaped to speak to that struggle in prayer, and it leads us to see that God is a Father who is altogether good, and therefore a God who will respond to his people when they pray. We can finesse this text all we want, but Tom Wright brings it directly home: "But, for most of us, the problem is not that we are too eager to ask for the wrong things. The problem is that we are not eager enough to ask for the right things."[4]

EXPLAIN the Story

This text virtually proves that Matthew 7 is more or less an eclectic collection of teachings of Jesus.[5] Judging does not clearly lead to the teachings on not giving out the gospel, and neither of those sections lead directly to the theme

---

2. In the notes of 6:7–15 we provide bibliography.

3. R. J. Foster, *Prayer: Finding the Heart's True Home* (San Francisco: HarperSanFrancisco, 1992), 179–90.

4. Wright, *Matthew for Everyone*, 1:72.

5. Hagner, *Matthew 1–13*, 173; France, *Matthew*, 278–79.

of prayer. Moreover, none of these sections leads naturally to the Golden Rule in 7:12. It is wise to let the Bible be what it is—in this case, a random collection of Jesus' teachings. But 7:7-11 itself is tidy: exhortations to pray are followed by promises (7:7). Verse 8 broadens verse 7. The exhortations and promises are anchored in the character of God (7:9-11).

Exhortations with Promises

Jesus' view of prayer is probably drawn from the Jewish wisdom or prophetic tradition (cf. Prov 8:17; Jer 29:13-14): ask and it will be given, and so on. In each of these there is a conditionless promise that God will answer the prayer. Of course, Jesus wasn't naive; this is part of Jesus' exaggerated rhetoric, and Jesus knew that his own disciples prayed and didn't get what they wanted (Matt 14:22-33; 17:14-21). This is why we have James 1:5-6, which can be read as a commentary on this text, as can James 4:3. Most importantly, it can be said that Jesus himself prayed and didn't get what he asked for (cf. Matt 26:39).

Realities push us to probe under the surface promises. Jesus teaches that his disciples are to go to God, ask him, and expect him to respond. Why does he need to say this? Because the disciples are wondering *if* God will answer their prayers. Thus, 7:7-8 isn't a promise that everything everyone asks will be given. Instead, it is addressing doubting disciples who need to be assured that God indeed loves them and that they can trust God (see John 16:23-24).

The Jewish tradition of sages or holy men illustrates the Jewish ideal of petitionary prayer. Thus, we think of Elijah (2 Kings 17:7-24) and Honi the Circle Drawer.[6] Here is the Mishnah's account of Honi (*m. Ta'anit* 3:8):

A. On account of every sort of public trouble (may it not happen) do they sound the shofar,

B. except for an excess of rain.

C. M'SH S: They said to Honi, the circle drawer, "Pray for rain."

D. He said to them, "Go and take in the clay ovens used for Passover, so that they not soften [in the rain which is coming]."

E. He prayed, but it did not rain.

F. What did he do?

G. He drew a circle and stood in the middle of it and said before Him, "Lord of the world! Your children have turned to me, for before you I am like a member of the family. I swear by your great name—I'm simply not moving from here until you take pity on your children!"

---

6. G. Vermes, *Jesus the Jew: A Historian's Reading of the Gospels* (Philadelphia: Fortress, 1981), 69-72.

H. It began to rain drop by drop.

I. He said, "This is not what I wanted, but rain for filling up cisterns, pits, and caverns."

J. It began to rain violently.

K. He said, "This is not what I wanted, but rain of good will, blessing, and graciousness."

L. Now it rained the right way, until Israelites had to flee from Jerusalem up to the Temple Mount because of the rain.

Prayer's Anchor: God's Character

Jesus anchors petition in God's goodness. Thus, if a son asks for bread, does any father (other than a creep) give instead a stone?[7] If that son asks for fish, does any father give him a snake? This father-son relation is pressed into service here by Jesus to focus on God's goodness. If we humans, who are evil,[8] are good enough to give good things to our children, how much more will God give to us! Why? *Because God is both better than us and is altogether good!* This perception of God's goodness can be found in Psalms 37:4; 84:11; and Isaiah 49:15, but we are also reminded of James 1:16–17. For both Jesus and James God is good, and God gives nothing but good things.

Matthew's version varies from Luke's in one significant way: Matthew 7:11 has "good gifts" while Luke 11:13 has "the Holy Spirit." Perhaps Luke thought that all good gifts are found in the Holy Spirit, or perhaps Matthew flattened "Holy Spirit" to "good gifts." Are there any textual clues about what specifically Jesus has in mind with "good things"? Some have suggested this refers to the necessities of life (as in 6:25–34), but the language of this text emphasizes not so much a particular kind of good thing but the goodness of God in responding to God's children with good things, including provisions.[9] God is good—God creates, orders, sustains, listens, adjusts, disciplines, elects, protects, guides, ransoms, saves, reconciles—and we could go on and on.

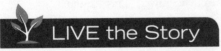

LIVE the Story

My experience teaches me that it is easier to make Christians feel guilty about their lack of a prayer life than it is to motivate them to become more active in

---

7. It is unlikely that Jesus is here alluding to other events in his life, though they do make for interesting parallels: cf. 4:3; 14:13–21; 15:32–39.

8. Jesus' take on original sin is not explicit here. Luz sees the "evil" as forming a rhetorical foil to God's goodness, while France warns about pressing this word to find original sin (Luz, *Matthew 1–7*, 359; France, *Matthew*, 281 n. 8). Allison (*Sermon on the Mount*, 157) proceeds to list all the sins that are implicit in the Sermon on the Mount.

9. For a good discussion, Keener, *Matthew*, 246–47.

prayer. The former (guilt) rarely produces the latter (active prayer). Jesus' words in this text may be the most insightful words in the entire Bible on how to motivate people to pray: *instead of using guilt to motivate, we need to cast a compelling vision of the goodness of our Father.* Knowing God's love, knowing God's goodness, and learning to embrace those attributes of God prompt us to pray.

When it comes to those from whom I have learned about prayer and whose example spurs me to more prayer, I can do no better than A. W. Tozer.[10] His practice, or better yet obsession, with bathing himself in the presence of God in prayer has been described by Lyle Dorsett:

> Although the author [of *The Pursuit of God*] never boasted about his devotional habits, those few who knew him well knew that the angular man with little formal schooling learned much about his Lord and his God in the secret place. Tozer spent incalculable hours in prayer. Most of his prolonged prayer time—with his Bible and hymnals as his only companions—took place in his church office on the back side of the second floor. He would carefully hang up his suit trousers and don his sweater and raggedy old "prayer pants" and sit for a while on his ancient office couch. After a time his spirit would drift into another realm. In time, he would abandon the couch, get on his knees, and eventually lie facedown on the floor, singing praises to the Lion of the Tribe of Judah.

Genuine prayer, Tozer reminds us, is about a passion for God and an obsession with entering his presence. God delights in our presence and delights in sharing his presence with us. We are summoned to enter.

Two Temptations

There are many temptations when it comes to our prayer life; I focus on two. First, we are tempted as humans to figure things out ourselves and to make things happen under our own power. Martin Luther offers a powerful reminder in our temptation to go at life on our own:

> The world is insane. It tries to get rid of its insanity by the use of wisdom and reason; and it looks for many ways and means, for all sorts of help and advice on how to escape this distress. But the shortest and surest way is to go into a little room (Matt. 6:6) or a corner and there to open your heart and to pour it out before God, filled with complaints and sighs, but also with confidence and trust that as your faithful heavenly Father He wants to give you His help and advice in this distress.[11]

---

10. See L. Dorsett, *A Passion for God: The Spiritual Journey of A. W. Tozer* (Chicago: Moody Press, 2008), citing from p. 121.

11. Luther, *Sermon on the Mount*, 231–32.

The second temptation is to think God is distant and uncaring. This temptation assails me at times. How so? Kris and I have been in Cape Town and Johannesburg, Sydney and Perth, Copenhagen and Aarhus, Vienna and Frankfurt, and from New York to Miami to Dallas to Chicago to Seattle, and right down the Californian coast to San Francisco, Los Angeles, and San Diego. We encounter a diverse world of people, entirely unknown to us and as busy as we are in their own worlds, and one has to wonder how in the world God can care about so many people at the same time. But this only reveals how earthly and earthy our conceptions of God are: the God of the Bible is so immense, omnipotent, and omniscient that for God, knowing each of us in the depths of our beings is an afternoon walk in Sydney's botanical garden. The God of Jesus knows us by name, knows our minds and hearts and emotions, loves us (anyway), and summons us, as it were, into the divine presence to lay out our requests. This is not a challenge to God so much as it is incomprehensible to humans. Jesus calls us to trust him when he says God knows, God cares, and God wants us to ask for what we want.[12]

Two Discouragements

The single biggest discouragement in prayer is unanswered, deeply felt petitions. Sometimes we ask God for something that doesn't matter that much, but when we ask for what we most want—the conversion of a friend or healing, employment, or justice in the face of massive injustice—and when we go before God time and time again with that single issue, and God seems distant or uninterested or flat-out does not answer our prayer (someone dies prior to conversion, someone dies without healing, or someone's life goes south because of unemployment), we can become discouraged about prayer.

I have no answer to the problem of unanswered prayer, and frankly the typical answers don't do much for me—that God does answer but not the way we expected, that we are to keep on praying, that we are out of God's will, that our motives are impure, that we are really only learning to adjust our wills to God's will, that we really don't want what we are asking, that the answers are given as "yes, no, or wait a little longer." None of these really get to the heart of the heartfelt yearning for God to act. I don't appeal here to mystery. Instead, I focus on who God is, and I continue to lay my petitions before that God in faith, trust, and hope. Sometimes hope lags behind our petitions, and sometimes hope sustains us. But I keep on praying because I believe God is good. Sometimes it is discouraging, and I'd be a liar if I didn't admit it.

---

12. John Stott provides three problems with what Jesus says here about prayer: that prayer is unseemly (for a sovereign God), unnecessary, and unproductive. See his pastoral discussions of each: Stott, *Message*, 186–89.

A second discouragement to petitions is that if God knows, why bother? If we think about this, it makes only partial sense. Some gifts are surprises, but often gifts come as a result of asking. Those who love others often ask one another for things, so God beckons us to ask—sure, God knows, but God also wants us to interact so that out of our love for God we petition God. I don't want to enter the lofty places of the debate about open theism and how much God knows (some think God knows all things while others think God interacts with humans at such a level that our communications with God actually result in God's comprehending things not previously knowable), but petitionary prayer can assume that God both knows and wants to know what we want. I believe that the broad sweep of the way in which prayer works in the Bible—and I'm thinking here of Jonah and the repentance of Nineveh—teaches us that God, in his sovereignty, has established a kind of contingency in the universe, and that God *genuinely interacts* with humans who pray in such a way that the universe changes as a result of our prayers.[13]

Two Beliefs

Theology reshapes prayer. What happens to our prayers if we really do believe that God is good? I am convinced that many of us, while we affirm that *God is good* and that God listens, do not act as if God cares and listens. In other words, we wouldn't be caught dead not affirming God's care for our every moment, but we act as if God is up there not all that bothered with us and our world, let alone something so small as our next putt on the golf course, our next answer on a test, or our next conversation with the one we love. But Jesus wants us to see in this text that our God is the Father who really does care and wants us to ask. We must learn to believe that God is good and answers our prayers. As Ulrich Luz says so memorably, "The certainty that prayer will be heard does not make it superfluous; it makes it possible."[14]

A second belief is that God is good because *God is Father*. The "ontology" of this text is not that we infer God's fatherliness from ours but that our fatherliness *is rooted in and emerges from God's*. Because God is Father, and because we as fathers respond to our sons with good gifts, we are to see our goodness not as something we produce and hope that God will imitate, but as something that derives from the goodness of God as Father.

Now, let's make this equal: we are not talking just about males here. We as mothers and fathers respond to our children (male and female) in good ways. We do this *because God has made us like himself*. The ontology of God—who

---

13. The best I've seen on this topic, though I don't always agree, is Tiessen, *Providence and Prayer*.

14. Luz, *Matthew 1–7*, 359.

God is, God as Father—shapes who we are and how we act. This is at the root of what Jesus teaches us here: *because God, the Father, is good, we see something of God in the simplest of kindnesses between parents and their children.* Our kindness, then, is a window—let's call it iconic in the Eastern sense—onto *who God is* and *what God is really like.* We are to learn to take this belief and let it flourish: if we are good and if we reflect God, God is even "good-er."

Two Questions

This exploration of prayer in light of who God is and how God treat us leads me to ask two questions as we finish this passage:

- What kind of parent doesn't give good gifts, so far as the parent is able, to her or his children? (If this is the way we are, we are to think of God as even better.)
- How much do we *not* have because we do not ask and we do not ask because we do not believe God is good—and yet every day we see or experience the goodness of parents blessing their children?

Let us pray to the Father of our Lord Jesus Christ, the Father who is good.

CHAPTER 20

Matthew 7:12

 ## LISTEN to the Story

[12]"So in everything, do to others what you would have them do to you, for this sums up the Law and the Prophets."[1]

Listening to the text in the Story: Exodus 19–24 (esp. 20–23); Leviticus 17–26; 19:18; Deuteronomy 6:4–5; 11:13–21; Numbers 15:37–41; Matthew 19:16–30; 22:34–40; Romans 13:8–10; Galatians 5:14; James 2:8; *b. Šabbat* 31a.[2]

Of the many ways to describe or articulate the Torah, two are pertinent in our text: one can either *multiply laws* so as to cover all possible situations, or one can *reduce the law* to its essence. Clearly the Bible shows the multiplication orientation in the Covenant Code (Exod 19–24, or 20–23), the Holiness Code (Lev 17–26), and the Deuteronomic Code (Deut 12–26). By the time of Jesus those codes expanded enormously: think Dead Sea Scrolls to the rabbis. Many Christians think multiplication means legalism, the perfect foil being rabbinic rulings,[3] while the essence approach is closer to liberalism, this time the foil being the über-tolerant. Some find solace in the Golden Rule, though more careful consideration of the Golden Rule, which is a variant on the Jesus Creed (Matt 22:34–40), reveals that Jesus is not giving either the legalist or the liberal a pat on the back. He wags his finger at both of them.

In summary, many are uncomfortable with the legal texts of the Bible, but Jesus wasn't. So Jesus *reduced the Torah to two points — loving God, loving others (the Jesus Creed) — not to abolish the many laws but to comprehend them and to see them in their innermost essence.* Jesus himself was law observant, but what distinguished his praxis was that he did so through the law of double love. To do the Torah through love is to do all the Torah says and more.

---

1. KNT: "So whatever you want people to do to you, do just that to them. Yes: this is what the law and the prophets are all about."
2. For more Jewish texts, see Talbert, *Reading the Sermon on the Mount*, 135.
3. See Aharon Shemesh, "Legal Texts," *EDEJ*, 877–80.

Of course, each of the two major alternatives carries its own temptations. The multiplication approach intends to make the law more (not less) doable by making problem situations clear. No one wants to fault this in principle; in fact, it is at the core of modern law throughout the world. It has always tempted some to a sense of superiority because of one's greater rigor. As well, some have virtually come to the conviction that they are worthy of God because of their moral condition of observance.

The reduction model has led at times to Antinomian freedom to the degree that one can sin it up in order to find the magnitude of grace in forgiveness. Others found in the reduction model self-justification to do what they wanted instead of what God wants.

The law is a good revelation from God and is the premier example of an Ethic from Above. Jesus reduced the Torah to its basics in order to make the Torah more understandable and doable. So we are back to the Golden Rule to see that Jesus does not abolish law (5:17–20) but establishes it: loving God and loving others. Or, doing to others what we want done to us.

EXPLAIN the Story

This text has no obvious connections to what is before or after. A quick look at Luke's parallels illustrates Matthew's collection of sayings:

7:1–5	➔	Luke 6:37–38, 41–42
7:6		[no parallel]
7:7–11	➔	Luke 11:9–13
7:12	➔	Luke 6:31
7:13–14	➔	Luke 13:23–24
7:15–23	➔	Luke 6:43–45, 46; 13:26–27
7:24–27	➔	Luke 6:47–49

Perhaps Luke scattered the sayings. Either way, the Golden Rule was part of the prewritten Sermon on the Mount and was probably in Q. Yet we cannot fail to observe that the Golden Rule of 7:12 officially closes the teachings of Jesus in the Sermon and *summarizes the essence of the Sermon.* It sounds somewhat like 5:17–20 (where Law and Prophets are mentioned), leading some to think it summarizes all that has been said from 5:17 to 7:11.

The Golden Rule (7:12a)

The first word of 7:12 in Greek is *panta*: "in everything." The language is emphatic. When "all" is combined with "whatever" (*hosa*; cf. RSV), one gets perhaps more than a simple "all."[4] And if one ties this to 5:17–20, it is reasonable to translate "in all things" or even "the sum of the matter." Twice Jesus probes into the essence of the Torah by appealing to self-love: here and in the Jesus Creed (22:34–40). As his followers were to love their neighbors *as they loved themselves*, so they as disciples were to do to others *what they would want others to do to them*. This principle is neither selfish nor narcissistic but expansive—we are to extend our self-care to others.

There is nothing complex about this most simple of moral maxims; its difficulty is in the doing, not in the knowing. There is a simple reciprocity at work: the very thing, whatever it is, that you want others to do to you, that is the very thing, whatever it is, that you should do to others. There is also nothing new in Jesus' Golden Rule. A similar saying is attributed to the great rabbi roughly contemporary with Jesus, Hillel (teacher of Gamaliel, who was the teacher of the apostle Paul). The story for Hillel's saying derives from the Babylonian Talmud (some three to four hundred years after Jesus and Hillel), but some trust it as an authentic remembrance of the historical Hillel:

> On another occasion it happened that a certain heathen came before Shammai [Hillel's more "conservative" rival teacher] and said to him, "Make me a proselyte on condition that you teach me the whole Torah while I stand on one foot." Shammai drove him out with a builder's cubit which was in his hand. When he went before Hillel, he made him a proselyte. He said to him, "What is hateful to you, do not do to your neighbor. That is the whole Torah. The rest is commentary. Go and learn!"[5]

Jesus' version is positive and Hillel's negative, and there is a difference when one frames something in either way. But we also need to exercise some caution here. If we press the distinction too much, we begin to dabble in speculative psychologizing if not a sense of superiority that Jesus' positive version trumps the negative version. But Jesus too can express his teachings in a negative, and Hillel can be positive, and both ways are an effective means of communication. Jesus' saying and Hillel's are almost certainly near equivalents.[6] A later text tips the balance in favor of not making any difference between the negative and the positive. The early Christian text *Didache* (1:2) provides Jesus' Golden Rule in the negative form: "First, love the God who made you, and second, your neighbor as yourself. And whatever you do not want to happen to you, do not do to another."

---

4. Other instances in Matthew are 13:46; 18:25; 28:20.

5. See *b. Šabbat* 31a. P. S. Alexander, "Jesus and the Golden Rule," in *Hillel and Jesus: Comparative Studies of Two Major Religious Leaders* (ed. J. H. Charlesworth; Minneapolis: Fortress, 1997), 363–88 (here p. 366).

6. Davies and Allison, *Matthew*, 1:687–88.

There's something radically important in the Golden Rule, and perhaps Matthew 5:43–48 is the place to find that radicality: self-love is the fertile ground for growing love for all, including one's enemies. The Ethic from Beyond finds its paradigmatic form in the Golden Rule.[7]

The Significance of the Golden Rule (7:12b)

The next line is profound: "for this sums up the Law and the Prophets." This has to be tied to two other statements by Jesus, both given in variant form in the Jesus Creed.

> Matthew 22:40: "All the Law and the Prophets hang on these two commandments." [The KNT has a more graphic and literal translation: *"The entire law hangs on (or 'from') these two commandments—and* that goes for the prophets, too."]
> Mark 12:31: "There is no commandment greater than these."

To these I want to add James 2:8: "If you really keep *the royal law* found in Scripture, 'Love your neighbor as yourself,' *you are doing right*" (italics added). There is a shocking claim made here by King Jesus for kingdom citizens: *the entire Torah is summarized by or hangs down in dependence from the Golden Rule*. In fact, James sees it as the capital command of the entire Torah. If you get that one right, you are the truly obedient and observant Jew! Three times the apostle Paul supports the Golden Rule, though again in the Jesus Creed (Lev 19:18) form:

> Romans 13:9: "The commandments, 'You shall not commit adultery,' 'You shall not murder,' 'You shall not steal,' 'You shall not covet,' and whatever other command there may be, are summed up in this one command: 'Love your neighbor as yourself.'"
> Romans 13:10: "Love does no harm to a neighbor. Therefore love is the fulfillment of the law."
> Galatians 5:14: "For the entire law is fulfilled in keeping this one command: 'Love your neighbor as yourself.'"

Two more grandiose terms are used this time by Paul in this reduction approach to the Torah: the love command sums up (Paul's term can be translated "recapitulates") the Ten Commandments and "whatever other command there may be"! Or, the "entire law" finds its goal and fulfillment in the observance of this one command to love others as oneself. The entire will of God is about learning to love others, or to treat others, the way we treat ourselves! So the NIV's "sums up" is one way of putting this.

---

7. For discussion, P. Ricouer, "The Golden Rule," *NTS* 36 (1990): 392–97.

 LIVE the Story

The Golden Rule sums up the whole ethic of Jesus: our calling as followers of Jesus, from morning to night, is to monitor our behaviors toward others in accordance with our own self-care. Jesus is not hereby encouraging selfishness but instead selflessness. This Messianic Ethic comes to us both as an Ethic from Above and Beyond.

Listen to Yourself

It may be against every grain in our bodies, especially if we are trained well in the theology of the Reformation to see ourselves as sinners and to know our need of grace, but we must learn that self-care is a grounding for how to treat others. Instead of being just self-care, however, this will lead to other-care. We must be willing to listen to ourselves first to make this happen. So when we see someone else in need, we have to ask ourselves "What would I want? How would I want to be treated?" Maybe the bracelet can be WWIW: "What would I want?"

Listen to Yourself at Home, in the Neighborhood, at Church

It is perhaps easier for us to do this in some contexts than in others, but when we tie the Golden Rule to the enemy-love teaching of Jesus in 5:43–48 and to the Jesus Creed in general, and when we see how Paul applied this in Romans 14 or James in James 2, we get the distinct mentoring focus that we are to listen to ourselves in all contexts. So we need to relate to our spouses and our siblings, our parents and our children, along the same line, learning to listen to the inner voice that says: "This is how I would want to be treated in this same situation."

We are to extend this as well into our neighborhood, as when we look after our neighbor's grass or mail when they are gone, just as our neighbors (Jim and Julie) look after ours when we are gone — and Kris and I are the major receivers on this one because we travel more than do Jim and Julie.

We are to do this at work. I think here of how my colleagues and I interact with one another; we ask each other to read what we are writing, and it is a good rule for us to say, "How would I want my stuff to be read by a colleague?" Perhaps many don't know how this works, but sometimes I give to my fellow New Testament friend and one of the editors of this series, Joel Willitts, or to my philosopher friend Greg Clark, something I've written, and basically I want them to make my piece better. But sometimes their suggestions mean I'm wrong or that I've got more work to do, and I think they want the same of me — but this is where the Jesus Creed and the Golden Rule become the genius they are: they ask us to love one another in such a way that we become better because of love and not just tolerated or accepted for whatever we want to be told about ourselves. We work with one another out of love, not competition or drudgery. We work with one another to make one another better.

The same applies in our churches. We need to think in the exercise of gifts of how we would want to be treated, and we need to treat others that way. Recently a former student came into my office and told me she was now working in an "über-charismatic" organization. They were a little too "in her face" about some things, and she asked my advice. We covered a few topics like learning to understand variety among Christians, but one of our solutions was that she needed to think about how she would want to treat someone or how she would want to be told if she were being a bit overbearing. So she agreed to think and pray about this and then chat with the person who had been a little too pushy with her. But the Golden Rule is of direct value in relationships in churches. It takes but a moment's thought to think it through: *How do I want to treat others? How would I want to be treated?*

Listening for Corporate Groups

I'd like to suggest that the Golden Rule is perhaps the most potent political weapon we Christians have today. And I don't say this because I'm Anabaptist but because *empathy* is at the bottom of the Golden Rule. If we as Christians with a faithful witness would set the example, not by way of reaction but by way of reasoned empathy, we might set the tone for more shalom in our world. Think about 9/11 and al Qaeda in light of the Christian's obligation to respond in all situations with the Golden Rule, of asking how we would want to be treated.

The Golden Rule leads us to a measured humility. Instead of immediate, visceral, angry reaction and plots of vindication—all normal human responses to injustice—perhaps we could ask this first: Did we do something to provoke this? What were the reasons the invaders gave for their violence? To be sure, no one here wants to justify their violence, even if we deserved it (and I don't think we did), but at least we need to back up enough to assess the situation and ask why in the world anyone would want to invade us. Perhaps we need to ask if our international policies are such that we are breeding hatred for our economy, our morals, and our culture when we think we are doing well. Perhaps we need to ask—following the Golden Rule—questions that make us turn inward first.

But international politics is just one example. What about at work? Can we apply the Golden Rule to our place of work? I'm a professor, so let me explore a few questions. If I were a student, would I want to be treated the way my students are treated? If I were an administrator, would I want to be treated this way? If I were a neighbor, would I want to be treated the way my school treats its neighbors? If I were an academic or sports rival, would I want to be treated this way? Do I treat colleagues the way I want to be treated?

This is the Law and the Prophets.
This is God's will.
This is Jesus' Ethic from Above and Beyond.

Any serious pondering of all of life through the Golden Rule is dangerous for our moral health because it will summon us — I know I feel this way just writing the above paragraphs — to live under the King and as one of his kingdom citizens.

If you listen to yourself in all of life, you will be led out of yourself into a life of loving others.

CHAPTER 21

Matthew 7:13–14

 LISTEN to the Story

¹³"Enter through the narrow gate. For wide is the gate and broad¹ is the road that leads to destruction, and many enter through it. ¹⁴But small is the gate and narrow² the road that leads to life, and only a few find it."

Listening to the text in the Story: Exodus 19:1–24:18; Deuteronomy 6; 12–26; Joshua 1–5; 23:1–24:28; Nehemiah 8:1–10:39.

The exodus, forming the covenant but especially the giving of the law, stands behind our passage. One is reminded of Moses' ups-and-downs Mount Sinai to meet with God and then with the children of Israel. The fundamental summons of Moses was for the people to do God's revealed Torah. "When Moses went and told the people all the LORD's words and laws, they responded with one voice, 'Everything the LORD has said we will do'" (Exod 24:3).

That summons from Mount Sinai is repeated by Moses in Deuteronomy 26:16–19:

> The LORD your God commands you this day to follow these decrees and laws; carefully observe them with all your heart and with all your soul. You have declared this day that the LORD is your God and that you will walk in obedience to him, that you will keep his decrees, commands and laws—that you will listen to him. And the LORD has declared this day that you are his people, his treasured possession as he promised, and that you are to keep all his commands. He has declared that he will set you in praise, fame and honor high above all the nations he has made and that you will be a people holy to the LORD your God, as he promised.

Exodus, Sinai, Jordan, Land—and at each major juncture in Israel's history the people of God are summoned to hear God's will and to commit themselves all over again—as if for the first time—to the Torah. Joshua 1–5

---

1. KNT: "nice and wide" and "plenty of room."
2. KNT: "tight squeeze."

tells that Story again, and this one ends with a Passover celebration at Gilgal, the place where the reproach of disobedience was removed. This ongoing pattern of summons to obedience, including Joshua's farewell (23:1–24:28), finds yet more echoes in Ezra's return from the Babylonian exile. The temple is rebuilt, another Passover is celebrated, and Ezra summons Israel to renewed commitment to obey the Torah (Ezra 1–6, 7:1–10; Neh 8:1–10:39). Over and over the pattern is God's act of redemption, the covenant is renewed, and the people are called to obey the will of God.

So when Jesus climbs the mount of this Sermon, assumes the posture of a teacher and lawgiver, issues forth his kingdom demands in ways that develop what Moses has taught, and then summons his followers to kingdom obedience at the end, only to descend the mount, we are obligated to see him taking the posture of the Final Prophet, the Messiah. The Sermon is that serious: this is the Messiah's revelation of God's will. The major difference, of course, is that Jesus connects his teachings to the inauguration of the kingdom. He swallows up each demand in the Sermon in this final section and says to his disciples, "Do this."

EXPLAIN the Story

First, Jesus gives a comprehensive summons in imagery: paths and gates (7:13–14). This is followed, second, by a warning about those who claim their gifts but fail in deeds (7:15–23). Third, Jesus concludes with a two-way warning in a parable (7:24–27). Our first passage (7:13–14) has a simple summons to enter through the narrow gate (7:13a) followed by the two options to Jesus' teaching (7:13b–14).[3]

The Summons (7:13a)

It is not uncommon for Jesus to summon people to "enter" the kingdom of God. Note Mark 9:47; 10:15; 14:25 as well as Matthew 5:19; 7:21; 8:11; 18:3. The most significant text of all these, and others could be listed, is Matthew 7:21: "Not everyone who says to me, 'Lord, Lord,' will enter the kingdom of heaven, but only the one who does the will of my Father who is in heaven." Within the scope of the concluding summons to the Sermon, "enter" (the Greek word is *eiserchomai*) is used for both "life" and "kingdom." The gravity of the summons is palpable: Jesus calls his followers to *enter* into the life of the kingdom in the here and now.

---

3. The gate precedes the path in these sayings; it is not entirely clear whether we are to think of that concretely—first a gate and then the path—or to see gate and path as more or less synonymous.

Everything hinges on the "gate," the entrance to cities and temples. What does this mean? Some restrict "gate" to the ethical vision or commands of Jesus from 5:1 to 7:12,[4] while others see Jesus himself along with his commands.[5] Jesus is the gate in John 10:9, and he is calling people to follow *him*; his demands are entailed in relationship with Jesus. The Messianic Ethic creates the Ethic from Above.

There is one reason the gate is "narrow": it is demanding discipleship.[6] It is demanding because it contrasts with the wide gate that leads to a broad road in 7:13b and compares favorably with the "small" gate[7] that leads to a narrow road in 7:14. The gate is narrow because it requires a person to turn from sin to follow Jesus, to do the will of God *as taught by Jesus*. It is narrow because it is the surpassing righteousness of 5:17–48, the deeper righteousness of 6:1–18, the single-minded righteousness of 6:19–34, and the wise way of life as seen in 7:1–11. In essence, the narrow gate is to follow Jesus by learning to live by the Jesus Creed and the Golden Rule (7:12). And the gate is narrow because of persecutions (5:11–12; 8:18–22; 10:17–25, 34–39; 24:9, 21, 29).[8] Is it possible to walk the narrow road?

> As long as I recognize this road as the one I am commanded to walk, and try to walk it in fear of myself, it is truly impossible. But if I see Jesus Christ walking ahead of me, step by step, if I look only at him and follow him, step by step, then I will be protected on this path.[9]

The Two Options: Destruction or Life (7:13b – 14)

These two options have been the source of considerable anxiety, some of it spiritually good and some of it unfortunately tragic. Jesus joins the two-paths of Deuteronomy 28 (blessings, curses) and a host of similar two-paths teaching in the ancient world. Perhaps the opening to the *Didache* puts it best:

> There are two ways, one of life and one of death, and there is a great difference between these two ways. Now this is the way of life: first, "you shall love God, who made you;" second, "your neighbor as yourself;" and "whatever you do not wish to happen to you, do not do to another" (*Did.* 1:1–2).

---

4. Luz, *Matthew 1–7*, 372; Turner, *Matthew*, 215.

5. Allison, *Sermon on the Mount*, 164; Guelich, *Sermon on the Mount*, 389–90.

6. Some debate if the gate is at the entrance to the path or at the end of the path; word order favors the former. See Quarles, *Sermon on the Mount*, 311–15.

7. I don't understand why the NIV has "narrow" in 7:13a and "small" in 7:14 for the same Greek term (*stenē*). Both should be "narrow," as in the KNT.

8. The Greek word behind the NIV's "narrow" is *tethlimmenē*, a perfect passive participle of the word group *thlibō, thlipsis*, often translated as "persecution." For the best discussion, Davies and Allison, *Matthew*, 1:700.

9. Bonhoeffer, *Discipleship*, 176.

This two-paths approach to ethics is a rhetorical way of simplifying in order to cast before a listener the gravity of the moral life. It is heard as an Ethic from Above. This sort of rhetoric forces everything into two options: wide versus small, broad versus narrow, destruction versus life, and many versus few. Everything is chosen for rhetorical severity in order to create moral gravity. The choice matters because it determines who enters the kingdom.

Is Jesus hereby being a radical exclusivist, or one who thinks few will enter the kingdom while the vast majority of humans (most of whom on the world's stage have not heard of Jesus) will be sent to hell? Or is this exaggerated rhetoric that ought to lead one to self-inspection instead of into theological speculation on the numbers of the saved? It is true that Jesus can use similar terms from different angles. Thus, 22:14 confirms our text with its "many are invited [called], but few are chosen." But Jesus can also say "many" from the east and the west will come into the kingdom (8:11), and Jesus' death liberates "many" (not few) from captivity (20:18). Yes, Jesus is exaggerating for rhetorical impact. But, yes, this raises the theological debate about who will be saved and on what grounds.[10] There is a threshold for Jesus, and his moral severity arises because he connects entrance into the kingdom with response to him (21:28 – 32; 22:1 – 14; 25:31 – 46).

What clinches this discussion for me is the Lukan parallel (Luke 13:23 – 24), which deserves to be quoted because it connects these words to final salvation: "Someone asked him, 'Lord, are only a few people going to be saved?'"

Jesus' response is notable: "Make every effort to enter through the narrow door, because many, I tell you, will try to enter and will not be able to."

There may be questions unanswered by Jesus, but it seems at least clear to this author that Jesus' lines about many and few are directly related to those who will be saved, that is, those who will enter the kingdom of God. It hangs on whether Jesus is one's Lord.

LIVE the Story

Followers of Jesus cannot be afraid to set the vision of Jesus, in which Jesus is King and humans are summoned to become citizens of his kingdom, in the context of a final judgment, nor can they be afraid of the simple framing of life into two options: following Jesus or not. As R. T. France says it so well, "This is not a matter of more or less successful attempts to follow the lifestyle

---

10. J. Hick et al., *Four Views on Salvation in a Pluralistic World* (Counterpoints; Grand Rapids: Zondervan, 1996).

of the kingdom heaven, but of being either in or out, saved or lost."[11] The Sermon is not theory: the Sermon itself gospels the gospel. The Sermon casts forth the image of Jesus and of his vision for how kingdom people are to live, and then Jesus looks his listeners in the eyes and summons them to choose to follow him. Sorting all folks into two seems brutal in our world, but we cannot soften the rigor of Jesus' words, nor can we fail to connect this summons to grace. Again, this is an Ethic from Above with incomparable gravity.

Final Accountability

You can't wander far into the Bible without recognizing that God holds people accountable and, as the Bible develops its Story, that accountability becomes a combination of this life and the age to come. Every day we all stand before God. Jesus stands upright in the middle of that orientation and says, "Follow me!"

The options are life and destruction. This is not the place to debate the nature of hell but instead to observe that our one life now determines whether our end will be *life*—and here we are to see the new heavens and the new earth, often depicted as an endless banquet of joy, peace, justice, and love— or *destruction*—and here one would think of eternal separation from God, whether one thinks of this in terms of conscious pain or even of a destruction that comes to an end. Some consider annihilationism to be too soft while annihilationists see it as a more just form of eternal consequences. Either view is, in my view, justifiable and consistent with Jesus.

But what we do not see in Jesus is an opportunity after death or the eventual salvation of all people. To be sure, whether one is an exclusivist, an inclusivist, or an accessibilist matters little in this instance; what matters is that Jesus calls us to account for ourselves before God. What we do now will determine what happens then. We need first to get ourselves postured so we hear this final accountability message of Jesus. Another way of saying this is to wonder aloud if our discussions about hell, how long it lasts, who goes there, and whether hell will be emptied might be distractions from the fundamental belief undergirding such discussions: Is one with Jesus or not? That's the question this text poses to its hearers.

Rigor

The intent of Jesus in these words is the rhetoric of clarity. He wants his listeners to see that life matters, that their moral life matters both now and for the age to come, and he wants them to decide to follow him. Yes, the two-ways sayings here are part of a rhetoric, but this rhetoric is used because for Jesus there is a rigor required to enter the kingdom of God. To enter the kingdom

---

11. France, *Matthew*, 287.

we must enter through the one and only gate. If the common view that Jesus is the gate is correct, we are called to focus on Jesus—we are to respond to Jesus and to summon others to respond to Jesus.

Because 7:13-14 is connected thematically in the summons to 7:15-27, we need to let "gate" get as expansive as Jesus makes it: the gate is Jesus, who calls us to "do" (we will see the emphasis on this term in the next two units) the will of God as he teaches it. So the gate is not just a mild association with Jesus or some kind of general affiliation, but a radical commitment to Jesus as the one who is King and Lord who shapes all of life for us. To enter the narrow gate is to enter into a relationship with the Jesus *who really is the King and Lord who saves and rules, and the relationship to Jesus entails following him.*[12]

A Song for Nagasaki

There are many stories of Christians who have surrendered their lives for Jesus because of his call and because they know that they will answer someday to God. The story of World War II is often told from the angle of the Americans and British and the winners. The story of Pearl Harbor emerges far more often through the story of the winners. But there are Christian stories from Japan, and I can think of none more eloquent and moving than the story of Takashi Nagai.[13]

Dr. Nagai was a convert from Buddhism to the Catholic Christian faith; he married a woman who had been praying for his conversion for years. When the American Chuck Sweeney chose not to drop the bomb on Kokura because of cloudy weather, he headed south and dropped it on Nagasaki. Dr. Nagai was at his radiology laboratory; his wife, Midori, was at home and was instantly burned beyond recognition and sent into the presence of God; his two children, with their grandmother, had been taken to the hills for protection, and they survived.

But Dr. Nagai's story is the focus here. It is a story of a man who knew what it meant to live a single-minded, devoted-to-the-Lord life in which his job was transformed into a gift to God and to the church community around the Urakami Cathedral. Here are some of his words about how he treated patients who suffered from the nuclear fallout and from death, while he himself was withering away due to radiation poisoning:

> Those words in the Sermon on the Mount "blessed are those who weep" should be taken literally by doctors. A real doctor suffers with each patient. If the patient is frightened of dying, so is the doctor.... Each patient becomes your brother, your sister, your mother, for whom you

---

12. McKnight, *One.Life*, 109-19, 183-92.
13. See P. Glynn, *A Song for Nagasaki: The Story of Takashi Nagai, Scientist, Convert, and Survivor of the Atomic Bomb* (San Francisco: Ignatius, 1988). I refer to and quote from pp. 148, 233-34, 238.

drop everything else.... I've come to understand that medicine is a vocation, a personal call from God—which means that examining a patient, taking an x-ray or giving an injection is part of the kingdom of God. When I realized that, I found myself praying for each patient I treated.

At the risk of his own health and before medical science comprehended the danger of radiation, Dr. Nagai knew that his patients were more important than his own life. Thus, he entered into a life of service, compassion, and suffering. Dr. Nagai's life was shaped by loving the neighbor whom God set before him. He said, "Our lives are of great worth if we accept with good grace the situation Providence places us in and go on loving lovingly."

Dr. Nagai learned in the months before the A-bomb altered the course of human history that his body was suffering from radiation-induced leukemia. That evening when he returned home filled with a heavy heart and knowing he had but three years to live, he told Midori of his condition. His biographer fills in the details of what happened:

> Then, quietly rising from the table, she lit the candles on their family altar. She knelt there in the austere *seiza* fashion, her head bowed before the crucifix her family had guarded through 250 years of persecution. He followed her and knelt likewise behind her, now noticing that her shoulders were shaking. She remained there in prayer until the emotional turbulence had subsided.

Then Midori said to Dr. Nagai:

> We said before we married ... that if our lives are spent for the glory of God, then life and death are beautiful. You have given everything you had for work that was very, very important. It was for his glory.

Nagai's response? "He was fighting to hold back tears, not for himself, but tears of gratitude. He sensed he was in the presence of holiness."

This is a beautiful story of Dr. and Midori Nagai's surrendering of themselves to God in the face of Jesus Christ, and the Lord's sacrificial call on their lives was embraced in the shadow of the cross of Jesus Christ. Dr. Nagai lived only a few more years, but his story is the story of a man whose entire life was a Christian song for Nagasaki.

Grace

The genius of the Protestant Reformation was its focus on the necessity of grace, or better yet, the pervasiveness of grace in the Christian life. Jesus doesn't here say anything like what many theologians would have preferred him to say; that is, he doesn't say, "Enter the narrow gate by recognizing that you are hopeless and helpless and in need of grace." Instead, he flat-out summons people to enter the gate. Yet the best understanding of the gate is that it is Jesus, and that leads us to this important conclusion: *union with Jesus Christ is the origin and source of all spiritual blessings and all discipleship.*

Jesus isn't here calling someone merely to a better moral life. Rather, his own presence looms in the entire Sermon as the one through whom God speaks, through whom God redeems, and through whom God reigns. So the "enter" demand is a summons to Jesus first and foremost. In other words, discipleship begins at the personal level of a relationship to Jesus as the King and Lord who saves and rules. Connection to Jesus unleashes the grace of God's bounty. Midori and Dr. Nagai entered into that very grace at the deepest level when they endured joyously their own sufferings in the light of the cross of Jesus' grace.

CHAPTER 22

Matthew 7:15–23

 LISTEN to the Story

15"Watch out for false prophets. They come to you in sheep's clothing, but inwardly they are ferocious wolves. 16By their fruit you will recognize them. Do people pick grapes from thornbushes, or figs from thistles? 17Likewise, every good tree bears good fruit, but a bad tree bears bad fruit. 18A good tree cannot bear bad fruit, and a bad tree cannot bear good fruit. 19Every tree that does not bear good fruit is cut down and thrown into the fire. 20Thus, by their fruit you will recognize them.

21"Not everyone who says to me, 'Lord, Lord,'1 will enter the kingdom of heaven, but only the one who does the will of my Father who is in heaven. 22Many will say to me on that day, 'Lord, Lord, did we not prophesy in your name and in your name drive out demons and in your name perform many miracles?' 23Then I will tell them plainly, 'I never knew you. Away from me, you evildoers!'"

Listening to the text in the Story: Deuteronomy 28; Psalm 1; Pick your prophet; Matthew 16:27; 25:31–46; 1 Corinthians 3:10–16; 2 Corinthians 5:6–10; Revelation 20–22.

Some of us don't want to preach this text because we don't like it; some of us don't want to preach this text because it aggravates every fiber in our theology; and some of us don't want to preach this text because it may drive some financially supporting or opinion-shaping people away. You can avoid these texts if you wish, but anyone who has spent much time with judgment texts in the Bible knows that the Bible *teaches that our final destiny is determined by works.* We may be saved by faith, but we are judged by works. Every judgment scene in the Bible is a judgment by works. I urge you to read the sampling of texts in the "Listening to the text in the Story" above.

Far too many think because they have "prayed to receive Christ," they are safe and secure. I don't want to dispute the all-sufficiency of Christ or the

---

1. KNT: "Master, Master."

importance of faith and God's grace, but far too many today are trusting in a onetime decision but show no marks of discipleship. Yes, some emphasize works so much one has to think they are saved by what they do. We are saved by Christ, but Christ saves us into discipleship. *Sometimes we need to sound like salvation is by faith so much that works are out of the picture, and other times we need to sound like works are so much in focus that we may sound like faith isn't the point ... and if we follow these biblical themes we will find the proper biblical balance.*

The rhetoric of Jesus here emphasizes works; I will do the same. His rhetoric is designed to put the fear of God in us about our moral condition; I will attempt to do the same. Jesus reveals here an Ethic from Below that expects behaviors shaped by an Ethic from Beyond. Some want to take the steam from his words with an Ethic from Below. What complicates this text is that Jesus focuses on deceivers and the deceived. Deceit finds its way into every religion, including Christianity. In fact, deceit was at work from the very beginning. Two sorts of deceit are found in our verses: some leaders deceive the people of God (7:15-20), while some deceive themselves (7:21-23). Jesus aims his words at the deceitful and deceived. They need to hear these words; because we don't know if we are in their camp, we need to hear these words.

EXPLAIN the Story

It is not entirely clear to me that 7:15-23 follows sharply from 7:13-14. Perhaps the broad-path folks of 7:13-14 are followers of the false prophets, or perhaps the false prophets prevent some from the narrow gate. What is clear is this: the Sermon reveals God's will as taught by Jesus; its invitation in 7:13-27 summons people to follow him.

There are two parts to this section:[2] the deceiver (7:15-20) and the deceived (7:21-23). The deceiver unit aims at the "false prophets" by warning them in 7:15a, by describing them (7:15b), and then by offering a method of detection (7:16a) that is explained in two illustrative analogies (7:16b-19) and summarized into a crisp statement (7:20). The deceived unit begins with a warning about the deceived—that is, about who will and who will not enter the kingdom (7:21); this warning is then restated with a concrete hypothetical illustration of how the deceived may make their claims (7:22), which is followed by Jesus' own final evaluation (7:23).

---

2. Pressing hard a unified connection of 7:15-20 and 7:21-23 needs to be tempered by the observation that Luke has these two sections in different places in his gospel (cf. 6:43-45, 46, and 13:26-27). This may well explain why Matthew 7:15a has "false prophets" while 7:21-23 includes exorcists and miracle workers with the false prophets. In other words, Matthew may have brought together two originally distinct sections.

The Deceiver (7:15 – 20)

In this text Jesus warns his followers about the false prophet: "Watch out for false prophets" (7:15a).[3] The verb translated "watch out" (*prosechō*) is also aimed at the hypocrites (6:1), the opponents of Jesus (10:17), the leaven of the scribes and Pharisees (16:6, 11, 12) — and we need to keep in mind as well 24:11, 24. There are four major leaders in Israel: the king who represents God over the people, the prophet through whom God speaks to his people, the priest through whom the people speak to God, and the sage, who observes realities of life for the people. The following graph illustrates the location of each between God and God's people.

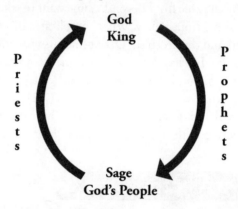

The implication of this chart for understanding is that a false prophet is one who stands between God and God's people falsely and deceitfully. We should restrict this warning to those who (1) make a claim to be speaking for God, but who (2) are not truly appointed by God and (3) fail to follow Jesus. While heresy[4] may be involved, the fundamental orientation in this text is that *they live disobediently.* Jesus' description of the false prophet could be the costume of a theater: outwardly they look like God's people (Matt 10:16; John 10:1 – 30), but their designs are ravenous (see Ezek 22:27 – 28; Acts 20:29; *Did.* 16.3).

Much scholarly effort has been spent in seeking to identify "false proph-

---

3. See 24:23 – 25; 1 John 4:1 – 3. For a technical study, G. N. Stanton, "Jesus of Nazareth: A Magician and a False Prophet Who Deceived God's People?" in *Jesus of Nazareth: Lord and Christ: Essays on the Historical Jesus and New Testament Christology* (eds. J. B. Green and M. Turner; Grand Rapids: Eerdmans, 1994), 164 – 80.

4. A person can be called a heretic only if that teacher of doctrine has been brought before a council, explained his or her errors, comprehended the errors, and refuses to change. There are a number of good studies, including H. O. J. Brown, *Heresies: The Image of Christ in the Mirror of Heresy and Orthodoxy from the Apostles to the Present* (Grand Rapids: Baker, 1988); G. R. Evans, *A Brief History of Heresy* (Blackwell Brief Histories of Religion; Malden, MA: Blackwell, 2003); B. Quash and M. Ward, *Heresies and How to Avoid Them: Why It Matters What Christians Believe* (London: SPCK/Peabody, MA: Hendrickson, 2007).

ets." Here are the options: Pharisees, Essenes, anti-Roman Zealots, Judean sign prophets from the 60s, Simon Magus, the Jewish Messiah Bar Kokhba, Gnostics, Paul and his circle of churches, Hellenistic antinomians, Christian enthusiasts, and law-observant Christians.[5] If we could know the specific audience Jesus had in mind with confidence, this list would not exist; since we can't, it is wiser to speak in general terms rather than in specific terms. Whoever they are, they claim to be followers of Jesus—calling him "Lord, Lord" in 7:21 and doing great deeds in his name (7:22). They are, then, *"Christian" false prophets*, who are to be contrasted with Christian true prophets (5:11–12; 10:41; 23:34).

Jesus offers a *method of detection*: fruit inspection reveals the true character (7:16a, 20). Fruit inspection, which is taught in other terms by Jeremiah (Jer 23:9–15), no doubt supplements prediction fulfillment (Deut 18:21–22) and orthodoxy (13:1–6). "Fruit" is explained in two illustrative analogies: first, grapes don't grow on thornbushes, and figs don't emerge from thistles. Second, good trees produce good fruit; bad trees produce bad fruit; good trees don't produce bad fruit; bad trees don't produce good fruit. The character of fruit reveals the character of the tree. Good trees are tended for their fruit; bad trees are cut down and burned (surely a metaphor for final judgment; cf. Matt 3:10; 5:22; 13:42; 25:41). There is no infallible method to detect deceitful leaders, and that is why we have further tests: 1 Corinthians 12:1–3; 1 John 4:2; *Didache* 11.5, 10.

So what does "fruit" mean? It is not hard for a Christian theologian to wonder if Jesus is teaching the priority of regeneration. Does he mean that good fruit comes from a grace-created regenerate tree, or is his focus more on fruit inspection that leads to judgment of character? I'm inclined to think he means the second option: there is less ground here to find grace, though it might be present, than to see in this analogy a warning that bad fruit means the person is bad (i.e., a false prophet).

So, again, what is the fruit? In context, there is only one conclusion: it refers to *doing God's will*[6] (cf. 7:17–20, which translates the Greek word for "doing," *poieō*, with the word "bears" five times; 7:21 uses "does" while 7:23 uses "evil*doers*," and then 7:24–27 is about putting into practice, and this language again translates the Greek word *poieō*). The implication is clear too: if the disciples hear someone making a claim to speak for God, they are to observe that person's life to see if that person *is doing God's will*. If so, they may be speaking for God; if not, they are false prophets.

What should the follower of Jesus do about the false teachers? Jesus is silent, and it makes us think of the parable of the weeds and wheat (13:36–43). We

---

5. Allison, *Sermon on the Mount*, 165–66; Luz, *Matthew 1–7*, 376–77.
6. Luz, *Matthew 1–7*, 378; France, *Matthew*, 291.

might have expected Jesus to say they should be removed from leadership or to urge his followers to run from them, but his focus is elsewhere. Jesus teaches his followers to observe their fruits so they can discern true from false. In our next passage Jesus says they will be finally judged. By implication the followers are to heed their own fruit observations and turn from the false prophets.

The Deceived (7:21–23)

Jesus is shadowboxing with enemies of the gospel in a hypothetical end-time judgment scene. The false prophets either petition Jesus or confess him as "Lord, Lord."[7] They support themselves by appealing to their prophecies, exorcisms, and miracle working. But Jesus counters that they don't do God's will and are evildoers. These people, in other words, deceive themselves into thinking they are kingdom people because of the gifts they have performed.

It is not uncommon for someone other than God's people to do mighty works (see Exod 7–8; Matt 24:23–28; 2 Thess 2:9–10; Rev 13:13–15). What is required to enter the kingdom is doing God's will (7:21). Followers of Jesus follow Jesus and his teachings; those who don't follow Jesus are not followers. The will of God is far more often works of compassion, as in Matthew 25:31–46 or James 1:25–27, than charismatic displays of might.

The deceived place before Jesus on the judgment day[8] what they have done—notice the triple emphasis: they have prophesied "in your name," and exorcised "in your name," and done miracles "in your name." These folks are affiliated with Jesus and claim to have done special acts through the power of Jesus, but they are denounced for two major missing elements. First, Jesus doesn't know them (25:12) and never has, which theologically indicates the absence of covenanted intimacy (Gen 18:19; Amos 3:2). Second, they are "evildoers" instead of doers of the Father's will. That Matthew 24:12 connects lawlessness (same term as here) with love growing cold suggests that these false prophets have no mercy or care for those in need. Because Jesus reduces God's will to loving God and loving others, it is not a stretch to see in the deceived in our text a colossal failure at the basics: the Jesus Creed or the Golden Rule.

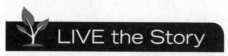

LIVE the Story

To whom does this text speak? Mark Allan Powell, as I have already mentioned, observed after years of teaching and preaching that pastors identify with char-

---

7. Cf. Matt 25:11; Luke 8:24; 10:41; Acts 9:4, where the double use of a vocative occurs.
8. This is the meaning of "on that day"; cf. Matt 24:19, 22, 29, 36; 26:29. For the rabbis, this term often referred to "the age to come." For references, see Davies and Allison, *Matthew*, 1:714.

acters in the text that ordinary laypersons don't.[9] Pastors reading the gospel texts about Jesus identify with Jesus and see themselves as Jesus to their congregations. The layperson identifies with the other characters of the text and begin to wonder if they are in or out. Put together for 7:15–23, this means the pastor will tend to see herself or himself as Jesus pointing out the hypocrisies of others while the layperson will wonder if he or she is doing God's will. While there are good reasons for the pastor to fashion himself or herself as an undershepherd for Jesus, there are better reasons for the pastor first to sit under the word of Jesus and to ask if she or he might be the false prophet.

The Preacher, the Pastor, the Priest, the Teacher

Mark Powell's theory will nearly always find a breakthrough. Why? There's probably not a pastor or a priest or a preacher preparing this text for a sermon who doesn't sense the eyes of this text staring at him or her. If we read 7:15–20 in light of 7:21–23, or the other way around, we see the connection: the false prophet is nearly synonymous with the prophet who prophesies in the name of Jesus, the exorcist who drives out demons in the name of Jesus, and the miracle worker who does mighty things in the name of Jesus. In other words, *the false prophet is the gifted leader who does not do the will of God in the ordinary elements of life.* The false prophet is the preacher, the teacher, the pastor, or the priest who has converted the splendor of a gospel calling into a job done well but whose moral life is indistinguishable from the common person of this world. The false prophet here is the leader who exercises the gifts of the Spirit with a flourish but who flounders at the personal level of following Jesus.

So before you climb into the pulpit this week, where your spiritual-gift persona is on full display, or if you are reading this text as a teacher or simply for study, I would urge you to turn the text into a mirror to let it ask you a simple question: Am I the false prophet of this text? Am I the person who exercises gifts well, who does things as a leader that many admire, but who is also the person who in my private life, in my home, in the quiet hours of the day, is not following what Jesus has taught in this Sermon? If that is the case, then I would urge you to fall to your knees, confess your sins, wait on the Spirit of God to cleanse your heart, and ask God to quicken in you the way of Jesus—the way of doing what he calls us to do.

Works Tell the Truth

Sensitive theologians are sometimes nervous about the way Jesus talks, and sometimes we need to exercise a special caution, but we need to trust that Jesus said what he wanted. No one is saved *by* works, of course; but everyone

---

9. See comment in the discussion of 7:1–5.

is *judged* by works because works are the inevitable life of the one who surrenders to, trusts in, and follows Jesus. Thus, you can tell the true charismatically gifted leader from the false *by their fruit* (obedience to Jesus).

This leads to a fundamental question: What kind of good works? And then to a deeper question under that one: How many do we have to do? When we turn Jesus' observations about fruit-as-works into quantitative counting, we are missing the point. Jesus' Ethic from Above and Beyond points to a problem: disobedient charismatic leaders — that is, those who are not loving of others, who do not show mercy to those in need, who are not meek and kind, and who are abusive at home. In theological categories, this text is not about soteriology but about moral integrity and a method of detecting where we stand when it comes to genuine discipleship.

So let's think of the sorts of fruit that Jesus would have had in mind and ask ourselves if they are visible in us. Do we show mercy to those who are in need? Do we care for the marginalized, unlike the rich man who did not concern himself with the poor man at his gate (Luke 16:19–31)? Do our neighbors think we are gracious and loving or obstinate and judgmental? Do we nurture love and patience in our own children? Do we serve our spouse as Christ serves the church? Is our charismatic gift so important that menial tasks have to be done by others? Or, put differently, do we expect our spouse to do all the dirty work around the home so we can carry on our holy business? Do we know the names of our congregants or are they "BIPs" (butts-in-pews)? Do those "under" us delight in working with us, or do they fear us?

No one is perfect, of course. But the charismatically gifted person is to be known for his or her fruit. And the fundamental fruit of the New Testament, especially for Jesus, is the Jesus Creed or the Golden Rule — and that is loving others and doing for others what we would want done for us. So, we ask, what have you done for others today? (Other than exercise your gift.)

But Works Are Not Infallible

Jesus' method of inspection is not the only one. There are other tests for the false prophet, but this text is not primarily about how to detect a false prophet. Instead, it is designed to probe into the life of the charismatically gifted leader in order to get him or her to realize that gifts are not enough, that the fruit of love in life is what matters most. If we take this as its rhetorical intent, we need also to recognize that wide-ranging conclusions drawn from this fruit inspection may miss the mark.

Reduced now: works will tell us if the charismatic leader is living right. But works can be faked too, so that works *alone* are not entirely adequate. Luther opined in his discussions of this text about how the Catholic leaders could be seen as folks who did good things, but time would eventually manifest their character; Calvin did the same.[10] Many have followed their lead to observe that while this test is more than adequate in making us examine ourselves and pointing out how some charismatic leaders don't have the life to back up their claims, sometimes works are inadequate as a test. Turned inside out then: works sometimes indicate a distorted theology, sometimes the attempt to earn favor with God, sometimes a personality disorder, sometimes little more than the habits of a former commitment, and sometimes a burst of enthusiasm.

Thus, let us not overdo works to the point that all that really matters is works. That's misusing what Jesus is saying here. One more time: the charismatic leader needs to ask if she or her exhibits behaviors expected for Jesus' followers.

Simple Acts, Extraordinary Powers

Simple acts are more valuable than extraordinary powers or spiritual gifts. For Jesus there is a categorical difference between charismatic giftedness and the ordinary fruit of love, compassion, and mercy. Perhaps we need to learn to ask ourselves, particularly if we are gifted leaders, if we value our gifts more than love, if we value the performance of a gift for the good of others or the gift of love for the good of others. When Jesus used "fruit" over against mighty charismatic gifts, he was getting at what mattered most. Do you show love to your neighbors, to your enemies, and to all those who happen to be on your path? Jesus is saying here that if you don't do the latter, he doesn't particularly care about your charismatic giftedness.

What Jesus is getting at is this: leaders are first of all followers of Jesus before they are leaders. If they forget that, they will hear these words of Jesus as a searching judgment.

One of my favorite South Africans is pastor Trevor Hudson, who serves a church in Benoni near Johannesburg. Trevor is in some ways South Africa's Dallas Willard or Richard Foster, focusing as he does on the inner work of the Spirit in spiritual formation. Trevor's ministry to the homeless and suffering in South Africa is well-known, but he tells the story of someone who makes what Jesus wants from us—ordinary acts of love and not just glorious giftedness—come to life.[11] It is the story of a West Indian woman in London who had just been told her husband had been tragically killed in a street accident; the woman suffered for days.

She sank into the corner of the sofa and sat there rigid and unhearing. For

---

10. Luther, *Exposition of the Lord's Prayer*, 268–80; Calvin, *Harmony of the Gospels*, 1:239–41.
11. Trevor Hudson, *Holy Spirit Here and Now* (Cape Town: Struik Christian Books, 2012), 171–72.

a long time her terrible trancelike look embarrassed her family, friends, and officials who came and went. Then the schoolteacher of one of her children, an Englishwoman, called and, seeing how things were, went and sat down beside her.

The teacher put an arm around the tight shoulders of the grieving wife. A white cheek touched the brown. Then as the unrelenting pain seeped through to her, the newcomer's tears began to flow quietly, falling on their two hands linked in the woman's lap. For a long time that was all that was happening. Then at last the West Indian woman began to sob. Still not a word was spoken. After a while the visitor got up and left, leaving her monetary contribution to help the family meet its immediate practical needs.

Trevor heard this story from John Taylor, who then with insight observes how such an experience needs to be interpreted. "This is the embrace of God, his kiss of life. That is the embrace of his mission, and of our intercession." This is what Jesus wants from us: not our gifts but our life, not what brings us honor but what serves the neighbor.

At the judgment Jesus will not ask us about our gifts. He will ask if our cheeks have touched the cheeks of those who suffer, if our hands have held the hands of those who endure pain, and if our gifts are directed at those who most need them.

CHAPTER 23

Matthew 7:24–27

 LISTEN to the Story

24"Therefore everyone who hears these words of mine and puts them into practice is like a wise man who built his house on the rock. 25The rain came down, the streams rose, and the winds blew and beat against that house; yet it did not fall, because it had its foundation on the rock. 26But everyone who hears these words of mine and does not put them into practice is like a foolish man who built his house on sand. 27The rain came down, the streams rose, and the winds blew and beat against that house, and it fell with a great crash."

Listening to the text in the story: Genesis 6–7; Deuteronomy 28; 30:15–20; Psalm 1; Proverbs 10:25; Ezekiel 13:10–16; 33:30–32; Matthew 21:28–32; 25:1–13.

This is the third element of the invitation at the end of the Sermon (7:13–14, 7:15–23, 7:24–27). This part of Jesus' invitation is a parable, a story that summons us to imagine a different world and, as a result of that imagining, to become different people called to work for a kingdom world now.[1] Jesus wants us to imagine two kinds of builders as two sorts of responses to the Sermon. Contrasts are a favorite way to gain an audience's attention in order to press the moral imperative, and this is even more the case when, with Israelites, one is delivering a word from God. That is, we have here again an Ethic from Above.

So we go back to Deuteronomy 28; 30:15–20 and to Psalm 1 for classic depictions, but the Sermon itself is filled with two-option thinking: Pharisees versus followers of Jesus (5:17–20), hypocrites versus followers of Jesus (6:1–18), good treasure versus bad treasure (6:19–21), good eyes versus bad eyes (6:22–23), God versus mammon (6:24), anxiety versus seeking the kingdom (6:33) — and this all swirls into a vortex of warnings in 7:13–27: broad way versus narrow way, good tree versus bad tree, doing versus not doing.

---

1. On parables, I cannot recommend highly enough the book by K. Snodgrass, *Stories with Intent: A Comprehensive Guide to the Parables of Jesus* (Grand Rapids: Eerdmans, 2008).

There is no mystery in understanding this parable. First, we get a parable about the person who both hears and practices (does) what Jesus has said in the Sermon (7:24–25). Second, we get a parable about the person who hears but does not practice the Sermon's teachings (7:26–27). The two parts are symmetrical:

> Hearing and doing versus hearing and not doing
> Wise versus foolish
> House not collapsing versus house collapsing

The parable rhetorically warns listeners what will happen to them in the final judgment. This issue of hearing and not doing is embedded in Israel's Story (cf. Ezek 33:30–32). There is nothing new here.

The Wise: Hearing and Doing

Instead of offering just a parable, Jesus begins each parabolic unit by telling his listeners exactly what sort of person he has in mind. The first person is described as one hearing and doing.[2] That is, they are sitting around Jesus as he gives this teaching, and they are the ones who hear and do what he says. One thinks here of the parable of the two sons (21:28–32) and the wise and foolish virgins (25:1–13). As there, so here: one is approved and one is not approved.

The approved one is "wise" (7:24), a term used in other places for those who are finally approved by God (24:45). Wise men, when building homes, find a rock-solid foundation on which to build.[3] I'm thinking of Nazareth, which is up in the hills but full of rock-solid material on which to build; of Sepphoris, where Jesus may have worked as a carpenter; and of Capernaum, where Jesus established his ministry and where the closer one got to the shores of the Sea of Galilee, the more likely it was that one would find a sandier consistency.

At work in this image of Jesus is perhaps a village along a wadi that in a sudden rainstorm can flood the homes along its path. Or does Jesus have in mind the temple?[4] It is difficult to know if Jesus has one specific place in mind, so we should perhaps focus on the general wisdom one gains from years

---

2. The emphasis of the present tenses in 7:24a (hearing, doing) is not so much to describe an ongoing hearing and doing, or a constant hearing and doing, but instead the present tenses sketch the acts in front of us as if they are happening before our very eyes. Sketched in C. R. Campbell, *Basics of Verbal Aspect in Biblical Greek* (Grand Rapids: Zondervan, 2008), 40–43.

3. It is fanciful to allegorize "rock" here into a reference to Peter (cf. 16:13–19); rather, "rock" refers to "hearing and doing."

4. Wright, *Matthew for Everyone*, 1:81. See also Wright, *Jesus and the Victory of God*, 292, 334.

of building: build on rock and the building will last; build on the sandier soil along the wadi and you will find your home in a heap. Storms are sometimes used as imagery for the trials of life (Ps 69:2), but here the storm is imagery for a person's entire life in the presence of God's final judgment (cf. Gen 6 – 7; Prov 10:25; Ezek 13:10 – 16; Nah 1:7 – 8).[5]

The Foolish: Hearing and Not Doing

The second person is the one, and again the language invites us to imagine this happening before our eyes, who hears the Sermon's teachings and does not do them. Instead of being wise, this person is "foolish," a term deep in Israel's Wisdom tradition (like Proverbs) and at times found on the lips of Jesus (see Matt 5:22; 23:17; 25:2, 3, 8). Jesus compares such a person to one who builds a house on top of sand, and when storms come, again with their rains and rising streams and winds, it collapses into destruction.

There is little dispute what these two consequences are: the first one enters the kingdom of God (cf. 7:13 – 14, 21) while the second one is destroyed (7:13, 27), is cast into the fire (7:19), and is separated from Jesus (7:23). The word in 7:27 is *ptōsis* (where it is a "great crash") while the word in 7:13 is *apōleia*, the more common word for "destruction." These are words of final disapproval from God in the great judgment, and one would be wise to avoid thinking these terms define the nature of the final condition (annihilationism or eternal conscious punishment).

LIVE the Story

Few have the courage of my friend and colleague Klyne Snodgrass to say what seems obvious from this text: "Anyone who hears Jesus' words and does not do them is a fool."[6] As Klyne has pointed out in a lengthy article, the word "hearing" often means "obeying."[7] I will pluck some courage here to urge us all to prevent our children from singing the song about this parable in way that creates fun and jollity. It may be fun for children to "all fall down," but to play with destruction is to do just that. The parable is one of the severest in the entire Bible.

The Aim of the Sermon Is Doing

So we come to the end of this Sermon and the invitation, the summons, or the challenge of Jesus is not simply to accept him or to believe in him (as if

---

5. Keener, *Matthew*, 255 – 56; Turner, *Matthew*, 221.

6. Snodgrass, *Stories with Intent*, 337.

7. K. Snodgrass, "Reading to Hear: A Hermeneutics of Hearing," *Horizons in Biblical Theology* 24 (2002): 1 – 32. I sketch his stuff in McKnight, *Blue Parakeet*, 98 – 103.

rational acceptance was his fundamental mission). The fundamental aim of the Sermon is to present Jesus and his kingdom vision for his kingdom people, and the only acceptable response to this Sermon is to embrace him, to accept the challenge; that means *to do what he says*. The Sermon is a Messianic Ethic from Above and Beyond, and it is designed for obedience by the messianic community. Ten times in 7:13–27 the word "do" or "practice" appears: 7:17 (2x), 18 (2x), 19, 21, 22 (negatively), 23 (synonym), 24, 26. The aim of the Sermon rhetorically was for Jesus to tell his disciples what he expected of his own and to get them to do what he said. But this isn't just Sermon stuff; I call our attention to other similar expressions in the gospel of Matthew, including 3:8, 10; 5:19, 7:12; 21:28–32, 43; 25:31–46.

"Doing" and "practicing" are more ordinary terms for the more substantial term often found in Matthew: *righteousness*. And this term too is important for comprehending the Sermon: righteousness (*dikaios, dikaiosynē*), a term describing behaviors that conform to God's will and, in particular for Jesus, behaviors that conform to the will of God *as he teaches it for the kingdom*. Thus, we think of 3:15; 5:6, 10, 20; 6:1, 33; 21:32. Jesus is calling his disciples into the way of righteousness.

Jesus is not alone; Matthew is not alone. Two other texts are worthy of our attention. The apostle Paul, when describing the ultimate aim of the Scriptures, says they are revealed to transform us:

> All Scripture is God-breathed and is useful for teaching, rebuking, correcting and training in righteousness, so that the servant of God may be thoroughly equipped for every good work. (2 Tim 3:16–17)

To be sure, the apostle was not thinking particularly of the Sermon but instead the Scriptures of Israel. Yet what he says applies all the more to the New Testament: the *aim of the Scriptures is to transform us into people who are ready to do every good work*. I can think of no more appropriate words for the aim of this Sermon.

And Jesus' brother James says much the same:

> Do not merely listen to the word, and so deceive yourselves. Do what it says. Anyone who listens to the word but does not do what it says is like someone who looks at his face in a mirror and, after looking at himself, goes away and immediately forgets what he looks like. But whoever looks intently into the perfect law that gives freedom, and continues in it — not forgetting what they have heard, but doing it — they will be blessed in what they do. (Jas 1:22–25)

Here we have all over again: hearing leads to doing or the hearing is totally useless. Martin Luther, a champion for gospel orthodoxy, says this well: "The doctrine is a good and a precious thing, but it is not being preached for the sake of being heard but for the sake of action and its application to life."[8]

Yet, Doing Is Not a New Law

The Sermon is not the Torah on steroids. The Sermon, paradoxically, continues to point us from the demands of Jesus to the Demander, from the laws to the Lawgiver, from what is taught to the One who teaches.[9] The Sermon begins with Jesus ascending, like Moses, the mount in order to speak to God's people how God wants the people to live. It begins, in other words, on a new Moses or a messianic theme. But we fail to read the Sermon aright if we read it as law. It is law, but the striking note is the audacity of the one who deigns to reveal the eschatological Torah for kingdom people.

We are driven, in other words, to see once again the words used by Matthew to close off the Sermon: "because he taught as one who had authority, and not as their teachers of the law" (7:29). What struck the listeners was the audacity of Jesus to do what Moses did. In the end, enclosing the Sermon as the first part of what runs from 4:23–25 all the way down to 9:35 is that Matthew is saying, "Here's Jesus!" The implication of his presentation is found right here in 7:13–27: "Either do what he says, or don't do what he says. It is your choice."

So, we dare not reduce Christology to ethics. Instead, the Sermon calls us to lift ethics into Christology. What echoes down through the corridors of history when this Sermon is read or preached is that Jesus, in the closing passage, clasped those very words to himself:

*Therefore everyone who hears these words **of mine**...*

To respond to the Sermon is not to respond to an ethical vision. To respond is to respond to Jesus. The proper response is to declare who he is by the way we live.

---

8. Luther, *Sermon on the Mount*, 281.
9. Guelich, *Sermon on the Mount*, 413.

Scripture Index

Subject Index

Author Index

We want to hear from you. Please send your comments about this book to us in care of zreview@zondervan.com. Thank you.